JOHN JACOB ASTOR

GREAT LAKES BOOKS

A complete listing of the books in this series can be found at the back of this volume.

PHILIP P. MASON, EDITOR
Walter P. Reuther Library, Wayne State University

DR. CHARLES K. HYDE, ASSOCIATE EDITOR
Department of History, Wayne State University

Advisory Editors

John Jacob Astor

Business and Finance

in the Early Republic

John Denis Haeger

Wayne State University Press Detroit

95 94 93 92 91   5 4 3 2 1

Library of Congress Cataloging-in-Publication Data

Haeger, John D.
    John Jacob Astor, business and finance in the early re-
public / John Denis Haeger.
        p.   cm. — (Great Lakes books)
    Includes bibliographical references and index.
    ISBN 0–8143–1876–2 (alk. paper)
    1. Astor, John Jacob, 1763–1848.   2. Businessmen—
United States—Biography.   3. United States—Economic
conditions—To 1865.
    I. Title.   II. Series.
    HC102.5.A76H34   1991
    380.1'092—dc20
    [B]   90–28518
                                                    CIP

Designer: Joanne Elkin Kinney

To Cecily and Meg

Contents

Illustrations and Tables

Preface

THERE ARE several reasons for embarking on a study of John Jacob Astor and the economic growth of the early Republic. First, Astor's business career encompassed America's formative economic years from the precarious days following the American Revolution to the emergence of an urban-centered manufacturing economy in the late 1840s. Change was the dominating motif of the period, and Astor either exemplified the varied economic, social, and political changes in his business career or he directly affected the course of events.

Astor is also a convenient vehicle for understanding the American economy because he participated in many phases of its development. He is best known as a merchant and fur trader. Astor participated in America's intrusion into foreign markets in Europe, the West Indies, and China, and he personified the intimate connections between westward expansion and national economic development. As he came to exercise a powerful influence over the American fur trade, for example, the New Yorker exported furs to Europe and China and imported goods for use in the urban markets on the East Coast and in western frontier communities. Few businessmen possessed Astor's extensive connections with the country's dominant political figures such as Thomas Jefferson,

James Madison, James Monroe, and Albert Gallatin; thus the New York financier was a central figure in important political issues such as the financing of the War of 1812, the chartering of the Second Bank of the United States (BUS), and the setting of government policies in relation to territorial expansion. Astor's career paralleled the economic, political, and territorial expansion of America's first half-century.

The New Yorker was also a barometer of the more mundane but nonetheless important changes in the business world. Although his contact with the fur trade and land speculation would seem to categorize him as a preindustrial entrepreneur, his methods and goals reflected a "modern" business mentality. The American Fur Company was among the most effective uses of the joint-stock company for a private business venture. Early on, Astor grasped the importance of cities and was among the first of the big-city developers. He purchased New York City lots, constructed and leased buildings, built theaters and hotels, and participated in innovative financial institutions like the New York Life Insurance and Trust Company.

This brief summary would suggest that Astor was an important figure in the life of the early Republic; yet he has been the subject of only one scholarly biography—published nearly sixty years ago by Kenneth Wiggins Porter—and virtually ignored by recent historians in studies of the American fur trade and the rise of New York City. Surely another look at Astor's career is appropriate if only to explain why historians have so neglected a figure that antebellum Americans respected as the richest and most powerful businessman of his day.

I would be remiss if I did not acknowledge the many people who contributed to the completion of this work. Most important were library staffs in this country and abroad who helped in my efforts to review both business and personal records connected with Astor's career. Although I visited most libraries, my visits were often quite brief and dependent on the willingness of others to oversee photocopy and microfilm orders. A partial list of institutions that provided me with valuable resources either at the library or by mail includes: Albany Institute of History and Art; American Philosophical Society; Baker Library, Harvard University; Beinecke Rare Book and Manuscript Library, Yale University; Chicago Historical Society; Clarke Historical Library, Central Michigan University; George Arents Research Center, Syracuse

University, Historical Society of Pennsylvania; India Office Library and Records, London; Library Company of Philadelphia; Library of Congress; Minnesota Historical Society; Missouri Historical Society; McGill University Library, Montreal, Canada; National Library of Scotland, Edinburgh; New York Historical Society; New York Public Library; New York State Library; Public Archives of Canada; Public Records Office, Kew Gardens, England; University of Aberdeen Library, Scotland; William L. Clements Library.

A number of individuals and institutions were also very helpful in the development of my ideas on Astor and the business revolution. Central Michigan University's Faculty Research and Creative Endeavors Committee provided funds for several trips to the East Coast and for visits to foreign libraries. The Research Professorship award from Central Michigan University provided a semester's leave to finish the first draft. My colleagues in the Department of History at Central Michigan University have been helpful and kind critics during several faculty seminars. Members of the Department of History at the University of Strathclyde, Glasgow, Scotland, provided many useful suggestions for setting Astor's career in a comparative perspective. A special thanks is due to Charles Ebel who identified valuable primary sources in Aberdeen, Scotland, and to James Ronda who has generously shared his insights into Astor's personality and the settlement at Astoria. Finally, Cecily Dickinson Haeger has provided extraordinary assistance with the formation of my ideas and the transformation of those ideas into readable prose.

CHAPTER ONE

Searching for the "Real" John Jacob Astor

A REASSESSMENT of John Jacob Astor must first confront the image of the New York financier that has persisted in popular and professional historical literature for more than a century. Despite the meticulous scholarship of Kenneth Wiggins Porter, Astor's biographer, the New Yorker remains an enigmatic and contradictory figure who rarely elicits dispassionate evaluation. Historians and social commentators alike have characterized the financier as either the epitome of the rags-to-riches fable or as the embodiment of an American Scrooge. His curious reputation, of course, resulted from his position among the first, the richest, and the most powerful of American businessmen. He came to personify nineteenth-century business leadership, and he became a favorite subject for both capitalism's apologists and detractors. It is little wonder that Astor has confused modern historians, for both friendly and hostile judgments about him come from highly suspect sources, including the reminiscences of his contemporaries, popular nonfiction biographies, and social reform tracts disguised as dispassionate scholarship. A brief review of this literature demonstrates that little lies often told eventually become big truths. A first step, then, in retelling Astor's story must be to neutralize the existing legend.

The earliest writings on Astor appeared in the 1840s before his death and were lavish in praise of his business acumen. Astor was partly responsible for this literature as he paid his friend Washington Irving to write an account of his attempt to establish an American foothold on the Pacific Coast before the War of 1812. Astor was concerned because two participants in the Astoria venture, Gabriel Franchére and Ross Cox, had already published accounts that raised questions about Astor's responsibility for the settlement's failure. Washington Irving published *Astoria or Anecdotes of an Enterprise Beyond the Rocky Mountains* in 1836. Irving presented Astor's side of the story, crediting him with a plan, magnificent in scope, that crumbled owing to the ineptitude and treachery of his employees and the shortsightedness of American government officials. The book was a success and improved Astor's reputation. An article on the fur trade four years later, for example, highlighted Astor's organizational role in the American fur trade.[1]

Astor's biography in *Hunt's Merchant Magazine* in 1844, and Moses Beach's lengthy description in *Wealth and Biography of the ... Citizens of New York ...* in 1845, however, were the most influential works for setting the tone and interpretation for all later defenders.[2] According to these sources, Astor personified what later became known as the Horatio Alger ideal—a penniless immigrant fleeing European oppression who seeks and finds his fortune in the New World. The young German supposedly utilized his ingenuity and organizational skills and parlayed a few breaks in America into both a monopoly control over the American fur trade and an important role in American commerce with China. He also foresaw the crucial importance of New York City and invested in the city's real estate, thereby substantially enlarging his fortune. These early descriptions never fail to stress that Astor's success directly benefited others; not only did he bring economic growth to New York City and the country but also to his own employees. Moreover, Astor was praised for his social consciousness and nationalistic fervor: he risked his fortune in attempting to establish Astoria, built a library for the city, and assisted other immigrants through bequests to the New York City German Society.[3] The following summary statement from *Hunt's Merchant Magazine* exemplified the laudatory nature of these early descriptions, "We neither possess the materials, nor claim the ability to sketch the life and character of one, whose name has passed into proverb as current as that of Croesus, who, for nearly forty years, has been characterized as, perhaps, the greatest merchant of this, if not of any age—the Napoleon of commerce."[4]

The article in *Hunt's Merchant Magazine* and Moses Beach's pamphlet must be used with great caution, for they provide a substantial amount of supposedly factual material about Astor's early background and business strategy that, in reality, reflected nothing more than the prevailing gossip or "wisdom" of the day. Astor's earliest defenders were New York City boosters who regularly embellished the facts of otherwise mundane occurrences in order to enhance the image of businessmen.[5] Popular writers, for example, described Astor's departure from his village of Walldorf, Germany, in marvelously romantic and prophetic language. The young man stopped just outside the town, sat down under a tree and, as he looked wistfully toward his home, pledged that whatever adventures lay ahead, he would always "be honest, industrious, and never gamble." When the young Astor arrived in America, after several years in England, he carried only seven flutes, and it was from this stake he built a huge fortune. A similar story circulated about Astor's first contact with the fur trade. He reputedly learned of the trade from casual conversations with fellow passengers on the way to America. Rather than a frightened twenty-year-old immigrant hoping to secure a foothold in America, Astor's biographers depicted a self-assured and shrewd businessman.[6] These stories are certainly questionable because Astor later recalled the events surrounding his arrival in America but failed to mention such fairly memorable details as the seven flutes or conversations regarding the fur trade.[7]

Although Astor's contemporaries generally had great respect for both his accomplishments and his character, negative comments predominated in the popular press after his death in 1848. The financier's last years had elicited tremendous interest throughout the country because he had been a public figure for many of his eighty-four years, because he seemed closely connected to the first generation of American political leaders, and because the size of his fortune had been the subject of endless rumors. Stephen Girard, who died in 1831, had been the only business figure of comparable stature, and he had left the bulk of his fortune for the establishment of a college and for improvements to his adopted city of Philadelphia. When Astor's will was published, Americans were amazed that his fortune dwarfed Girard's estate and that he had left the major portion of his money to his family through a trust to be administered by his son, William. Compared to Girard, in fact, Astor left a miniscule sum to charity and public endowments.[8]

Horace Greeley, Whig politician, newspaperman, and reformer, reflected the public dismay of Astor's life in his *New York Tribune* obituary. Overall, Greeley praised the financier's hard work and skill and urged American youth to emulate his career. Greeley, though, was critical of Astor's parsimony and the questionable dealings during the War of 1812 when he profited from the sale of government bonds to support the war effort. Greeley was also writing in the aftermath of the overthrow of Louis Philippe in France and was conscious of the tide of social and political reform about to engulf Europe. Consequently, he challenged the social utility of massive personal fortunes and suggested new laws for limiting their size. Although Greeley was certainly not a radical revolutionary, he was committed to the improvement of American labor's position and to the necessity for equal access to economic resources such as land. Greeley's attack partly reflected the sentiments of radical land reformers such as Irishman Mike Walsh who branded Astor's profits from rents as "legalized plunder." Noting Astor's accumulation of thousands of acres of agricultural land and his stupendous holdings of New York City lots, Greeley recommended that new laws should be passed that taxed personal income and limited individual ownership of land to one thousand acres.[9]

James Gordon Bennett, editor of the *New York Herald,* was not as kind as Horace Greeley. He reprinted Astor's will on the front page of the newspaper and then presented an editorial that charged the financier with hoarding wealth that really belonged to the people of New York City. Bennett reasoned that half of Astor's fortune came from the increased value of Manhattan real estate, an increase that resulted not from the financier's efforts, but from the "industry of the citizens of New York." Bennett was especially agitated because Astor's lawyers had created a trust arrangement that protected his fortune and guaranteed that his heirs would benefit for several generations. "The great object of the will," Bennett wrote, "is to create an Astor dynasty . . . and to keep up this dynasty by entailing the property upon the regular successors of the individual for ages to come."[10] The publicity surrounding Astor's will impressed upon mid-nineteenth-century Americans the realization not only that capitalism created marked disparities of wealth but also that it allowed such fortunes to pass from one generation to the next.

Horace Mann, the puritanical Massachusetts educational and social reformer, expanded the attack on Astor a few years later in a short essay entitled *A Few Thoughts for a Young Man*. This piece reflected both the ambivalence of Americans toward great wealth and the symbolic importance of Astor himself. Mann warned his readers, "the millionaire is as dangerous to the welfare of the community in our day, as was the baronial lord of the Middle Ages."[11] Not only was making money a somewhat degraded calling according to Mann, but great fortunes surely enslaved the sons and daughters of the wealthy by depriving them of the opportunity to work and achieve self-fulfillment. The owners of great fortunes were morally acceptable only if they benefited society by using their money for charitable purposes. In Mann's judgment, Astor failed on humanitarian grounds—especially compared to Stephen Girard—and "he was hoarding wealth for the base love of wealth, hugging to his breast, in his dying hour, the memory of his gold and not of his redeemer."[12] Within a few years after his death, many Americans viewed Astor as a wealthy man who may have earned his fortune through great business skill but who failed to assume the responsibilities of the good steward.[13]

The harsh criticism of Astor that followed his death did not go unanswered. Charles Bristed, Astor's grandson, immediately responded to the charges of Horace Mann in *A Letter to Horace Mann*. He argued that Astor was interested in both the public good and national goals, citing the financier's attempt to establish an outpost at Astoria and his interest in a library in New York City. Bristed was especially angered by Mann's comparison of Astor to Stephen Girard, who had endowed a college. Bristed pointed out that Girard's motives were antireligious because he insisted that no religious influence could exist at the college. Bristed, though, admitted that his grandfather's will was niggardly in terms of its public benefactions, but he blamed this defect on Astor's lawyers who, in the financier's enfeebled later years, had determined the provisions of the will.[14]

Despite Bristed's defense and an occasional laudatory biography, the most influential studies of Astor from the 1840s until Kenneth Wiggins Porter's scholarly biography in 1931 were predominantly hostile. James Parton, who wrote a biography in *Harper's Magazine* in 1865, was perhaps the most influential architect of Astor's negative image in the nineteenth century. Parton was among the most famous early American historians. Over his long career, he specialized in biography and published works on Albert Gallatin, Thomas Jefferson, Benjamin Franklin, Andrew Jackson, and Aaron Burr. He also wrote regularly for the *North American Review* and *Harper's Magazine*. Parton generally held Whiggish views about society and politics. His biography of Andrew Jackson, for example, praised Jackson's forthright views but found him intellectually and emotionally unfit for office. Parton's standard was Thomas Jefferson whom he considered a man of great learning and moral vision.[15]

Parton's book on Astor was not his best effort as he presented an often confused and contradictory image of the financier. The author praised Astor for his business skill in organizing the fur trade, his daring attempt to establish Astoria, and his construction of buildings in New York City. Although Parton admitted that money-making was a perfectly legitimate activity, he observed, "like every proper and virtuous desire[,] it may become excessive, and then it is a vice." Although he never charged Astor with any specific immoral or illegal acts, he conveyed the impression that the financier was a miser and therefore morally flawed because of his excessive attachment to money. To demonstrate his parsimonious character Parton interviewed Astor's friends and enemies and repeated virtually all the negative stories about him then floating about New York City—without checking their veracity.[16]

Parton also depended heavily on an 1855 biography of Astor written in German by "Philip Oertel" (the pseudonym of W. D. von Horn) that provided a highly romanticized and unsubstantiated account of Astor's early family life. Parton used these materials to create a lasting character portrait of John Astor. His father was supposedly a drunkard who provided few amenities for his growing family of four sons and a daughter. John Jacob was apparently an unhappy youth who was alienated from his stepmother and unable to form close friendships with other youths in the village of Walldorf. The financier's later neurotic behavior toward money and his inability to assume the social responsibilities of great wealth were, according to Parton, directly related to the unhappiness of his childhood. "If, in later life," Parton wrote, "he overvalued money, it should not be forgotten that few men have had a harder experience of the want of money at the age when character is forming."[17]

Parton's biography alongside a few reminiscences of Astor's contemporaries were the chief sources for the stories that constitute the Astor legend so prevalent in the literature of the late nineteenth century and so influential with twentieth-century popular and professional historians. These early writers never revealed the source of their information, for the obvious reason that many stories were either grossly exaggerated or pure fabrication. It was not unusual, of course, for nineteenth-century historians to enliven the narrative or even to use apocryphal stories in order to make a point; the problem is that these stories continue to surface in modern-day historical works on John Astor.

For example, Parton created the image of Astor as a miserly old man by describing his last years in pitiful detail. The New Yorker was supposedly nourished at a woman's breast at the age of eighty-two and tossed in a blanket for exercise when he was no longer able to walk or ride in a carriage. Despite his infirmities, the old man was concerned, supposedly, with extracting every last cent out of his investments. Parton related one incident in which Astor's real estate agent came to see the financier during his morning excercise:

> The old man cried out from the middle of his blanket,
> "Has Mrs. _____ paid the rent yet?"
> "No," replied the agent.
> "Well, but she must pay it," said the poor old man. "Mr. Astor," rejoined the agent, "she can't pay it now; she has had misfortunes, and we must give her time." "No, No," said Astor; "I tell you she can pay it, and she will pay it. You don't go the right way to work with her."[18]

Parton also retold a story he allegedly heard in 1834 from the captain of a vessel that had transported Astor from Europe to America. As storms and the accompanying rough seas buffeted the ship, Astor became seasick and terrified. Oblivious to the desires of other passengers, he tried to bribe the captain into returning to port, so he could disembark. The story fitted Parton's overall theme—that Astor was a man of considerable moral weakness.[19]

The Astor legend also included numerous stories of the financier's preoccupation with even small amounts of money. After subscribing to John James Audubon's *Birds of America,* Astor supposedly refused to pay the artist even though he made five trips to Astor's home.[20] Similarly, Astor was riding one day about the French countryside after a painful fistula operation. His companion, a doctor, became quite concerned when the financier appeared to be in great pain. When the doctor inquired as to his condition, the financier admitted that his pain was a minor concern compared to the fact that he was worried over losing 1 or 2 percent on an investment.[21]

Astor was also credited with truly phenomenal greed. Joseph Scoville (who wrote under the pseudonym of Walter Barrett) in his multivolume *The Old Merchants of New York City* described an arrangement whereby Astor, De Witt Clinton, and Gouverneur Morris were negotiating to buy the Louisiana Territory from Napoleon. Their plan was to sell the territory to the United States and collect an advance, or commission, of 2½ percent, for a profit of $30,000. Not only did the story demonstrate Astor's hunger for profit, but it also reflected another common theme to his detractors—his lack of patriotism. Indeed, some critics even suggested that the New Yorker had established Astoria in order to build his own nation. The literature contains so many fanciful and apocryphal tales that Kenneth Wiggins Porter once remarked that Astor himself must have devoted his old age to making up such stories for the gullible public.[22]

The nineteenth-century image makers, then, were generally impressed with Astor's business skill and accepted the fact that his fortune was acquired by legal, although often manipulative, means. Parton especially stressed the financier's incredible fortitude and persistence in learning the details of markets in China and Europe. Parton, though, was suspicious of Astor's speculation in agricultural lands and city lots, for he believed such holdings inevitably slowed the process of economic development. Moreover, Parton and other critics insisted that Astor was morally corrupted by his money, for he refused to contribute his time and skill to public concerns. He was, according to James Parton, a money-making machine:

> It is only when we regard his mercantile exploits that we can admire him. He was, unquestionably, one of the ablest, boldest, and most successful operators that ever lived. "He could command an army of five hundred thousand men," exclaimed one of his admirers. That was an erroneous remark. He could have commanded an army of five hundred thousand tea chests, with heavy auxiliary force of otter skins

and beaver skins. But a commander of men must be superior morally
as well as intellectually. He must be able to win the love and excite
the enthusiasm of his followers. Astor would have made a splendid
commissary-general to the army of Xerxes, but he could no more have
conquered Greece than Xerxes himself.[23]

Few works on Astor appeared throughout the rest of the nineteenth century, but in the early twentieth century, Burton Hendrick renewed the attack with an article in *McClure's Magazine*
entitled "The Astor Fortune." Neither Hendrick nor *McClure's*
could be considered scholarly or even unbiased. The magazine was
a major outlet for Progressive writers and regularly ran investiga-
tive articles on selected capitalists and industries while paying
scant attention to the substantiation of allegations or identifica-
tion of sources. Hendrick worked for *McClure's* from 1905 to 1913,
and during that time he plunged energetically into the social critique of American society. His most famous piece was an investi-
gative report in 1906 on "The Story of Life Insurance." Age later
softened Hendrick's reformist zeal and improved his skills as an
historian. In 1919, he wrote the *Age of Big Business* for Yale's
Chronicle of America Series and later a biography of Andrew Carnegie; in these books, he demonstrated a grudging admiration
for the captains of industry. Hendrick also later won three Pulit-
zer Prizes.[24]

In 1905, when he wrote his critique of the Astor fortune,
though, Hendrick had one goal: to demonstrate that John Jacob
Astor and his descendants had acquired a fortune by unethically, if
not illegally, manipulating the New York City real estate market.
Unlike earlier historians, Hendrick would not concede that Astor
possessed uncommon business skills, only avarice and luck. Astor's
crime, according to Hendrick, was that he purchased land in the
early nineteenth century on the outskirts of New York City and
then simply sat by "with no anxiety, no sleepless nights, no work"
and waited for the city to expand so he could profit from the increase in the land's value.[25]

Hendrick further charged that Astor often acquired land
through mortgage foreclosures during periods of economic depression, thereby profiting from the misfortune of others. He was especially critical of the fact that the financier typically leased his land
and buildings for no longer than twenty-one years. At the end of
that period, according to Hendrick, the property reverted to As-

tor's greedy hands, even though the tenant might have erected buildings and paid yearly rents. "Thus year after year," the author complained, "Astor compelled his fellow-citizens to improve his property, pay his taxes, and yearly tribute besides."[26] Hendrick buttressed his indictment with colorful stories borrowed from James Parton that pictured the elderly financier attempting to foreclose a mortgage just a few days before his death. The reformer's anger, though, was actually directed at Astor's descendants who continued to trade in New York City real estate and displayed their wealth as members of the city's aristocracy. In Hendrick's mind, real estate fortunes were socially and economically reprehensible because, unlike the fortunes amassed by the railroad and steel barons, the Astors demonstrated no skills, took no risks, and contributed nothing to the country as a whole.[27]

Hendrick's attack on the Astor fortune was mild compared to that of fellow New Yorker, Gustavus Myers, whose portrait of John Jacob and William B. Astor in his three-volume *History of Great American Fortunes* firmly established the malevolent Astor image in American literature and among professional historians of the twentieth century. Because popular authors and professional historians have so frequently consulted Myers's study, it deserves extended comment. Originally published in 1910 in three volumes, Myers's *History of Great American Fortunes* proved so popular that Random House published a revised one-volume edition in its *Modern Library* series in 1936, and thus gave it the status of an American classic.[28]

In the publisher's blurb and according to many literary historians ever since, Myers's book was a product of the Progressive period. Unlike his contemporaries who wrote scathing exposés based on hearsay and sensational half-truths, the critics claimed that Myers was a dedicated historian who used government documents and private manuscripts to present the "truth." In 1936, the publisher wrote that Myers's volume was distinguished by reasoned judgments and conclusions supported by incontrovertible sources. No one, claimed the publisher, had yet challenged either the author's evidence or his conclusions.[29] In 1941, Myers earned a Guggenheim Fellowship for his studies of bigotry in the United States. Despite his popularity and reputation in literary circles, his description of John Jacob Astor cannot stand as good history, for he deliberately misused evidence, depended on hearsay, and ignored contrary facts and interpretations.[30]

The bias and distortion of Myers's *History of Great American Fortunes* can be fully understood only if one realizes that the author was a dedicated social reformer whose early background created an empathy for the poor and disdain for the rich. His parents were immigrants who endured grinding poverty and frequent family separations. When he was fourteen, Myers left home and lived with strangers in order to work in a factory for the support of his family. He later admitted that these early experiences colored all his later thinking:

> I mention these circumstances because, although my individual lot, they had a profound awakening influence in early life in shaping my sympathy for the underdog and clearing my vision in youthful years to the effects of oppressive environment and social injustice in general. My developing grievance was not so much personal as social, resulting in a spirit of rebelliousness against conditions which racked so many people in my immediate view.[31]

Myers surmounted, but never forgot, the poverty of his early years. After completing high school, he worked on the *Philadelphia Record,* but within a year he moved to New York City. While serving as a staff reporter for several New York newspapers, Myers's interest in politics and social reform grew and he joined the New York City Social Reform Club. In this organization, Myers became entranced with the Progressive notion that "facts" concerning wealth, housing, law, and government that are clearly presented to the educated public would be sufficient to produce social reforms.[32] His first publication, "History of Public Franchises in New York City," was a detailed investigation into the granting of franchises to transportation and electrical companies by New York City's municipal government. Not only did he uncover numerous instances of corruption by city and business leaders but he also revealed that many private fortunes had grown from the unholy alliance between men of capital and elected government officials.[33] In 1901, Myers published *The History of Tammany Hall,* through private subscriptions because no publisher was willing to face the wrath of the New York City political machine. Utilizing much of the information uncovered during his research on the franchises and the evidence accumulated during the Tweed investigations, Myers demonstrated the corrupt and venal nature of the Democratic party. Alexander Callow, who has written extensively on Boss Tweed and New York City politics, claimed that Myers's book was the best factual history of Tammany Hall but flawed because of the author's passionate antiparty views that distorted his interpretations.[34]

In the process of writing his first books, Myers became convinced that many of the country's great fortunes were built upon corrupt foundations and not the result of the ability, enterprise, and thrift so often described elsewhere.[35] After the publication of his book on Tammany Hall, the reformer next immersed himself in a study of America's wealthy, and in 1910 he published his most famous work in three volumes, *History of Great American Fortunes*. Despite Myers's claim that his only desire was to allow the facts to speak for themselves and that he was not presenting a damning exposé, his work was the product of his socialist, anticapitalist views. Before analyzing Astor's financial career (and I suspect long before collecting the evidence), Myers declared, "the great fortunes are natural, logical outcomes of a system based upon factors the inevitable result of which is the utter despoilment of the many for the benefit of a few."[36] The problem, in other words, was the capitalist system that encouraged fraud, cheating, and gross disparities of wealth. The author described the commercial system of the early nineteenth century as "founded upon a combination of superior executive ability and superior cunning— not ability in creating, but in being able to get hold of, and distribute, the products of others' creation."[37]

Given Gustavus Myers's starting point, it is understandable that his evaluation of Astor would be entirely negative. Using selected excerpts from federal documents, he tried first to build a case that Astor's American Fur Company was a monopoly that not only operated above the law but also effectively destroyed American Indian cultures in its search for profit. In a rather bizarre example of refusing to analyze one's own evidence, Myers argued that Astor bought beaver skins for $1.00 each in western New York and then sold them in London markets for $6.25; he reinvested the profits in English goods and sold these goods, in turn, to fur traders and Indians. The author concluded that Astor could make a profit of $10.00 per skin. Although Myers considered himself an economic historian, he seemed strangely ignorant of the costs of purchases, transportation, packaging, and marketing that affected price in the early nineteenth century. Even though information on prices and markets was available to Myers in federal government documents and in the American Fur Company account books, he neglected to consider it.[38]

Myers also stressed Astor's corruption of American government officials particularly Lewis Cass, governor of the Michigan Territory, and Thomas Hart Benton, senator from Missouri. Similar to his earlier books on Tammany Hall and the franchise evil, the reformer wanted to demonstrate that men of wealth inevitably undermined the political process. Yet Myers presented no evidence to substantiate his charge that Thomas Hart Benton was an Astor mouthpiece in Congress.[39] The more likely explanation was that Benton, a westerner and proponent of expansion, gladly supported Astor's American Fur Company, in order to achieve his own political goals.

The more damning charge was against Lewis Cass who, while governor of the Michigan Territory, supposedly received a $35,000 bribe from Astor. Myers's source was a 1909 newspaper article reporting a $35,000 entry under Cass's name in a ledger of the American Fur Company. The newspaper then surmised that the $35,000 payment was to assure that Cass gave Astor all the fur trading licenses he requested. The bribery charge was based on no evidence of wrongdoing whatsoever, only that American Fur Company monies were transferred to the governor of the Michigan Territory.[40] Even though Myers assured his readers that he had inspected the actual ledgers in which the Cass payment was recorded, no subsequent historian has ever discovered the entry in the American Fur Company account books. Nevertheless, many popular authors continue to repeat this charge of Astor's venality; and, even those historians who acknowledge the flimsy evidence still take Myers's account seriously.[41]

Myers's condemnation of Astor's fur business was mild compared to his analysis of the New Yorker's real estate operations. The landlord/landowner was society's true parasite, Myers claimed, for he contributed nothing to society's progress. "Society worked feverishly for the landowner such as Astor," Myers explained, "every street laid and graded by the city; every park plotted and every other public improvement; every child born and every influx of immigrants; every factory warehouse and dwelling that went up all these and more agencies contributed toward the abnormal swelling of his fortune."[42] Following closely Burton Hendrick's 1905 *McClure's* article, Myers claimed that Astor increased his landholdings during the depression of 1837. Without a single case to prove his point, Myers simply assumed that the financier regularly foreclosed mortgages in the 1840s and threw his tenants into the street, thus driving them to stealing, prostitution, and even suicide. To further demonstrate Astor's ruthlessness, Myers somberly pronounced, "not a single instance has come down of any act of leniency on Astor's part in extending the time of tenants in arrears."[43]

Despite the fact that Myers carefully poured through the municipal records of New York City and federal government documents, his efforts, which ought to have been directed toward weighing the evidence, were unfortunately bent on collecting isolated facts with which to indict capitalism and its leaders. It may be that his earlier works on Tammany Hall and the franchise system were built upon substantial documentary evidence, but his portrait of Astor was based on a very brief, highly selective reading of government documents; on the gossipy work of James Parton; and on the unsubstantiated allegations of Burton Hendrick. Although Myers's work can stand as a Progressive critique of wealth and wealthholding in America, it must be discarded as an acceptable study of John Jacob Astor.[44]

Until Kenneth Wiggins Porter's scholarly biography in 1931, Myers and Parton were the principal authorities on Astor. However, a number of works appeared before 1931 that contributed substantially to his negative image. Perhaps the most influential was James Gallatin's *A Great Peace Maker: The Diary of James Gallatin*. . . . James Gallatin was the son of Albert Gallatin, Jefferson's secretary of the treasury, and for a quarter-century one of America's most respected diplomats. He was a friend of John Jacob Astor, assisting him with introductions to top government leaders at the time of the Astoria project and during the efforts to reestablish the Bank of the United States (BUS) in 1815 and 1816. Astor later served as Gallatin's investment counselor when the latter was out of the country, either as ambassador to France or on numerous diplomatic missions. The friendship between the two men was substantial enough that in 1815 Astor tried to persuade Gallatin to become a full partner in his various business endeavors.[45]

Even though his father and Astor were friends, James Gallatin despised Astor and through his *Diary* helped to create the financier's image as a crass, uncouth, and illiterate German immigrant. Authors still delight in relating James Gallatin's stories of how

Astor used his knife to eat peas and ice cream at a dinner party.
Even more damaging and revealing of the financier's supposedly
boorish and plebian background was Gallatin's description of a
quiet family dinner in Paris when Astor, seated next to Gallatin's
sister, Frances, wiped his fingers on her dress sleeve after mistak-
ing it for a napkin.[46]

At first glance, these stories seem so insignificant as to require
no further comment, yet they have reappeared in the works of
later historians. As a result, it seems necessary to challenge their
authenticity. First, they have no independent corroboration whatsoever. No other primary source commented on either Astor's uncouth demeanor or general illiteracy. Indeed, the opposite case
could be made. Astor was known as a lover of classical music and
surrounded himself with literary men such as Washington Irving
and Joseph Cogswell. Second, James Gallatin was a hostile witness. He hated Astor for a number of reasons, including the fact
that he unsuccessfully courted Astor's youngest daughter Eliza.
Moreover, he was jealous of the New Yorker's great wealth, especially as his father constantly worried over his own precarious financial position. After several lengthy residences in various
European capitals, James Gallatin considered himself a member
of the international aristocracy. He was a Francophile as well and
had great distaste for Astor, a German immigrant. Finally, historian Raymond Walters, Jr., after a careful analysis of Gallatin's
Diary, has shown that substantial portions dealing with political
affairs were totally fabricated. Thus, historians must completely
discount Gallatin's description and look elsewhere for clues to Astor's character and demeanor.[47]

In addition to Gallatin's *Diary,* the Astor legend was given
support when William J. Ghent wrote the essay on Astor for the
Dictionary of American Biography in 1928. Although an editor for
the *DAB* in the 1920s, Ghent came to that position after an extensive background that included social reform and socialist politics.
Trained as a printer, the author joined the International Typo-
graphical Union as a young man and soon began writing on social
reform topics as an independent socialist. Immersing himself in
New York City politics of the 1890s, he helped establish the Social
Reform Club to bring together workers and middle-class intellectuals and served briefly as editor of the *American Fabian.* In 1899,
he helped manage the publicity for Samuel "Golden Rule" Jones's
campaigns for mayor of Toledo and governor of Ohio. In 1903, he

organized the X Club in New York in order to provide a meeting place for progressive intellectuals like Lincoln Steffens and Charles Beard. He joined the Socialist party in 1904 and helped form the Rand School of Social Science of New York City in 1906. Ghent was a popular speaker and active party worker. In 1911, he became secretary to Socialist Congressman Victor Berger and helped draft an old age pension bill.[48] The author's socialist views were perhaps best reflected in his book, *Our Benevolent Feudalism*. In this work, he acknowledged the powerful influence of industrialists and bankers and the inevitability of financial consolidation. He predicted a Fascist state in America in which the financial leaders would rule benevolently for the masses, thus ensuring all citizens a share of the economic bounty.[49]

Ghent's views changed markedly with the outbreak of World War I. First, he refused to support the Socialist party's repudiation of the war effort and then became wary of the Communists during the 1920s. In *The Reds Bring Reaction*, (1923) he argued that capitalism was the only sure defense against the Communists. In 1927–1928, he accepted a position as staff writer and assistant editor for the *DAB* and wrote many entries on economic and frontier subjects. Indeed, by this time in his life, Ghent was more interested in the history of westward expansion than in the political issues that had dominated his earlier life. He eventually published several books on western themes, including *The Road to Oregon*.[50]

Ghent's analysis of Astor's career was remarkably judicious given his earlier political beliefs and his total dependence on the works of James Parton and Gustavus Myers. He correctly highlighted the major preoccupations of Astor's life: the fur trade, China trade, and Manhattan real estate; yet he retold many of the apocryphal stories that first appeared in James Parton. Ghent slavishly followed earlier interpretive schemes and concluded that John Astor was so obsessed by the desire to make money that he regularly violated the law and acceptable moral standards in his business ventures. In a passage based squarely on Myers and Parton, Ghent concluded:

> The stories of his exteme parsimony as well as of his exacting acquisitiveness as creditor and landlord are many, and his merciless aggression in prosecuting the fur trade is attested by official documents that

cannot be questioned. His influence at Washington, combined with his great wealth and his extensive organization, enabled him to carry on his operations with a high hand. . . . His men shared with other traders, and of course with his approval, in the work of debauching the Indians with liquor in order to get their furs more cheaply. The amassing of wealth was his ruling passion, and few devices that could contribute to that end, were neglected by him. Though in his later days he wished to be portrayed as a broad-minded patriot and even a humanitarian, there is evidence that this ruling passion still possessed him at the close.[51]

Arthur D. Howden-Smith buttressed this conclusion in his popular biography of Astor published in 1929. Howden-Smith utilized the existing secondary literature with its plethora of colorful Astor anecdotes and added only minor twists to the basic theme. Howden-Smith accepted the general belief that Astor was morally flawed owing to an excessive pecuniary drive, but he further stressed the impact of Astor's German ancestry. Writing in the aftermath of World War I and the ethnocentric climate of the 1920s, Howden-Smith attributed Astor's failure to successfully establish the Astoria outpost in 1812, his supposed mistreatment of subordinates, and his miserly ways to his German nationality and character. In the author's mind, Astor never understood the American democratic spirit. Moreover, Howden-Smith implied that Astor was unpatriotic because of his frequent absences overseas and his close ties to the British and Canadians in the fur trade.[52]

Although Parton, Myers, Howden-Smith, and many other writers created a negative image of John Jacob Astor in American literature and history, there were occasional positive descriptions before Porter's scholarly biography in 1931. However, these books were as unreliable as the anti-Astor literature, for they routinely praised the financier without a critical evaluation of either primary or secondary materials. In 1915, for example, Elizabeth L. Gebhard wrote *The Life and Ventures of the Original John Jacob Astor* with the clear intention of rehabilitating his reputation. Her fascination with the financier was undoubtedly motivated by the fact that a member of her family had emigrated in 1771 from the same German village (Walldorf) that produced Astor. Gebhard chose to ignore the attacks of Gustavus Myers, retelling instead the story of Astor's hard work, prescient understanding of the fur and land markets, and philanthropic undertakings such as the establishment of the Astor Library. In the dedication of her book, she expressed her romantic belief concerning the major significance of Astor's career: "To the boys who courageously work their own way."[53]

The Horatio Alger theme—hard work, moral integrity and perseverance ultimately produce success—dominated the pro-Astor literature. Matthew H. Smith, who frequently wrote on New York's financial community, for example, believed that the New Yorker's immense fortune was the result of his dedication to business tasks. He further stressed Astor's care of the less fortunate and related the surely apocryphal story that the financier operated a soup kitchen from the rear of his own house. The author further claimed that Astor paid his employees good salaries and cared for their social and religious welfare. He related an incident in which the financier allowed a particularly religious clerk to attend church on Sunday despite the pressure of getting a ship ready to sail with the tide, "You need not come tomorrow . . . ," Astor supposedly told the laborer, "I am glad we have one Christian among us. You go to church, and pray for us poor sinners hard at work."[54]

Perhaps the most well-known book of this genre was Elbert Hubbards's *Little Journeys to the Homes of the Great Businessmen.* Hubbard added nothing new to the basic story of Astor's career, yet his eagerness to invent new stories and even dialogue demonstrated the continuing development of the Astor legend. Hubbard, for example, presented what he claimed was Astor's own assessment of the characteristics of a successful businessman:

> The man who makes it the habit of his life to go to bed at nine o'clock, usually gets rich and is always reliable. Of course going to bed does not make him rich—I merely mean that such a man will in all probability be up early in the morning and do a big day's work, so his weary bones put him to bed early. Rogues do their work at night. Honest men work by day. It's all a matter of habit; and good habits in America make any man rich. Wealth is largely a result of habit.[55]

Kenneth Wiggins Porter's two-volume scholarly biography in 1931 was, indeed, a remarkable accomplishment given the contradictory images of Astor that had become part of American history and literature. Porter was the first historian to utilize the primary sources that included the Astor letterbooks at Harvard University's

Baker Library and the American Fur Company letterbooks and account books. Porter also traveled to, or corresponded with, libraries such as the New York Historical Society, the New York Public Library, the Missouri Historical Society, and the Public Records Office in London. He was so conscious of Astor's sullied reputation and the mountain of folk stories that he tried to authenticate every source. In general, he questioned—although he did not discard—most of the information of a personal nature in both James Parton and Gustavus Myers.[56]

Porter's biography, however, was not a glossed-over defense of the New Yorker; instead, he strove to present a balanced and judicious assessment based on all the available evidence. Porter was unable to rehabilitate John Astor despite his questioning of the legend and his inability to uncover any damning evidence against him. He acknowledged the financier's business skill and his success, but he just could not accept that any man who had accumulated so much money had either worthy motives or a clear conscience. Porter's ambivalence about the New Yorker's career showed in his avoidance of strong judgments on Astor's business accomplishments and strategies. Unfortunately, this ambivalence confused Porter's readers: he left the image of Astor as a plodding merchant who exercised only a minimal impact on the society, politics, and business system of his day.

Porter's uncertain interpretation, I believe, resulted first from a flawed technique for evaluating evidence. Porter's research methods failed him at critical junctures when he might have emerged from a welter of conflicting sources and endless detail to present firmly grounded conclusions. Surely, Porter was making a conscious effort to avoid the mistakes of earlier writers like Myers and Parton, who were in the service of ideas and goals beyond an objective study of Astor. But Porter's zeal for objectivity was misdirected. He treated each primary source as if it had equal weight. Rather than discard a story about Astor that was based solely on gossip and hearsay or weeding out unreliable witnesses, instead, Porter attempted to find a middle ground—to discover a point at which all the sources were consistent. His incredibly detailed and thorough research eventually drove him back to his own deeply held assumptions when advancing broad generalizations.

Perhaps one example demonstrates Porter's methodological quagmire. He faced conflicting testimony relating to Astor's family background in the German village of Walldorf and his first years as a businessman in America. Did the financier come from a poor family? How do we account for his rapid advancement from the time he left Walldorf at the age of sixteen to 1792 when he had become a merchant of moderate, if not substantial, means? The Astor legend was built on the notion that the financier had shown great initiative and literally pulled himself from a wrecked family life to work his way from Walldorf to London where he stayed for four years with a brother who was in the business of manufacturing musical instruments. He then went to New York City in 1784 where he eked out an existence that included—depending on which sources you read—delivering bakery goods in the city streets, making toys and selling them along the docks, and beating furs in the backrooms of a retail merchant; this combined with treks into the wilderness of New York State to barter with the Indians for furs. A few years later, he operated his own music and fur store. In these accounts, the financier's early years thereby demonstrated both incredible grit and business acumen.

Unfortunately, most of these supposed facts cannot be substantiated and all came from undocumented and biased sources such as Moses Beach and James Parton.[57] Porter's mistake was to take these sources seriously rather than to exclude them for reasons of bias, distance from the events and personalities, and factual errors. If Porter had discarded them, he still had solid evidence in neutral sources such as legal documents, ship manifests, and newspapers pointing to a far different interpretation of Astor's early years: that Astor came to America with a substantial financial stake and hardly represented a climb from rags to riches.[58]

Adding to the burden of his unwieldy research techniques, Porter's ambivalent views of John Astor were the product of a clash between the influence of his own environment and his assumptions about economic society. In the 1920s, he worked at the Harvard Business School's Baker Library alongside N. S. B. Gras who was then pioneering the historical study of American businessmen. Porter's study of Astor was part of a series, the *Harvard Studies in Business History,* edited by Gras. Although there were surely no conscious efforts to force Porter into a defense of Astor, the Harvard Business School in the late 1920s was, nevertheless, an unlikely place to spawn a damning indictment of America's first business hero. In these early years, Gras and his followers were constantly trying to raise money to continue their work, resulting in business biographies that were often nonconmittal on social and political issues.

Yet Porter might well have been pulled in such a direction, for he was a socialist and a deeply religious man who wrote hymns and prayers when not occupied with his historical studies. His basic distrust of businessmen and capitalism rarely crept into his work, but the few occasions when it did were vivid. For example, he compared Astor and Stephen Girard, his Philadelphia contemporary, in terms of business ethics, commenting that "both were honest, at least within the restricted sense which that term implies in 'commerce.' "[59] Porter thus faulted Astor for lacking concern for his fellow man, possessing an overwhelming desire for profit, and limiting his involvement in national and social issues. These character traits, the author understood to be a result of the New Yorker's extreme unhappiness and poverty as a young man. In essence, Porter exhibited the same distrust of commercial life and lukewarm judgments of Astor's character as had James Parton who had written almost sixty-five years earlier.[60]

The end result of Porter's totally dispassionate, thoroughly professional, and completely objective study was two extraordinarily long volumes (over thirteen hundred pages) that were confusingly organized and lacking an overall thesis. These volumes are among the legion of often-cited but rarely read books in American history; despite the laudable research, Porter's study failed to alter the legend of Astor first created by Parton and Myers. One need only read Harvey O'Connor, John Terrell, Lucy Kavaler, and Virginia Cowles to realize that contemporary popular authors would sooner reach for James Parton and Gustavus Myers than consult the primary sources or Porter's study.[61]

Both Lucy Kavaler and Virginia Cowles's books were clearly popular accounts and were treated as such by historians and the reading public, but the O'Connor and Terrell volumes have gained a measure of scholarly acceptance and therefore require additional comment. Harvey O'Connor had written several scathing criticisms of other American millionaires, including Andrew Mellon and the Guggenheims, before taking on the Astor family. His reputation for radical politics, moreover, eventually found him cited for contempt in 1954 by Senator Joseph McCarthy's witch-hunting Senate Subcommittee on Investigations. Besides his obvious anti-business stance, O'Connor's book on Astor suffered from a lack of research into the primary sources and a complete dependence on Parton and Myers. He regularly cited the popular legends (e.g., Parton's story of the elderly financier berating his rental agent for not collecting from a destitute widow) in order to picture the financier as an immoral and greedy capitalist.[62]

John Terrell penned the most thorough modern condemnation of John Astor. Terrell, though, violated most of the canons of both professional and amateur history, yet his failures were understandable given his background as a prolific author of novels and children's books. When he set to work on a volume of history, he lacked a clear notion of the historian's methods and goals and often lapsed into the novelist's techniques. For example, he attributed thoughts and ideas to Astor that cannot be substantiated. Thus, he described the young Astor dreaming of empires as he read books by candlelight on far western exploration. Similarly, he charged that Astor wanted to form his own nation on the Pacific Coast, not just establish a fur trade depot at Astoria. Terrell's evidence was a letter of Thomas Jefferson's in which the latter expressed a hope that the region west of the Rockies would someday form a separate nation. Terrell assumed that Astor had planted this notion in Jefferson's mind as part of a grand scheme to take the territory. Not only was Terrell's interpretation ludicrous but it also took Jefferson's letter completely out of context.[63]

The Astor mythology has a unique way of staying alive in historical literature at least, in part, because the stories of the financier's excesses make good reading. Norman Gras and Henrietta Larson's widely used textbook on business history, for example, retold many of these tales, although it presented a balanced interpretation. Ben Seligman's general history of American businessmen, *The Potentates,* not only accused Astor of illegal business methods but even managed to produce new stories to prove the point. According to Seligman, Astor was so boorish that he would "remove the chewing tobacco from his mouth before a visitor to draw designs on the window."[64]

In general, modern historians have supported the dominant Parton–Myers interpretation and have come to believe that Astor was a crook. Consequently, today's historians often neglect Astor either by excluding him from textbooks on American economic and political history or by mentioning him briefly as a fur trader or as a symbol of capitalistic excess.[65] William Barney's recent interdisciplinary study of nineteenth-century America does not even mention Astor, neither does Robert Wiebe's *The Opening of American Society*.[66] Richard Bartlett's excellent study of westward expansion entitled *The New Country* virtually ignores Astor's influence and refers to him as the "exploitative miser."[67] W. J. Rorabough in *The Alcoholic Republic* blamed the New Yorker for corrupting both the fur traders and the Indians. In a statement demonstrating the author's dependence on W. J. Ghent's *DAB* article, Rorabough concluded, "It is fair to state that Astor's wealth came from selling liquor rather than buying furs, a fact that may explain why later, with a touch of conscience perhaps, he gave money to the temperance movement."[68] Finally, a recent summary of Astor's career in the multivolume *Biographical Dictionary of American Business Leaders* repeated the usual stories of the New Yorker's unhappy youth and of his arrival in America, while questioning his business practices and ethics.[69]

For over a century, then, most historians have eagerly embraced a negative image of John Astor based on flimsy or, at the very least, inconclusive evidence. The durability of this interpretation can only be explained if we go beyond Astor's career and investigate his contemporaries, later historians, and the reading public—all of whom viewed the New Yorker through distorted lenses. Astor's contemporaries lived and wrote during the 1840s and 1850s when nationalistic fervor, particularly in cities like New York, produced a marked hostility toward German-born citizens. Many New Yorkers questioned Astor's patriotism not only because of his heavy accent but also because he continued to live in Europe for long periods. Moreover, the size of the financier's fortune challenged mid-nineteenth-century conceptions of America's open democratic society. To many observers, Astor had transplanted European class traditions into America when he established a trust in his will that perpetuated the family fortune for generations to come.

Ironically, the New Yorker's reputation later suffered from the follies of family members because much of the hostile writing against him was really directed toward subsequent generations. By the 1840s, William B. Astor, John Jacob's son, controlled the family business and apparently he and later his son, John Jacob Astor II, flaunted their aristocratic lifestyle and continued to make the Astor name synonymous with Manhattan real estate.

Unfortunately, the family produced a number of truly arrogant dilettantes who delighted in public opprobrium.

William Waldorf Astor was the best example of this tradition. He was a lawyer and politician who served briefly as a New York State assemblyman and later as a senator. He ran twice unsuccessfully for the U.S. Senate, although in 1882 he entered publc service when President Chester Alan Arthur appointed him ambassador to Italy. But Astor disliked his countrymen and finally expatriated himself and took up life as a conservative English gentleman. He bought a liberal newspaper, the *Pall Mall Gazette,* and turned it into a vehicle for conservative thought. He also published a magazine in which he wrote a spirited defense of the original John Jacob Astor. In this article, he criticized American laws and customs, which he felt were unduly antagonistic toward the rich. In a truly boorish statement, William Waldorf Astor announced, "It has always seemed to me a truism that we owe to wealth the greatest advantages and pleasures that life can offer in education, in the comforts and refinements of home, in the embellishments of art and in the delight of travel."[70] It is little wonder that historians and public commentators could not separate the character and business of the original Astor from the descendants who smugly guarded the fortune and carried the Astor name.

Finally, over the years, professional historians have had difficulty in correctly evaluating John Astor because they held a substantial bias against his two major economic activities: the fur trade and land speculation. Early studies of the fur trade were interested either in the fate of the Indians or in the colorful personalities of the traders rather than in the business itself. Only the most recent literature has examined the economics of the fur trade, its business organization, and the entrepreneurial skills of its leaders.[71] In a similar manner, historical literature has expressed great animosity toward land speculators who supposedly reaped great profits from the sale of land at the expense of yeoman farmers. Land speculators, like fur traders, were not thought to have contributed to the productive use of the land or to related transportation, banking, or urban development. Because John Astor was heavily involved in both the fur trade and in land speculation, his image as a grasping and selfish businessman whose wealth produced no improvements for the larger society was virtually unamimous. Historians today no longer hold such one-dimensional views of extractive economic activities, and both fur traders and land speculators have been considerably rehabilitated in recent literature.[72]

In conclusion, then, this analysis of the literature on John Astor demonstrates the need for a fresh appraisal free of the rhetoric of over a century of historical writing. I do not intend to redo Porter's important study, although I acknowledge my debt to Porter's thorough research. My own analysis of Astor's career departs substantially from the methodology of previous historians. On many points of fact and particularly on questions about the financier's personality and motives, I have discounted highly suspect authors such as Moses Beach, James Gallatin, Gustavus Myers, James Parton, and John Terrell unless there is specific corroboration of facts and opinions in the primary sources. It seems to me historians, like lawyers, should discount "bad" evidence.[73]

No biography can be definitive, of course, because each author utilizes different materials and perspectives and builds on the work of many other historians. I have benefited substantially from the existence of primary sources that were not available to others or difficult for them to access. The American Fur Company Papers today are readily available on microfilm and contain perhaps the most thorough and detailed record of any antebellum business organization. Similarly the Albert Gallatin Papers, which contain a lengthy correspondence between Gallatin (then secretary of the treasury) and Astor reveal the latter's political and economic motives and a good bit about his personality. The Gallatin papers are particularly important because the main collection of the Astor papers at the Baker Library, Harvard University, and at the New York Historical Society are noticeably lacking in personal materials. I suspect that either Astor himself or his descendants carefully culled any "damaging" materials from the collections.

I also have benefited from substantial advances in both the theoretical and methodological approaches to economic history that have occurred over the last twenty-five years. Two perspectives dominate this study, thus providing an organizational and interpretative framework. First, I have used what social scientists refer to as entrepreneurial and modernization theories: not as strict paradigms, but as general guides to understand to what extent Astor was an innovative force. Did he change the methods of conducting business or develop new products and institutions or

inspire substantial changes through his example? Why did he succeed on such a grand scale? Did he have a clear business strategy
or was his success a matter of luck?[74]

My second perspective is a product of the first and helps to
answer the questions posed earlier. My reading of Astor's career
places him squarely in what historian Thomas Cochran has referred to as "the business revolution" in the American economy
and, thus, conflicts with the broad interpretative framework of Astor's first biographer, Kenneth Wiggins Porter.

Porter's biography of Astor was written under the tutelage of
Norman S. B. Gras, who was among the first and most important
interpreters of American business and economic development. According to Gras and Porter, merchants and businessmen from the
colonial period to the advent of manufacturing in the 1840s had
very limited control over their businesses owing to their inability
to control markets. They had few employees, lacked institutional
or corporate structures, and rarely affected political and economic
events. The difficulties of sea and overland travel created huge
risks, so that, for protection, merchants diversified their activities
beyond trade, carried more than a single product, and shipped to
many ports and markets. The lack of communication and the dangers of travel often meant that ship captains left port unaware of
market prices and traveled the international markets for a year or
more in a haphazard search for profitable exchanges. The businesses of merchants were simply organized (typically in partnerships with other merchants) to protect against risks. Other than
one or two clerks and ship captains, these merchants did not
worry about the intricacies of large staffs and the strategies of
market capitalism. The merchant's day reflected the unhurried
pattern of the trade world of the time, with a morning trip to the
counting house, leisurely lunch, and an afternoon gathering with
other merchants.

According to Gras and Porter, gradual changes began to take
place in the preindustrial world of the general merchant by the
late 1780s as American foreign trade increased in the aftermath of
the American Revolution. As artisans and farmers sought wider
outlets for their products, merchants specialized in a single line of
commerce such as furs, iron, and cotton; and this specialization in
the business world increased the volume of goods moving through
the economic system. Banks expanded rapidly, particularly in
the first decades of the nineteenth century, as did other financial

institutions such as insurance companies and savings and loan associations. The building of roads and canals knitted together population and markets that had expanded to the West. Government attitudes changed as both state and federal authorities promoted business and economic development.[75]

Historians, though, disagree substantially on the significance of these economic changes. Alfred Chandler, who has carried on the study of American business first begun by Norman Gras and Kenneth Porter at the Harvard Business School, has argued in his important book, *The Visible Hand,* that these changes did not alter business practices even as late as 1840 and that merchants remained unsophisticated in both business strategy and structure. According to Chandler, businessmen were still at the mercy of market forces and unable to control the volume or price of goods in the marketplace. Consequently, they made few efforts to alter institutional structures, to apply new managerial strategies, or to refine accounting procedures. For Chandler, the great breakthrough was the railroad that, because of its speed, moved a significantly higher volume and greater variety of goods through the system. In order to control the railroads and the flow of goods, businessmen then developed the modern large-scale corporation with its multidivisional structure and its salaried managers. For the first time, managers, what Chandler calls the visible hand, exerted control over the marketplace. So it was that a business revolution accompanied the great manufacturing and technological changes associated with the onset of American industrialization in the 1840s.[76]

Chandler, Gras, and Porter are not mistaken, but there is today a significant literature that suggests they have overemphasized the impact of technology and the railroad and thereby have failed to recognize the significant changes in business behavior, strategy, and structure that occurred from the 1780s to the beginning of the railroad. Thomas Cochran is the most articulate exponent of this view. He dates the beginning of American industrialization in the early national period, arguing that not only had there been significant manufacturing breakthroughs but also that changes in the business system—such as the development of the corporate form and the appearance of institutions for pooling capital—were fundamental to creating an institutional structure that supported industrialization. Cochran saw the railroad as the final rather than the first step in creating an industrial society.[77]

My argument throughout this book is that Cochran's perspective offers a far clearer lens through which to see the significance of Astor's business career. The New Yorker stood at a period of great transition and although he occasionally stayed with accepted modes of thought and action, more often he seized on new opportunities and experimented with different strategies and structures. How else does one begin to explain the creation of the first American dynasty that mixed old and new markets—furs and tea—and pursued that quintessential American business activity—urban development and promotion?

CHAPTER TWO

The Early Years, 1763–1794

AT THE core of the generally negative interpretations of John Jacob Astor's character and business influence, in the works of authors from James Parton to Kenneth Wiggins Porter, was the belief that the young Astor suffered an unhappy childhood at the hands of a derelict father and an overbearing mother in uncertain, if not deprived, economic circumstances. Thus Astor, supposedly alone and penniless, undertook an odyssey of emigration that brought him first to England, then to America, and ultimately to a vast fortune unmatched in mid-nineteenth-century America. The struggle, however, left deep and lasting scars, and these early historians nearly all agreed that Astor was obsessed with accumulating an ever-larger fortune and rarely spent his bounty in a socially constructive fashion.[1] However, another look at Astor's early years demonstrates that he was not the embodiment of the Horatio Alger story but, instead, arrived in America with a moderate financial stake and appeared to struggle far less than most of his contemporaries. In effect, nearly all interpretations of John Astor attached great significance to his early life; yet all these interpretations were based on flimsy, if not completely inaccurate, evidence.

John Jacob Astor was born 17 July 1763 in Walldorf, a small German village not far from Heidelberg in the Duchy of Baden. He was the fifth child of Jacob Astor and had three older brothers and two sisters in addition to a half sister. His mother died when he was less than five years old, but his father soon remarried. We know little about Astor's family life. His father was primarily a butcher by trade, of moderate means, and probably held some minor legal position at some time during his life. The young Astor and his siblings were members of an artisan class and had received a basic education and religious training through local tutors and at a local school.[2]

John Astor could hardly look forward to a bright future in Walldorf. At the end of the eighteenth century, small German towns were economically stagnant. The immense changes of the Industrial Revolution were decades away, and village life still revolved around the rhythm of an agricultural society. Walldorf and the surrounding countryside was an insular and provincial society. Both artisans and farmers sold their products in stalls at local fairs and markets in the town center. There were, as yet, few middlemen in the trading patterns; thus there was an ill-defined middle class in the villages. In small towns especially, artisan and craftsmens' guilds controlled prices and products and limited access to the trades. Apprenticeship systems were rigidly fixed and often family connections were essential to learning a trade.

The artisan's life was neither easy nor secure. As the eighteenth century progressed, life became more difficult not only owing to continued political upheaval but also because of demographic and economic changes. Population was increasing throughout Europe—particularly in Baden—and this placed enormous strain on the traditional agricultural society. In Baden-Württemberg, agricultural reforms had ended primogeniture and established a freehold system and partible inheritance. The farms grew smaller and more inefficient and this drove farmers into the cities. Yet, in the cities, mobility was limited because employment in the trades and crafts had not increased sufficiently. German village life throughout the eighteenth century was a status-bound society with few or no avenues of social mobility.[3] No wonder that many Germans were dissatisfied and restless. Emigration both to England and America was widely acknowledged as an attractive outlet for relieving the economic pressures.[4]

Obviously, John Astor's decision to leave Walldorf was motivated by these economic pressures as well as by a variety of more personal concerns. Even though his father was an artisan, there

must have been little need for apprentices as none of his older siblings had undertaken that vocation. Indeed, Astor's brothers
sought opportunities outside Walldorf. His oldest brother, George,
emigrated to London where he manufactured and sold musical instruments. Another brother, Henry, somehow found his way to
New York City in the 1770s, probably stopping first in London and
then coming to America with the British army in a noncombat
role. In New York City, he eventually chose his father's craft and
became a butcher. A third brother, John Melchior, remained in the
Walldorf region as a farmer.[5] By the time John Jacob reached the
age of sixteen, there was probably little doubt that he, too, would
seek to escape the confines of village life. But for him the decision
to emigrate was easier, for he had family connections both in New
York and London, In 1779, therefore, John Astor left Walldorf and
headed for London to join his brother.[6] He remained in London for
four years, living initially with his brother and working with him
in manufacturing flutes and other musical instruments. During
this period, he developed a lifelong affection for classical music
and established contacts with London manufacturers such as
Shudi and Broadwood.[7] Here, young Astor also acquired a modest
financial stake as well as mercantile experience and connections.
When the American Revolution ended, he sailed to Baltimore on
the *North Carolina* arriving in March 1784.[8]

Nineteenth-century historians such as James Parton deliberately created a myth for dramatic effect about Astor's arrival in
America, and it has obscured both his goals and financial circumstances. He arrived in America neither penniless nor without
prospects; rather, he came with four years' experience as assistant
to his brother and probably also as a salesman for his brother's
manufactured products. Indeed, one of the purposes of his voyage
to America was to investigate the market for musical instruments
and supplies. Consequently, he carried samples from his brother's
factory.[9] On his first day in Baltimore as he wandered among the
streets near the wharf, he met a local merchant, Nicholas Tuschdy.
Tuschdy not only allowed Astor to live with him for a short period
but also agreed to display some of Astor's samples in his store. Astor remained in Baltimore about three weeks before making his
way to New York City to survey the markets and economic conditions there and to meet his brother Henry.[10]

Astor, in fact, repeated a fairly common pattern among aspiring
merchants and businessmen on both sides of the Atlantic Ocean at

the end of the Revolution. He attempted to establish or reestablish economic contacts between England and America. Astor's first trip to America was not, then, the emigration of a poor, though precocious, young man; instead, it was an exploratory journey in which he intended to decide for himself and his London contacts whether to commit additional effort and capital to American markets.[11]

Astor must have been startled at New York City's appearance in 1784. The American Revolution had devastated the political, social, and economic structure of the city. In 1775, New York City had a population of 22,000, the majority compactly housed within a mile of Fort George at the tip of Manhattan. When Saint Paul's Church was built on Vesey Street to the North in 1766, people considered this location to be in the country. New York was a commercial emporium at this time and only Boston or Philadelphia could claim a more vibrant trading economy. The slips along the East River were the hub of commercial activity, with retail and trade establishments a block or two inland, particularly on Queen and Dock streets. Although many merchants lived on the top floor of their retail establishments, there were also clearly identified residential neighborhoods for the wealthy as well as some segregation of class and economic activity.[12]

The Revolution altered this physical and demographic structure. By the middle of 1776, with the threat of combat and British occupation, New York City's population had fallen from 22,000 to 5,000. But the population swelled again as first American soldiers came and, after their defeat at the Battle of Long Island in late 1776, the British took over the city for most of the war. In addition to the permanent residents, the city's population surged to 31,000 with the influx of soldiers and Loyalists from throughout the colonies. British occupation, though, was disastrous as the soldiers fortified many public places and also converted commercial buildings and private residences to military barracks. The military government certainly felt under no obligation to attend to the normal responsibilities of municipal government. Refuse littered city streets, and normal repairs on docks and bulkheads were neglected. To further exacerbate conditions major fires hit the city in 1776 and 1778 destroying approximately one-fourth of the settled area. Finally, the city's commerce was totally disrupted. When the war ended, the British soldiers and their Loyalist supporters deserted the city leaving behind an empty shell to the remaining 11,000 inhabitants.[13]

Ironically, New York City's hardships created many opportunities for aspiring businessmen. Its location as a port was unmatched, and the war's end carried the potential for a return to a favorable business environment for residents. The departure of the Loyalists opened new opportunities for mercantile careers, to say nothing of the speculation that resulted from the forced sales of Loyalists' property.[14] Timing has always been a crucial ingredient of success, and John Jacob Astor came to New York City at the precise moment of its emergence as the commercial and financial center of the new nation. By 1786, its population has grown to 23,000; by 1790 it was 31,131.[15]

When Astor arrived in New York City in the spring of 1784, his search for opportunity centered in rather disparate fields: music and fur trading. He carried with him some sheet music and musical instruments with which to establish contacts among the city's retailers. He hoped to establish a formal arrangement with a general merchant who would regularly import from London's specialized music stores. If the market seemed to warrant it, Astor may have considered locating in New York City as an importer. In addition, the fur trade also intrigued him, an interest he carried with him from London, the center of European fur markets and the headquarters of the Hudson's Bay Company. Astor also had met and talked extensively with a German-American fur merchant while on board ship en route to America. As his contacts with the music business were well established, he utilized profits from the sale of his musical wares to invest in furs, which he purchased either at auction in the city or from retailers.

Astor did not remain long in New York City, departing in June or July for London. There he sold the furs at a profit; and, based on his experience both with musical instruments and furs, he decided to settle in America. He quickly arranged his personal and business affairs. He also established business arrangements with London firms like Shudi and Broadwood, a leading piano manufacturer, and with Robert Backhouse, who supplied goods, mainly blankets and trinkets, for the fur trade and who sold furs in London and continental markets. By November or December 1784, Astor had once again set out for America, only this time he intended to settle permanently.[16]

Astor's movements in 1785 and 1786 cannot be pieced together with total accuracy, although we know that he both traded furs and imported musical instruments and that his prospects seemed bright. In the fall of 1785, he married Sarah Todd, who apparently brought a small dowry to the marriage as well as a distant connection to the well-known Brevoort family.[17] In 1786, Astor lived and sold musical supplies at 81 Queen Street in a building owned by his mother-in-law. In May 1786, he advertised in the *New York Packet* that he had "just imported from London, an elegant assortment of musical instruments, such as pianofortes . . . the best of violins, German flutes, clarinets, . . . fifes, the best Roman violin strings, and all other kinds of strings, music books and paper, and every other article in the musical line, which he will dispose of on very low terms for cash."[18] This advertisement alone provided clear evidence that Astor was a merchant of moderate means, for he obviously had credit with London exporters and an ability to finance at least part of a large inventory. The popular stories that Astor was beating furs in the backrooms of New York merchants or that he was selling trinkets along harbor docks are obviously total fabrications.[19]

But Astor was not single-mindedly pursuing the music business; indeed, he had already decided that the fur trade offered more lucrative rewards. The fur trade had been central to both the British and French colonial establishments in North America. In the colonial period, the great trade center was Montreal. Traders set out from Montreal along the Saint Lawrence River and pushed deep into the Great Lakes and Mississippi River basins in their search for pelts. These French adventurers inevitably clashed with British traders who were moving westward from the second major center of the North American fur trade at Albany, New York. Thus the fur-trade industry became a flashpoint of the imperial wars of the eighteenth century.[20]

The American colonists at Albany provided substantial competition for the French at Montreal. Albany was a central location, situated in a natural break in the Appalachian Mountains, which permitted traders easy access to the West as well as a convenient point of transshipment for furs and manufactured goods moving on the Hudson River to and from New York City. With the defeat of the French and the resulting Treaty of Paris in 1763, Albany gradually declined as a fur-trade center. The northern routes to the interior from Montreal were faster and more efficient. Moreover, Montreal merchants—now dominated by the British—established better organization and control as trade expanded westward.[21]

The American Revolution subsequently confirmed Montreal's dominance in the trade. The revolutionary war, of course, completely disrupted the access of Albany merchants to British goods and the fur markets in London. Many traders such as Simon McTavish left Albany and relocated in Montreal in order to pursue the trade and to support the British blocked American participation in the fur trade as well as expansion to the West. Rigid controls were established to regulate the number of traders and the quantity of goods allowed into the interior. After the Revolution, the British sought to maintain control of the fur trade and Montreal's hegemony by prohibiting the export of Canadian furs to the Americans.[22]

British actions surrounding the 1783 Treaty of Paris that ended the American War of Independence gave Montreal a virtual, although temporary, monopoly over the North American fur trade. The treaty stipulated that the British government relinquish the rich fur-bearing region in the Great Lakes controlled by Montreal traders. The Americans received a northern boundary from Lake Superior on angle to Lake of the Woods and from there to the Mississippi River. At the same time, the treaty called for Great Britain to abandon its military posts in the western territory at places such as Mackinac, Oswego, Detroit, and Niagara. Yet Montreal merchants protested vigorously. Subsequently, the British government, through its representative in America, General Frederick Haldimand, refused to abandon British forts in American territory, citing the vague language of the treaty which did not specify a precise time for withdrawal. British presence, particularly at Oswego, blocked American access to Lake Ontario and the possibility of renewed fur trade, by means of the established route west from Albany. Moreover, the British were also entrenched on Mackinac Island, thereby preventing American intrusions along Lake Huron and west to Lake Michigan and the Mississippi River tributaries.[23]

Neither the American government nor the mercantile community initially provided much resistance to the British position in the trade. The Confederation government, of course, was neither politically nor militarily capable of challenging the British presence in the Old Northwest. Moreover, American interest at first was centered on formulating a coherent Indian policy and settlement program in the Ohio Valley. American merchants, on the other hand, were in a poor position because they lacked capital and a domestic market for furs. The Americans also faced severe restrictions in trying to ship furs to foreign markets such as London or to obtain British manufactured products. For the time being, the North American fur trade was entirely in British hands.[24]

Given the control of British Canadians centered in Montreal over the North American fur trade, one wonders why a young enterprising German immigrant would have desired to participate in the industry. Unfortunately, records are not available on Astor's motivation, although some evidence—business letters, newspaper advertisements, shipping manifests, and customs receipts—do reveal the broad outlines of Astor's strategy and challenge existing descriptions of his early years.[25] Astor had sufficient capital from his first days in America to purchase furs and sell musical instruments on a reasonably large scale. From his first trip to New York in 1784, Astor realized that he could secure modest profits in purchasing furs at both Albany and Montreal for sale in American markets and overseas.[26] He had no intention of challenging the entrenched Canadian interests.

John Jacob Astor's early fur-trade business had three centers of operation: New York City, Albany, and Montreal. New York City was important first as a market center. As early as 1788, he advertised furs for sale in the city hoping to attract hat and clothing manufacturers. New York was also the center from which Astor shipped overseas to foreign markets. Obviously, it was necessary that he possess a full range of business contacts in the city.[27]

In the first few years, Astor established business relationships with two important New York City merchants: Robert Bowne and William Backhouse. Both men were general retailers who occasionally purchased furs and supplied goods for traders. William Backhouse was particularly important, for he was also tied to the London firm of Thomas Backhouse and Company, which by 1790 accepted furs from Astor and shipped goods (e.g., blankets and other woolens) for use in the Indian trade. Astor's ties to Backhouse were particularly strong, for in 1792 Astor christened his second son William Backhouse; Backhouse's wife, Anna, stood as a baptismal sponsor.[28] Moreover, Astor's later business partners, particularly William Laight and Cornelius Heeney, had themselves been connected with William Backhouse.[29]

Astor's connection to Bowne is unclear; numerous sources have commented that Astor worked for Bowne, but it is more likely that he was involved in a form of agency relationship, that is, Astor assumed responsibility for obtaining furs in a market such as Albany and Bowne shared in the purchase price or disposed of them in New York City.[30] Astor's close ties to Bowne and Backhouse were quite beneficial, for both men were older, settled merchants with important connections in New York City's mercantile community. Bowne, for example, was a founding member of New York's Chamber of Commerce in 1784 and a director of the Bank of New York in 1785. In addition, along with William Backhouse he was a member of the Board of Governors of the New York Hospital.[31]

A succession of business relationships, which sometimes constituted full-fledged partnerships and at other times may have only been a type of agency agreement, characterized Astor's early years in New York City. Such business arrangements were typical of fur merchants who changed partners yearly and often had several partners at one time, depending on the type of fur or the location of the market. For Astor, this pattern permitted him to raise capital, obtain credit, share the risk, and divide the various responsibilities associated with the fur business. For example, in the early 1790s, he formed a partnership with Cornelius Heeney, a man who had worked previously as a clerk for William Backhouse. During this period, Astor spent a substantial amount of time at the fur markets in Albany and Montreal, and Heeney kept the account books and wrote the necessary business letters. The association with Heeney lasted from at least 1792 to 1795, after which time Heeney broke off their arrangement and became a general merchant.[32]

Astor also had a business partnership with Peter Smith in the late 1780s and early 1790s, a relationship that included a connection to the fur resources of upstate New York centered in Albany. Like Astor, Smith had come to New York City in 1784; he first became a clerk and later opened a retail store that specialized in books. More than likely, Smith found this pursuit unrewarding; by 1787, he had relocated near Little Falls, New York, a key juncture on the route west from Albany to the Mohawk River and Lake Ontario. Here Smith was in a suitable location to purchase furs from traders. However, he moved again within a year to Old Fort Schuyler, later Utica, where he opened a store that carried a regular inventory of goods for the fur trade.

Throughout the 1790s, Astor regularly visited Albany and occasionally stopped at Utica on his annual fur-buying trips to Montreal. Albany was by now the former center of the American fur trade, and, although now in decline, it still served as the central collecting point for furs. Moreover, in earlier years, a thriving trade in furs and manufactured products existed between Albany and Montreal; these communication routes Astor clearly utilized to his advantage. Smith and Astor had an agreement in which Smith provided Astor with a dependable source of furs and Astor supplied trade goods and marketed the furs. Even after the end of their formal agreement, Astor continued to accept furs on commission from Smith for many years.[33]

Montreal was the most important location for Astor's fur business, for the simple reason that it was the best market for obtaining furs and the center of the North American fur industry. Consequently, the young Astor understood and accepted the industry's organizational structure and deftly cultivated business relationships with the existing power structure. His skills were immediately apparent.

Astor recognized that his position as an American fur trader was quite limited. In the 1780s, Montreal merchants controlled the trade in both Canada and the United States. Furs came from three broad areas. The Detroit region was the transfer point for outfits exploiting the territory south of the Great Lakes such as along the Wabash and Maumee rivers.[34] Mackinac was a second central collecting and distributing point. From here traders moved west and south to Green Bay, Chicago, the Illinois River, and the upper Mississippi River. By the 1790s, the Canadians were even challenging the Spanish and French traders from Saint Louis. Indeed, by 1793, Charles Gratiot, a leading Saint Louis trader, obtained goods and shipped furs from Mackinac through Montreal to London.[35] The third trading region was located at Grand Portage, which was the gateway to the Far West and the incredibly rich harvests of the Athabasca region.

The Montreal fur trading community, nevertheless, was worried because so much of the trade was drawn from American territory. A government report prepared in 1784 estimated that the total annual output of furs was valued at £154,000 with nearly two-thirds of that trade coming from Detroit and Mackinac. In 1790, John Inglis of Phyn, Ellice and Inglis, reported the fur harvest's value at £200,000, of which £100,000 came from American territory. Of that £100,000, the Detroit region produced 40 percent and Mackinac accounted for 60 percent. Of the remaining £100,000 gathered in Canada, nearly half came from the far Northwest or Grand Portage region.[36]

These figures help explain the business strategy of Montreal merchants in the late eighteenth century. They prosecuted the fur trade in American territory—referred to as the southwest trade— as vigorously as possible, knowing that the Americans might at any moment assert their control over American territory. Consequently, the Montreal merchants pressured British officials in Quebec and London to relax many regulations governing the trade. By 1791, the government no longer required licenses and permitted the use of liquor in the trade. Simultaneously, the great mercantile houses such as McTavish, Frobisher and Company; Forsyth, Richardson and Company; and Todd, McGill and Company petitioned the government to protect the western posts—if not to negotiate a completely new treaty strengthening the British position. Nevertheless, many Canadian traders, who decided that only by expanding farther west could they protect the trade from the uncertainties of international diplomacy, focused all their attention on the Grand Portage region or the Northwest trade.[37]

The constant expansion of trade territories to the west and the volatile political situation along the border produced a simultaneous movement on the part of Montreal merchants to reorganize the structure of the fur business. In the late eighteenth century, the fur trade was a highly individualistic, openly competitive, and often ruthless business. It can, perhaps, be most closely compared to the early days of the steel and oil industries when many independent producers battled for a share of the marketplace. The trade itself was conducted over a vast geographic area that extended from the capitals of North America to Lake Superior and beyond to the foothills of the Rocky Mountains. Moreover, the markets for the sale of furs included North American cities—mainly Baltimore, Philadelphia, and New York—and international capitals—London and Paris—as well as centers in Russia and China.

Between the gathering of the furs and their sale in the marketplace, several levels of business activity existed. This division of function and responsibility was the result of transportation difficulties and the vast distances. No one individual could efficiently both trap furs and sell in the distant marketplace because the cycle from production to final sale could take up to three years.[38]

On the bottom rung of the fur business were the Indians, who most often trapped the animals and then sold the furs to traders who periodically visited their tribal lands. Fur traders, usually of French and British descent, were the Indians' principal contact.

They transported the furs from the interior to central collection points at Detroit, Mackinac, and Grand Portage, exchanging them for goods such as blankets, beads, firearms, and liquor that then constituted the basis for exchange in the following trade year. At Detroit and Mackinac, the traders negotiated with independent merchants or associations of merchants such as John Askin or Grant, Campion and Company, middlemen who accepted the furs and passed on the goods they received from Montreal. Particularly prosperous traders might bypass the western wholesaler and carry their furs directly to Montreal where they bargained with another, higher level of middleman such as James McGill, Benjamin and Joseph Frobisher, or Simon McTavish.

These Montreal traders were usually organized in partnerships and acted as the linchpins in the North American fur trade. They supplied goods to firms in the interior at Mackinac and Detroit and assembled furs for shipment to the London marketplace. The Montreal firms usually either employed or formed direct relationships with interior agents. They also possessed equivalent ties to mercantile agents in London. The merchants in London were responsible for the sale of furs either at auction or to wholesalers from Europe as well as for the purchase of goods from manufacturers. Although the variations in this trade pattern were endless, the price of furs in the London marketplace determined the profits for everyone along the chain from the traders in the interior to wholesalers at Mackinac and Detroit to the merchants in Montreal.[39]

Finally, all the industry's participants were united in a series of interlocking credit arrangements that carried over a two- to three-year period; each, in turn, was both a creditor and debtor. The traders advanced goods to the Indians in hopes of securing enough furs to justify their investment; the traders were simultaneously indebted to their Detroit or Mackinac suppliers; in turn, the suppliers were indebted to their Montreal connections; finally, the Montreal firms were indebted to the London merchants. No one along the route profited from excess competition that drove up fur prices or from glutted markets when all furs reached the market at the same time. Obviously organization and cooperation might reduce risks and increase profits; this need was extraordinarily important in the 1780s given Britain's tenuous hold on American territory south of Canada.[40]

The North West Company established in 1783—by far the most important and most powerful organization—was one that profoundly affected John Astor's career. It brought together traders and merchants from the interior, Montreal, and London in an effort to lessen the effects of competition and to secure financial advantages from the very act of organizing. A powerful group of Montreal businessmen saw that their competition for supplies and furs adversely affected prices. Moreover, they depended on bidding for the services of traders who, in turn, struggled against one another in the interior. It made good economic sense to bring a limited number of people into a formal organization, thereby avoiding duplication of function and cutthroat competition while sharing equally in the profits.[41]

The theme of organization and combination in the trade, however, must not be overstated. Despite the North West Company's dominant position in the trade, the industry was large and reasonably profitable, thus allowing many independent Montreal businessmen and smaller companies and partnerships to pit their skills against the North West Company. There existed as well internal shifts and quarrels within the North West Company that destabilized the industry for many years. For example, the North West Company was primarily interested in the Far West trade, but the company also maintained an interest in the southwest trade operating from centers at Mackinac and Detroit.

Astor cautiously inserted himself into this volatile business situation by never challenging Canadian hegemony and by simply using Montreal as a place where he could buy furs from anyone willing to sell. Beginning in 1787, Astor made regular trips to Montreal, stopping en route at towns like Albany and Champlain. He was usually in Montreal during the summer when the furs arrived from the interior. He would stay for several months to take advantage of periodic auctions and the opportunities to purchase from independent traders as well as those associated with the North West Company. In the early years, he formed a business relationship with Alexander Henry the Elder, who was one of Montreal's most famous traders and explorers. Although Henry was not a member of the original North West Company, he later joined the firm. Henry provided Astor with vital contacts in the city's fur trade community; when Astor returned to New York after the summer season, Henry served as Astor's agent throughout the rest of the year.[42]

The size of Astor's Montreal trade in the late 1780s must have been fairly extensive. He rented a warehouse in Montreal in 1787 to store furs.[43] He often purchased in volume if the few surviving business agreements can be considered typical. In September 1789, he signed a contract with Ephraim Santford, a Montreal fur trader, to purchase fifteen thousand muskrat skins for approximately £825. Similarly in August 1789, he contracted with William Hands of Detroit for the delivery of fifteen thousand muskrat skins. Each of these contracts required the trader to deliver the next year's harvest at a prearranged price. Thus Astor hoped to stabilize the price and guarantee a certain volume of furs rather than be forced to compete with the larger companies and partnerships at the time the furs arrived in the market.

These promissory agreements, which attempted to control volume and price, often proved difficult to fulfill, obliging Astor occasionally to take legal action against traders for noncompliance. Obviously, it was difficult to predict the exact price furs would bring in a year's time, and traders might wish to avoid a prearranged contract with Astor if they thought a higher price might be obtained in the open market. On the other hand, Astor might well desire to avoid a preexisting contract if the fur prices fell precipitously; on one occasion, Astor was sued by a trader for failure to purchase furs at an agreed-on price.[44]

The extent of Astor's early fur-trade business can also be discerned from newspaper advertisements in New York City from 1786 to 1794. In April 1788, he highlighted the arrival of "an elegant assortment of Piano Fortes," but he also mentioned that he would buy and sell "for cash" all types of furs.[45] In October 1788, he enlarged his advertisements of furs and announced that "He gives cash for all kinds of furs; and has for sale a quantity of Canada furs, such as beaver, beaver coating; raccoon skins, raccoon blankets, and spring muskrats; which he sells by large and small quantities—a considerable allowance will be made to every person who buys a quantity."[46] These advertisements plus the contracts with Montreal merchants demonstrated Astor's growing importance as a fur merchant. Not only do they indicate that he purchased and sold in quantity but also that he often had partners and that his music and fur businesses were of sufficient volume that he could offer discounts and credits to purchasers.

Marketing furs purchased in Canada was not easy, yet Astor early penetrated markets in both the United States and Europe. British regulations forced Astor to ship all furs purchased in Canada first to London before reexport owing to a prohibition against direct trade between Canada and the United States. There obviously existed a healthy market for furs in the United States and Europe because Astor calculated that he could pay the duties, shipping, and insurance charges and still make a profit. In September 1788, for example, he employed Rosseter Hoyle, a Montreal merchant bound for London, to carry furs for him valued at £783. Astor paid Hoyle an 18 percent commission on the transaction, from which Hoyle was obliged to pay all shipping and insurance charges. On reaching London, Hoyle was to divide the parcel, sending half on to New York City and the rest to Rotterdam, Holland. Most likely, he consigned the furs in Holland to yet another middleman who sold them on commission.[47]

Astor also shipped furs overland from Montreal into the United States, thus avoiding British trade laws. This was legal according to American law because there was a specific exemption from American duties for furs and hides imported into the United States. Clearly, there were greater profits if one could avoid British duties and had exemptions from American duties. Yet there were some risks as the British still controlled military posts on Lake Champlain (even though nominally in American territory), and the British could seize furs being exported from Canada. Yet the dangers of arrest and seizure were small because British authorities exerted little effort to stop the overland trade between Canada and upstate New York. Astor easily moved furs across the border through contacts both in Canada and the United States. Often Alexander Henry shipped parcels for Astor to either Pliny Moore in Champlain or Peter Sailly in Plattsburg (Astor's agents), who were located in northern New York State just over the Canadian border. At other times, Astor made the overland trek himself and accompanied the furs all the way from Montreal to New York City.[48]

By the early 1790s the overland fur trade increased substantially, as did Astor's importance to the major Canadian traders such as the North West Company because markets in Europe and China began to decline. As part of the British Empire, Canadian trade was closely regulated and all furs usually headed first to London before sale or shipment elsewhere. In Europe, prices were unstable and markets often nonexistent due to periodic warfare. Whereas England was often directly involved in this warfare, the

United States enjoyed a position of neutrality, thus allowing American merchants, like Astor, to ship furs directly into European markets. This caused the North West Company some anxiety especially as the Continent took approximately three-eights of the annual fur harvest from North America.[49]

Equally threatening to the North West Company as well as other Canadian merchants was the inability to expand into a growing market in China. In the eighteenth century, Canadian furs reached China only with great difficulty. British trade laws required that furs first be shipped to England. Yet the East India Company, which controlled all trade to China through a British government monopoly, was not particularly interested in trading furs. Thus the North West Company sent furs through other firms and agents: first to Russia, then overland through Siberia. Yet this route had closed because of a war between Russia and Turkey and a Chinese ban on Russian fur imports in 1791.[50]

The struggle for access to the China market brought Astor into close alliance with the Canadian merchants and ultimately catapulted him onto the world stage. China had fascinated the Canadians throughout the seventeenth and eighteenth centuries. The earliest French explorers from Montreal first envisioned China as they traveled west with the cry "La Chine" ("On to China"). Eventually the point of open navigation south of Montreal for all fur-trade voyages was known as Lachine.[51] In the late eighteenth century, Canadian interest increased as traders from Montreal pushed farther west into the Athabasca region and explored routes to the Pacific Coast. Captain James Cook, who explored several rivers along the Northwest Coast in the late 1770s raised the possibility of water communication from the coast into the interior. Peter Pond, a partner in the North West Company, knew of Cook's voyages when he began to explore the rivers running from Great Slave Lake and Lake Athabasca to the Pacific Coast. His hope was also to open the riches of the China market for voyages direct from the Pacific Coast. Yet Pond was unable to convince the British government to finance further explorations in the early 1780s, and, similarly, his proposal in 1785 to the Confederation Congress elicited no enthusiasts in the infant American Republic.

Yet Pond's ideas stirred other Canadians. As early as 1781, Alexander Henry the Elder, who later became John Astor's agent in Montreal, had been with Pond on this expedition and was convinced of the possibility of shipping furs direct from the Northwest

Coast to China. In 1781, he outlined a plan for a great expedition of discovery that would pinpoint the location of rivers from the mountains to the Pacific Coast. In 1785, Henry drafted a visionary scheme for forts and trading posts all along the Northwest Coast where rivers flowed into the sea. Here Indians would bring animal pelts for trade; these would be combined with sea otter and seal pelts and shipped to China.[52]

But it was Alexander Mackenzie who proved the most articulate exponent of Canadian expansion and demonstrated the feasibility of the Pacific trade. Mackenzie had wintered in the Far West with Peter Pond in 1787 and then made two remarkable exploring expeditions to the Pacific Coast in 1789 and 1793. On his return, Mackenzie spent over a decade in frustrating attempts to convince British officials of the great profits awaiting, if only funds were made available for settlements along the Pacific Coast and for formation of a company that would utilize a route crossing the entire continent from east to west.[53]

While Henry and Mackenzie dreamed of a transcontinental fur trade and a Pacific outpost at some future date, Canadian traders, particularly the North West Company, had an immediate need to reach markets in China and Europe. Here was Astor's opportunity, for the company required a knowledgeable trader as a partner or agent who could ship their furs from an American port, thereby avoiding British trade laws. Of course, Astor was already familiar with the European trade, yet he was also extraordinarily well informed about China. He could not have been unaware of the first American voyages to China. In 1784, the *Empress of China* had shipped locally gathered furs, ginseng, and specie on a direct voyage to Canton. The ship returned in May 1785 with a cargo of tea, silks, and decorative items. These were quickly sold and returned a profit of approximately 25 percent to the investors. The commercial possibilities of voyages to China quickly captivated Americans at a time when many British markets in the West Indies were closed to them.[54]

In New York City, Philadelphia, Boston, and Salem, merchants rushed into the trade. Within a year, five other American ships were on their way to Canton. The Boston merchants were the most active and sent voyages first to the Northwest Coast to gather the valuable sea otter pelts, which the Russians called "soft gold." They sent two ships, the *Columbia* and *Lady Washington* in 1787. During the period 1789–1790, fourteen American ships brought back 3,093,200 pounds of tea to the United States.[55] The federal government recognized and encouraged this trade and passed legislation that required American vessels to pay a tax of only six to twenty cents per pound on tea brought directly from China in American vessels, whereas they levied fifteen to twenty-five cents per pound for tea imported in foreign vessels.[56]

Astor's ties to the China trade, though, extended well beyond just a casual interest. He was linked by marriage to three successful sea captains, two of whom had experience in the China trade. His wife's brother, Adam Todd, was a sea captain; and a niece married Stewart Dean, master of the second American vessel to make a voyage to Canton. His wife's nephew, John Whetten, was also in the China trade and later became a frequent partner in Astor's China trade.[57] Of course, Astor also knew of the Canadian excitement over the China market and most surely listened to Alexander Henry's great plans while staying at his home in the early 1790s.[58]

But the key connection was William Edgar, who Astor probably first met through their mutual acquaintance, Alexander Henry. Edgar was an Irish immigrant who came to Albany in the 1760s and entered the fur trade. Soon he moved on to Detroit where he conducted a trade in furs until the early 1780s, frequently in association with the North West Company and Alexander Henry. In 1783 or 1784, he moved to New York City and became a general merchant. His profits from the fur trade must have been substantial because in 1785 he informed his friend, Alexander Henry, that he intended to become a China trader. Perhaps Henry moved him in this direction, for Henry most clearly described his own fascination with China in letters to Edgar. In 1787, a ship bearing Edgar's name left for Canton; and over the next decade he continued this trade and became one of New York City's best-known merchants.[59] Given the connections among Alexander Henry, William Edgar, and John Astor, then, the North West Company logically sought out Astor and Edgar when they decided to avoid British trade laws and to ship the North West Company's furs to China by way of New York City.[60]

The North West Company's first "Adventure to China"—its heading in the account books—was planned in 1791 and undertaken in 1792. Alexander Henry and McTavish, Frobisher and Company held a 50 percent share; the remaining 50 percent consisted of other North West Company partners plus John Astor and William Edgar. The Americans were compensated with a share or commission on the sale of the return cargo. The venture began with the shipment of furs from Canada to the United States over the northern border, more than likely through Astor's agents, Peter Sailly in Plattsburg and Pliny Moore in Champlain. In New York City, the furs were loaded on two American ships, the *America* and *Washington*. Edgar owned the *America*.[61] The outbound cargo consisted of furs and ginseng and on return the ships carried silks and teas. The American partners, among them Astor and Edgar, then sold these products in American markets. A second voyage was undertaken in 1793 with a cargo that included forty thousand beaver skins and had a total capitalization of £279,894. A third voyage followed the next year, and there were plans for a fourth in 1794. Astor and Edgar were probably involved in the initial voyages, but plans for the 1795 trip involved Philadelphia merchants.[62]

The North West Company was disappointed in the financial returns from the "Adventures to China." They lost £13,484 in 1792; £16,260 in 1793; and £22,824 in 1974. Two factors were preeminent in these failures. First, the outgoing cargoes primarily consisted of furs, and if specie were not included, the traders were unable to export sufficient teas and silks to make the return voyage profitable. The China trade was a delicate balance. The Canton market desired furs but few other American products; thus each voyage depended on huge profits on the return cargoes. The North West Company's profit margin was even narrower because the American partners received a large share of the profits on the sale of teas and silks.[63]

John Astor, however, benefited enormously from these early China voyages. He received a guaranteed share in the return cargoes, and his standing grew in both the New York and Montreal business communities. By the early 1790s, then, Astor was a merchant of some stature, and already he had begun speculating and investing in other ventures. In August 1792, for example, while staying at Alexander Henry's home in Montreal, the New Yorker signed an agreement with Phillip Liebert, a former surgeon for the American army during the revolutionary war. Liebert claimed that the American government owed him $390 (Spanish) plus a pension for seven years. Astor agreed to press the American government for payment on a contingency basis. If he succeeded in obtaining the full sum, Astor was to pay Liebert $1,000 (Spanish) and then keep the remainder. Astor would receive only three-fifths of any smaller settlement. Although Astor undertook at least two such speculative claims, he apparently was successful at neither.[64]

One exceptionally good index of Astor's early success as a merchant was the size of his land investments. He first explored the opportunities for land development in Lower Canada along the border with the United States. The Canadian government opened vast areas for settlement by offering land to investors who would then survey, subdivide, and sell to small farmers. In 1792 and 1793, Astor and other business partners, among them Alexander Henry, petitioned for a tract or township ten miles square. On his own, Henry also petitioned for another township directly adjacent. Astor gained title to approximately one thousand acres, and he and his partners expended considerable capital for development. The minimum surveying and subdivision costs were £657; in addition, the developers sought to attract settlers by laying out roads and constructing a few farm houses. On another parcel, Astor pledged £2,400 for development costs. Even though he never saw this scheme through to completion, it is significant that he possessed the necessary capital to consider such projects.[65]

Astor's interest in land as well as the success of his mercantile endeavors was particularly evident in his purchase of two tracts of twenty thousand and seventeen thousand acres, respectively, in the Mohawk Valley known as the Charlotte River and Byrnes Patent lands. Originally, this land belonged to Sir William Johnson, the British Indian agent, who retained title even after fleeing to Canada during the American Revolution; on his death, the title had passed to relatives. Astor first began investigating a purchase in 1793, no doubt with the full acquiescence of his business acquaintance, Peter Smith, who lived in the land's vicinity and would be responsible for its oversight and development. In 1794, Astor, after contacting Johnson's relatives on one of his trips to England and assuring himself that the title was reasonably clear, purchased the land for £10,466. He shared the investment with Peter Smith, who took one-half and William Laight, a former partner of Astor's friend William Backhouse, who was responsible for one-third. Astor thus was only a one-sixth partner, although he and Laight shared all the initial cost because Smith borrowed the money for his share from Astor at 7 percent interest. Again, Astor hoped that the land could be subdivided, with minimal development expenses, and then sold in small parcels to settlers.[66]

All businessmen, even successful ones, make mistakes, and Astor most certainly regretted this purchase. No sooner had he completed the purchase than he discovered that the title was defective and that some settlers within the tract claimed that they already had purchased their lands from Sir William Johnson. Unfortunately, Sir William Johnson was now dead and all his papers had been destroyed when he fled the territory at the outbreak of the American Revolution. Before the partners could sell any parcels, then, they had to clear the title. Obviously, they could settle with the numerous settlers who claimed title or attempt to gain full title in the courts. For nearly eight years, Astor, Laight, and Smith pursued a combined strategy that involved court suits and a search for additional heirs and evidence of title. There seems little doubt that Astor and his partners were legally correct, for they eventually secured a copy of Johnson's will indicating that he had maintained full title to all lands. Obviously the settlers either misunderstood the terms of their leases with Johnson or, less kindly, they attempted to defraud Astor in the confused climate governing land titles of British citizens in America. After the courts finally recognized Astor's title in 1799, a compromise was struck with the settlers that allowed them to secure title to their lands at a price generally between $2.50 and $7.50 per acre, the sum payable over a ten-year period. The investment hardly returned a profit given the cost of legal fees and the time involved.[67]

Even at this early date, Astor also invested in New York City lots. In 1789, for example, he purchased two lots and four half-lots from his brother, Henry. In 1790, he purchased a lot and building at 40 Little Dock Street for £850; this then became the site of his own office and residence. The following year he purchased additional lots in the dock area. In a very short period, the financier had expended approximately $7,000 on Manhattan real estate, which he was then prepared either to sell or lease.[68]

By 1794, ten years after his arrival in America, John Astor at the age of thirty-one, was a merchant of diverse business interests and considerable importance in New York City's mercantile community. His personal life reflected this success. In 1790, for example, he moved from a building owned by his mother-in-law at 81 Queen Street to a new office at 40 Little Dock Street in the heart of the business district. In 1794, he moved again to 149 Broadway, although he appears to have still lived above his office. No doubt his moves were also caused by a growing family that by 1794 included a daughter, Magdalen, and two sons, John Jacob, Jr., and William Backhouse. Astor now appeared in New York City business directories either as a furrier or fur merchant.[69]

Typical of city merchants, he joined organizations that increased his business associations. He purchased a share in Magdalen's name in the Tontine Coffee House when it was built in 1792. The Tontine Coffee House served both business and social clienteles. Merchants met there daily to exchange information on recent ship arrivals and market prices and to purchase insurance for ships and cargoes.[70] In 1790, Astor joined the Mason's Holland Lodge Number Eight, where he associated with other important New Yorkers, like De Witt Clinton and Henry Livingston. Clinton and Astor subsequently became close friends and political allies.[71] Astor's emigrant background more than likely led him to join the German Society of New York in 1787; in the 1790s he was a member of the German Reformed Church. Astor's arrival as a merchant of some stature and means was confirmed also when Gilbert Stuart painted his portrait in 1794. Astor had joined an elite company of aristocrats and politicians—Aaron Burr, John Jay, and Robert Livingston—whose portraits Stuart also painted in the period 1793–1794.[72]

In 1794, it had been just fifteen years since Astor had left his German homeland and immigrated to England during the tumultuous years of the American War of Independence, and only a decade since he arrived in Baltimore with a modest financial stake. So far the young merchant had experienced little privation and struggle; indeed, he appears to have been extraordinarily fortunate. The disordered state of American business following the Revolution, particularly in New York City, undoubtedly contributed to numerous business opportunities. Astor's genius lay in perceiving the open market for furs and in his willingness to travel extensively throughout his adopted land and to Montreal, the center of the North American fur trade. Although he conducted a small trade in musical instruments in the 1780s and 1790s, by 1793, he was already the most important American fur merchant then operating in the Montreal and London markets. The profits were good, if not spectacular, and advanced the young German to an important, although not yet a first-rank, position within the New York mercantile community.

Yet Astor was still only a minor figure in the international fur trade controlled by the British. His profits were consistently limited owing to England's regulation that all furs be shipped first to London. Moreover, the British continued to occupy the western posts at key locations such as Oswego, Detroit, and Mackinac, and this presence blocked the direct movement of furs into American markets and maintained British alliances with the Indians. But great changes were on the horizon in 1793 as American envoy John Jay journeyed to England to resolve the lingering trade problems between the United States and Great Britain. At the same time, France had declared war on Great Britain, and this opened a substantial trade for neutrals like the United States and weakened British resolve to maintain a military presence in the American West. Although Astor was not an actor on this international political stage, he was an opportunist who stood ready to pounce on the economic opportunities that would soon materialize.

Chapter Three

Furs and Tea

Astor Builds a Fortune, 1794–1807

IN THE lives of most self-made men, there is a period of intense business activity, little distracted by either political or social concerns, in which success crowns nearly every move and in which both economic and political power slowly accrue. Such is the case with John Jacob Astor's business life from 1794 to 1807. At the beginning of this period, Astor had reached the stage of moderate wealth in New York City, yet he was still relatively young (thirty-one) and undistinguished from a host of contemporaries in similar circumstances. By 1807, he had moved well beyond other business-men to attain a position of very substantial wealth—probably in excess of $1 million. He now had entree to leading political officials such as De Witt Clinton and Albert Gallatin, and his focus shifted from purely business endeavors to embrace economic and political concerns on a world stage. The source of Astor's fortune was the fur trade. At first, his markets were limited to the United States and Europe, but in 1800 he added China. He then became a major importer of teas and silks into domestic and foreign markets. This expansion occurred slowly and cautiously, with as little risk as possible, over a twelve-year period.

To understand the significance of Astor's business career at this time we also need to enlarge our perspectives in order to try to grasp not only why Astor was successful but also to understand what his career reveals about the role of business and businessmen in the American economy. Essentially Astor operated much as businessmen would a century later; indeed, the surprising characteristic of his business was the extent to which he sought control of supplies and markets, followed carefully designed strategies, and often influenced the flow of business events.

Despite the fact that Astor's main interest was the fur trade, an industry that admittedly was in its waning days, nevertheless, it was one of the most "modern" in its organization and practice, forcing Astor to react and adapt more quickly than many of his contemporaries in other businesses. Before 1794, the Canadians, through a series of complex partnerships and companies, controlled the fur supply. This reality forced Astor to limit his activities initially to purchasing furs in Canada for shipment into American and foreign markets. Yet from 1794 to 1807 Astor took advantage of political and economic events to secure a greater supply of furs and to capture a larger share of markets in Europe and China.

In modern business analysis, Astor's actions would be referred to as vertical integration: backward to capture a dependable supply; forward to assure a stable market outlet. There is no need to push this analysis too far. Astor was not a twentieth-century businessman. He continually had to deal with primitive institutions, the vagaries of wind and weather, the lack of instant communications, and the political and economic realities of early nineteenth-century America. Nevertheless, the most striking aspect of Astor's business career is how much he resembled modern businessmen in his thinking. I suspect he would have been quite comfortable in a room with Andrew Carnegie and Henry Ford. Historians have been far too eager to create gaps between the general and specialized merchants of early America, the manufacturers of the antebellum period, and the corporate executives of industrial America. Changes in business practice and organization were far more gradual, and there seems little doubt that John Astor built his business empire through market and institutional strategies normally attributed to later historical periods.[1]

Astor benefited enormously from favorable economic conditions throughout the 1790s and early 1800s. From the early 1790s, America's foreign trade grew at a substantial pace, with American ships penetrating every corner of the globe. The warfare that wracked Europe and led to the opening and closing of ports in the French, British, and Spanish possessions both on the Continent and in the New World disrupted European commerce, but overall it was a bonanza for a neutral carrier like the United States. Our trade with Latin America was especially significant, with nearly one-third of all American exports from 1790 to 1812 going to the West Indies and Latin America. The chief ports were Havana and Santo Domingo. American traders also moved easily into French, Spanish, and Dutch ports when the European powers proved unable to protect their colonial markets during frequent periods of European warfare at the century's end.[2]

It was in this period as well that America increased both its carrying and reexport trade. The reexport trade saw American ships carry goods from South America, the Orient, and French and British colonies in the West Indies first to seaports such as New York, Philadelphia, and Boston. Depending on the demand, these goods were then reexported to Europe. The stopover in an American port theoretically made such cargoes neutral. Before the Napoleonic Wars, these goods might have moved directly to Europe in foreign ships without passing through American ports or being transported by American ships. Table 1 indicates the astounding growth of the reexport trade. In some years its dollar value exceeded that of our own exports.[3]

Not only did American shipping increase, but also Americans came to control the vast majority of goods moving into and out of American ports. In 1789, only 54 percent of the tonnage in America's foreign trade was in American hands, but by 1795, Americans controlled a remarkable 91 percent of the tonnage. The federal government encouraged this trend through laws that charged much higher tariffs on goods arriving in foreign vessels and that extracted discriminatory tonnage duties. For example, the Tonnage Act of 1789 required all foreign-built and foreign-owned vessels to pay a duty of fifty cents per ton on entry into an American port, whereas American vessels were required to pay only six cents per ton. American ships engaged in the coastwise trade (i.e., traveling from one American port to another) had to pay tonnage duties only once, whereas foreign ships had to pay tonnage duties each time they entered an American port. This regulation assured American traders a monopoly of the short-haul trade along the coast. Similarly, tariff laws were designed to protect American

Table 1

Total Foreign Trade of the United States, 1790–1808

Year	Domestic Exports	Foreign Reexports	Total Exports	Total Imports
1790	$19,666,000	$ 539,000	$ 20,205,000	$ 23,000,000
1791	18,500,000	512,000	19,012,000	29,200,000
1792	19,000,000	1,753,000	20,753,000	31,500,000
1793	24,000,000	2,110,000	26,110,000	31,100,000
1794	26,500,000	6,526,000	33,026,000	34,600,000
1795	39,500,000	8,490,000	47,990,000	69,756,000
1796	40,764,000	26,300,000	67,064,000	81,436,000
1797	29,850,000	27,000,000	56,850,000	75,379,000
1798	28,527,000	33,000,000	61,527,000	68,552,000
1799	33,142,000	45,523,000	78,665,000	79,069,000
1800	31,841,000	39,130,000	70,971,000	91,253,000
1801	47,473,000	46,642,000	94,115,000	111,364,000
1802	36,708,000	35,775,000	72,483,000	76,333,000
1803	42,206,000	13,594,000	55,800,000	64,666,000
1804	41,467,000	36,232,000	77,699,000	85,000,000
1805	42,387,000	53,179,000	95,566,000	120,600,000
1806	41,253,000	60,283,000	101,536,000	129,410,000
1807	48,700,000	59,643,000	108,343,000	138,500,000
1808	9,433,000	12,997,000	22,430,000	56,990,000

Source: Emory Johnson, et al., *History of Domestic and Foreign Commerce of the United States,* 2 vols. (Washington, D.C.: Carnegie Institute, 1915), 2: 20.

markets as well as raise revenue. In some cases, as with tea, foreign shippers were required to pay both higher tariff rates than Americans plus an additional surcharge. Congress obviously wished to encourage the American takeover of the China trade.[4]

New York City, like other ports such as Baltimore and Philadelphia, benefited enormously from the favorable trading conditions. In New York City, the exports of the port grew from a value of $5.4 million in 1794 to $13.3 million in 1797, to 26.3 million in 1807. Trade statistics from this period do not even begin to measure the tremendous increase in the domestic trade. Not only did agricultural products flow from the interior into the city but also American manufacturing increased its output. These factors then attracted more workers and stimulated additional retail businesses. In 1790, New York City had a population of 33,131 and this number grew to 60,489 in 1800 and 96,373 in 1811. At the same time, the infrastructure of a dynamic economy began to take shape in New York City. New banks, for example, formed to handle merchant and businessman's needs for short-term credit. Yet even as late as 1799, New York had only two banks, the Bank of New York and a local branch of the Bank of the United States (BUS). But then two additional institutions formed: Aaron Burr's Manhattan Company and the Merchants' Bank.[5] Although there were fluctuations in the value of imports and exports as American commerce was continually harassed in the West Indies and in the Mediterranean, nevertheless, the general trend was a steady increase in trade, manufacturing, and retail businesses. The historical conditions were absolutely perfect for Astor. In essence, he was in the right place at the right time.

In the 1790s, Astor's fur business was simply organized because he was still dependent on the Canadians. Although he purchased a small number of furs in upstate New York, he was forced to rely heavily on yearly trips to Montreal where he purchased furs from independent traders, the North West Company, and at auction. With the British still occupying all the western posts, there was no chance for him or any other American to contest Canadian control of the trade in the American West, particularly around the Great Lakes. All this western bounty flowed northeast along the Saint Lawrence River basin to Montreal and Quebec. In addition, British trade regulations required Astor to ship any furs purchased in Montreal to Great Britain before reshipment to New York. Even though the British often ignored the existence of a substantial overland trade in furs from Montreal to New York City, they rigidly enforced the regulations by sea. These trade barriers were sufficient to block any substantial American intrusion into the Canadian monopoly of the trade. Astor thus survived in the late 1780s and early 1790s by cooperating with Montreal merchants in the purchase of furs.

The Jay Treaty, which was signed between Great Britain and the United States in 1794, although not ratified in the United States for another two years, was the event that first permitted John Astor, ever so gradually, to break from Canadian domination. The Jay Treaty marked the beginning of an evolutionary change in British policy toward the United States and Canada that continued well into the nineteenth century. By the early 1790s, the British government desired a working arrangement with the American government based on political and economic realities. The Americans were slowly moving westward, and, despite numerous setbacks, the British knew that soon the Americans would win the battle against the recalcitrant Indian tribes. At that time, the British would face an open confrontation with American troops for control of the western posts at Michilimackinac (now Mackinac), Oswego, and Niagara. General Anthony Wayne's defeat of the western tribes at the Battle of Fallen Timbers, followed by the Treaty of Greenville in 1795, was clearly indicative of America's increasing strength in the West.

The British government also was weakening in its support of the Canadian fur trade. In the early 1790s, the fur trade was an economically profitable business producing, on average, about £200,000 in exports from Montreal and Quebec. Probably half that sum came from the Great Lakes and upper Mississippi River, areas that clearly belonged to the United States. British fur-trade interests in Canada and England were conscious of the American threat to their livelihood and pressured government officials in Canada and London, stressing the fur-trade's economic value and its political importance to maintaining Indian alliances. In the early 1790s, the fur-trade lobby persuaded the British government to support the concept of an Indian barrier state in the West. Its boundaries were conveniently drawn to include the prime fur-trade regions of the American West. British diplomats quickly abandoned the idea when it met with a cold reception from the Americans.[6]

Although it took decades to fully evolve, the British government slowly altered its thinking and came to understand that the fur trade was "peanuts" when stacked against the economic bounty that might be gained by closer trade relations with the Americans. The major attraction was the potential market for British manufactured goods in the expanding American market. English merchants also still desired a settlement of their claims against the Americans from the revolutionary war. Significantly, John G. Simcoe, the first lieutenant governor of Upper Canada (modern Ontario), although occasionally supportive of the fur traders, believed that the province's future was in agriculture. Moreover, the British government viewed the American question as a minor affair compared to the enormous struggle with France for hegemony then taking shape on the European continent. The signing of the Jay Treaty thus marked the *beginning* of the economic and political decline of the Canadian fur-trade industry and the opening of new opportunities for American interests.[7]

Two clauses of the Jay Treaty had immediate significance for John Astor and for the most important Montreal firm, the North West Company. First, the British finally agreed to abandon the western posts in American territory, thus opening the possibility that furs, gathered in the Great Lakes region, could move over American rivers and roads direct to New York City. Second, the Canadians were allowed to trade directly with American ports, ending all regulations that required furs to be shipped to London first. John Astor was now free to buy furs in Montreal and ship them directly to New York or to Europe without extra duties or the risks of an overland journey from Montreal to New York City. It also gave him the ability to ship Canadian furs all over the world without first passing through the London markets.[8]

As soon as news of the Jay Treaty reached America in 1794, John Astor sought to capitalize on its terms. He hurried first to Montreal where he conferred with Alexander Henry and other partners in the North West Company. Essentially, Astor proposed that he should now become a full-fledged partner or shareholder in the North West Company responsible for shipping the company's furs directly to China and to Europe from New York City. Even though Canadian fur traders could trade with the United States, they were still unable to enter European markets because of British trade regulations and intermittent warfare. Moreover, the East India Company controlled all British trade with China. Astor's proposed partnership would allow the North West Company to avoid all British trade laws and the East India Company's monopoly. The opportunity for larger profits seemed possible for both Astor and the Canadians.

After making his proposition to Montreal merchants, Astor went to England in late 1794 and spoke with the North West Company's London partners. While his proposal was under consideration, he traveled to the Continent where he established contacts and negotiated arrangements for the import of furs and teas with commission merchants in cities, such as Hamburg and Bordeaux. In August 1796, he returned to Montreal and learned that the North West Company had rejected his proposal, despite the efforts of his friends, Alexander Henry and James Hallowell.[9]

Astor's inability to strike a deal with the North West Company had two major causes. First, the company was internally divided over the wisdom of pursuing the China trade because of losses sustained in earlier ventures. Simon McTavish and John Fraser, who were then establishing a permanent base for the North West Company in London, were never in favor of sending furs to Canton. They believed that Canton received the best North American furs, whereas the London market received inferior pelts. Second, the North West Company, under the influence of Alexander Mackenzie, who disliked Astor personally, was reluctant to give Astor a major share in the fur trade. Thus, the North West Company decided against a formal American connection and sought to arrange their own shipments into Europe and China from American ports. Astor, though, continued to purchase furs from the North West Company and accepted the company's furs on commission for sale in domestic and foreign markets. However, he was never a partner or shareholder in the firm, but only one of several New York merchants who handled the company's furs.[10]

At this time, the North West Company also explored the possibility of opening its own American agency. In 1795, Simon McTavish, the chief Montreal partner, first discussed the notion with Alexander Mackenzie. In early 1798, Alexander Mackenzie came to the United States and arranged with a New York firm, Seton, Maitland and Company, to undertake a joint venture to Canton, with the return voyage stopping to trade Chinese goods in European ports. Mackenzie and his partners in the North West Company paid $35,000 for a ship, *Northern Liberties,* which then sailed under the names of the American partners. To increase the voyage's profitability, the vessel carried $40,000 in specie, in addition to $40,000 worth of furs, for the purchase of teas and silks. Mackenzie also investigated the possibility of sending vessels to other European ports such as Hamburg.[11] But Mackenzie's efforts to operate from American ports to reach China were not generally successful and led to discussions within the North West Company over the expense of the Canton trade. In 1800, John Fraser, a London partner, blamed poor returns on the company's inability to work with the Americans, "It's a pity you have not been able to manage the establishment of a house at N. York," he wrote to his Montreal associates, "if you could find a steady, clever American you could rely on, it might still be an advisable measure."[12]

Even though the Canadians were unsuccessful in reaching European and Chinese markets, John Astor still could not dramatically expand his business, nor was he in a position to challenge the North West Company's control of the American fur trade. Despite the Jay Treaty and the British surrender of military posts in

American territory, the British military and Canadian traders were still the dominant presence in the Great Lakes region. After departing from Mackinac Island, for example, the British moved to nearby Saint Joseph's Island. Leaving Detroit, they crossed the river and constructed a post at Fort Malden. Astor also still lacked the resources to form an American company capable of competing with the North West Company, with its approximately one thousand traders and fur exports valued at £370,000 in 1801. In addition, the Canadians had several key fur-trade settlements around the Great Lakes, for example, at Green Bay, and they owned two smaller vessels (between twelve to fifteen tons each) and one of seventy-five tons, the *Otter;* these transported furs and goods on the lakes.[13]

Equally troubling to John Astor and other American fur traders was the fact that the Jay Treaty did not exclude British traders from American territory. Instead, it recognized the rights of traders from both nations to move freely back and forth across the border. This treaty provision unleashed an intense exploitation of American territory by Canadian traders, who were aware that someday the Americans would totally exclude them from the region. Anxiety over the future unleashed another period of vicious competition that caused a split among the North West Company's partners. By 1796, some elements of the North West Company including Forsyth, Richardson and Company; Alexander Mackenzie; and Leith, Jamieson, and Company shifted their focus away from the southwest trade around the Great Lakes and moved to exploit the trade farther west and north. Alexander Mackenzie simultaneously pushed his partners and the British government to establish a post on the Northwest Coast in order to seize military control and to ship furs directly to Canton. Eventually these dissenting elements came together in the XY Company, or New North West Company, and competed directly, from 1796 to 1804 with the "Old" North West Company.[14] Astor knew that he could not enter this competitive environment on an equal basis, so he purchased furs at advantageous prices from both sides.

Not only was the business environment in Canada inimical to Astor's dramatically expanding his business but also American laws and trade regulations were not especially favorable. British manufactured goods such as blankets were still the mainstay of the trade's barter system, and Astor could not buy goods as cheaply as the Canadian traders because of America's protective tariffs. Astor was reluctant to use American textiles because they were so inferior to the British goods. There was little incentive, then, for Astor to supply traders, except on a small scale. In addition, the American government required American traders to purchase licenses and restricted the use of alcohol, thereby weakening their ability to compete with Canadian traders. The establishment of the federal government's factory system also hindered Astor's ability to expand. Chartered by Congress in 1796 to purchase Indian furs in exchange for manufactured goods, the factory system was intended to gradually wean the Indians from their dependence on the British by providing an "American" competition in the fur trade. Astor did not want to compete with his own government in such trade.[15]

For all these reasons, Astor remained a one-dimensional fur broker. He purchased furs in Canada and in American territory for sale in American and foreign markets, but he did not get involved in the hiring nor in the supply of traders. Despite the fact that earlier historians described John Astor as late as 1800 as a general merchant—implying that he traded many different products such as furs, glass, pianos, and woolens—the evidence actually points in a different direction. By the early 1790s, Astor had specialized as a broker in the fur trade, buying furs principally in Canadian markets and then selling them in the United States, Europe, and China. In the late eighteenth century, he listed himself in New York City directories as a furrier or fur merchant; and unlike general or diversified merchants in the city, he did not have a continuing advertisement in the commercial newspapers like the *New York General Advertiser*. Instead, Astor advertised only when he had acquired special shipments, and these advertisements almost always concentrated on furs and goods from China.[16] The only exception to Astor's specialized business was that he continued to import pianos and organs until the early nineteenth century. Yet, as these goods did not appear in his newspaper advertisements, it is reasonable to assume that Astor (owing to his earlier connection to London manufacturers of musical instruments) imported these items on commission for other merchants.[17]

Customs receipts do indicate that Astor imported many smaller parcels, particularly from Germany and England. These goods, in addition to European furs, included muskets, shot, powder, muslin, blankets, and woolen goods. Such goods were clearly linked to the fur and China trades. Muskets, powder, muslin, and blankets were used as exchange items to obtain furs. Moreover, the surprising fact, in admittedly fragmentary records, was the small number and dollar value of retail goods handled by Astor. Kenneth Porter estimated that Astor imported goods valued at between $11,000 and $21,000 in the early 1800s, yet when an average voyage to China brought in $250,000 in teas and silks, these other imports were indeed small in comparison.[18]

Given all the handicaps deriving from Canadian control of the trade, Astor, nevertheless, expanded his business at the end of the eighteenth century. In the terminology of business analysis, Astor first adopted a strategy of backward integration: to secure a larger and more reliable supply of furs harvested in American territory. At the same time, he integrated forward, that is, he expanded his control over the markets. This move inevitably led him into the China trade.

Astor's attempts to secure a reliable source of supply were quite cautious. He did not want to supply traders or import trade goods because these steps would have meant open competition with the North West Company. Consequently, he continued to make annual trips to Montreal to purchase furs from various Canadian sources, including the main partners of the North West Company. In 1800, for example, he and Alexander Henry jointly purchased a large number of muskrat skins during the auctions in an effort to control the market; in 1805, Astor acquired furs valued at £16,000 in one transaction with Parker, Gerrard, Ogilvie and Company. There was no lingering animosity from his earlier overtures to become a partner because he had become quite friendly with members of Montreal's fur-trade aristocracy. He occasionally was invited to meetings of the Beaver Club, the prestigious organization that included all the great merchants, and he was frequently entertained in their homes. A good indication of Astor's reputation and prestige in the trade was that Alexander Ellice, who was a London partner in the North West Company, sent his son, Edward, to New York City in order to learn the fur-trade business from an American, John Astor.[19]

Astor's policy was to develop access to many suppliers, thereby allowing him to purchase wherever the price was most advantageous. In the first decade of the nineteenth century, Astor was successful in expanding his sources beyond the Montreal market. He purchased from suppliers in New York State such as William

*John Jacob Astor, 1805. Courtesy of Astor Family
Papers, Rare Books and Manuscript Division,
The New York Public Library, Astor, Lenox, and
Tilden Foundations.*

Fowler in Albany and Peter Smith in Utica. He also moved farther
west and purchased furs from middlemen in Mackinac and Detroit. To establish his own control of the American trade he often
transported furs over the Great Lakes to New York City, thus bypassing Montreal. He increasingly employed agents such as Henry
Brevoort, Jr., his wife's nephew, who traveled through Ohio to
Detroit in 1803–1804, purchasing furs from independent traders.
P. l'Herbette, the son of a French merchant who marketed Astor's

furs in Europe, was given a modest amount of capital in 1804 to purchase furs in western New York and in the Old Northwest. On other occasions, Astor accepted furs from Detroit, Albany, and Mackinac traders and sold them on commission through his London and European connections.[20]

In due course, the New Yorker pushed as far west as Saint Louis. In 1799, he had helped a London merchant close an account with Charles Gratiot and Auguste Chouteau, both of whom traded along the Mississippi and Missouri rivers. Astor used the opportunity to propose a formal arrangement in which Gratiot and Chouteau would consign all their furs to him, shipping them over the Great Lakes to New York City, thus bypassing their normal business contact in Mackinac and Montreal. Astor proposed to sell the furs through his agents in Europe and to supply goods to the Saint Louis traders. Although Gratiot responded favorably, Chouteau was not willing to give Astor a permanent foothold in the Saint Louis region. He preferred to maintain informal contacts with the New Yorker.

Astor, though, was in an enviable position as a fur broker. He could pick and choose particular furs and search for the best price not only from various Canadian interests but also from traders working in the interior of North America. As he did not supply goods to the traders, he avoided the risk of moving supplies back and forth to the interior, of carrying accounts, and of dependence on a single supplier.[21]

As he developed a reliable network of fur suppliers, Astor also increased his presence in domestic and overseas markets. Unfortunately, the evidence is spotty on the number and value of furs he sold during the late 1790s and early 1800s. His advertisements appeared more frequently in New York City commercial newspapers and revealed that he held a large and varied stock of furs. Hat and clothing manufacturers were his major customers in the domestic markets.[22]

More important to business expansion, however, was his penetration of European markets. On his trip to England and the Continent in 1795–1796, Astor had established contacts with numerous merchants who were to purchase his furs or to sell them on commission. The time was propitious because the Canadians still had to ship directly to London unless they sold in American markets or shipped under American registry. With Great Britain often at war, the Canadian traders were unable to ship into

European markets. At this point, Astor did not own any ships, but rather purchased space on the numerous vessels that frequently traveled between New York City and London, Hamburg, and Le Havre. In November 1803, for example, he shipped thirty-six large casks and six bales of furs valued at $36,000 on board the *Oneida Chief* bound for London. In April 1804, he sent furs valued at $5,000 to London.[23]

Throughout these early years, most shipments were small and spread among continental ports and London because the European fur markets were quite diverse and competitive. London was the center, and great auctions were held there in January, February, and March, attracting buyers from all over Europe. Here Astor's furs were sold in competition with the annual harvests of the North West Company, the Hudson's Bay Company, and Russian and German suppliers. There was also a brisk trade among middlemen who bought and sold furs outside the auction system. In the spring, the fur markets shifted to the Continent where traditional fairs were held in key trade centers such as Leipzig, Frankfurt-am-Main, and Novgorod. The fairs, such as the annual one in Leipzig, were particularly well known for the availability of fine furs and both buyers and sellers from France, Germany, Russia, England, and the United States moved from booth to booth along crowded streets seeking the best buy. Astor again worked through established commission houses, particularly in Hamburg and Le Havre. Not only did he sell his own furs but he often purchased Russian and German furs for export to the United States.[24]

European and American fur markets were unstable and limited, so that Astor, like the Canadians, increasingly saw the China market as potentially the most profitable. Astor knew that he could export furs and then purchase teas and silks, thus securing profits on both ends of the voyage. Furs brought very high prices in China because Chinese homes were unheated. By the end of the eighteenth century, the tremendous risks formerly associated with the journey owing to unfamiliarity with the routes and markets also were gone. By 1799–1800, eighteen American ships journeyed to Canton and returned with over 5 million pounds of tea. The next year, there were twenty-three American ships with outgoing cargoes valued at $2,562,000 and imports of 5 million pounds of tea. By 1801–1802, the number of American ships increased to thirty-two and exports were valued at $3,742,194 and tea imports of 5,740,734 pounds.

Even though statistics were poorly kept in these early years, two facts distinguished this trade. First, the Americans were the major foreign power at Canton next to the English, who controlled the majority of trade through the East India Company. In 1799–1800, there were only three Danish vessels and one Swedish ship besides the Americans and English. In 1800–1801, twenty-three American ships and seven foreign ships traded there. In 1802–1803, when there were thirty-four American ships, foreign ships numbered only ten: five Swedish, two Russian, two Danish and one French.[25]

The second distinguishing feature of the China trade was that the dollar value of imports and exports was quite substantial given the small number of American ships involved. For example in 1804–1805, the first year for which reliable statistics exist, thirty-four American ships carried exports valued at $3,555,818, or an average per ship of $104,582. These same ships imported teas and other Chinese products worth $3,842,000. There were obviously substantial profits to be garnered in the China trade even though, in dollar value, it amounted only to approximately 1 percent of the total value of American trade in 1804.[26] More significant from the viewpoint of John Astor was the fact that, with only a few ships participating in a highly specialized trade, there was the potential for windfall profits. Astor, moreover, was the most important American fur trader, thus he controlled one of the most valuable exchange products in the China trade.

Astor significantly expanded his participation in the China trade beginning in 1796–1797. At first, he purchased space on ships owned by other merchants. In 1798, for example, Astor owned only part of the cargo on the *Ontario* captained by his wife's nephew, John Whetten. His portion consisted of 590 otter skins, 35 beaver skins, and 615 fox skins as well as 25 peculs of ginseng. (A pecul equaled approximately 133 pounds.) Ginseng, which had been exported on every American voyage since the *Empress of China,* was a well-known and valuable product in China. The Chinese believed that ginseng could restore health and had positive effects on sexual potency. After reviewing commodity prices received from the previous trade year at Canton, Astor expected to sell the otter skins at $7.00 per skin, beaver at $5.50, fox at $2.00

and the ginseng at $200.00 per pecul.[27] Whether Astor received his asking price cannot be determined, but his estimates would have returned $10,552.50. In 1799, New York commercial newspapers carried Astor's advertisements for Chinese products such a hyson tea, nankeens, and India silks imported on the *Ontario* and other vessels.[28]

In 1799, Astor purchased cargo space on the *Mary,* a ship owned by New Yorkers John McVickar, Lawrence Van Zandt, and Coster and Company. He exported seven casks of ginseng, weighing 2,407 pounds and valued at $1,686, and five casks of furs valued at $6,782. The furs sold for $13,816, and the ginseng returned $7,876 for a total of $21,692. Astor's return was over two and one-half times the estimated value. The ship's owners charged Astor a 15 percent commission on the sale and then invested the remaining money for him in teas, silks, and nankeens.[29] Astor advertised and sold these products in 1800 to retail merchants. No evidence exists that Astor ever owned a store from which Chinese or European goods were sold over-the-counter. Stories of Astor standing behind a counter as a simple shopkeeper were the creation of nineteenth-century writers anxious to show the millionaire's climb from rags to riches.[30]

Although these voyages undoubtedly yielded profits, the high commission charges plus the insurance and cartage fees paid to others convinced the financier that he should expand his own investment and become a full shareholder in these voyages. In 1800, he was a partner in the voyage of the *Severn*. Other investors included William Laight, who had shared land purchases with Astor, and Laight's son, Charles. The vessel carried 1,023 beaver skins, 351 fox skins, 103 otter skins, 4,769 bolts of camlets (cloth made from silk, wool, and other mixed fibers), 132 peculs of ginseng, 27 peculs of cochineal (scarlet dyes made from insects in Central America and also used as an antispasmodic medicine), and 30,753 seal skins. The *Severn* remained in Canton from October to late December 1800 and returned to New York on 11 May 1801 carrying a cargo that included 500 chests of black tea, 1,517 chests of green tea, China wares, nankeens, and silk goods.

With John Whetten as captain, the *Severn* undertook a second voyage—with a similar cargo as that of 1800—in early 1802 and arrived in Canton on 10 June 1802. This ship also carried $43,000 in specie because the money received from the sale of furs would not purchase teas and silks sufficient to fill the vessel for the return voyage. Astor now regularly had a large share in the entire venture. Simultaneously, he shipped furs on other vessels out of Philadelphia and Boston and imported teas on a commission basis. The vastly expanded scope and profitability of his business was reflected in the fact that by 1800 he no longer lived over his own office at 149 Broadway, and had purchased a separate office-warehouse at 71 Liberty Street. In 1803, he changed residences again and moved to a more prestigious address, 223 Broadway.[31]

Because of the increased volume of his business in China, Astor now decided to expand further. He first became a majority shareholder on each voyage, and then he decided to build his own ships. But this decision was far more significant than simply an expansion of an existing business endeavor. For the first time in his career, Astor assumed responsibility for an entire operation that was extraordinarily complex, heavily capitalized, and involved employees and agents in several countries. The increased involvement in the China trade represented a quantum leap, moving Astor from the status of trader to executive manager and decision maker. Until this venture, he had always shared the risks and fitted into operations where others, such as the leaders of the North West Company, made the policy decisions, calculated the costs, and assumed the greatest risk.

The first indication of Astor's new role in the China trade occurred in May 1803 when the *Severn* sailed again for Canton with Astor as the principal owner and John Whetten as a minor partner. In 1804, Astor became the sole owner of the *Severn;* the next year he and his partner, John Whetten, had New York shipmakers Eckford and Beebee build a new vessel, the *Beaver,* specifically designed for the China trade. Weighing 427 tons and capable of carrying 1,100 tons of cargo, the ship had two decks, three masts, and was 111-feet long and 29-feet wide. It was the equal of the East India Company ships known for their size and capacity. Most American vessels in the trade were smaller and stressed speed over capacity, but Astor obviously saw possibilities in carrying a larger volume.[32] In 1805, probably in partnership with others, the financier christened another ship, the *Magdalen,* named after his eldest daughter. The *Magdalen* was considerably smaller, weighing just 255 tons. Its inauguaral voyage was made in 1806. A short time before this voyage, Astor had sold the *Severn,* but he still owned two ships. For the next four years, he usually had one vessel on the outward voyage and one on the return from China.[33]

The selection of the cargo was the most important business decision on which the success of a voyage depended. Astor knew from past experience that ginseng and furs would constitute the principal exports. He also needed to be aware of the mix of furs so that various types were sent in quantities reflecting the needs of the market and thus capable of bringing the highest prices. He regularly gathered news of prices at Canton from vessels returning to New York, Boston, and Philadelphia so that he could gauge which furs would sell best in a given year. For example, the voyage of the *Severn* in 1800 carried 30,573 seal skins and only 1,023 beaver skins, whereas in 1804 the *Severn's* cargo consisted of 3,000 seal skins and over 6,000 beaver pelts. In 1805, the *Beaver* carried 24,275 rabbit and 2,500 otter skins, but no beaver pelts. Cargoes included other items in smaller quantities such as cochineal, quicksilver, iron, and cotton. Each vessel carried bullion or specie in order to purchase additional teas and silks, thus increasing the voyage's profitability. The variation in specie exports can be seen in the following: 1803 voyage of the *Severn*, $62,000; 1804 voyage of the *Severn*, $160,000; 1805 voyage of the *Beaver*, $62,000; 1806 voyage of the *Magdalen*, $111,000; 1807, voyage of the *Beaver*, $96,000.[34] The acquisition of such large amounts of specie was itself a difficult task, and Astor often bought and sold bank stock to secure the necessary amounts.[35]

With the specie and products on board ship, the outward bound cargoes were usually valued between $160,000 and $175,000, although Astor certainly hoped to sell the products at a considerable advance.[36] Each outward bound cargo, then, was worth $200,000, at least in terms of its exchange value for the purchase of teas and silks. On most voyages, Astor was not solely liable for this amount. Like venture capitalists before him, he often carried the specie or goods of other traders, either for a percentage share or on commission. For example, John Whetten was a shareholder in the *Magdalen;* and, in 1807, Astor sold additional shares in that vessel to Elias Kane and Company and Corp, Ellis and Shaw.[37]

Astor's outbound cargoes reflected the general imbalance of America's China trade. Specie was always an important ingredient because the fur sales, ginseng, and miscellaneous products never by themselves netted sufficient profits to purchase a return cargo. Tables 2 and 3 summarize America's China trade from 1804 to 1808, giving the type and total number of furs, the value of specie, and the total dollar value of merchandise and cargo. The total

Table 2
American Imports into Canton

Season	No. of Ships	Specie	Percentage Specie	Value of Goods	Total Value
1804–1805	34	$2,902,000	81.6	$ 653,818	$3,555,818
1805–1806	42	4,176,000	78.4	1,150,358	5,326,358
1806–1807	37	2,895,000	74.6	982,362	3,877,362
1807–1808	33	3,032,000	76.9	908,090	3,940,090

Source: "Statement of American Imports and Exports at Canton, 1808–1818," Great Britain, House of Commons, *Report by the Lords Committee Appointed Select Committee to Inquire into the Means of Extending and Securing the Foreign Trade of the Country, and to Report to the House . . .* , 1821, vol. 7, pp. 314–315.

value of merchandise sent to Canton was only 18 to 25 percent of the cargo's value, which meant that specie constituted 75 percent of all imports into China in those years. Astor had an advantage over other China traders because he had a dependable fur supply. Thus, he often sent more furs and made greater profits; consequently, he carried less specie. Most other traders would have bought furs in America at market prices. In essence, Astor was not solely dependent on the sale of the return cargo of tea, but rather the sale of furs in Canton was a crucial element in the profitability of his China trade.[38]

Of course, before any cargo left port, Astor, as the principal business organizer and manager, had numerous additional concerns that ran the gamut from the selection of a captain to outfitting the ship. The selection of the captain was perhaps the most

Table 3
American Furs Imported at Canton

Season	Total No. of Furs	Sea Otter	Seal	Beaver	Neutra and Fox	Rabbit
1804–1805	270,136	11,003	183,173	8,756	67,200	—
1805–1806	195,409	17,445	140,297	34,464	—	3,400
1806–1807	298,946	14,251	261,330	23,368	—	—
1807–1808	130,606	16,647	100,000	11,750	2,009	—

Source: "Statement of Number of Furs Imported into China by the Americans in the Following Years, 1804–1827," Great Britain, House of Lords, *Papers Relating to the Trade with India and China . . .* , 1829, vol. 109, p. 43.

crucial decision, for in addition to his normal duties on the early China voyages, either the captain or a business agent for the owners (called the supercargo) was responsible for sale of the cargo, which included judging the fairness of prices offered by Chinese merchants. The captain or supercargo also purchased the return cargo and again had to assess the quality and price of teas and silks. Usually this individual was a minor shareholder in the voyage, thus increasing his interest in negotiating the best possible prices. The largest China traders such as Russell and Company from Boston had permanent agents in Canton in the early nineteenth century, but Astor delegated these responsibilities to the ship's captain. He knew most of these individuals through his frequent partner, John Whetten. Year after year, Astor employed the same captains—John Cowman, Stewart Dean, William Howell, and John Whetten. On later voyages, he employed supercargoes; after the War of 1812, he appointed an agent, Nicholas Ogden, who resided throughout the year in China.[39]

Although captains were given some discretion, Astor directed, as far as possible, the captain's decisions. There was little doubt that Astor was the boss, a message that he typically conveyed in lengthy instructions before a voyage's departure. Astor would inform the captains of the prevailing prices in the market, what price he expected for each type of fur, and what price he would pay for particular varieties of tea. The New Yorker also selected and determined the rate of pay for the captain, minor officers, the common seamen, and sailors with special skills such as ship's doctor and blacksmith. Typical of Astor's instructions were the following to Captain Daniel Greene in 1813:

> You want in the first place one or two very clever fellows as officers, and if you get them, . . . it would be the more agreeable, there is a man here who has been the first mate with Capt. [John] Ebbets, he is not very clever, but if we cannot do better we must take him. The ship ought to have 25 hands all told, but I think you had best have 30, of these 8 or 10 should be prime seaman, which are plenty here at $14, the remainder half hands & landsmen those I think you best engage. . . . I would like that one or two were somewhat of Blacksmiths, one copper, one house carpenter, one or two ship carpenters, or more if to be had reasonable, one sailmaker, and a tailor might not be amiss.[40]

No ship could leave port before being adequately provisioned and outfitted. These tasks might include new sails and having the ship's bottom recoppered to prevent the formation of barnacles that would slow the passage. Finally, Astor had to determine the amount of insurance to carry on each voyage, a premium of from 8 to 10 percent, on a value that included the ship and cargo minus the specie carried on board. However, from the few examples that remain it does not appear that he tried to insure the venture's full value. For example, the 1806 voyage of the *Beaver* was insured for $30,000 and the 1803 voyage of the *Severn* at the same figure. When we add the costs of insurance premiums, the provisioning and outfitting costs, and the dock and loading fees to costs for the vessel, one can understand the immensely more complicated nature of Astor's business in the early nineteenth century.[41]

An important decision for both the safety and profitability of the voyage was the selection of the route. There were two principal choices. Some ships left East Coast ports with American manufactures and stopped first in Europe. Here they traded for European goods or acquired Spanish dollars to facilitate the purchase of China goods. Then the vessels would round the Cape of Good Hope and perhaps stop again in the East Indies or India, garnering additional products for exchange.

Astor, however, chose a different route because he already had products the Chinese desired—furs. His ships left America traveling south around Cape Horn—a far more dangerous passage than around Cape Hope—and then headed across the Pacific Ocean. There were still risks at this point from the weather and hostile nations. Nearly all China traders carried heavy armaments such as muskets and cannons. Astor, for example, equipped the *Beaver* with twelve cannons. Along the way, some ships stopped at islands to secure seal skins and almost all stopped in the Hawaiian Islands for reprovisioning before proceeding on to Canton. Although Astor did not participate in the Northwest Coast trade until 1809, a substantial number of other ships left the Hawaiian Islands and sailed to the Northwest Coast where they might trade with the Indians for a season to secure the skins of seals and otters. This voyage had additional risks that included the extended time for the passage, hostile Indians, and fluctuating prices in the Canton markets. Although voyages that stopped along the Northwest Coast might require nearly two years, Astor's more direct routes, stopping only occasionally for sealskins and provisioning, usually took less than a year for a round trip. For example, the *Severn* left New York in May 1803 and arrived at the Whampoa anchorage outside Canton on 2 September. It began the return voyage on 2 December 1803 and arrived back in New York in April 1804. The *Beaver,* however, made the circuit in ten months. It left New York in May 1805, arrived in Whampoa in September 1805, and departed from there in December and was back in New York on 26 March 1806.[42]

Astor encountered a maze of legal and cultural regulations in the China trade. Within traditional Chinese society and the Confucian social system, merchants and mercantile activities were tolerated but considered fundamentally dishonorable. Even though this strict viewpoint may have dissipated by the end of the eighteenth century, the Chinese government still assumed a superior attitude toward foreigners and closely regulated their trade and contact with Chinese society.[43] Canton was the only port open to foreigners, and ships were not allowed to sail either directly to Canton on the Pearl River, a distance of seventy miles inland, nor could they sail sixty miles upriver to Whampoa, the principal anchorage for foreign vessels. The first stop was at an outer island, Heungshan, with its port of Macao, a Portugese outpost since the seventeenth century. Here the captain received a permit, or *chop*—in addition to a Chinese pilot—that permitted passage to Whampoa.

At Whampoa, where ships were loaded and unloaded, the westerners were completely under the control of the *cohong*. The *cohong* was a group of merchants, usually twelve in number, who had obtained a license from the Imperial Chinese government to trade with foreigners ("barbarians").[44] Each *hong* merchant was an independent businessman and often traders like Astor preferred to deal with the same *hong* trader year after year. At Whampoa, Astor's vessels also hired both a *comprador* and a linguist through the *hong* merchant. The *comprador* provisioned the ship both while it was in harbor as well as for its return passage. His fees, not counting the cost of provisions, was usually $200 to $300. The linguist was an interpreter and thus the primary link for the foreign trader. Soon thereafter, the captain came in contact with the officers of the *hoppo,* the chief custom's official who measured the vessel and then charged a tax, based on its size, usually in the range of $2,000 to $3,000. Next was the *cumshaw,* a tribute of approximately $2,000 paid to the emperor for the privilege of trading at Canton. After paying numerous other small duties, the *hong* merchant, who purchased the inbound cargo, finally sent sampans to unload and transport it as well as the ship's officers to Canton.[45]

On arrival at Canton, approximately twelve miles further up the river, the ship's captain and supercargo were still sealed off from the city proper and confined to a series of buildings called *hongs*, or factories. Each factory belonged to a separate country where its traders and their agent, the *hong* merchant, stored both the imports and exports. Of course, the English factory, the headquarters of the East India Company, was the most elaborate. The captain and later permanent agents maintained sleeping quarters at the factory throughout the trade season. However, the Chinese took great care to make the sojourn at Canton as uncomfortable as possible to prevent the foreigners from establishing any permanence there. No women were allowed at the factories and the foreigners' movements were restricted to the immediate environs and a few streets adjacent that contained the shops of Chinese merchants. All negotiations over the return cargo were conducted in the factory and its surroundings, an area of probably not more than one-quarter of a square mile. Before this restrictive system began to break down in the early nineteenth century, most permanent representatives of American companies and other foreign nationals left the factories once the trading season ended and retreated to Macao, which was more like a European city.[46]

While at Canton, the captain or supercargo conducted negotiations for the return cargo. Astor, of course, already had alerted his agents to the prevailing prices in the market for teas, decorative items, silks, and nankeens. There was nowhere near the amount of guesswork that one might suppose during this era. Because *hong* merchants were in competition with one another, however, captains and supercargos did negotiate for the most favorable prices.[47]

Tea, of course, was the principal export to supply American consumers, who had been drinking it twice a day since the mid-eighteenth century. Teas were purchased usually while they were still in baskets for easy inspection, then they were packed in chests weighing three- to four-hundred pounds. The tea leaves were poured into the chests and then crushed as coolies repeatedly walked over them. The finer grades of tea, however, were packed by hand. If the whole process was not supervised, either inferior grades of tea could be substituted or chests might be improperly weighed. Astor alerted his agents to be careful at this stage of the transaction.[48]

Nankeens and silks were the next most important exports on Astor's ships. Silk was used for women's garments, whereas nankeen, a brownish yellow cloth that had a durable texture was used in making men's trousers. As late as 1840, *Hunt's Merchant Magazine* reported Chinese nankeen was "unrivalled by any of the cotton fabrics of Europe" and that silks, "notwithstanding the improvement made in this branch of industry in Europe, and particularly in our own country [the United States] still continue to be largely exported from China." Other exports found on Astor's vessels included sugar, cassia (a spice substituting for cinnamon), alum, China root (such as ginger and turmeric), chinaware, and lacquered ware.[49]

Table 4 lists American exports for each year from 1804–1805 to 1807–1808, and gives an overall view of the major exports by volume for all American ships and a dollar value for the year. Table 5 specifies Astor's export of China goods for three years from 1805 to 1807. Several observations help to place Astor's trade in perspective. First, the New Yorker had only two ships involved in the trade and only one ship carrying exports in a year, although he more than likely exported smaller shipments on other vessels. Nevertheless, his exports were only a small part of the total China trade, despite the fact that he is among the most well-known traders. Assuming the value of Astor's cargo in 1805–1806 at $175,000, which would have been an above-average cargo, he carried no more than 3.4 percent of the total American exports from Canton of $5,127,000. Second, the list of Astor's exports demonstrates his reliance on tea and nankeen, a pattern also followed by most other merchants. The popular, but more expensive decorative items were never the profitable part of this trade.[50]

The return voyage was of critical importance to the whole venture. The outward voyage had carried furs and specie, and although profits were made on the sale of furs, the ultimate profitability depended on the prices received from the sale of teas and other Chinese goods. Vessels, thus, were carefully loaded so that all available space was utilized. Captains in these early years were conscious of the need to arrive in New York City in early spring. This was the optimum time for the sale of goods to jobbers and commission merchants and for the preparation of cargoes for vessels headed to Europe and elsewhere after the winter slowdown.[51]

Once his ships reached American shores, Astor, along with many other merchants, profited from the numerous trade regula-

Table 4
American Exports from Canton*

Season	No. Ships	Tea	Cassia	Silk	Sugar	Nankeen	China	Total Value
1804–1805	34	94,189	4,143	9,385	1900	2,648,000	3080	$3,842,000
1805–1806	42	122,887	3,135	24,960	124	2,808,000	3535	5,127,000
1806–1807	37	118,527	1,447	17,680	885	1,764,000	2690	4,294,000
1807–1808	33	70,681	2,088	20,400	1400	2,922,000	4194	3,476,000

Note: Measurements are chests (approximately 300 to 400 pounds) of tea; pieces of nankeen; and peculs (approximately 300 pounds each) of cassia, silk, sugar, and China.

Source: "Statement of American Imports and Exports at Canton, 1808–1818," Great Britain, House of Commons, *Report by the Lords Committee Appointed Select Committee to Inquire into the Means of Extending and Securing the Foreign Trade of the Country, and to Report to the House . . . ,* 1821, vol. 7, pp. 314–315.

tions that favored American over foreign vessels. Not only did Americans pay fewer custom's duties on China products, but they were able to avoid taxes altogether if the goods were shipped to a foreign port within a year. The warehouse or drawback system allowed merchants, after careful itemization of the cargo and the

Table 5
John Astor's Exports from Canton, 1805–1807*
(Voyages of *Severn* [1805], *Beaver* [1806], *Magdalen* [1807])

	Severn	*Beaver*	*Magdalen*
Black tea	732	947	1,150
Green tea	1,209	2,251	2,148
Nankeen	788	918	351
Chinaware	116	147	165
Chinaroot	105	47	—
Silk piece goods	20	36	44
Alum	210	—	—
Silk thread	—	3	6
Cassia	—	134	—
Lacquered ware	—	2	—
Raw silk	—	—	5
Tortoise shell	—	—	3

Note: Measurement is in chests for tea and peculs for the remainder.

Source: EIC, 1804, p. 149; 1805, p. 159; 1806, p. 158; and Lists of Astor's Vessels in the China Trade, AP, BL, 13.

posting of suitable bonds, to store teas and other products in government-approved warehouses until the cargo was reexported. Sometimes, the government allowed the better-known merchants to use their own warehouses for storage. If reexported within one year, then all duties were canceled. If the teas were held longer, the duties were partially canceled. If the cargo eventually was sold in the United States, then duties were paid at that time. Astor's return voyages usually carried teas and silks worth more than $175,000, on which duties were approximately 12 percent. In a nation chronically short of capital, this system was of tremendous benefit to merchants. It allowed them to hold their products until the best price in the most suitable market could be found.[52]

Astor's most important market for exports from Canton was in the United States. Already a nation that had adopted the tea-drinking habit, the market consumed approximately 2.5 million pounds a year. Nankeen and silk were also quite important. Astor sold these goods in a variety of ways. First, he often advertised large lots for sale in New York City newspapers, hoping to interest wholesalers and retailers. Second, he consigned the goods to auction houses, although this method was used more frequently after 1815. Third, he sold teas and silks outright or on commission to commercial correspondents in cities along the Atlantic Coast. In the latter case, Astor retained title and control over the acceptable price, giving the agent a small commission on the sale. In Philadelphia, Astor's agents were William and Joshua Lippincott; in Baltimore he worked through Henry Payson; and in Boston, John Dorr was his principal contact. On occasion, he sold to his friends in Montreal, such as Parker, Gerrard, Ogilvie and Company. Yet the cities and agents changed constantly as Astor continually searched for the best price and market. Thus, it took three to four years for Astor to sell the contents of a single cargo, so that teas and silks received in 1805–1806 would not be fully accounted for until 1808–1809.[53]

The most distinctive aspect of the market for tea—and by extension all the China products—was the extent to which merchants used both domestic and foreign markets. Foreign markets took, on average, a little less than half of all tea originally imported into the United States. Consequently, Astor was constantly dividing his cargo, placing some in storage and sending other consignments to foreign ports. A few examples demonstrate the complexity of the process. The *Beaver* arrived in New York City in

March 1806 with a cargo of teas and silks. In April, Astor sold part of this cargo to Baltimore merchants and shipped it to them on board the Schooner *Fortitude*. Astor also reexported part of the *Beaver's* cargo and sent it to commercial agents in Puerto Orotava, Tenerife, for sale on commission. On other occasions, Astor sold goods to agents in Saint Thomas and Havana. Other cargoes of tea and nankeen were sent to Europe, where the favorite ports were Hamburg and Le Havre. In 1802, for example, Astor sent 4,508 pounds of tea to Joseph Pitcairn in Hamburg and 18,541 pounds to Strobel and Martin in Bordeaux. All Astor's shipments to Europe were on board the vessels of other merchants and captains, for he was not then involved in importing European goods into the United States. At this stage of his mercantile career, he preferred sales for cash or extended credit for up to four months at 4 percent interest. Astor's business was almost exclusively related to the fur–China-trade nexus, and he sought his profits in the sale of these products. Philip Hone, a business contemporary, described best the essential nature of his business:

> The fur trade was the philosopher's stone of this modern Croesus; beaver-skins and muskrats furnished the oil for the supply of Aladdin's lamp. His traffic was the shipment of furs to China, where they brought immense prices, for he monopolized the business; and the return cargoes of teas, silks, and rich productions of China brought further large profits; for here, too, he had very little competition at the time.[54]

How profitable were Astor's fur and china trades? Unfortunately, the answer cannot be as specific and detailed as economic and business historians might like. Astor's remaining business records for this period are spotty, giving only a partial account of fur shipments to Europe and China, with little indication of prices paid and received. Moreover, the pattern of business activity in the fur and China trade did not yield year-end statements of profit and loss. Furs that Astor purchased in Montreal in September or October might not be shipped to Europe or China until the following spring and probably not sold until late summer or fall. In the China trade, moreover, Astor might import a large cargo in the spring, but the teas and silks were often not completely sold for three or four years. Astor treated each China voyage as a distinctive venture and kept track of expenses such as commission fees, auction costs, shipping charges, cartage, duties, and tariffs, and he subtracted these costs from sales. He also noted money gained from interest on credit sales. Although, for the period from 1800 to 1807, we do not have a complete accounting of sales from any ship, nevertheless, there are a remarkable series of accounts, covering the period from 1816 to 1819 that provide information on the markets and sale prices of all teas and silks. These records indicate that a single voyage would usually yield $200,000 in gross sales. Also, Astor commented in 1815 that he usually had $800,000 actively involved in the fur and China trades, a sum that probably also reflected his capitalization in the first decade of the century.[55]

Astor's other business activities at this time also hinted at the enormity of his profits from the fur and China trade. For example, in 1801–1802, he used surplus capital to purchase New York City lots worth $125,000; by 1809 he had invested an additional $400,000. Astor also bought bank stock and continued to purchase agricultural lands in western New York. In 1806, he purchased the Park Theatre in New York for $50,000 and then leased it to managers. He also became influential with the other "movers and shakers" in New York City's financial and political communities and counted among his friends men such as De Witt Clinton, John Hone, and Albert Gallatin. By 1807, then, John Astor had emerged into the very first rank of businessmen in the early Republic.[56]

Business success apparently also brought Astor a measure of family happiness, comfort, and social recognition. He was a member of the Knights Templar Order and the Masons and a leader in the German Reformed Church, the leadership of which often met at his home.[57] Since 1803, Astor resided in one of the city's best neighborhoods at 223 Broadway in a house originally built by Rufus King. There, he and his wife, Sarah provided a comfortable life for a family that in 1807 included five children: Magdalen, born 1788; John Jacob, Jr., born 1790; William Backhouse, born 1792; Dorothea, born 1795; and Eliza, born 1801. Although his wife traveled rarely, if ever, Astor regularly had the older children accompany him on business trips. It should not be surprising then that Magdalen, who was the first to wed, married a business contact of her father, Adrian Benjamin Bentzon. He was a Danish citizen, governor of Santa Cruz (now Saint Croix), an island in the Danish

West Indies, until dispossessed by the British in early 1807 shortly before his marriage.[58]

The years from 1795 to 1807, then, were exhilarating for Astor. At age forty-four in 1807, he had accomplished a great deal. His business expansion had been steady and cautious, yet each year profits grew. With more capital at his command, Astor now stood at another turning point in his career, and one that ultimately transformed him from another of New York's first-rank merchants into the subject of myth and legend. Astor was about to catapult onto the world stage in a daring move that he would ultimately live to regret.

CHAPTER FOUR

Astoria

Initial Plans, 1807–1809

ASTORIA WAS the name of the Pacific Coast settlement that John Astor's employees established on the Columbia River in 1811. Although it was subsequently lost during the War of 1812, Astor always prided himself on the venture's boldness and blamed others for its failure. The enterprise was so extraordinary that many of the participants such as Ross Cox, Gabriel Franchére, Wilson Price Hunt, Duncan McDougall, Alexander Ross, and Robert Stuart either maintained diaries of their experiences or wrote books describing the events. Astor collected the diaries, journals, and letters connected with the planning and support of the settlement, and in 1834, he employed his friend Washington Irving to write a history of the enterprise. The financier wished to rehabilitate and protect his reputation after criticisms of his role had appeared in books by Astorians Gabriel Franchére and Ross Cox. Irving then hired his nephew, Pierre Irving, to assist with the basic research while both spent many hours at Astor's estate, Hell Gate, on the East River near New York City. Irving's conclusion left no doubt that

> Mr. Astor battled resolutely against every difficulty and pursued his
> course in defiance of every loss. . . . Had he been seconded by suitable

94

agents and properly protected by government, the ultimate failure of his plan might yet have been averted. . . . It is painful at all times to see a grand and beneficial stroke of genius fail of its aim: but we regret the failure of this enterprize in a national point of view; for, had it been crowned with success it would have redounded greatly to the advantage and extension of our commerce.[1]

Since the publication of Washington Irving's *Astoria, or Anecdotes of an Enterprise Beyond the Rocky Mountains* in 1836, the participants and later historians have argued about Astor's intentions in establishing the colony and the causes for its failure. Although Washington Irving, in what most historians believe was a reasonably accurate portrayal of the events, credited Astor with great daring, Hubert Howe Bancroft blamed Astoria's failure on the financier's "mania" to obtain wealth and to monopolize the fur trade. Bancroft had only scorn for Washington Irving's account and accused the author of deliberate falsification. Hiram Chittenden's *The American Fur Trade of the Far West* was a bit less sanctimonious, concluding that Astor's plan for a Pacific settlement was sound but that mistakes in judgment by Astor, his subordinates, and the federal government destroyed the settlement. James Ronda's recent account, however, has supplanted these old quarrels and reestablished Astoria's importance in the history of western exploration.[2]

Astoria is also a crucial event in evaluating John Astor's economic vision and business skill. Not only was it his most complex organizational undertaking, but also it involved diplomatic negotiations with Great Britain and Russia. There are several factors that are central to understanding Astor's participation in the venture. First, Astor's primary motivation was economic and involved a broad plan that included the establishment of a settlement to serve as a trading center on the Pacific Coast in addition to control of the fur trade in the Old Northwest. Second, the Astoria enterprise was affected by political and diplomatic events of the period, particularly by warfare in Europe, by the political and economic contest all along the boundary between British Canada and the United States, and by the erratic conduct of American diplomacy with Great Britain. Finally, chronology was especially important as Astor changed plans many times in reaction to events and, subsequently, moved in directions that were not envisioned when the project began in 1807.

In the first decade of the nineteenth century, Astor constantly maneuvered to expand his involvement in the fur trade. He had experienced great success in exporting furs to China and in importing teas and silk into Europe and the United States. He also had acquired a fur supply that did not depend solely on purchases in Montreal and London, and this supply contributed to cost savings and greater control. Although in the early years of the decade, Astor was not yet able to challenge the dominance of the North West Company, conditions had altered by 1806–1807. The New Yorker became not only more powerful but also the Canadian fur trade was weakened as the fur markets in England and Europe were disrupted by the Napoleonic Wars.[3]

Astor's position in the Great Lakes fur trade also benefited from the expanding American presence in the Old Northwest. The westward movement of American military troops and the establishment of new factories for the Indians east of the Mississippi River such as at Mackinac and Chicago challenged British influence over the Indians. In addition, the federal government had created a revenue district in the Old Northwest with Mackinac as the port of entry. Here duties were levied on trade goods shipped from the East Coast, duties which the Canadians believed were unfair because they were typically calculated on the value of the goods at Mackinac rather than at Montreal or New York. By estimating the value at Mackinac, American officials included the value-added by transport, a major component of the price, and thus justified a considerable increase in the duty. Canadian worries over America's increasing control were only exacerbated by continued clashes between the North West Company's traders and American officials. In 1805, for example, Captain David Duncan, the collector at the port of Mackinac, seized two canoes that the North West Company claimed were not liable for duties because they had stopped at Mackinac solely to take refuge from inclement weather and were, in fact, en route to Canadian trading territories.[4]

But it was Astor who gained most from America's movement into the Far West. President Thomas Jefferson was determined to challenge the British presence and influence along America's northern boundary, and he believed that the fur trade was an arm of American diplomacy. In 1803, Jefferson had purchased the Louisiana Territory and immediately sought to exploit its commercial potential. He was aware of the substantial American trade on the Northwest Coast where ships gathered seal and sea otter pelts and then carried them to China. He also knew of the Canadian explorations for a route to the Pacific Coast and had read Alexander Mackenzie's book, *Voyages from Montreal . . .* , that urged a transcontinental fur trade and an outpost on the Pacific Coast. Mackenzie not only identified a site on the Columbia River as the central outpost for British control but also characterized the project in competitive, nationalistic terms, "By opening this intercourse between the Atlantic and Pacific Ocean, and forming regular establishments through the interior, and at both extremes, as well as along the coasts and islands, the entire command of the fur trade of North America might be obtained.[5]

Because of the Canadian threat, Thomas Jefferson sent explorers, Captain Meriwether Lewis and William Clark, in 1803 to find an American fur-trade route that utilized the Missouri River and crossed the mountains to the Pacific Ocean. Such a route would give American fur traders an advantage over the British, whose route was far to the north. While Lewis and Clark moved west, General James Wilkinson, governor of the Louisiana Territory, sent Lieutenant Zebulon Pike to search for the source of the Mississippi River. As he explored north along the river, Pike also identified the most logical sites for military and trading posts that would bring the Indians into alliance with the American government.[6]

British fur traders were acutely aware of American intrusions in the Far West when Governor Wilkinson, with the support of Secretary of State James Madison, issued a proclamation in 1805 prohibiting all but American traders from operating in the Louisiana Territory. The British government formally objected to this order as a violation of the Jay Treaty, which had guaranteed free movement back and forth across the border for both British and American traders. The Americans argued, however, that the Louisiana Territory was not then part of the United States and so not covered under the Jay Treaty.[7]

In the first decade of the nineteenth century, the Canadian traders streamlined their trading organizations in an effort to blunt the effects of American pressure along the border and to prevent any challenges from American traders such as Astor. After a bitter struggle everywhere in the West between factions of the North West Company and independent traders from 1799 to 1804, the dominant partners realized that cutthroat competition was unproductive, especially since the Americans threatened to take over the trade south of Lake Superior. Consequently, in 1806 an agreement was signed dividing the western fur trade. The North West Company was henceforth to trade north of Lake Superior, and a new company, the Michilimackinac Company, composed of four Montreal firms, two of which were also members of the North West Company, were to trade south of Lake Superior in the Midwest and upper Mississippi regions. The agreement included elaborate provisions for dividing geographic regions and outfits and even provided for arbitration if issues between the companies could not be resolved through discussion.[8]

Although Astor knew of the struggles in the interior and of the effects of American expansion on Canadian traders, events closer to home were more influential in stimulating his proposal for an American fur company and an outpost on the Pacific Coast. The return of Lewis and Clark to Saint Louis and the subsequent reports of their journey to the Pacific Coast were of seminal importance. Lewis and Clark demonstrated that traders could cross the continent to the Pacific Coast; and, although not an all-water route, it was clearly sufficient for many commercial purposes. Lewis and Clark left no doubt that this "American" route was superior to the Canadian trail to the north, would give the Americans control of the fur trade, and would help counteract British influence over the Indians.

Meriwether Lewis also presented Thomas Jefferson with a comprehensive plan for conducting the fur trade. Furs could be collected in the interior, on both sides of the Rocky Mountains and along the Missouri River, and then shipped directly to Canton from an outpost on the Pacific Coast at the Columbia River. He questioned, though, whether the heavy and sometimes fragile goods from China could be transported over the mountains to the East. Clearly, he anticipated that American merchants would continue their practice of sending vessels to the Northwest Coast to collect furs for sale in Canton. Finally, Lewis alerted Thomas Jefferson to the fact that he had proposed a risky and expensive commercial project requiring government assistance: "If the government will only aid, even in a very limited manner, the enterprise of her citizens I am fully convinced that we shall shortly derive the benefits of a most lucrative trade from this source."[9] Even though Lewis had outlined his plan in a letter to Jefferson, it was widely published in late 1806 in newspapers, including the *National Intelligencer* and the *New York Post*. Consequently, along with Washington Irving's claim that Lewis and Clark's trip was essential to Astor's planning, it is safe to assume that Astor had read Lewis's letter.[10]

The New York financier must have been intrigued by the possibilities of an American route, but why suddenly in 1807 did he feel that he could successfully risk an immense capital and challenge the Canadians? Political and diplomatic considerations were essential to his decision. A key event occurred in June 1807 when a British warship, the *Leopard,* fired on the American frigate *Chesapeake* off the coast of Virginia. The *Chesapeake* suffered twenty-one casualties, extensive damage, and the humiliation of a British boarding party that removed four suspected deserters. This encounter was the culmination of years of unresolved commercial and diplomatic issues that included impressment, questions of American rights as a neutral trader during wars in Europe, and territorial and Indian problems along the borders.

On hearing of the *Chesapeake* affair, Jefferson prepared the country for war; within his administration that summer and early fall, war seemed imminent. Jefferson, General Henry Dearborn, secretary of war, and Albert Gallatin, secretary of the treasury all talked of the necessity of an invasion of Canada to neutralize the British military in the west. In September 1808, Gallatin even wondered whether five hundred American troops should be sent to Detroit to supplement the garrison there.[11] By October, the war fever had dissipated somewhat and the administration—led by Secretary of State James Madison and Albert Gallatin—decided to use American trade as a diplomatic weapon to force the resolution of outstanding issues. To this end, Congress passed the Embargo Act in December 1807, prohibiting all trade with foreign ports. Despite its passage, the war threat was not over. In January 1808, for example, Jefferson jotted a note to Albert Gallatin expressing his belief that the government needed to encourage merchants who were willing to risk their capital in the Indian trade. Strong alliances with the Indians, Jefferson argued, would help the United States on the western frontier should war occur.[12]

In January 1808, John Astor outlined a plan, breathtaking in its economic and political scope, that envisioned an American Fur Company powerful enough to challenge the British–Canadians along the entire northern boundary from east to west. Could there have been a better time for such a venture? Harassed continually by American officials, the Canadians already feared an American takeover of the trade. With the passage of the Embargo Act and the continuing war threat, Astor perceived an opportunity to gain greater control of America's fur harvest and simultaneously to meet the objectives of American foreign policy. He discussed the idea with business acquaintances in New York City in late 1807 and early 1808 and then set forth the details, at the request of De Witt Clinton, in a letter to him on 25 January.

Astor realized that Clinton's support was important to the plan's success because of his positions as both mayor of New York City and a New York State senator. Astor frankly stated that Clinton's willingness to request a charter of incorporation from the New York State legislature for the American Fur Company was the plan's essential first step. As Astor and Clinton were already friends, sharing membership in the same Masonic Lodge and having similar views about the necessity of commercial expansion, Astor's request was favorably received. Over the next several years, Astor and Clinton were in constant communication with Astor a frequent breakfast and dinner guest at Clinton's Richmond Hill home on New York City's outskirts.[13]

Astor's letter to Clinton is an extraordinarily important document because it reveals the financier's ability to merge economic and political objectives as well as his strategy *before subsequent events would dictate changes*. He first observed that the purchase of furs from the two major Canadian companies, the North West and the Michilimackinac, was no longer an acceptable business practice. These furs, Astor wrote, were actually trapped in American territory and then shipped to Montreal or London with extra duties and transportation charges. "It is a fact known to yourself," Astor claimed, "that we are obliged to draw 3/4 of our furs for home consumption from Canada I suppose annually to an amount of $400,000."[14] Instead, Astor proposed to establish an American corporation, headquartered in New York, with a capital of approximately $2 million that would operate in American territory across the entire continent. Astor intended to take over the existing network of private traders and partnerships in New York State and the Old Northwest; on the upper Mississippi and Missouri rivers, he planned to construct a series of trading posts "on the route made by Lewis to the sea."[15]

Astor predicted success for his American Fur Company, for it would possess two advantages over the Canadian companies. First, he claimed that the routes for the transportation of furs to market were more numerous, more direct, and substantially cheaper because he could utilize either the Mississippi River or the Great Lakes to reach the Mohawk River valley and thus come to Albany and New York City; to the west there was the Missouri River and the overland route to the Pacific Coast. The Canadians, on the other hand, had no alternative but to transport furs over the Saint Lawrence River to Montreal. Astor was aware that they had yet to establish the potential of an overland passage to the Pacific Coast in Canadian territory. Moreover, the Hudson's Bay Company actually blocked the North West Company's route to the Pacific Coast because it held title to lands in the Canadian Northwest and refused access to rival traders.

Astor also cited his ability to send furs directly into any markets he chose, whether in Europe or China. The Canadians, of course, had to ship most furs to London before distribution to Europe or China, and in the latter, they could not share fully in the profits of return cargoes. The British East India Company jealously guarded its monopoly of the Canton trade. It occasionally granted the North West Company a license to ship furs to Canton, but this license was restricted and did not permit the North West Company to export teas and silk. Astor knew that the China trade was not profitable unless the return voyage could be part of the enterprise.[16]

There are additional points in Astor's letter to Clinton that are crucial to understanding later events. First, in January 1808, Astor had not decided whether to establish a major settlement on the Columbia River; this idea matured later, following negotiations with the federal government and the Canadian fur-trade companies. Second, Astor definitely wanted a charter of incorporation, solicited Clinton's help in obtaining one, and desired to secure as many shareholders as possible. He did not initially perceive going it alone, nor was he grasping for a monopoly over the trade. He was acutely aware of the diversity of private interests in the trade both in the Great Lakes and at Saint Louis, where he had contacts with Charles Gratiot and the Chouteau family. Unless one assumes that Astor was the world's greatest gambler, the historian must accept the financier's statement, "You will readily conceive that few men of property will consent to engage in a trade where they would be willing to employ but a part and perhaps a small part of the property, that they should for the sake of the advantages arising from that expose their whole fortune. I am therefore of opinion that a company equal to the object cannot be formed unless in corporation."[17]

Astor also pointed out to Clinton that his idea offered advantages to the federal government, and thus he might reasonably expect their assistance. An American fur company, Astor reasoned, would permit the government to close its trading factories in the trans-Mississippi region. The financier obviously knew of Thomas Jefferson's desire to surrender the fur trade in the Far West to private American companies and traders. Jefferson hoped to save government resources and use them to improve the factory system east of the Mississippi River. Initially, Astor argued that the federal government might consider just one or two companies in the Far West, thereby protecting the Indians from competition between companies; but he later dropped any such notion as impractical given the existing competition.[18] Astor's letter to Clinton, then, was not a final proposal but an outline of a strategy and a plan that would evolve over the next several years.

Clinton was very supportive of Astor's proposal; thus the financier took the next step and wrote to President Thomas Jefferson in February 1808 presenting the most general outlines of the plan and specifying its usefulness in terms of Indian relations. Astor also indicated that he would proceed only if the federal government gave its *approbation*—a term Astor used to mean formal approval. Jefferson discussed the New Yorker's proposal with members of his administration and had Secretary of War Henry Dearborn investigate Astor's business reputation. Astor subsequently visited Washington in early March, where he met with Albert Gallatin, but it appears unlikely that he spoke with Thomas Jefferson at this time. Nevertheless, Astor received encouragement in Washington as the recent passage of the Embargo Act combined with war clouds on the horizon suggested the need for an American initiative in the fur trade. Moreover, both Jefferson and Gallatin were committed to exploration of the Far West, to the curtailment of British influence over the Indians, and to the utilization of the fur trade as an arm of diplomatic policy.

Astor subsequently returned to Washington, at Thomas Jefferson's request, in late April to explain in more detail the American Fur Company's business and diplomatic significance. He could not have hoped for a more influential and receptive audience, which included Jefferson; Gallatin; General Henry Dearborn, secretary of war; and James Madison, secretary of state. At this meeting, Astor placed increased emphasis on the establishment of an outpost on the Columbia River, probably because he knew that Jefferson favored this notion. He also revealed his intention to buy a half interest in the Michilimackinac Company, the most important Canadian firm operating on the Great Lakes and upper Mississippi River. In the discussions that followed, Astor again asked for government approval, or *approbation,* of his plans, and military assistance for the Pacific Coast settlement in case of war.[19]

The exact context of the discussions and the promises, implied or explicit, offered by government officials in March and April 1808 are the subject of considerable disagreement among both the participants and later historians. Astor came away from his late April meeting convinced that the government was enthusiastic and willing to close the factories in the trans-Mississippi West and provide military aid for the Columbia River outpost. Yet he did not assume that he had been granted monopoly privileges, and neither did he ask for them. But there was confusion over the level of government involvement. The only written documentation that he ever received was a vague letter from Thomas Jefferson dated 13 April 1808 that directly responded to Astor's earlier letter of February and preceded their late April conversations. Astor would later argue that he had received personal assurances, behind closed doors, that went considerably beyond Jefferson's somewhat cautious endorsement in a letter to the New Yorker:

> I learn with great satisfaction the disposition of our merchants to form into companies for undertaking the Indian trade within our own territories. . . . The field is immense, & would occupy a vast extent of capital by different companies engaging in different districts. All beyond the Mississippi is ours exclusively, and it will be in our power to give our own traders great advantages over their foreign competitors on this side of the Mississippi. You may be assured that in order to get the whole of this business passed into the hands of our own citizens & to oust foreign traders who so much abuse their privilege by endeavoring to excite the Indians to war on us, every reasonable patronage and facility in the power of the executive will be afforded.[20]

It may be that Astor's later bitterness toward government officials originated here with his failure to discern the nuances in Jefferson's letter. By late April 1808, both Gallatin and Jefferson had realized that the executive could not promise direct aid to any private merchant; although they supported Astor's plan, they could only provide "general assurances of the protection due to every citizen engaged in lawful and useful pursuits."[21] But it would be a mistake to imply that the federal government was in any way lukewarm to the New Yorker's proposal, and Jefferson and Gallatin surely encouraged Astor. It suited the goals of both the federal government and Jefferson so perfectly that Jefferson's views of the company expressed to Meriwether Lewis in July 1808 probably reflected the hopes of all concerned:

> A powerful company is at length forming for taking up the Indian commerce on a large scale. They will employ a capital of 300,000 D.[dollars] and raise it afterwards to a million. The English Mackinac Company will probably withdraw from the competition. It will be under the direction of a most excellent man, a Mr. Astor, merch't of New York, long engaged in the business, & perfectly master of it. . . . Nothing but the exclusive possession of the Indian commerce can secure us their peace.[22]

The extent of government support for John Astor's scheme was demonstrated indirectly as well by the famous incident involving Chinese businessman, Punqua Winchong. In July 1808, Samuel Mitchell, senator from New York, requested an exception to the Embargo Act so that an "esteemed citizen" of China could return for his grandfather's funeral. Jefferson permitted Winchong to charter a ship for this purpose, hoping to gain the good will of business classes in China. Winchong secured a vessel, none other than the *Beaver,* owned by John Astor. Although Astor was prohibited from carrying more than $45,000 in goods—presumably these belonged to Winchong—according to the Embargo Act, he could carry a return cargo consisting of teas and silk that he owned before the Act's passage. By early August, the voyage had become public knowledge. Philadelphia merchants, some no doubt Federalists sensing a chance to embarrass the administration, charged that Winchong was nothing more than a common laborer and that Astor was deliberately avoiding government legislation. He clearly was not alone in his attempt at such chicanery because, at the time, Jefferson and Gallatin were inundated by similar requests from merchants. By the time Jefferson and Gallatin suspected that the exemption might be fraudulent, Astor's ship had sailed. Whether Astor intentionally misled Gallatin and Jefferson cannot be stated with certainty, yet the incident plainly revealed the federal government's eagerness at this juncture to encourage any project even remotely connected to John Astor.[23]

Along with his efforts to secure the *approbation* of the federal government, Astor also shepherded a charter of incorporation through the New York State legislature. Between his trips to Washington in early March and late April, he also visited Albany to discuss the charter with members of the legislature and to discuss strategy with De Witt Clinton, who introduced a bill into the legislature to incorporate the American Fur Company. The charter easily passed the Senate, but attracted considerable discussion in the House before receiving approval in April 1808.[24]

Astor and his lawyers had created a stockholding corporation very similar to other quasi-public companies then securing approval in New York State. No doubt, Astor wished to clothe his enterprise with a public purpose similar to turnpike and bank corporations. According to the charter, the American Fur Company would secure "great public utility, by serving to conciliate and secure the good will and affections of the Indian tribes toward the government and people of the United States, and may conduce to the peace and safety of our citizens inhabiting the territories bordering on the native Indian tribes." As an "American" fur company with such lofty public purposes and diplomatic advantage, the charter also stipulated that all stockholders had to be American citizens.[25]

The charter further specified that the American Fur Company was to last for twenty-five years, with renewal possible, and that its capital stock was initially to be $1 million at $500 per share, which after two years could be raised to $2 million by calls for further payments on each share of stock. The company was permitted to elect a board of directors as soon as one thousand shares were sold and payments of $25 per share were made. The charter permitted the company to reserve one-third of the stock for its employees in a manner similar, no doubt, to the profit-sharing pattern of the North West Company. Astor's business partners in selling stock included at least two people—William Edgar and Edward Laight—directly connected with him in China ventures and land investments. These men were aware of the risks associated with the project, and each sought to obtain at least a dozen wealthy stockholders to assume part of the burden. Astor once observed that, if a large number of businessmen subscribed for stock, he would willingly reduce his own investment to expand the pool of stockholders.[26]

With a charter for the American Fur Company in hand and convinced that he would have federal government support, Astor arrived in Montreal in the fall of 1808 with a two-part proposition intended for the Michilimackinac Company and the North West Company. His strategy was to avoid competition with the Canadians and to use the tense political climate along the border and the Embargo Act as well to urge them to sell their American holdings. Astor apparently made no secret in Montreal of the magnitude of his undertaking and talked freely of his intention to cross the continent and establish an outpost on the Pacific Coast. Whether many Canadian merchants were intentionally misled or simply misunderstood, they concluded that the New Yorker possessed a monopoly charter from the federal government. To the Canadians, therefore, Astor appeared to be a truly formidable competitor.[27]

Essentially, Astor offered to buy out the Michilimackinac Company's interests in American territory for $550,000, taking all their goods both in Montreal and in the trading territories. At the same time, he wanted a related agreement with the North West Company in which each signatory agreed to refrain from trading across national boundaries set by the Treaty of Paris in 1783. Of course, Astor was attempting to gain a free hand in the Missouri River territory. However, the Canadians rejected the offer, and apparently made a counterproposal that set the sale price at $700,000 for full compliance.

In late December 1808, Astor realized that he was a long way from an agreement. The Canadians were reluctant to surrender the southwest trade and Astor was apparently unwilling either to pay their price or to enter into a cooperative agreement. In late 1808, he visited Albert Gallatin in Washington where they agreed that Astor should hold firm, particularly as control of the Michilimackinac Company and its trade with the Indians would be critical in the case of war. Astor's thought, at this point, was that so long as British trade was totally banned by the Embargo Act and later by the Nonintercourse Act, there was no reason to discuss any further joint ventures with the Canadians.[28]

The Canadians were stalling, and Astor knew it. Early in 1809, the Michilimackinac Company appeared ready to sell, but then they suddenly withdrew the offer. Astor surmised that the British government prevented the sale for fear of losing control of the Indians.[29] Although the New Yorker overestimated the British government's interest, he was correct in his assumption that the Canadians were consciously trying every device to save their investment and prevent America's political and economic takeover along the northern border. Indeed, Canadian moves from 1808 to 1812 profoundly affected Astor's plans.

The Canadians could hardly mistake the American government's intent to secure its borders in the West. After the Embargo Act was passed, the North West Company had sent a representative, George Gillespie, to Washington in an attempt to negotiate exceptions for British goods utilized in the fur trade. Trusting that the American government eventually would ease the restrictions, the Michilimackinac Company outfitted twenty canoes and sent them into American territory to trade. When the first boats entered the Niagara River, near an American fort, the customs collector and military authorities attempted to stop the traders because they had not filed papers concerning their cargoes, which was a requirement of the Embargo Act. Shots were fired, six vessels were halted and expropriated, and the others were chased into the open waters of Lake Ontario. The British ambassador to the United States, David Erskine, wrote an angry letter of protest to Secretary of State James Madison referring to the incident as a "gross and unprovoked outrage."[30] The Montreal partners of the Michilimackinac Company were no less upset. In a petition to Governor Craig of Lower Canada, they highlighted the significance of this incident and the necessity for action by the British government, "Your memoralists have for some time seen progressing, with extreme concern, a systematic plan to drive the British Indian traders from American territory, by every species of vexation; and they must soon succeed, if His Majesty's Government does not take up their cause with decision."[31]

In the years from 1808 to 1812, the leading partners of both the Michilimackinac Company and the North West Company also sent a barrage of petitions and memorials to British officials in Canada and London and, as well, dispatched personal representatives to the Foreign Office and the Colonial Office in London. A number of pamphlets were published in England acquainting the public with the importance of Canada; in 1809, a group was formed called the Committee of British North American Merchants. Its most active member was Nathaniel Atcheson, who wrote *American Encroachments on British Rights* in 1808, and penned a long letter in 1810 to Lord Wellesley, foreign secretary, outlining the whole case for aid to the fur-trade interests in Canada. In 1811, the Canada Club was formed in London representing these same merchants. Modeled on the Beaver Club in Montreal, this group met regularly and provided an organized lobby in London for fur-trade interests.[32]

But what did Canadian fur traders hope to accomplish through all these lobbying efforts? In fact, their goals were highly changeable and depended on the diplomatic situation. At first, they hoped for changes in the Embargo Act and the relaxation of American duties. Yet they knew that, soon, Canadians would be forced to give up trading in American territory. Still, they wished the British government to secure a provision in any negotiation that would give traders a "liberal pecuinary allowance . . . for the sacrifice of their trading establishments and Indian debts." Most important in all the petitions and writings of this period was the Canadian insistence that the crucial issue was the land west of the Mississippi River and the establishment of trading posts along the Northwest Coast. The fur supply in the West and access to the Canton market were as important to the Canadians as to the Americans. Thus Astor's plan propelled the Canadians into action. The message to the London diplomats could not have been more specific: you must challenge American claims to the mouth of the Columbia River, Montreal and London fur traders urged, and limit American influence along the northern border. Canadian petitions to the British government included specific references to Astor's American Fur Company, which the Canadians believed had government support for an expedition to the Northwest Coast.[33]

The North West Company also hoped for direct aid from the British government for their own enterprise on the Pacific Coast. They wanted clear title to land, which was then under the control of the Hudson's Bay Company, from Fort William west to the Pacific Coast. In addition, the North West Company argued for an end to the East India Company monopoly so that direct trade could be carried on from the Northwest Coast to Canton. Finally, they asked for a monopoly charter to compensate for the risks of expansion. Clearly the North West Company wished to challenge Astor on the Pacific Coast; and while they negotiated with Astor from 1808 on, they simultaneously petitioned for, and discussed, a program of political and financial aid with the British government. The discussions between Astor and the Canadians, then, were multisided, and just as Astor huddled closely with Albert Gallatin, so the Canadians moved under the watchful, although somewhat disinterested, eyes of the British government.[34]

Two major factors—the lack of progress of the Canadian negotiations and the Embargo Act and its successors—forced Astor by late February 1809 to make dramatic changes in plans for the American Fur Company. Initially, he had conceived of a two-step program that would begin with the acquisition of the Michilimackinac Company and the establishment of control over the southwest trade. Then he hoped to expand the American Fur Company west of the Mississippi River with a chain of posts along the Missouri River, ultimately with an outpost on the Columbia River. Although he continued to pursue an arrangement with the Michilimackinac Company, while competing with it in the Great Lakes region, he now decided to push ahead with plans for trade in the Far West. With both the Embargo Act, which prohibited all trade, and the less restrictive Nonintercourse Act of March 1809, Astor was prevented from obtaining trade goods from England and shipping furs into British and French markets. However, with the Nonintercourse Act he could trade with China, making the Pacific venture more attractive. Astor also was forced to reconsider his original strategy because only a few capitalists had purchased American Fur Company stock owing to the unsettled economic conditions within the United States and the uncertainty of the Canadian negotiations.[35]

Astor's change in plans was indicated first to Albert Gallatin in May 1809 when he announced that he was sending a ship with traders and Indian goods valued at $50,000 to the Columbia River. This trip was specifically designed to establish contacts with the Indians and to explore a site for settlement. Simultaneously he "hoped" to buy out the Michilimackinac Company. And with the trade goods acquired in that purchase, he would later send an overland expedition to establish a chain of trading posts along the Missouri River. The overland group, Astor projected, utlimately would rendezvous with the traders coming east from the Columbia River. It is important to note how sketchy were Astor's ideas of the Pacific venture. The Missouri River posts were the most important objective, whereas the Columbia River settlement was purely exploratory. Conscious of the diplomatic overtones in this venture, he indicated that he would also send about fifty people, forty-five of whom would be American citizens, to establish "American" interests in the trade.[36]

Astor's May 1809 letter also revealed his close ties to the federal government as well as the nonofficial nature of federal government support. He informed Albert Gallatin that he wished the government to receive early notification of his plans in order that government officials such as military officers would not interfere with the movements of the overland expedition. In a rather oblique statement, surely made to elicit federal assistance, Astor asked for any advice that Gallatin had "as it being the intention to take no step of any importance without the knowledge of Government & to act as much as possible consistent with its wishes." The New Yorker, nevertheless, left no doubt that the amount of capital and effort that he committed depended on government *approbation*. He specifically asked Gallatin, if the government "still intended" to withdraw its factories from the Indian country after the American Fur Company went into operation—an idea they obviously had discussed either in person or by correspondence.[37]

Astor's letter to Gallatin also revealed his knowledge and worry over the competition of traders at Saint Louis. He knew, for example, that trading interests had flocked to Saint Louis after the return of Lewis and Clark and that men like Ramsay Crooks and Robert McClellan already had undertaken trading ventures north and west along the Missouri River. Most threatening to Astor's plans, though, was the Saint Louis Missouri Fur Company that was being formed in 1809 under the direction of Manuel Lisa, Pierre and Auguste Chouteau, William Clark, and Reuben Lewis, brother of the explorer. Given the cast of characters, Astor felt compelled to ask whether this company had the direct patronage of the government. Basically, Astor wanted assurances that he was on equal ground with the competition. Yet he also told Albert Gallatin, if only to establish his superiority in the eyes of government officials, that he doubted whether the Missouri Fur Company had the necessary capital, as he did, to challenge the British.[38]

Astor's decision to move toward the Pacific received an enormous boost in the summer of 1809 when he was visited by Andrei Dashkov, the newly appointed Russian consul in Philadelphia and a representative of the Russian-American Company. This organization had established its fur-trade headquarters at New Archangel (Sitka) on the Northwest Coast. Dashkov knew of Astor's reputation as a China trader and of his plans for the Pacific Coast, so his proposal was quite simple: he wanted Astor to supply the Russian colony at New Archangel with goods and ship its furs into the Canton market.[39] This proposal, of course, was completely outside Astor's thinking in 1807–1808, and yet he quickly perceived the economic advantages for the fur trade and the equally important repercussions for American foreign policy.

There were several reasons for the Russian overture. Beginning in 1808, the Russian and American governments had expanded diplomatic relationships with trade as the prime motivation; as a consequence, they moved from representation by consuls to ambassadors. Russian activity in the fur trade and in North America was nothing new; indeed, the Russian-American Company had been chartered in 1799 to coordinate efforts. It was modeled on the East India and Hudson's Bay companies and was to serve as an agent of Russian expansion. Its North American headquarters at New Archangel, though, was difficult to supply from the centers of Russian population, for it involved overland transportation across Siberia to the Russian port at Okhotsk. Company leaders and government officials had tried several alternatives. In 1803, an expedition set out from Kronstadt on the Gulf of Finland to sail around the world to test the possibility of supplying the colony and to explore other areas along the Northwest Coast. The government also investigated the feasibility of establishing formal relations with the Spanish colonies in California, but the Spanish government declined.

In addition to the problem of supply, the Russians had political problems with China and were not allowed to ship furs directly to Canton. Russian furs had access to China only through interior ports of entry on the Russian–Mongolian frontier. Russian furs sold at Canton, therefore, did not garner great profits because of the dangers and expense involved in a cumbersome transportation route to market.[40]

From 1800 to 1809, the Russians had developed partial solutions to their economic problems, but these measures also created new worries. The Russian governor at New Archangel, Alexander Baranov, had entered into several trade agreements with American ship captains who sold him supplies for the colony and shipped its furs to Canton. However, this trade was irregular and undependable.

The Russians also were alarmed by the increasing American presence along the coast. In particular, they objected to the fact that Americans sold firearms to the Indians, leading to increasingly hostile tribes. Finally, many Russian officials had territorial ambitions to the south along the Northwest Coast toward the Columbia River. Baranov had sent more than one expedition to the Columbia River region, and he and company officials were aware of the westward progress of the Canadians. In 1808, Russia's foreign minister, Nikolai Rumiantsev, wrote the American consul in Saint Petersburg asking the American government to stop the trade in firearms and to recognize Russian trading rights and territories on the Northwest Coast. Later, when Andrei Dashkov first arrived in the United States in 1809, he again requested American officials to take action. The American government, though, flatly refused to negotiate either a boundary settlement or to exert control over the actions of American merchants.[41]

Consequently, the Russian consul, Dashkov, decided that an *exclusive* trading arrangement with a merchant such as Astor would accomplish great benefits for both countries: I doubt that a meeting of the minds ever took place more quickly. Dashkov and Astor both believed that other American traders would be driven off the coast and that Astor alone could supply the Russian colony with its goods and transport its furs to Canton. Both men also saw an alliance of the American Fur Company and the Russian-American Company as a device to squeeze the North West Company, which both knew hoped to locate a port between the Columbia River to the south and the Russian colony to the north.[42] Astor once described his Russian strategy as a lesson that he had learned from the Canadians, "Long experience, clearly bought by the different Canada traders, has proved, both, that the Indian trade can not be carried on, but by companies, and that, when two companies come in contact, they must join and come to a friendly understanding or both be ruined."[43]

Throughout the summer and fall 1809, Astor readied a ship, the *Enterprise,* for this first voyage to the Pacific Coast directly connected with the Astoria project. Astor had contemplated sending a vessel to the Pacific Coast as early as May 1809, but his conversations with Andrei Dashkov added important new responsibilities to the trip and delayed its departure. John Ebbets, the captain, was selected because he had previously sailed to the Northwest Coast, New Archangel, and China while employed by

Boston merchants. The singular importance of this venture was also demonstrated by the fact that the *Enterprise* was to carry a supercargo, Daniel Greene, who also had sailed to the Pacific Coast and Canton.[44] The *Enterprise* was loaded with a large and varied cargo, consisting of supplies for the Russian colony and goods for trade with the Indians along the coast. For example, there were eighteen hogsheads (a large barrel or cask) of sugar worth $3,241, ten hogsheads of tobacco valued at $2,083, thirty-four hogsheads of molasses worth $3,079, and an extensive amount of brandy, rum, and gin valued at $5,621. The cargo also included thread, flour, callicoes, jackets, trousers, shirts, shoes, and writing paper. The value of the cargo was over $28,000, and Astor's total investment was close to $80,000 given the value of the ship, provisions, insurance, and wages for the crew.[45]

Astor, then, had two principal objectives in dispatching the *Enterprise*. First, the ship was to stop along the Northwest Coast, particularly near the Columbia River and "prepare the Indians for a friendly reception to some white men who would come to stay with them."[46] By fall 1809, Astor already was preparing for another sea voyage and an overland trip to the Columbia River in 1810. The *Enterprise*'s second objective was to sail from the Columbia River to New Archangel and there propose a formal commercial arrangement between Astor and the Russian colony. The *Enterprise* sailed only with a tentative agreement between Astor and Dashkov that in no way committed Governor Baranov at New Archangel to purchase the *Enterprise*'s cargo. Ebbets, though, carried with him detailed instructions from Astor and full authority to negotiate for the cargo's sale and to arrange for the sending of additional vessels for up to three years.[47] Simultaneously, Astor intended to pursue a far-more-comprehensive arrangement with the Russians through diplomatic channels both in the United States and Russia. Until the *Enterprise* sailed from New York in November 1809, then, all Astor's plans for the Pacific venture had been on paper only, but now he had taken the first steps in the riskiest and most costly venture of his business life.

By late 1809, three major characteristics of the Astoria venture were evident. First, the federal government in the person of Albert Gallatin and Thomas Jefferson was very much aware and in support of Astor's efforts to capture the Great Lakes and Far West fur trades. Clearly, public policy and private interests were on a course of mutual advantage. Second, Astor's plans were in a state of constant flux. He had started originally with a vision of capturing the American fur trade by initially gaining control of the Canadian interests in the Great Lakes by purchase and then moving toward the Pacific Coast. However, shifts in American trade legislation and Canadian unwillingness to negotiate quickly made the Far West trade and a Pacific Coast outpost a more accessible goal. The Russian overture fit perfectly with his plans for the coast. Third, Astor was making all the decisions and managing an increasingly complex venture that cut across the diplomatic affairs of three nations—the United States, Russia, and Great Britain—and that required increasing amounts of capital and organization. Yet he still intended that all his initiatives eventually would be part of a stock company—the American Fur Company—in which he would be a major, but not the only, stockholder. The challenge from this point forward was to create an entity or enterprise that in effect encouraged people to become stockholders.

CHAPTER FIVE

Exploration and Incorporation

Astoria, 1809–1812

THE DEPARTURE of the *Enterprise* for the Columbia River and New Archangel in November 1809 began a period of intense business activity on Astor's part. In these years his wealth, power, and business skill were everywhere evident: he personally organized the Pacific Fur Company in order to establish a settlement on the Pacific Coast and negotiated contracts with the Canadians and Russians to secure his territorial control of the American fur trade. But it would be a mistake to think that Astor controlled events. His success or failure often hinged on the judgment of his employees on the Pacific Coast and in the interior as well as on the territorial and political ambitions of government leaders in Saint Petersburg, London, Montreal, and Washington. In an age where news traveled slowly, Astor committed both men and money to the Astoria venture and then waited many months before learning of the outcome. Historians may be able to fault Astor for mistakes in judgment and overall conception but not for any lack of determination, decisiveness, or nerve.

Even as he wrestled with the Russian overtures and prepared for Ebbets's voyage, Astor continued to work on plans for the southwest trade and the overland and sea expeditions to the Pacific Coast. In late 1809, he still anticipated a Canadian decision on his offer to purchase the interests of the Michilimackinac Company in American territory and to mutually respect each nation's territorial boundaries in the areas west of the Mississippi River. In February 1810, North West Company representatives, John Richardson and William McGillivray, came to New York to negotiate with Astor. Their position at this point was desperate because they were making plans for another trade season, yet the Michilimackinac Company still could not ship goods into, nor furs out of, American territory owing to America's restrictive trade legislation. Astor clearly had the upper hand, and he forced a tentative agreement in which he became a 50 percent owner of the Michilimackinac Company. The North West Company's agents further agreed to take a share of between 30 and 50 percent in the Pacific Coast venture. Final approval of this agreement, however, depended on the assent of North West Company partners both in the interior and in Montreal. Although the Montreal partners were favorable, they sent a representative, George Gillespie, to Fort William in order to secure the approval of the interior traders.

Astor's subsequent actions and business strategies, though, had to consider various contingencies. He knew that it would take considerable time to secure Canadian approval, perhaps as much as a year. Therefore, he continued with plans for the Astoria project and prepared to compete directly with the Canadians, but he also allowed for the possibility that an agreement might be signed by all the North West Company's partners. By March 1810, Astor also had adjusted his conception of the Pacific initiative. He now conceived of a permanent settlement on the Columbia River. Traders would assault the Pacific Coast in a two-pronged offensive: one group by sea and another overland along the Missouri River and across the Rocky Mountains. Astor no longer intended to establish trading posts on the Missouri River, rather the expedition was to explore potential sites for these posts. A chain of trading posts across the country was planned for a later date, probably when, and if, the Pacific settlement succeeded.[1]

Astor's organizational structure for the Pacific venture was the Pacific Fur Company. Unlike the projected American Fur Company, in which he meant to sell stock, the Pacific Fur Company was an intermediate step to finance the initial expeditions to the Pacific Coast while preparations continued for the larger, parent concern, the American Fur Company. In March 1810, therefore, Astor signed a preliminary agreement to establish an outpost on the Pacific Coast with three disgruntled members of the North West Company: Duncan McDougall, Alexander McKay, and Donald McKenzie. These men were experienced traders, and one, McKay, had accompanied Alexander Mackenzie on his trips to the Pacific Coast in the 1790s. Joining these men in New York for discussions with Astor was Wilson Price Hunt, a Saint Louis merchant. Astor had contacted Hunt in the spring or summer of 1809 concerning his willingness to join the venture. Ramsay Crooks, Robert McClellan, and Joseph Miller, who were experienced traders on the Missouri River, were also associated with Hunt from an early date. They were especially important because they knew the traders and business people in the Saint Louis fur-trading community, particularly the competition headed by Manuel Lisa, which would have to be faced in any overland expedition to the Far West.[2]

After Astor's lawyers had finished an extraordinarily long document of thirty clauses, the Pacific Fur Company became a reality on 23 June 1810 when the various partners or their proxies signed the final contract. It was not a corporation but rather a partnership uniting Astor, who controlled one-half, or fifty shares, with his Canadian and American partners. McKay, McKenzie, McDougall, and a new partner, David Stuart, each held five shares; Hunt and Crooks, five shares; and McLellan and Miller, two and one-half shares each. Fifteen shares were to be reserved for future partners, of whom Astor could nominate four. Any new partners, though, had to be skilled in the Indian trade, and none could hold more than three shares.

The partnership was an uncommon opportunity for the hardy and adventurous. Essentially, the New York financier assumed all the financial risks; the traders mortgaged their lives. Astor agreed to provide all the capital up to a maximum of $400,000 and bear all losses for five years, although profits would be distributed according to shares. In addition, Astor pledged to send supply vessels to the settlement in both 1811 and 1812 as well as provide $200 for clothes and supplies each year for each trader. These supplies were to be purchased in New York and sent out on yearly vessels. The company was to last for twenty years. The partners, though, reserved the right to dissolve the company within five years if it proved unprofitable.[3]

Astor structured the Pacific Fur Company on the model of the North West Company. The partners, or shareholders, were divided between the winterers, who traded in the interior, and the merchants, in this case, John Astor, who was responsible for purchasing trade goods and selling furs. Winterers were obligated to the company for terms that ranged from five to seven years. After five years, the traders were allowed to come East on a furlough before returning to the Pacific Coast. On the coast, the wintering partners had full authority to make decisions respecting the trade. The company was to hold an annual meeting on the coast at which new policies and procedures could be adopted binding on all concerned. Astor, though, had not surrendered control over the company's decisions. As Astor held 50 percent of the shares, had the right to nominate additional partners, and had appointed Wilson Price Hunt as his agent (who controlled another five shares), there was little doubt that Astor controlled the company—or so he thought!

The contract establishing the Pacific Fur Company also contained two clauses that set forth Astor's hope, that at some future date, he would finalize agreements with the Michilimackinac and North West companies. At that point, Astor planned to disband the Pacific Fur Company and merge the whole venture into the American Fur Company. Article twenty-six specified that Astor could "make any arrangements with the North West Company . . . to extend the business" and article twenty-eight allowed Astor "to make over his shares and Interest in the said Concern to the said Corporation [American Fur Company]."[4]

Before signing the final agreement, Wilson Price Hunt and the Canadian partners went to Montreal to recruit a full complement of traders and clerks for the Pacific Fur Company's land and sea expeditions to the coast. In *Adventures of the First Settlers on the Oregon or Columbia River . . .*, Alexander Ross recalled that Alexander McKay wrote and asked him to come to Montreal where, in May 1810, he saw the "gilded prospectus" of the Pacific Fur Company. Despite efforts of the North West Company in Montreal to downplay the venture's significance, the "golden prospects" held out by McKay and Hunt were sufficiently alluring to entice twenty-four voyageurs. In addition, Russell Farnham, Gabriel Franchére, Donald McGillis, Benjamin Pillet, and Alexander Ross signed on as clerks. Franchére wrote later that he was motivated by a "desire to see other countries joined with the wish to make a fortune."[5]

By early July 1810, the overland party was set to go. Wilson Price Hunt and Donald McKenzie were to share command. Although Hunt was essentially a merchant with little wilderness experience, McKenzie had been a trader for ten years with the North West Company. Even though they shared command, Hunt, as Astor's agent, was the senior partner. The reason for Hunt's control was obvious. Astor was well aware of the diplomatic significance of the trip and of the continuing difficulties between America and England. His discussions with Albert Gallatin and Jefferson produced general agreement that ultimately they all desired to squeeze the Canadians out of the trade. With this in mind, Hunt determined that only one canoe and approximately fourteen traders would depart overland from Montreal. He intended to hire additional "American" traders in Mackinac and in Saint Louis when he arrived at those points. The strategy was to have enough Canadians to keep the North West Company interested in a joint arrangement (should that come to pass) but not so many Canadians that they would control the expedition. Hunt's hiring practices were evident to Alexander Ross, a Canadian trader, who commented later that Hunt "gave a decided preference to Americans."[6]

The overland party left Lachine south of Montreal on 5 July 1810 and arrived at Mackinac on approximately 26 July. Washington Irving claimed that the trip was delayed by the desultory pace of the Canadians who balked at taking orders from the neophyte woodsman—Wilson Price Hunt. Throughout the Astoria venture, there was an understandable tension between Hunt and McKenzie and between Canadian and American traders. Nearly all primary accounts also reflect a bias, depending on their "Canadian" or "American" perspective.

After arriving at Mackinac, Hunt was joined by Ramsay Crooks, whom he had personally recruited as a partner in the venture because of his experiences on the Great Lakes and upper Missouri River. Crooks insisted that they try to hire additional explorers (rather than traders) because they were skilled with rifles and prepared to face hostile Indians who might be encountered on the upper Missouri River. But the employment of additional men was not easy. It was summer on Mackinac Island;

and, if the accounts of Irving and Ross are accurate, the island was full of traders who spent most of their days drunk and disorderly and in no mood, yet, to consider employment for the upcoming winter. Word spread quickly around the small island about this company, however, and the potential fortunes that might accrue to its traders. By the time Hunt reassembled his group in early August, it had grown from fourteen to thirty traders.

So far, Hunt was on schedule. The overland party left Mackinac in early August on two barges loaded with traders and goods. They were bound for Green Bay on Lake Michigan. Then they were to go up the Fox River and down the Wisconsin River to Prairie du Chien and from there on the Mississippi River to Saint Louis. The arrival there in early September allowed adequate time to recruit additional traders and to replenish supplies before departing to seek a winter headquarters on the Missouri River.[7]

Saint Louis proved a somewhat hostile environment. Manuel Lisa's Missouri Fur Company viewed Hunt's group as direct competition to its interests on the Missouri River. Yet Hunt had innumerable business connections of his own in the city, especially Joseph Miller who was a company partner. Miller had already secured supplies for the overland group and had promoted the project with prospective traders. With Miller's assistance, Hunt was able to leave Saint Louis in late October to journey up the Missouri River as far as possible before winter set in. At this point, the expedition consisted of about twenty riflemen and forty voyageurs—plus supplies—loaded on two keelboats and two barges. By 16 November, they had traveled 450 miles to the mouth of the Nodaway River, where they encamped for the winter.[8]

Hunt stayed at the winter encampment until early January 1811 and then left the group to return to Saint Louis. This move was according to previous plans because Hunt wanted to check for any last-minute instructions from Astor. Moreover, he had decided that the expedition needed an interpreter and additional riflemen. Hunt also must have been delighted to leave the company because the severe winter had already taken a substantial toll with petty bickering between Yankees and Canadians and a few desertions. Hunt received instructions in Saint Louis that only increased these tensions. Astor now appointed Hunt the sole commander of the overland expedition, dropping any fiction that this was a shared venture with the Canadians. These new orders reflected Astor's growing certainty that a cooperative venture with the North West

Company in the Far West was unlikely. Therefore, he did not want the Canadians to have decision-making powers over the expedition. Hunt left Saint Louis again in March 1811 and joined his unhappy company at Nodaway on 17 April. Within four days, the entire party, consisting of approximately sixty men loaded on four boats, pushed up the Missouri River toward the Rocky Mountains.[9]

The second assault on the Pacific Coast was by sea. These traders left Montreal and headed for New York in several groups, beginning in July 1810. In New York City, a ship, the *Tonquin,* was being outfitted for the voyage. Astor personally hired additional personnel for the ship's company that would be crucial for the settlement: a blacksmith, silversmith, cooper, and several carpenters.

The group was delayed approximately five weeks in New York City. During this period given the tense international situation, Astor and the Canadians evidenced considerable unease with the joint venture. Led by Alexander McKay, several Canadian traders visited Daniel Francis Jackson, the British ambassador to the United States, who was in New York City, and explained their participation in Astor's enterprise. The Canadians inquired about their status and responsibility if war were to break out between the United States and Great Britain. After listening to the description of Astor's proposed settlement on the Pacific Coast, Jackson apparently allayed their fears and assured them that in case of war they would be viewed as British citizens—not as enemies.

The possibility of war also worried Astor, particularly as he had been unable to sign an agreement with the North West Company. Given Astor's close ties to the federal government and the diplomatic and political significance of the enterprise, it is not surprising that Astor selected Lieutenant Jonathan Thorn, who was on furlough from the U.S. Navy, to take command of the *Tonquin.* Thorn had seen military action against the Tripoli pirates and was cited for bravery by Stephen Decatur. When the *Tonquin* left New York City on 6 September with a crew of twenty-two and thirty-three passengers, it received a military escort from the American frigate, *Constitution,* to protect it from British cruisers intent on impressment. No one on board possibly could have missed the military and political significance of this expedition.[10]

The voyage of the *Tonquin* was an unparalleled disaster. Almost from the first day at sea, Captain Thorn showed his unfitness for his first command. Thorn was unable to adapt to his peculiar position as captain of a vessel with a unique cargo that necessitated sharing command with the partners of the Pacific Fur Company. He treated all the passengers as common sailors, and many of these individuals, who were partners in the enterprise, were not willing to accept orders and verbal abuse. Astor must share at least part of the blame for this situation. His desire to form a close association with the federal government led him to select an untested naval lieutenant for a task requiring uncommon tact and diplomacy.

Thorn's problems stemmed from an insecurity in his own judgment, from an overzealous attempt to protect American interests, and from a nationalistic bias against the Canadian traders. Thorn refused to recognize the hierarchy that existed within the Pacific Fur Company. Thus, he insulted the company's artisans when he moved them into the cramped quarters of the common sailors. Thorn, obviously worried over the loyalty of the Canadians, restricted their movements to particular parts of the deck and required all lights to be extinguished by 8:00 P.M. These tactics insulted the traders and provoked several confrontations, none more dramatic than when Alexander McKay and Thorn stood nose-to-nose. At one point, Thorn threatened to "blow out the brains of the first man who dared to disobey his orders." Only the gentle intercession of David Stuart, a Canadian partner, prevented further hostilities.

In December 1810, when the ship stopped at the Falkland Islands to renew its water supply, Thorn sailed away and left a party of nine persons on shore who had missed the signal for departure. This group, included three of the Pacific Fur Company partners—Duncan McDougall, Alexander McKay, and David Stuart—as well as Alexander Ross who later described the incident. When the shore party realized that the *Tonquin* was headed for the open sea, they all boarded one small boat and rowed frantically for six hours in pursuit of the ship. According to accounts by Ross and Gabriel Franchére, they would have perished except that Robert Stuart, who was on board the *Tonquin,* grabbed a pistol and threatened to kill Thorn unless he waited. From that point on, Thorn and his passengers rarely spoke and mutual hatred grew. It was little wonder that several crew members deserted when the vessel arrived in the Hawaiian Islands.[11]

Desertion may have been the wise choice, for Thorn had yet to make his most disastrous mistake. After leaving the Hawaiian Islands, the *Tonquin* reached the Pacific Coast and the mouth of the Columbia River on 22 March 1811. Here, Captain Thorn was confronted by dangerous sandbars across the river's mouth, bad weather, and rough seas. Rather than wait for a shift in the winds, Thorn ordered his first mate and a small crew into a dinghy to take soundings in the channel. They were immediately swamped and all disappeared. But Thorn was not to be deterred and sent other boats on the same mission. Eventually, the *Tonquin* entered Baker's Bay, but the effort had cost the lives of eight men.

The first days on the coast were extraordinarily busy. The most immediate task was to select a site for the settlement. For two weeks, small parties explored both sides of the inlet; finally on 11 April, they chose a spot on Point George about twelve miles from the river's mouth on the south bank. Then the entire group began clearing a site for the post, a task of great difficulty given the size of the trees and the thickness of the brush. It took nearly a month just to clear an acre of ground. Almost immediately they planted a small garden and also set to work on the foundation for the first building, a store and temporary shelter measuring about twenty-six by sixty feet. When its foundation was laid, the group named the settlement Astoria.

Almost from the moment of their arrival, Indians had come to observe the work and to trade. Indeed, during the early days, some Canadians remained on board ship trading for furs. However, the settlers were not yet sure of the Indians' intentions, and as Ross, in his usually exaggerated prose, described the scene, "Every man, from the highest to the lowest, was armed with an axe in one hand and a gun in the other; the former for attacking the woods, the latter for defence against the savage hordes which were constantly prowling about."

To add to their problems, the rainy and cold climate and a poor diet brought illness. Ross and McDougall remembered that on some days there were only a half-dozen men able to work. In these early days, some men deserted with the intent of crossing the mountains to return home.[12]

Once arriving at the settlement, Duncan McDougall, the leader among the Canadian partners, took command. Thorn, having unloaded only part of the settlement's supplies, left to trade with the Indians and to explore farther north on the coast. Thorn planned to return to Astoria, but neither he nor the *Tonquin* was ever seen again. Although there are no reliable accounts of precisely

what happened, Thorn apparently insulted local chiefs at one of
his trading stops along the coast. With incredible arrogance and in
direct violation of Astor's warnings, Thorn allowed the Indian on
board ship. The Indians subsequently attacked and killed the entire crew. During the encounter, the powder magazine exploded destroying the *Tonquin*. The traders at Astoria were unaware of the
Tonquin's fate until October 1811 when an Indian visitor told them
the story. I doubt that Thorn's passing elicited much sorrow. His
folly, however, cost lives of crew, traders, and Alexander McKay, a
partner. Moreover, the *Tonquin*'s destruction left the settlement
without necessary supplies and military hardware as they faced
their first winter on the coast.[13]

Despite the difficulties, the Astoria settlement did gain a foothold. From the first day of their arrival, the fur trade was brisk.
Within two months, they explored along the Columbia River and
moved overland to the north with the intention of establishing sat-
ellite trading posts. They had intended also to trade along the
coast but the *Dolly*—a vessel whose frame was brought out on the
Tonquin—was only twenty-five tons and unsuitable to the task.
The Astorians tried to use it on the rivers to haul supplies, but
here, too, it proved unwieldy. Nevertheless, the trade was so good
that they had difficulty in controlling the number of Indians who
daily arrived at the settlement.[14]

Through their contacts with the Indians, the Astorians soon
learned that they were not alone on the coast. Other traders were
located to the north, and they surmised that these men must be
representatives of the North West Company. In July 1811, David
Thompson, the Canadian explorer and North West Company
agent, suddenly arrived at the Astorians' newly constructed dock.
Neither Thompson nor McDougall was exactly sure what stage negotiations had reached between Astor and the North West Company in the East. Thompson, however, informed McDougall that
his latest news (which was inaccurate) was that the winterers of
the North West Company had accepted Astor's offer of a one-third
partnership in the Pacific venture and that the final details were
now being worked out between Astor and the Montreal partners.
The Astorians were genuinely pleased with this news because no
one wished to engage in a brutal competition on the Pacific Coast.
No further commitments were made by either side while awaiting
further developments in the East; but Thompson, who was then on

Astoria in 1813. Courtesy of Clarke Historical Library,
Central Michigan University.

his way back to Montreal, offered to carry letters from the Astorians to Astor that described their safe arrival and willingness to accept their new partners. Indeed, there was a strong sense of common purpose at this point. Thus on 22 July 1811 when Thompson's party left, he was accompanied for some distance by David Stuart, Alexander Ross, and about seven traders from Astoria who journeyed up the Columbia River to establish an interior post. In late July, Stuart founded a post at Okanagan, perhaps five hundred miles from Astoria.[15]

At the Astoria settlement, there was continued progress. A second building near the storehouse was finished and served as a residence for inhabitants. Worries over the Indian threat increased daily, and work began on a stockade.[16] Yet the whole settlement was uneasy with the knowledge that Wilson Price Hunt and the overland contingent were now long overdue. By late fall

1811, the Astorians surmised that the groups had met some horrible fate crossing the mountains. They were partially correct.

When Wilson Price Hunt broke winter encampment in April 1811, his party included approximately forty Canadian voyageurs and twenty hunters. They initially traveled in four boats, one mounted with guns, and all having sails. The plan was to follow the route of Lewis and Clark up the Missouri River, but nothing seemed to go as planned. Their major concern was a report of hostile Indian tribes along the Missouri River, but equally bothersome was the threatening presence of Manuel Lisa of the Missouri Fur Company, who traveled alongside them for a brief portion of the journey. After meeting three hunters on the trail, who had recently crossed the mountains by another route to the south, Hunt decided to leave the Missouri River and head overland passing through modern-day South Dakota and Wyoming. Hunt's decision is difficult to understand because John Astor's major purpose had been to explore locations for fur-trade posts along the Missouri River. It may be that the Indian threat appeared so certain that Hunt felt he had no other choice. Both Ramsay Crooks and Robert McClellan had encountered Indian hostility recently in other ventures on the Missouri River, and they may have urged this change in plans. Hunt's decision, though, was a crucial error and an example of how little control Astor exerted once events were set in motion.

The overland trek was a nightmare. Washington Irving's *Astoria* and Hunt's own diary vividly described the group's misfortunes. Hunt lost the trail in the mountains and ran so short of food that he split the expedition. Each party then set out to find their own way across the mountains. These groups did not begin arriving at Astoria until 18 January 1812, when Donald McKenzie and Robert McClellan arrived with a small party of nine; on 15 February, Hunt straggled into Astoria with a party of thirty-three. Ramsay Crooks did not appear until May 1812 and then only after traders from Astoria accidentally met Crooks and his traveling companion who were so "emaciated . . . that our people for some time could scarcely recognize them to be white men."[17] The severe tribulations of the overland journey which included starvation, injuries from falls on treacherous mountain passes, spills on river rapids, and attacks from Indians left many Astorians unable to go on. Not only were there deaths and desertions along the way, but Crooks and Robert McClellan gave up their shares in the enterprise and decided to return to the East. Nevertheless, the small settlement at Astoria, which had numbered approximately seventy people, was buoyed by the arrival of the overland parties, and together they made plans for the trading season ahead.[18]

Astor in New York City knew nothing of the progress of the overland and sea expeditions throughout 1810 and 1811. Nevertheless, he had to presume that they would reach the coast. In the meantime, he continued to negotiate with both the Canadians and Russians in order to reach business decisions he hoped would ultimately lead to the control of the fur trade under a single umbrella—the American Fur Company.

When Hunt's overland party and the *Tonquin* left in the summer and fall of 1810, Astor's discussions with the Canadians were unsettled. Astor was really negotiating with two separate entities—the Michilimackinac Company, primarily interested in the southwest trade in American territory, and the North West Company, whose interests were to the north and west. He had met with representatives of the Michilimackinac Company and had agreed to purchase a 50 percent share in that company. He also had offered the North West Company a one-third share in the Pacific venture.[19] Even though the winterers of the North West Company consented, the Montreal merchants withdrew their commitment in early 1810. By this time, they undoubtedly believed that David Thompson and the traders of the North West Company, who were then pushing toward the Northwest Coast, would establish a prior claim there. Montreal merchants were also hopeful that after extensive lobbying they would receive help from the British government in establishing a settlement on the coast. In May 1810, moreover, the American government reopened trade with Britain, thus allowing the Canadian companies to move goods and furs into and out of American territory. All these events weakened Astor's negotiating position. His response was swift and direct. He immediately ordered a supply of goods from England to provide direct competition to the Canadians in the southwest trade in the summer and fall of 1810.[20]

By late fall 1810, circumstances again had changed. No sooner had Astor ordered goods from England for the southwest trade, than he reopened discussions with the Canadians. More than likely, Astor initiated these negotiations when he visited Montreal in October 1810 and conversed with the Montreal partners on business and social occasions.

Two events motivated changes in their attitude. First, the United States had warned that trade restrictions would be reinacted unless Great Britain altered its economic policies. Second, several Montreal merchants, who held shares both in the North West Company and the Michilimackinac Company, purchased all the shares in the Michilimackinac Company. They renamed it the Montreal Michilimackinac Company and indicated to Astor that they desired a permanent settlement in the southwest trade. They now realized that Astor was already moving toward the Northwest Coast and was also fully capable of seizing the southwest trade. William McGillivray, thus, came to New York City, and on 28 January 1811, Astor signed the long-sought-after agreement. The contract united the American Fur Company and the Montreal Michilimackinac Company in a new firm to be known as the South West Company.[21] Its title was significant: the South West Company was to stand equal with the North West Company in power and geographic scope.

Astor had compromised his original goal substantially in order to secure this contract. Originally, he had desired to close the Canadians out of the fur trade in American territory along a northern boundary extending all the way to the Pacific Coast. Instead, this contract reflected a desire to avoid competition and share the fur supply in the southwest where each side had substantial interests. This business strategy, placing cooperation over competition, was clearly articulated in the agreement:

> Whereas experience has proved that the People, Supplies and Materials for carrying on that trade are best procured in part from and through Canada, and in part from and through the State of New York; consequently an opposition between Companies so circumstanced would be productive of certain loss to both, whilst a reciprocal Communication of the advantages arising out the localities would assure a Materials benefit to each.[22]

The American Fur Company became a reality with the negotiation of this contract. Astor had assumed a 50 percent interest in the property and establishments of the Montreal Michilimackinac Company in the territory of the United States in order to pursue the trade jointly for five years. There was a further clause that gave Astor two-thirds, rather than half, the trade, were the U.S. government to withdraw its factories. Once again, Astor obviously thought, based on his previous conversations with government officials, that the factories would be removed. Each firm was to purchase 50 percent of the goods needed for the trade and each firm was to send an agent yearly to Mackinac for settling the annual accounts. Astor perceived this arrangement as an intermediate step before the total exclusion of the Canadians from the trade could be realized. The Canadians, on the other hand, saw it as a means of preserving some part of the American trade for another five years or until diplomacy or war dictated another solution.[23]

The agreement also had several important provisions relating to the North West Company. This firm agreed not to pursue any trade in American territory, except that connected with the South West Company. With this provision, Astor really had gained control of the trade in American territory. However, another clause specified that the agreement had "no application whatsoever to any Countries beyond the ridge of the Rockey Mountains [nor] the river Missouri nor to the North West Coast nor in the Pacific Ocean."[24] Astor knew, then, in January 1811 that he was in a competitive fight to control the Far West trade. From this point on, he must have worried about the number of Canadians he had allowed into the Pacific Fur Company in the hope that a joint arrangement would eventually ensue. It was also at this point that he had written Wilson Price Hunt and given him total command of the overland party.

Alongside his efforts to solidify business relationships with the Canadians, Astor also pursued a formal agreement with the Russians. When Astor sent John Ebbets in the *Enterprise* to New Archangel in 1809, the New Yorker had outfitted an entire vessel with the hope that the Russian governor, Alexander Baranov, would purchase the cargo on the advice of the Russian consul, Andrei Dashkov. The New Yorker, of course, had limited the risk. If the Russian overture failed, Ebbets was prepared to trade with the Indians along the coast. But Astor preferred the Russian trade connection.

Negotiations with the Russians at New Archangel failed to proceed smoothly, despite Astor's gift to Baranov of a large quantity of wine. The first problem was a slight delay and embarrassment

because Baranov and his immediate staff were unable to read
Astor's letters, which were written in English and French. Eventually, the captain of a Russian naval vessel translated the
documents.[25] The Russians also did not trust Ebbets, despite the
fact that Dashkov had written an accompanying letter assuring
Baranov that Astor was in no way connected with the American
government. Serious difficulties also occurred because Baranov
thought that the goods were too expensive. Astor had not listed
the original prices nor the markup for transportation, thus Baranov was understandably wary. He worried too, that a formal, long-
standing agreement needed higher government approval, and as
he was planning to return to Russia soon, Baranov was reluctant
to risk his superiors' disfavor.[26]

Despite all the problems, Ebbets and Baranov reached an understanding. No doubt Dashkov's endorsement helped convince
Baranov that the political and economic advantages justified a few
risks. In the end, Baranov purchased the bulk of the cargo, worth
approximately $26,000. He paid in beaver, seal, and otter skins,
which Ebbets later sold in Canton. Ebbets also transported to
Canton a large Russian fur inventory for a 5 percent commission
on the sale plus a transportation charge. He further agreed to return to New Archangel with Chinese goods. Baranov hedged on an
extended contract, preferring to await the outcome of more formal
negotiations in Saint Petersburg. He did indicate, however, that if
Astor would justify his prices, additional vessels would be welcome
while negotiations were underway.[27]

In early 1810, though, Astor was completely unaware of
Ebbets's discussions with Baranov as he prepared a complex trade
proposal for the Russian government and the Russian-American
Company. Astor assumed that he and the Russians possessed a
common goal, which was to drive away other American and foreign
traders and to bring stability and control over the Indian trade. In
essence, Astor hoped that a contract between the American Fur
Company and the Russian–American Company would prevent the
North West Company from establishing outposts on the Pacific
Coast. The New Yorker, therefore, proposed to furnish the Russian
establishments with supplies at an agreed upon markup on current prices in New York City. Astor initially proposed a 150 percent markup. Second, Astor agreed to carry Russian furs to
Canton on commission. Third, he proposed to divide the fur ter-

ritories and Indian trade on the Pacific Coast between the two companies. Astor suggested fifty-five degrees latitude to mark the boundary and in this way "to prevent as much as possible any interference of trade from the Canada North West Company who are making their way fast towards the coast in high latitudes and who intend soon to be in contact with the Russian company."[28]

Finally, Astor wanted access to Russian markets. He asked the Russians to reduce the heavy tariffs on foreign fur imports only for the American Fur Company. Astor evolved a totally spurious argument that, if the American Fur Company had market advantages in Russia, it would be a stronger company in challenging the North West Company elsewhere—an outcome that the Russians would supposedly desire. Basically, Astor desired reciprocity: Russian furs entered the United States free of duty, and, therefore, he desired an exemption from Russian tariffs only for the furs of the American Fur Company.

By April 1810, Astor had finished his Russian proposal, so he began the political maneuvering necessary to make it a reality. He spoke first with Andrei Dashkov, the Russian consul and representative of the Russian-American Company in Philadelphia; but in July 1810, Dashkov was eclipsed by Count Fedor Pahlen, newly appointed ambassador from Russia. Astor immediately sent his son-in-law, Adrian Bentzon, a former Danish diplomat, to Washington to talk with Pahlen.

The timing could not have been more opportune. Count Pahlen already had met with both Albert Gallatin and President James Madison, but he was disappointed that the American government still refused to control American ships operating on the Pacific Coast. Pahlen's dissatisfaction pushed him directly into Bentzon's hands, who described Astor's detailed plan that would effectively divide the Northwest Coast between the American Fur Company and the Russian American Company. Pahlen embraced the idea enthusiastically, although he cautioned that the higher councils of the Russian-American Company and the Russian government would make the final decision. However, Pahlen commented that its anti-English tone would appeal to Nikolai Rumiantsev, the Russian foreign minister.[29]

Bentzon was extraordinarily secretive during his stay in Washington, refusing to send a report on his discussions to Astor through the mail. He also urged Astor to refrain from writing

letters and holding discussions with government officials, preferring to postpone all discourse until such time as they could speak
personally. Bentzon, in fact, visited with both James Madison and
Albert Gallatin at this time, but he did not reveal the full scope of
Astor's plan.[30]

For the next few months, Astor worked assiduously on the Russian initiative. He personally visited with Fedor Pahlen, discussed
the terms of an agreement extensively with Bentzon, and finally
approached both James Madison and Albert Gallatin for their assistance. Astor apparently asked for official government sponsor-
ship. Although the New Yorker's plan offered a solution to the
friction between the Russians and Americans on the Northwest
Coast, President Madison absolutely refused official patronage to
the scheme because the government could not approve Astor's
scheme to acquire exclusive trading rights in Russia or on the
Northwest Coast. Interestingly, President Madison's letter to Albert Gallatin on the subject said nothing about Astor's proposal to
divide the coast at the fifty-fifth parallel, presumably because this
was an agreement between two companies, not two governments.

Madison may have adhered to constitutional scruples in refusing to assist Astor in his efforts to secure monopoly trading rights,
but the federal government, nevertheless, was wholeheartedly in
support of Astor's establishment of an American presence on the
Northwest Coast. In pursuit of this, Astor sent Adrian Bentzon to
Russia to negotiate an agreement with the Russian-American
Company, and Madison informed our ambassador in Russia, John
Quincy Adams, of the federal government's informal support of this
effort. In March 1811, Albert Gallatin secured passage for Adrian
Bentzon on the American frigate, *John Adams,* then bound for Europe. Astor's close tie to the federal government was evident once
again when George Erving, while on a special diplomatic mission
to Denmark, was forced out of his cabin onto a sofa in order to make
room for Bentzon and his wife, Magdalen [Astor's daughter].[31]

By October 1811, Bentzon was in Saint Petersburg for discussions with the Russian-American Company and with the Russian
government through the office of Foreign Minister Nikolai Rumiantsev. From the start, Bentzon pushed hard for the privilege of
annually importing furs up to a value of 200,000 rubles ($48,000)
free of duty. The Russian-American Company, though, adamantly
resisted granting this request as it would lessen their monopoly
status in the market. The Russian government, moreover, was not

persuaded that an exception to prevailing Russian trade policies was justified. Yet Bentzon appeared so committed to this proposition that many Russians believed that it was his major objective.[32] Eventually, he accepted defeat on this issue and then moved quickly to form an agreement between the American Fur Company and the Russian-American Company. It was signed in Russia in May 1812 and then sent to New York, where Astor signed it in December.[33]

Similar to the contract establishing the South West Company, Astor's Russian overture produced considerably less than he had hoped for. The agreement pledged each company to respect the hunting and trading spheres of the other but did not set any absolute boundaries. They agreed to act in concert "to remove outsiders who may wish to derive advantages from hunting, fishing, or trading" but did not specify how this was to be accomplished. The American Fur Company was given a monopoly in supplying the Russian colony, so long as the prices for goods were acceptable, and the right to carry Russian furs to Canton should the colony's governor so desire. The contract was to last for four years. Because this was a weak trade agreement at best, Astor had failed to build a wall against the North West Company's intrusion onto the Pacific Coast.

Why was Astor unable to secure a more binding agreement? Basically, the Russians did not trust the New Yorker or any other American because of worries over the safety of their colony and its possible expansion in the future. The Russians were also unhappy with the price of goods received from Astor. Essentially, the Russians only signed the agreement because they saw a chance to eliminate other American traders, particularly those who sold weapons to the Indians.[34]

During the negotiations with the Russians and the Canadians, Astor also rethought the organizational and financial structure for his ventures. He had not intended to assume the entire financial burden, which was approximately $500,000 by 1811. Astor's own rough estimate was: cost of goods, ships, and men on the *Enterprise, Tonquin,* and *Beaver,* $320,000; overland party, $24,000; cost of goods for interior trade with the South West Company, $120,000. In February 1811, he turned his attention to the American Fur Company, which had yet to go into operation; indeed, excluding his own interest, only one hundred twenty shares had been sold. Astor blamed the slow stock sales on the political climate created by trade restriction, on the threat of war, and on the defects in the corporate charter. Consequently, he asked De Witt Clinton to lobby in the state legislature for revisions in the American Fur Company's charter that would strengthen the company and make it more attractive to investors.[35]

Astor wanted several changes. First, he desired to extend the American Fur Company's charter from twenty-five to forty years. The financier knew now that it would be more than ten years before any substantial profits could be returned, thus he wanted to assure investors of the company's extended life. Second, he wanted the charter amended so that foreign capitalists could purchase stock. This amendment would also allow Astor to merge the South West and Pacific Fur companies, composed of foreign shareholders, into the American Fur Company. Third, the financier requested an expansion of the company's banking powers so that it could issue notes for payment of debts. This request added to its existing authority to issue bills of exchange in order to facilitate the movement of goods and furs. Finally, the New Yorker wanted to reduce the number of directors from nine to either three or four in order to guarantee secrecy of operation given the ongoing relationships with the Canadians and Russians. Of course, such a provision would increase Astor's power substantially and reduce the need to consult with other capitalists. He wanted the stockholders' money, not their advice.[36]

Even while seeking to improve the American Fur Company's organizational structure, Astor continued to honor his previous commitments to the Astoria enterprise. In October 1811, he sent another ship, the *Beaver,* to resupply the Astoria settlement and to bring goods to the Russian settlement at New Archangel. Astor still did not know whether either the *Tonquin* or Hunt's overland party had reached the coast. Therefore, he instructed the *Beaver's* commander, Captain Cornelius Sowle, to make contact with Wilson Price Hunt and Captain Thorn of the *Tonquin.* If he failed to find settlers on the coast, Sowle was to send a well-armed party to explore along the shore. Astor had confidence, though, that at least one party had made it to the coast. Thus the *Beaver* carried additional adventurers bound for Astoria, including a partner, John Clarke, and six clerks. One of the clerks, Ross Cox, later wrote a rather bitter description of the whole episode. In addition, there were fifteen American laborers and six additional Canadian voyageurs. Astor deliberately sent more Americans than Canadians because he was now conscious of the need to protect American interests. He had received false intelligence from England that the North West Company had sent a vessel from London to establish a British settlement on the Pacific Coast.[37]

The *Beaver* carried a full supply of goods for Astoria. Even though later accounts, particularly by Alexander Ross, accused Astor of deliberately sending inferior goods, the charge was illogical; Astor already had extensive capital invested and would not have deliberately jeopardized the settlement with inadequate supplies. Astor, however, often was unable to send the best quality axes and woolens because American trade restrictions made it impossible to obtain British goods. Nevertheless, the inventory of the goods on board the *Beaver* was impressive both in quantity and variety. Total merchandise intended for Astoria was valued at $32,452 and included: woolens; beads and cloth for trade; implements such as axes, a forge, awls, saws, and chisels; foodstuffs such as sugar, molasses, and liquor in substantial amounts; three boxes of books that included historical studies, poetry, economic tracts, and newspapers; and clothes such as shoes, hats, coats, and vests.[38]

The *Beaver* not only was to supply Astoria but also to stop at New Archangel with additional supplies for Governor Baranov. By the time the *Beaver* sailed in October, Astor had received letters from Alexander Baranov, the Russian governor, and John Ebbets whose ship, *Enterprise,* had traded at New Archangel in 1810, which indicated Baranov's unease with the lack of information concerning prices. This time Astor sent a pricelist indicating the dollar and ruble value of every item destined for New Archangel totaling $22,342 or 92,960 rubles. Andrei Dashkov again sent an accompanying letter testifying to the fairness of Astor's prices. So intent was Astor on strengthening the arrangement with Baranov that he did not enclose a commission or transportation charge. Instead, he allowed Baranov to determine the appropriate markup on the goods.[39]

At the same time that Astor expanded his operations in the interior of the United States and on the Pacific Coast, he increased, almost as a necessity, his trade with China. His efforts to garner an increased supply of furs obviously meant that the number of ships involved in the China trade and the importation of teas and silks into the United States also would increase. Crucial to understanding this expansion was the fact that when the provisions of the Embargo Act were reduced in 1809, it opened the China trade, even though access to English fur markets remained closed. In 1809, therefore, Astor dramatically expanded the number of ships in which he was full or part owner. He sent both the brig *Sylph* and the *Beaver* to China in 1809. In addition, the *Tonquin, Enterprise,* and *Beaver* were to stop first on the Pacific Coast but then carry furs from the Northwest Coast to China before returning with teas and silks to New York City. Astor reexported a portion of all cargoes to European markets; by 1810, the size of his business was so large that it justified the purchase of the brigs, *Adolphus* and *Powhattan* just to carry goods to Europe.[40]

By the end of 1811, John Astor had become the dominant force in the American fur trade. The South West Company represented his partial takeover of Canadian interests and the establishment of a premier position among American traders in the region from the Mississippi River to the East. The Pacific Fur Company's outpost at Astoria scooped Canadian efforts in the same area. The agreement with the Russian–American Company promised to increase his control of fur supplies along the Northwest Coast and to block Canadian efforts to gain a foothold north of Astoria. The distinguishing characteristics of Astor's initiatives were size and organization. The financier clearly wanted the largest share of the fur supply, and in controlling his own transportation, he would be able to bargain effectively in the Chinese and European markets. Astor was following a classic business strategy of vertical integration and simultaneously building a firm, the American Fur Company, to control the entire operation. Astor's equally classic efforts at horizontal integration were also important. When appropriate, he sought alliances with other business interests—the Canadians and Russians—to stifle competition and share markets.

The Astoria enterprise, then, represented an extraordinarily broad grasp of worldwide market conditions and a willingness to conduct business across the boundaries of several national states. He, of course, was motivated almost solely by economic realities, but his vision fit perfectly the diplomatic needs of the U.S. government. From 1807 on, John Astor had slowly weaved his way into the confidence of several government officials such as James Madison, De Witt Clinton, Thomas Jefferson, and Albert Gallatin. Except for Gallatin and Clinton, he was not a close friend of these politicians but rather a businessman who the government knew might well advance American interests along the northern border with Canada and on the Pacific Coast. By late 1811, Astor had become not only one of the country's wealthiest businessmen but also an influential national figure.

CHAPTER SIX

The War Years, 1812–1814

THE WAR of 1812 brought extraordinary challenges for John Astor. The onset of the war coincided with his Pacific venture at Astoria, which was only just underway, and his partnership with the Canadians in the South West Company was barely a year old. War also disrupted his trade with Europe and China. Yet Astor continued to pursue his business interests in the changed markets and political climate of the war years. He now became more involved with political officials because his initiatives on the Pacific Coast and in the Midwest fur trade had diplomatic and political significance. Some in the administration, such as President Madison and Secretary of the Treasury Albert Gallatin, believed that control of the fur trade was tied to the war effort, thus, they allowed Astor innumerable opportunities to link his business objectives with America's war aims. The federal government also needed Astor's money and contacts when its disastrous financial policies forced it to borrow operating funds from private capitalists. Astor was hardly unique, but his career during the War of 1812 was a clear example of the intimate relationships among politicians and businessmen in the early Republic.

Astor's ability to influence the federal government and secure assistance for his fur business and foreign trade was in large part due to his willingness to assist Secretary of the Treasury Albert Gallatin during the war years. Gallatin's difficulties actually began in 1811 when Congress refused to recharter the Bank of the United States (BUS). Unlike many Republicans, Gallatin had supported the bank because it provided a uniform currency, facilitated the movement of government revenues, and provided short-term loans. The bank, though, had many enemies, including those who doubted its constitutionality and state bankers anxious for credit expansion. At a time when Congress was discussing commercial restrictions and even war with England, nationalists objected to the fact that the BUS had a large number of British stockholders.

Astor had very personal reasons for favoring an end to the bank. The New York branch had closed his account in late 1810 after he withdrew a large amount of specie to purchase pounds sterling. Apparently, some bank officials questioned his patriotism after he sent money to Canada; others were simply peeved at his sudden withdrawal. When the bank closed in 1811, Astor assured Gallatin and President Madison that he and his friends would be more than willing either to assist the Treasury Department with a $2 million loan or to purchase government bills that could be used as a circulating medium.[1]

Although Gallatin did not accept Astor's offer of help in 1811, he became more interested when government finances deteriorated with the outbreak of war in 1812. The federal government had depended on revenues received from the tariff, but these funds had declined dramatically from $13.3 million in 1811 to $9.2 million in 1812. At the same time, expenditures rose to $22 million. Gallatin went back again and again to Congress, warning of the necessity for tariff increases and internal taxes. In February 1812, Congress doubled the tariff, and then in March authorized a loan of $11 million dollars. This effort to raise funds was painfully slow, although Gallatin eventually sold $8.1 million in government bonds, primarily to state banks. Congress also authorized a $5 million issue of Treasury notes in June 1812. These notes paid 5¼ percent interest and were redeemable in one year. To enhance their appeal, the Treasury made them acceptable for the payment of government obligations such as tariff duties and taxes. None of these measures, however, solved the Treasury Department's problems as wartime expenditures outran receipts by $28.5 million in 1812. In February 1813, Congress authorized a new loan of $16 million; at this point, Gallatin turned to Astor and other capitalists for help.[2]

Gallatin wanted eastern capitalists to take $10 million of the new government bond issue. Astor agreed to help raise the money and contacted his friends in New York City and Baltimore, while Gallatin solicited help from the Philadelphia merchant and banker, Stephen Girard. Astor also brought David Parish into the discussions. Parish, who was a member of a European banking family, had resided in Philadelphia since 1806, where he operated as an American agent for international financiers involved in the export of Spanish silver to Europe. He also owned over two hundred thousand acres of land in northern New York. Astor, however, failed in his first effort as a loan contactor. Parish balked because the prospects for peace were so dismal, whereas many other New York financiers were either opposed to the war itself or worried because Congress had not provided a special fund for the loan's repayment. Gallatin subsequently tried to sell the loan publicly, but this effort raised only about $6 million.[3]

Unable to secure public support, Gallatin was obliged to offer Astor, Girard, and Parish more favorable terms in exchange for their assuming responsibility for the remaining $10 million of the government loan. After extensive correspondence, Gallatin met with the three financiers in Philadelphia in April 1813 to conclude an agreement. Gallatin later recalled that Astor was the primary organizer, even though he was not the largest subscriber. Astor agreed to take $2,056,000 in bonds and Girard and Parish accepted $8 million, at a rate of $88 per $100 bond, bearing an annual interest of 6 percent and redeemable after 31 December 1825. In addition, the financiers received .25 percent commisson on the bond sales.[4]

The $16 million loan was insufficient alone to resolve the government's financial problems. War expenditures continued to rise and tariff receipts to fall. The government was forced to float additional issues of Treasury notes—$5 million in February 1813 and $10 million in March 1814—and another bond issue of $25 million.[5] In late April 1814, Astor, Girard, and Parish proposed to subscribe for an additional $8 to $10 milliion if the government would again discount the bonds to perhaps $88 and allow a commission on the sale. Astor explained to Secretary of State James Monroe that, whereas the government could hardly expect to sell these bonds to small purchasers in the United States, nevertheless, he and other financiers could successfully interest their commercial contacts throughout Europe. Astor and his friends had one additional condition: they wanted to invest the proceeds from European bond sales in trade goods, which then could be shipped into the United States. However, when Secretary of the Treasury George Crawford refused to alter the existing embargo on all foreign trade, Astor withdrew from the negotiations.

By this point, Astor had assumed a fairly belligerent stance toward the federal government. He no longer had an influential contact in Washington as Albert Gallatin was in Europe attempting to negotiate an end to the war. Astor was also angered by the government's restrictive trade measures that made it nearly impossible to get ships to Europe. Finally, he had failed to secure military support for his Astoria settlement, and thus he was not inclined to assist the federal government.[6]

By taking responsibility for selling the government loan when other capitalists refused, Astor and his friends were certainly more patriotic than many capitalists. The war was unpopular, and the federal government experienced great difficulty raising money. It issued $61 million in bonds from 1812 to 1814, but only $45 million were sold and less than $8 million at par—sometimes discounts were as high as 20 percent. However, Astor's patriotic motives were usually enmeshed with practical concerns. Loan contracting offered him a good opportunity to make money and increased his leverage for requesting government assistant for his business endeavors.

By mid-1814, Astor along with many other politicians and financiers was convinced that the country's financial condition was precarious and that only a new national bank offered a solution. The major problem was inflation caused by the note circulation of state banks and the issue of Treasury notes. In late summer 1814, banks in all areas of the country, except New England, suspended specie payments. This suspension failed to reduce business activity, and conditions worsened as banks continued to issue notes without any promise of redemption. As a result, bank notes circulated at various discount rates, depending on the bank's reputation. As state banks lent money to the government and conducted government business, the government received its payments in depreciated notes. There was also a significant sectional and party dimension to the banking crisis. New England and some New York banks, typically those in Federalist hands and opposed to the war, continued to redeem notes in specie but refused to lend money to the government.[7]

The country's financial crisis had practical ramifications for government bondholders such as John Astor. Throughout 1814, the value of government stock continued to drop precipitously. Astor, anxious to sell government bonds to other capitalists, faced the possiblity of huge losses, unless faith in the government's fiscal stability could be restored. Astor's profit opportunity on the $16 million loan depended on his ability to sell bonds above the $88 per bond that he paid to the government. In May 1813, he was confident in the fiscal system and refused to sell bonds at $92.50, a price that would have yielded a small profit. Later in the year, as inflation went unchecked, he sold bonds at $90. By late 1814, the course of the war and the state of government finances had pushed the market price to a low of $66 per bond. Just before the end of the war, Astor expressed considerable regret in having sold $150,000 in government bonds at $75, a loss of $13 per bond.[8]

In 1814, therefore, Astor became one of the major proponents of reestablishing a national bank, and there can be little doubt that his major incentive was a desire to protect his financial investment. He was not alone in this effort, for both Federalist and Republican financiers recognized the problem. In January 1814, for example, New York and Philadelphia businessmen had petitioned Congress for a new bank; Congressman John Calhoun had floated a plan for a bank in Washington; Jacob Barker, a New York Republican and loan contractor, had developed a proposal that called for a national bank based on subscription in specie; and Isaac Bronson, a well-known Federalist banker had initiated a correspondence relating to a new bank with David Parish.[9]

In March 1814, Astor along with David Parish and Stephen Girard seized the direction of the bank initiatives. Obviously, they wanted a bank that reflected their interests. They also wished to short-circuit financiers such as Jacob Barker who speculated in government bonds, thereby driving the price down. Astor traveled to Washington where he circulated a plan for a bank that provided for stock subscriptions in government bonds and allowed the bank to lend money to the government. Simultaneously, both Parish and Girard recruited Philadelphia businessmen and politicians, among them lawyer Alexander J. Dallas, who had close ties with Republican politicians in Washington, such as Secretary of the Treasury William Jones. However, this first effort ended abruptly. As yet there was no widespread agreement on the location of the bank or on the government's role in the bank. Many politicians and conservative businessmen also questioned whether the government's own bonds should be used for stock subscriptions. When rumors circulated in Washington in the spring of 1814 that peace was imminient, the administration felt less pressure to secure additional money; and the demand for a new bank dissipated.[10]

The issue reappeared later that summer with substantially greater urgency. By then, the peace rumors had proved illusory, the British had burned Washington, and a general suspension of specie payments was well underway. In August, Astor held a meeting in his New York home with a group of capitalists who supported a national bank. Out of this meeting came a proposal for a national bank based on real estate mortgages rather than government bonds or specie. No doubt, this provision was meant to encourage the support of Federalists like Isaac Bronson, who opposed the notion of a bank that accepted the government's own bonds in payment for stock. Although Astor never favored this plan, he was eager to compromise in order to stop the slide in the value of government bonds. He sought support for the idea and corresponded with Dennis Smith in Baltimore and Alexander Dallas, Stephen Girard, and David Parish in Philadelphia. Dallas subsequently sent the plan to Secretary of State James Monroe along with a letter of support from Astor. If the government supported the idea, Dallas volunteered his services to assume the soon-to-be-vacated position of secretary of the treasury. Anxious to resolve the government's financial crisis and aware of the New York-Philadelphia bank initiatives, Madison then appointed Dallas as secretary of the treasury.[11]

Throughout September and October 1814, Astor wrote many letters and met with capitalists, among them Dennis Smith and David Parish; they gradually came to the conclusion that a bank based on real estate would not work nor would it gain political support. Consequently, along with Secretary of the Treasury Dallas, they formulated a new plan that allowed private capitalists to use government bonds and Treasury notes to pay for their bank stock. The institution closely resembled the first BUS, as both the leadership and stock subscriptions were shared between the public and private sectors. But conservative financiers were appalled. They considered the new bank nothing more than a fancy scheme for government bondholders to become bank stockholders. Isaac Bronson, a Federalist banker from New York City, commented, "What a cursed besotted people! To submit to have a war costing them hundreds of Millions fastened upon them, that a dozen gamblers might make fortunes, by furnishing money to carry it on; and when failing of their object; to give them a bank for the avow'd purpose of cheating the nation out of 50 millions of Dollars to in-demnify them"[12]

In early October, Astor joined other large government bond-holders in Washington as the crucial vote in Congress approached. There was significant opposition to Dallas's plan, especially to the provisions allowing the bank to be intertwined with the govern-ment and its bondholders. John Calhoun, who at first had sup-ported the plan, presented an amendment to the legislation that would have divorced it from the government and required stock subscription to be paid in new Treasury notes issued specifically for that purpose. Calhoun's amendment horrified Astor. He wrote to the congressman pointing out that although Calhoun's proposal might well create a stable bank, it did nothing to solve the more immediate crisis of declining public credit and government insol-vency. After substantial debate and numerous compromises, Con-gress eventually passed a bill creating a commercial bank that was unresponsive to the country's financial dilemma. On the ad-vice of Secretary of the Treasury Dallas, President Madison vetoed it in early January 1815.[13]

By this time, Astor was disgusted with the endless bickering among politicians, and somewhat chagrined, no doubt, at the ani-mosity directed toward those who held government bonds. He thus withdrew from further involvement with the bank issue. Even though the bank proposal was a failure, Astor had been a key fig-ure throughout the war in all the government's efforts to raise money either through loans or through the establishment of a bank. As we shall see, Astor deftly exerted this influence whenever his private business endeavors required government assistance.

Just before and during the War of 1812, the New York finan-cier needed the federal government's assistance because existing laws hampered his ability to prosecute the Midwest fur trade. In January 1811, Astor's American Fur Company and the Canadians formed the South West Company in order to trade, on joint ac-count, in the Great Lakes region for five years. Each party pur-chased 50 percent of the trade goods and split the profits and losses. As diplomatic relations with Great Britain worsened, govern-ment officials, including President James Madison and Secretary of the Treasury Albert Gallatin, considered Astor's participation in this company an important step in establishing American influ-ence with the Indians and in securing the border. Yet in March 1811, the federal government reestablished trade restrictions against Great Britain, thereby prohibiting British trade goods from being shipped into American territory. The law was especially harmful to Astor because only recently he had ordered British goods worth $10,000. These goods had been imported at Montreal and shipped, along with the goods of his Canadian partners, to Saint Joseph's Island, the British headquarters for the fur trade north and east of Mackinac Island. Existing American laws, though, prevented the South West Company from moving these goods into American territory.[14]

The effect of the American legislation was disastrous for the South West Company. Astor's agent, Henry Brevoort, Jr., who had gone to Montreal in March 1811 and then traveled with the Canadian partners to Saint Joseph's and Mackinac islands, reported that goods could not be moved into the Great Lakes region and that the Indians blamed the American government. In 1811, Brevoort expressed the viewpoint of American traders that the Congress had "wantonly deprived an independent people of their usual supplies, without providing substitutes. The traders must return to their wintering posts; & when they are asked why they bring no goods, the whole blame will be thrown upon the Am: Govt., whose measures & policy were [as] before, but too obnoxious, toward the natives."[15]

Conscious that America's political interests along the border necessitated positive relations with the Indians and that his fur-trade business would benefit as well, Astor undertook, rather heavy-handedly, to use his influence with political officials. In summer 1811, he wrote President Madison asking for an exception to the law so that trade goods could be shipped into the United States. Madison, however, informed Astor that Congress had not allowed for presidential exceptions to the legislation, as was the case with the Embargo Act. Astor next decided to petition Congress for a specific exception to the legislation and prepared for this effort by trying to enlist the support of former President Jefferson and Albert Gallatin, secretary of the treasury.[16] He asked Gallatin to present his request to the Committee on Indian Affairs, as long as he saw "nothing impolitic or otherwise improper in it."[17]

Astor's letter to Jefferson thanked the former president for his earlier support and warned of the threat of Indian hostility against America for cutting the flow of trade goods. Astor asked

Jefferson to write President Madison and urge his support of Astor's petition to Congress. Even though Jefferson admitted that America's restrictive trade legislation should not have included the Indian trade, he absolutely refused to intervene. In rather strong language, he told Astor that his request for assistance was improper: "From meddling however with these subjects, it is my duty as well as my inclination to abstain: they are in hands perfectly qualified to direct them."[18]

Despite Jefferson's rebuff, Astor submitted a petition to Congress in late March 1812 asking for an exception to the trade law. The New Yorker was aware of the war threat and played upon this fear in his petition to Congress and in subsequent letters to Albert Gallatin. He warned that America was in danger of losing its Indian alliances and that arms and ammunitions were among the goods on Saint Joseph's Island. In early May 1812, he tried to bluff Gallatin with a threat to withdraw from the Indian trade, thereby allowing the British to reestablish their dominance. At this time, Astor's name also headed a petition from New York merchants to Congress that urged continued trade restrictions in preference to open hostilities.[19]

Eventually, Astor's pleading and the reality of a country moving toward war forced the president to act, even though Congress had not yet disposed of Astor's petition. The president allowed Astor to ship his goods into American territory and to deposit them with custom's collectors while Congress debated the general question of exceptions to existing trade laws. Presidential action, however, had come too late, for on 18 June 1812 Congress declared war.[20]

The war declaration forced Astor quickly to change his strategy in regard to his furs and goods in Canada and in American territory. His actions later led to charges that he had informed the British of the war declaration before such news could reach American military pesonnel on the frontier. The charges were probably true, although Astor was not intentionally unpatriotic; rather, he thought only of protecting his business interests.

As soon as he learned of the war declaration, Astor wrote, through several different channels, to his agents in Canada and on Mackinac Island in the hope of rapidly moving all his furs and goods into American territory. Albert Gallatin included one of these letters in a War Department mailpouch bound for General William Hull at Detroit. General Hull later charged both Gallatin and Astor with betraying American interests, but Gallatin dismissed the accusation by pointing out that Hull already had received news of the war in an earlier letter.[21] However, one of the financier's clerks in New York City sent a letter to a Montreal associate concerning the war declaration. Toussaint Pothier, a South West Company employee at Montreal, who was loyal to the British government, learned of the letter's contents. He then carried news of the war's outbreak to the British commander on Saint Joseph's Island by 3 July, before the War Department had alerted American troops at Mackinac Island.

Astor's mistake was in not realizing the extent to which the British were prepared for war along the border. He knew of the buildup of British troops in Canada, indeed, he had written Gallatin about their numbers after a trip to Montreal in 1811. Yet in late June 1812 he naively wrote to Gallatin that the declaration of war would take the Canadians totally by surprise. Hardly! Since early January 1812, Sir George Prevost, the British commander-in-chief, had been enlisting the military assistance of traders from both the North West and South West companies. They were prepared to strike at Mackinac Island with the onset of hostilities in order to regain control of the fur trade. On 16 July, a British detachment, bolstered by Canadian fur traders, surprised the Americans on Mackinac Island and forced them to surrender without a shot being fired.[22] Although Astor can hardly be blamed for this attack, the incident exhibited a single-minded concern with protecting his business to the exclusion of all other considerations.

Another striking example of this single-mindedness was Astor's effort to get his furs out of Canada after the war's outbreak. While in Washington in late June 1812, he asked Albert Gallatin to write Peter Sailly, who was collector of customs at Rouses's Point near Plattsburg in upstate New York and a former business acquaintance. Gallatin informed Sailly of the congressional directive that allowed American merchants to import goods from Canada that had belonged to them before the outbreak of war. Merchants were to post a bond with the collector while awaiting a congressional decision as to whether the importations were legal. Astor desired Gallation's support just to assure that his movement of goods across the border would not be misconstrued as smuggling. Astor was not alone in these efforts; many New York and Boston merchants moved goods from Canada into the United

States in 1812 and early 1813. Of course, this trade created immense confusion because it was difficult to tell whether goods were a continuing trade, which would be in violation of law, or goods acquired before the outbreak of war. Eventually, Congress canceled all fees and penalties connected with these imports.[23]

Even though Astor was not unique among merchants, he certainly pursued his interest with exceptional zeal and utilized his connections on both sides of the border. For example, at the same time that he obtained Gallatin's letter to Peter Sailly, Astor also secured a passport from Attorney General William Pinkney to travel to Canada (now enemy territory) in order to facilitate the movement of his goods. Astor went first to Plattsburgh where he waited, so that friends in Canada (most likely South West Company associates Forsyth, Richardson and Company) could obtain a safe passage from the British commander. He was in Montreal by 9 July 1812 to receive his share of furs from the South West Company's storehouse. He accompanied twenty-seven bales across the border, probably in late July, and later received a much larger cache valued at $50,000.[24]

In late 1812 and early 1813, the New Yorker successfully obtained additional Canadian furs worth approximately $250,000. These furs most likely came from interior posts to Montreal as part of the South West Fur Company's operations. Astor easily acquired passports for his agents to move in and out of Canada. His old friend and trading associate from the 1790s, Pliny Moore of Champlain, New York, helped these agents negotiate with American custom's collectors. Astor was especially careful during this period to stay within the law in order to avoid any activity that might hint of smuggling and thereby result in loss of his furs. His agents received carefully worded instructions "not [to] expose my furs to danger and not to use any illegal means to get them into this State."[25]

For example, in late 1813, the New Yorker had three agents in Canada, including his nephew, George Astor, to make certain that nothing went awry in moving a $200,000 fur shipment into the United States. His instructions to John Day reflected his cautious attitudes, "I believe you have already a pretty good idea of my views—tho desirious to make some business I am equally so to avoid risks—some I know must be run, but let be as little as possible."[26]

Astor, though, was not above testing the law and the authorities. He once instructed his associate, John Day, to inform Customs'

Collector Peter Sailly before entering Canada that he might return both with furs and trading goods. Items such as beads and blankets were obviously needed for the fur trade in the United States, but Astor did not own them before the war. If Sailly gave his assent, Day was then instructed to purchase trade goods in Montreal. In the event Sailly said no, Day was simply to forget the trade goods rather than smuggle them and risk confiscation of the furs.[27]

Efforts to obtain furs during the war were not confined solely to Canada. Conscious that war would disrupt normal supplies and markets, Astor knew that furs would bring high prices. The financier, thus, wanted to continue his fur trade throughout the Midwest, so that at war's end he could quickly reassert his dominance in the business. Thus, he reestablished business relationships with Saint Louis merchant Charles Gratiot, who purchased furs for Astor from 1812 to 1815.[28]

In the Great Lakes region, Astor's principal agent was Ramsay Crooks, who had returned from Astoria after suffering so terribly on the overland trip to the Columbia River. In 1813, Crooks was employed on a partnership basis to supply goods to independent traders and to purchase furs. On occasion, particularly when Astor was less hopeful for peace, Crooks was directed to sell furs to hat manufacturers and merchants throughout Pennsylvania, Virginia, Ohio, and Kentucky.[29]

Crooks also helped Astor regain furs that were on Mackinac Island when it fell to the British in 1812. No incident was more revealing of Astor's curious pursuit of business interests during the war and of the ironic rules that governed warfare in the nineteenth century. In October 1813, the financier sent Crooks to Mackinac Island to obtain furs that he owned as a South West Company partner. While stopping in Detroit on his way to Mackinac, Crooks learned that American military forces planned to retake the island, and he gained permission to accompany the troops in the summer of 1814. The military considered Crooks an asset because he knew the island and could provide valuable information about the trails leading up to the British fort.

Astor, though, was unwilling to wait on American troops. In April 1814, he visited Gallatin and Secretary of State James Monroe, and secured permission to send a vessel under a flag of truce to Mackinac Island to secure his furs. The government's permission was contingent on Astor's gaining of a similar order from the British. The New Yorker had already sent his nephew,

George Astor, to Montreal to talk to the Canadians. In June, McTavish, McGillivray and Company interceded for Astor with British commander Sir George Prevost. The latter granted permission with the understanding that the South West Company agent on Mackinac Island, Toussaint Pothier, would determine precisely how many furs belonged to Astor.[30]

Before George Astor could charter a vessel and reach Detroit, the military expedition, with Crooks along, was on its way. After stopping to burn British buildings at Saint Joseph's Island, the

Mackinac Island under British rule, 1813. Courtesy of
William L. Clements Library, University of Michigan.

American forces landed on Mackinac Island in early August 1814. No effort had been made to conceal the attack, and the British and Indian forces picked off the Americans on the narrow trails leading up to the fort. The next day, under a flag of truce, the Americans recovered their dead stopping only to ask whether Ramsay Crooks could remove Astor's furs from the island. Even though the British agreed, the commander of American naval forces, Captain Arthur Sinclair, refused as he had not yet decided whether to renew the attack or retreat.[31]

Eventually, American military forces decided to return to Detroit, and Crooks was unable to secure Astor's furs. However, both British and American commanders promised that he could return to Mackinac Island. George Astor subsequently arrived with a ship, and he and Crooks then retrieved the furs from Mackinac Island. Even by early nineteenth-century standards, the presence of the two men in pursuit of private profit amid so much death and destruction seemed particularly callous. Captain Arthur Sinclair, who allowed the vessel to pass under the flag of truce, was obviously bemused and wrote to Secretary of the Navy William Jones, charging that Astor had transported goods and furs that were probably obtained after the declaration of war.[32] Official Washington paid no attention to Sinclair's charges; indeed, the whole incident was a stark example of Astor's tremendous influence in Washington during the war.

So it was that Astor managed to secure a reduced, but nonetheless ample, supply of furs during the war. The majority were sent to markets in Europe, although many were sold in New York City. In October 1812, for example, he held a large auction offering the pelts of 59,557 muskrats, 6,817 raccoons, 1,454 fishers, 795 otters, plus 2,956 pounds of beaver skins and a substantial assortment of other pelts. Furs were also sent through commercial correspondents in American cities; for example, John Bryan, an Albany merchant, purchased 4,000 martin skins for him in early 1813.[33]

Another difficult problem during the war years was obtaining trade goods (e.g., blankets and beads) acceptable to Indians and independent traders. Without access to British imports, Ramsay Crooks had to purchase goods from merchants in Ohio, Kentucky, and Pennsylvania. In late 1813, Astor advanced $30,000 for this purpose. He also obtained manufactured items from commercial correspondents in Europe and along the East Coast. Indeed, on at least one occasion, he obtained trade goods from London suppliers who shipped the items to the neutral Russian ambassador, Andrei Dashkov, who then forwarded them to Astor.[34]

With the frequent intercession of government officals, the New York financier was also able to maintain a European trade throughout the war years. Of course, this trade was vitally important because Europe was the best market for Astor's furs and teas. Moreover, Astor partly depended on the European trade to obtain goods used in the Indian trade.

European commerce, nevertheless, fluctuated constantly from 1812 to 1815. Astor had to contend with the trade and embargo policies of two governments, Great Britain and the United States. The British also blockaded America's eastern ports during the war, but the blockade was not evenly applied. It was difficult to get ships in and out of New York City and Philadelphia, but Boston was relatively open.

American policy was about as inconsistent as the application of the British blockade. In general, the Republican Congress used trade restrictions as a war policy that, if used to deny products and profits to Great Britain, might hasten the end of the war. However, the administration was lax in its enforcement, and the government permitted some merchants, who obtained trading licenses from either the United States or Great Britain, to ignore the regulations. Of course, any ship on the open sea was liable to search and seizure; thus merchants, such as Astor, sought to obtain licenses both from American and British officials that allowed them to pass unmolested. Licenses were granted to ships for any number of reasons, including claims of neutrality or their use as diplomatic couriers. Throughout the war, many Federalist merchants obtained such licenses but then supplied the British with food and even military equipment. Astor's use of the licenses, however, was solely to get his ships safely from American ports to Europe. Despite taking precautions, he lost two ships, the *Adolphus* and the *Caroline,* during the war.

In July 1813, the federal government prohibited the use of British trading licenses and made a vessel subject to seizure. In December 1813, regulations were further tightened when Congress embargoed the export of all goods and produce. But this law was relaxed in May 1814. Consequently, the pattern of Astor's trade with Europe fluctuated with British and American laws.[35]

This disrupted pattern of foreign trade changed the character of the cargoes on Astor's vessels. Although his major exports were still furs and teas, he added cotton, flour, tobacco, and sugar. The diminished and often undependable supply of furs and teas as well as the necessity for sending ships fully loaded precipitated the change. Thus, when the *Caroline* sailed from Charleston in 1813, it carried three hundred to four hundred casks of rice and over five hundred bales of cotton. Similarly, return cargoes were more varied. Although he often tried to import European furs, ship inventories incuded wines, juniper berries, burrstones, and glass. On occasion, Astor brought ships home in ballast— as he did with the *Enterprise* from Lisbon in March 1813—or, if the return voyage appeared too risky, he ordered the ship sold in Europe.[36]

Despite all these difficulties, Astor was extremely adept at monitoring the regulations and manipulating government officials in order to move his goods to and from Europe. A classic case was the voyage of the *Hannibal* in July 1813. After its return from China in late October 1812, it immediately set out for Europe loaded with furs and teas and returned to New York City in April 1813. By this time trade restrictions had tightened and Astor needed a special license. His business ally, the Russian minister Andrei Dashkov, provided an opportunity for obtaining one. Dashkov wanted to get French General Jean Moreau, who was living in exile in the United States, to France in order to assist in the overthrow of Napoleon. The British admiral in charge of the blockade was only too happy to assist in any undertaking that would undermine Napoleon. Astor volunteered his ship, *Hannibal,* for Moreau's transportation to Europe.[37] The American government probably was unaware of the voyage's purpose, but the apparent involvement of the Russian ambassador would have assured the ship permission to leave port. Albert Gallatin and James Bayard had only recently departed for Saint Petersburg, where they were to join with our Russian ambassador, John Quincy Adams, to begin negotiations for peace with England under a Russian offer of mediation. Thus the American government was unlikely to stand in the way of the voyage of the *Hannibal* given the parties involved; indeed, Astor even offered to carry government dispatches for President Madison.[38]

The purpose of Moreau's return to France was a minor consideration to Astor given the opportunity to move a fully loaded vessel to Europe. He also sent several business representatives on the *Hannibal,* including his son-in-law Adrian Bentzon and C. C. Cambreling. The vessel's cargo consisted of teas and furs, worth approximately $60,000, and tobacco and coffee valued at $27,000. These goods were to be sold and the profits reinvested in products such as Danish lamb's wool, rabbit furs, and manufactured goods for the Indian trade.

Bentzon and Cambreling, though, had instructions to wait a brief period before loading a return cargo. Bentzon went to Saint Petersburg in order to follow the course of peace negotiations while Cambreling sought favorable prices for European furs and goods.[39] In the event peace came, Cambreling was to sail immediately for Canton and buy teas, silks, and nankeens sufficient to fill three ships that were then to sail to Boston, Baltimore, and New York. As Astor wrote to Cambreling, "You know pretty well my views relative to the object, which you are about to obtain by a voyage from Europe direct to Canton, provided a certain event tak's [sic] place [peace] in which case expedition will decide the fortune of the speculation out as well as home. I can have no doubt, but that if you are fortunate to get to Canton with certain knowledge, you may make good speculations."[40]

However, peace did not come because Great Britain refused the offer of Russian mediation. Cambreling and Bentzon, thus, had to change plans. Astor was not anxious to have any vessel return under American registry because American trade policy had tighened considerably by late summer 1813. Bentzon was given the option of either selling the *Hannibal* or undertaking one or two voyages from Europe to Canton under foreign registry. The *Hannibal,* though, remained in Europe almost a year before returning to New York in November 1814 under neutral colors and a different owner. Because Astor still controlled the cargo, which consisted of Russian furs, glasses, lamps, and numerous small manufactured items, the change in the ship's ownership was a legal fiction to avoid the trade embargo.[41]

The circumstances surrounding the voyage of the *Caroline* were similar to those of the *Hannibal.* Astor had purchased the *Caroline* in the spring of 1813 to ship goods to Europe. He also arranged to carry dispatches from Andrei Dashkov to the Russian government. To further insure the vessel's safe passage Astor had a partner on the voyage who also served as supercargo, C. M. Baumhauer, an official of the Russian consular staff. Astor, though, warned

Baumhauer to destroy his letter of instruction and partnership agreement so that, if the vessel were stopped, British authorities would not learn of its American connection. Leaving from Charleston, the ship carried a cargo of cotton and rice. The ruse failed, and the British captured and condemned the *Caroline*.[42]

From late summer 1813 to midsummer 1814, Astor reduced his involvement in European voyages. He told his agent in Europe, Adrian Bentzon, to ship goods only in neutral vessels. This decision was partly related to the unsuccessful voyage of the *Caroline* and the tightening of both American and British trade regulations. He also was pessimistic about the chances for peace after the Russian mediation failed. As he wrote to one of his ship captains in late 1813, "Times are so extremely uncertain & changes so frequent & quick that a man who wishes to adopt a plan today is obliged to change it tomorrow."[43] During this same period, the New Yorker reduced his purchase of trade goods and his investments in bonds. Explaining this policy to his Baltimore commercial correspondent, Henry Payson, he wrote "It will be well for men who wish to live in comfort to be out of debt, I am more so than I have been for many years, of notes I have scarce any out."[44]

Astor, though, renewed trade with Europe in late summer 1814 when Prsident Madison relaxed the trade embargo. He owned a one-eighth interest in the *Flirt;* and in October 1814, he shipped furs worth approximately $6,000 to his commercial agent in Bordeaux. His return cargo consisted of Russian and German furs. The financier's ship, *Fingal,* also left for Europe in October 1814 with a small cargo and carried diplomatic dispatches to the American peace commissioners. The captain was instructed not to risk a return voyage unless peace seemed imminent. The *Fingal* returned to New York City in May 1815, just after the war's end, with a cargo of furs and manufactured goods.[45]

The voyage of the *Boxer* in late 1814 demonstrated Astor's conviction that sometimes high prices and profits justified greater risks. For nearly a year, he had collected furs from Canada and the Midwest. He had withheld them from sale in the United States in the hope that prices would be much higher in Europe. In September 1814, he purchased the *Boxer,* a vessel of 275 tons, which was both fast and heavily armed. The cargo consisted of eight to ten thousand deer skins, two thousand otter skins, one thousand red foxes, one thousand bear skins, one thousand fishers, and fifteen hundred muskrats. Captain James Clark had orders to sail direct to the French port, Nantes, and to consign the cargo to Astor's business agent there. He was then to load a return cargo of European furs and manufactured goods and return directly to New York. Typical of Astor's treatment of his captains and an indication of expected profits, Captain Clark received a regular wage of $50 per month and two bonuses of $500 and $600 for successfully completing the outward and return voyages. Lesser pay and bonuses were given to the first and second mates.[46]

Although Astor maintained a small trade with Europe during the war his experiences in the China trade were altogether different. The longer voyage to China involved more risks of seizure at sea. The British, moreover, controlled Canton and prevented the movement of American ships in and out of the port. Statistics revealed the effectiveness of the British embargo on the China trade. American imports at Canton were $3,132,810 in 1811–1812; $1,453,000 in 1812–1813; and only $451,500 for the years 1813–1814 and 1814–1815. Exports revealed a similar dramatic decline. In 1811–1812, American exports from Canton were valued at $2,771,000; in 1812–1813, $620,000; and for the combined trading seasons of 1813–1814 and 1814–1815, only $572,000.

The British embargo at Canton also affected Astor's ship *Beaver* under Captain Cornelius Sowle. Sowle had left New York in October 1811 bound for the Northwest Coast, then he had sailed to Canton, arriving in February 1813. He chose not to challenge the British blockade and remained in Canton until war's end. Astor was displeased with his captain's timidity, and he wrote numerous letters suggesting alternative plans. At first, Astor urged him to buy China goods and prepare to sail when peace was declared. In 1814, when peace seemed a distant hope, he gave Sowle permission to sell the vessel. By early 1815, the financier was more confident of peace and willing to take a few risks. He urged Sowle, who had not sold the vessel, to sail home with a small cargo.[47]

Despite the fact that the war prevented trade with Canton, Astor had a substantial inventory of teas and silks for American and European markets. The New Yorker had been fortunate that two of his vessels, the *Enterprise* and the *Hannibal,* arrived in New York with teas, silks, and nankeens shortly after war began. The *Enterprise* had been Astor's first vessel sent to the Columbia River in 1809, and then it had sailed north to New Archangel. Captain Ebbets traded on the coast and in Canton for two years before returning home in June 1812 with a full cargo. The *Hannibal* had originally sailed from New York and arrived in Canton in January 1812 with a cargo of seal, beaver, and fox skins in addition to $85,000 in specie. The *Hannibal* returned home in October 1812 with a cargo valued at $250,000.

Throughout the war years, Astor carefully marketed these China goods. He advertised in New York newspapers in 1813 and 1814, and he sent teas to commercial correspondents such as Henry Payson in Baltimore and William and Joshua Lippincott in Philadelphia. Astor, of course, constantly altered his prices based on the vicissitudes of the war, and he continually wrote his business agents about acceptable prices for teas and nankeens.[48]

Astor was less cautious in late 1814 with the relaxation of the American embargo and the possibility of peace; and similar to his actions in Europe, he decided to risk a voyage to Canton. He purchased the brig *Macedonian* for $27,000 and spent an additional $15,000 outfitting it for sea. The cargo of furs and ginseng was small, valued at only $30,000. The financier gambled, however, that if peace came, the return cargo of tea would be worth $300,000. Despite the potential for windfall profits, Astor still tried to reduce his risks. The vessel itself was chosen because of its speed. He also tried, unsuccessfully, to sell a one-quarter interest to a Baltimore merchant. Finally, as with so many of his other voyages, Astor somehow managed to secure government assistance. When the *Macedonian* put to sea in January 1815, it was accompanied by several U.S. naval vessels, including the *President,* commanded by Stephen Decatur, bound for the Pacific Ocean. American naval vessels encountered the blockading British fleet. Even though the *President* was captured, the *Macedonian* managed to escape the combat and pursuing British ships. It arrived safely in Canton in July 1815.[49]

In both his trade with China and Europe, then, Astor maintained a reasonable level of activity throughout the war. He placed his limited supplies of teas and furs on both domestic and foreign markets when prices were high; and he exported and imported goods, most often with government assistance. Even with his access to government officials, though, Astor was unable to totally control events. In Astoria, the one enterprise that he most wanted to succeed, Astor learned the limits of his personal influence.

When war began in June 1812, Astor knew immediately that Astoria faced potential problems. He had been informed of the settlement's successful establishment and of Captain Thorn's fatal encounter with the Indians. He could only hope that the *Beaver,* which had left New York in November 1811 under Cornelius Sowle, had arrived at Astoria with supplies and additional colonists. His greatest worry was the North West Company, which might use the outbreak of war to encourage the British government to move toward the Pacific Coast. Thus Astor undertook numerous efforts to resupply his settlement, particularly with arms and ammunition, and to secure military assistance from the American government. These attempts again demonstrated his self-interest pursuit of business affairs, his organizational abilities, and his influence with national politicians.

The New Yorker's first effort to bolster Astoria's defenses was undertaken without the knowledge of the American government. In July 1812, he wanted to send military supplies to Astoria, but the British blockade of New York harbor prevented the departure of any vessel. Thus Astor sent two agents, William J. Pigot and Richard Ebbets to England in September with £12,000 and introductions to his London business correspondent, Thomas Wilson. Pigot and Richard Ebbets purchased a ship, the *Forester,* and a cargo. They sailed under British colors in February or March 1813 for the Pacific Coast. But the voyage was a fiasco. There were desertions and a mutiny; by the time the *Forester* reached the Pacific Coast in 1814, Astoria was already under British control. The voyage was only the first of several misfortunes connected with Astoria during the war.[50]

Regardless of the *Forester*'s fate, which Astor would not know for over a year, he still had to continue with his original plan to resupply Astoria with goods and manufactured products. Both the Astoria settlers and the Russians at New Archangel, expected a resupply ship in 1813. As before, the value of the cargo would be substantial, approximately $35,000, and Astor, conscious of the risks involved, sought military assistance from the government. It should be recalled that, at this moment, Astor was also negotiating with Albert Gallatin to take a large part of the government's $16-million-bond issue. Clearly Astor and government officials recognized the link between Astoria and the bond issue.

In January 1813, after preliminary discussions with Albert Gallatin, Astor went to Washington for appointments with Secretary of State James Monroe and Secretary of the Navy William Jones. Before committing additional resources on the coast, Astor wanted to know "whether the government . . . have or will assert any claim to that, or any part of that country, and whether the government will deem it expedient to take possession and give protection to the infant establishment which has been made." He specifically requested forty to fifty soldiers who would assist his men in repelling any British attempt to capture Astoria. In many subsequent conversations and letters, Astor argued that Astoria was of strategic value to military control of the Pacific Ocean as well as a strategic commercial site.[51] Neither Secretary of State Monroe nor President Madison ever responded to the financier's request, despite his constant pressure. Invariably, Astor's letters to Gallatin concerning the government loan also contained inquiries about when the executive branch would decide an assistance for Astoria.

The New Yorker's appeals carried a sense of urgency. The Astoria settlers included a large number of Canadians, Astor said, "who may join any force sent by the North West Company or the British government."[52] He also informed James Monroe that he had received information that the North West Company was sending a vessel, the *Isaac Todd,* to the Columbia River, although at this point he was not sure of its intent.[53] Astor's growing impatience was also occasioned by the fact that his ship, the *Lark,* waited in New York harbor to sail for the Pacific Coast. He had delayed its departure in hopes that the government would give him both a military escort and troops. Exasperated with government delays, he sent the *Lark* anyway, after having received a pass through the British blockade on the pretext that the ship was Russian and headed for New Archangel. The American government also gave it a passport to avoid any problems with the American navy. On 6 March 1813, the *Lark* left New York port only to be wrecked in a storm near the Hawaiian Islands in August 1813.[54] Disaster thus ended the New Yorker's second major attempt to aid Astoria.

Shortly after the *Lark* had sailed, Astor once again pushed for military assistance. The timing was propitious for applying pressure as he was just completing arrangements for subscribing to the $16 million loan. Writing to Secretary of State James Monroe, he again requested a military vessel, mentioning specifically either the *Hornet* or the *Argus,* which were known as fast transports. Astor's plea carried the disturbing new information that the North West Company had indeed sent the *Isaac Todd* to the Pacific Coast with a military force of eighty men and twenty heavy guns. The federal government reacted this time and ordered a military vessel, the *John Adams,* to sail immediately for the Pacific Coast. Astor agreed to send, within a few months and at his own expense, a ship with supplies both for the military and the Astoria settlement. But the financier's luck failed again when, at the last moment, Secretary of the Navy William Jones, rerouted the *John Adams* to the Great Lakes where the demands of the war seemed more compelling.[55]

Astor became increasingly frustrated and angry over his inability to secure government assistance, and events only exacerbated this feeling. In June 1813, Robert Stuart arrived in New York City after a year's journey overland from Astoria. The trip was extraordinarily significant because Stuart had demonstrated the feasibility of the overland route through the South Pass in the Rocky Mountains to the Pacific Coast. More than ever, Astor realized that, with government help, he could capture the interior western fur trade.[56] At the same time, Astor received correspondence from London friends that confirmed his worst fears. The British government, bending to pressure from the North West Company, had sent a naval escort along with the *Isaac Todd* to the Pacific Coast. Astor wrote despondently to a friend in July 1813, "I fear the war will ruin if not destroy us in that quarter, in peace we should have done well, in war we can do nothing and are exposed to danger from the British and . . . the North West Company. Our government ought to have afforded us some aid, but nothing has been done and nothing is to be expected."[57]

Astor's information was sketchy in early July 1813; if he had known the full scope of the British intentions, he might have given up at this point. In fact, the *Isaac Todd* sailed in a British convoy consisting of the *Phoebe, Raccoon,* and *Cherub.* The *Phoebe* and *Isaac Todd* were to rendezvous at the Columbia River with a group of nearly one hundred North West Company traders who were headed overland to the coast. The captain of the *Phoebe,* James Milligan, had explicit orders "to protect and render every assistance in your power to the British traders from Canada, and to destroy, and, if possible, totally annihilate any settlements which the Americans may have formed either on the Columbia River or on the neighboring coasts."[58] The North West Company also had managed to secure a license from the East India Company that would allow the *Isaac Todd* to carry furs from the Pacific Coast to Canton, where they could be sold.[59]

Despite his fears and frustrations, the New Yorker made one last attempt in July 1813 to obtain help for Astoria. He again asked Secretary of the Navy William Jones for a military force of twenty-five or thirty men. He also wanted the government to transport them; if a naval vessel was not available, he offered the use of his ship, the *Enterprise,* on reasonable terms. The New Yorker was now belligerent. Claiming that he already had a half-million dollars invested in the project, he wanted the government to finance a rescue mission given the "national" advantages that had already resulted from his efforts. He specifically mentioned the establishment of a claim on the Northwest Coast and Robert Stuart's discovery of the overland route. In late July 1813, Astor wrote a memo to President Madison before a scheduled private meeting summarizing all his previous arguments. He added as well his recollection that, as far back as 1808, the federal government had promised military help for Astoria. Madison agreed that some action should be taken and referred the financier once again to Secretary of the Navy Jones. The two men apparently reached an agreement, and in early August, Jones ordered the *Siren* to prepare for a mission to the Pacific Coast. For his part, Astor outfitted the *Enterprise* with goods for both Astoria and the Russian colony to sail in convoy with the *Siren.* The government again changed its plans for reasons that are not clear, and the *Siren* never sailed. Astor soon thereafter cancelled orders for the *Enterprise* to sail.[60]

By late November 1813, Astor abandoned all further efforts to assist Astoria. The reasons for his decision were understandable. With Albert Gallatin out of the country as a peace negotiator, Astor lacked his strongest advocate in government; thus the New Yorker knew that only further disappointment would result from efforts to secure government assistance. He also felt deserted by Thomas Jefferson whose influence he had requested by letter in October 1813. Jefferson, though, wrote an odd letter in return that praised the financier as a great explorer and colonizer that history would surely remember. Yet Jefferson also revealed a sudden confusion about the original purpose of the Astoria settlement and referred to it as the "germ of a great, free and independent empire on that side of our continent." Jefferson assured Astor that the federal government would protect the "independence" of Astoria at any peace conference.[61] Astor could only have surmised that Jefferson no longer envisioned the Pacific Coast as an integral part of the United States. Adding to the financier's sense of helplessness was a government order establishing a strict embargo in late 1813, which would have made it impossible to get the *Enterprise* out of port in any case.

Astor's decision not to risk additional resources was the prudent course. In late 1813, he could still hope for a little luck: perhaps one of the relief ships would make it to Astoria or perhaps the Astorians could hold out against the British naval expedition. Moreover, he had a reasonable chance of securing his objectives as part of a peace settlement. Albert Gallatin was a member of the peace commission, and in March 1814, James Monroe sent a special order to the commissioners alerting them to the fact that the United States should not surrender the settlement on the Columbia River.[62] Typical of the ironies of nineteenth-century communication, though, as Astor debated in his own mind whether to temporarily abandon Astoria, it already was under the control of the North West Company.

The story of Astoria's capture began in May 1812 when the first resupply ship, the *Beaver,* under the command of Cornelius Sowle arrived at Astoria. No one there knew of the impending war and prospects seemed bright. Sowle not only brought a full supply of trade goods and needed manufactured items and munitions but also additional traders, clerks, and partners to raise the total number at the settlement to more than one hundred. During that summer, the traders built a lodging for the mechanics and an infirmary. The partners also aggressively pursued the fur trade. Several posts were established in the interior, where traders gathered furs throughout the winter and then returned to Astoria in the spring. The northern posts—at the mouth of Okanagan River, Spokane House at the junction of the Spokane and Little Spokane rivers, and the She-whaps post on the South Thompson River— provided direct competition to the North West Company. In addition, posts were established on the Clearwater and on the Willamette rivers.

The partners also had agreed that Wilson Price Hunt, the chief agent, and Cornelius Sowle, captain of the *Beaver,* would leave the settlement to explore and trade north along the coast, a task that Jonathan Thorn on the *Tonquin* should have originally accomplished. Hunt then planned to stop at New Archangel with supplies for the Russian colony, gather their furs, and then stop once again at Astoria before the *Beaver* sailed for Canton, probably some time in late October 1812.[63]

Plans changed rapidly as first bad luck and then war intruded on Astoria. Wilson Price Hunt and Cornelius Sowle sailed uneventfully to New Archangel and there sold the goods invoiced at $22,342 to Governor Baranov for $58,417.87. Astor allowed Baranov to set the price, which was based on a markup for transportation costs and a sales commission. Hunt and Sowle received payment in seal skins, which were stored on Saint Paul's Island in the Bering Sea. On their arrival at the island, a storm damaged the *Beaver* and forced it to sail to the Hawaiian Islands for repairs. Rather than return to Astoria, Captain Sowle decided now to sail directly to Canton. Wilson Hunt, though, stayed in the Hawaiian Islands and awaited the arrival of Astor's second supply ship, the ill-fated *Lark,* due to stop there en route to Astoria. These decisions were perfectly logical given the circumstances, but Hunt and Sowle were unaware of the declaration of war and the wreck of the *Lark.*[64]

In January 1813, Donald McKenzie returned to Astoria from his post at Spokane House where he had heard from Canadian traders that war had been declared. Of course, this information changed everything. With the absence of Wilson Hunt, the two principal partners then at Astoria, Donald McKenzie and Duncan McDougall, were both Canadians, as were the majority of clerks and mechanics. As Gabriel Franchère expressed it, "Upon learning the news, all of us at Astoria who were British subjects and Canadians wished ourselves in Canada."[65]

However, this statement did not suggest that the Astoria personnel were suddenly British patriots; on the contrary, both Canadian and American traders looked for a way to avoid a confrontation. They desired, under the circumstances, to protect their financial interests, while maneuvering between the competing claims of loyalty from their employer and the British government. Consequently, they held what Franchère referred to as "a sort of council of war" among the partners and clerks and agreed that they could expect no more goods or supplies from Astor because ports would be blockaded owing to war. Because they had expected Hunt's return in the late fall 1812, they also were convinced that he had, by now, met the same fate as Captain Thorn and the *Tonquin.* They decided, therefore, to leave Astoria either in the spring or early summer so that they had sufficient time to begin an overland journey to the East. Messengers were sent to traders at the interior posts with news of the decision.

This decision seemed even more appropriate after nineteen North West Company traders arrived at Astoria in April 1813 in canoes flying the British flag. They brought the news that a North West Company vessel, the *Isaac Todd,* would soon arrive, although at this point no one was aware of the accompanying military vessels. Nevertheless, the presence of the North West Company traders threatened the Astorians, and they worried that they would lose all the furs in storage. These furs, of course, were their only chance for profit from the venture. On 3 June 1813, the partners and clerks met again and decided to pack up everything at once and start overland for Saint Louis.[66]

Yet another change in plans occurred in late June 1813 when the Astorians realized the dangers of leaving in such haste without the necessary provisions or horses. Moreover, the partners desired to hold on after the wintering traders returned to Astoria with 116 packs of furs, a much greater number than anyone had expected. Consequently, they postponed the abandonment of Astoria until 1 June 1814—unless, of course, they should receive goods or instructions from Astor to remain. The decision reflected little support for either side in the war, rather it revealed the Astorians' desire to protect their own economic interests.

In order to secure as much advantage as possible in the time remaining, the Astorians and the North West Company traders made several practical business arrangements. The Astorians gave up their northern posts to the North West Company in return for the company's withdrawal from other areas. They also sold provisions to the North West Company in return for a promise of supplies and horses the following spring. With an abundance of traders, the Pacific Fur Company allowed several, including Ross Cox, to accept employment with the North West Company.[67] These decisions by the Pacific Fur Company partners were certainly understandable and appeared at the time preferable to either military confrontation or open competition.

A short time later on 20 August 1813, Wilson Hunt, who had been stranded in the Hawaiian Islands, arrived back at Astoria on board the *Albatross.* After learning that the relief ship *Lark* from New York had been lost in a storm, Hunt had chartered the *Albatross* for passage back to Astoria. By this time, Hunt had learned of the war, and probably suspected that the *Beaver* would be unable to leave Canton to provide help. Hunt, nevertheless, was displeased with the decision to abandon Astoria, particularly since the fur trade and the trade with the Russians appeared so promising. He soon realized that there were few alternatives and formally agreed with the decision. He departed six days later on board the *Albatross* to purchase a vessel in the Hawaiian Islands that could be used to remove traders, goods, and furs from Astoria. In case he was unable to return, all agreed that Duncan McDougall had complete authority to provide for the closing of the post. This task included "making any arrangements [the Astorians] may be able to make with whoever may come forward on the part of the N.W. Co."[68]

Despite the intentions of all concerned to leave the country with the furs and goods of the Pacific Fur Company intact, in September 1813, Duncan McDougall was confronted with the arrival of the North West Company's overland military expedition, composed of approximately seventy-five traders. They had specific orders to take Astoria as soon as the *Isaac Todd* and its accompanying British frigate arrived. McDougall had no choice now but to negotiate the best deal possible both for himself and the Pacific Fur Company—although Astor later blamed him for surrendering the goods and furs. What Astor expected of McDougall is difficult to fathom, since McDougall might easily have lost everything. With the North West Company forces camped just outside the stockade at Astoria, McDougall had only one negotiating point: he possessed provisions for the winter as well as furs and trade supplies. Neither side wished a military confrontation; these men, after all, were traders who had but a limited amount of time to conclude a "practical" arrangement before the arrival of the British navy, when all goods and furs would be confiscated and treated as a prize of war.[69] Neither the North West Company nor Pacific Fur Company's traders appeared concerned with the national interests of either the United States or Great Britain.

The negotiations between the two fur companies took approximately two weeks in a tense atmosphere; finally, on 16 October 1813, Duncan McDougall sold all the furs, provisions, and manufactured items of the Pacific Fur Company to the North West Company. After completing a detailed inventory of all buildings, goods, and furs both at Astoria and the interior posts, a market value and sale value was assigned for each item. For example, all arms and cannons were sold at original cost, all buildings were sold at approximately $500 each, whereas only 50 percent of the market value was allowed for dry goods, stationery, and tobacco. Total inventory value of buildings and goods amounted to $19,117 and the furs were valued at $39,173, for a total of $58,290. However, $14,000 of the $58,290 was to be used for the payment of wages to the traders.[70] Thus Astor was to receive approximately $44,000 from the sale of Astoria.

The end of the Astoria venture followed quickly after the bill of sale. Scarcely a month later, 30 November 1813, the British ship *Raccoon* arrived with Captain William Black and John McDonald, a partner in the North West Company. The British convoy had faced numerous difficulties after leaving England. After rounding Cape Horn, it was decided to transfer some of the North West Company personnel from the slow-sailing, *Isaac Todd* to the *Raccoon*. On arrival, Captain Black found the North West Company in possession of the site. Not only was there no military engagement to be fought but there was no share in the Astoria prize for the British vessel. Nevertheless, Black conducted a formal ceremony and claimed the settlement, which he renamed Fort George, for Great Britain. Black then left Fort George in the control of the North West Company.[71]

When Hunt returned in February 1814 on board the ship *Pedler,* which he had purchased in the Hawaiian Islands, he found the British in possession and had little choice but to confirm the agreement to sell all the furs and possessions to the North West Company. Hunt departed in March with the American traders and headed for New Archangel and further trade with the Russian colony. Some of the Canadian traders also decided to leave the coast at this time, including Gabriel Franchére and Donald McKenzie, but they took an overland route through Canada to Montreal. It was from this party that Astor learned of the fate of Astoria in September 1814.[72]

When the New Yorker financier learned of the agreement, he was incensed at the low prices allowed for provisions and furs. Astor was probably correct in his own estimate that furs—including 17,705 beaver, 12,454 muskrat, 907 land otter, and 68 sea otter skins—would have sold for $100,000 at Canton. The provisions and trade goods, Astor estimated, were worth another $100,000. Astor also felt betrayed because Duncan McDougall and other Canadian traders went to work for the North West Company after the sale of Astoria. McDougall was even granted a partnership in the North West Company in July 1814.[73] Astor's bitterness over these losses was surely increased by the knowledge that his plan was workable. He had proven that furs could be collected from the interior, that a post on the Columbia River was both feasible and profitable, and that both furs and goods could be transported overland. Without the complications of international diplomacy, he would have succeeded! Although the financier pledged to redress what he believed was an unfair agreement "while I breath & so long as I have a dollar to spend I'll pursue a course to have our injuries repair'd."; in fact, there was nothing more he could do. In November 1814, the *New York Gazette and General Advertiser* carried a notice that the Pacific Fur Company had been dissolved.[74]

The loss of Astoria during the war has been the subject of a great deal of controversy and recrimination, both on the part of the participants and later historians. John Astor and, later, Washington Irving, blamed the treachery of Duncan McDougall, the principal Canadian partner of the Pacific Fur Company; the failure of the federal government to live up to its promises to provide military aid; and the mistakes of Cornelius Sowle and Jonathan Thorn, captains, respectively, of the *Beaver* and the *Tonquin*. Alexander Ross, a Canadian member of the Pacific Fur Company, blamed Astor himself for sending inferior goods to the coast and for issuing confusing and contradictory orders to his agents. Early historians of the event such as George Bancroft and Hiram Chittenden faulted Astor for hiring all the Canadian traders in the first place.[75]

The issue of who was to blame tends to obscure the precise order of events and involves the historian in repeating the justifications of the principal actors. In retrospect, it seems more important to observe that Astor's conception of Astoria was economically sound, but timing and luck were not his allies. Astor gambled and lost. He knew when he started that war clouds threatened the enterprise and probably miscalculated the level of government interest and support. Yet if just one of the government's relief ships (the *John Adams* or *Siren*) or one of Astor's rescue efforts (the *Lark* or the *Beaver*) had succeeded, the result would have been quite different. But what, in fact, happened was probably best expressed by Astor in a letter to Ramsay Crooks in September 1814 as the story of Astoria's fate first became known to him, "Was there ever an undertaking of more merit of more hazzard & enterpriz attended with a greater variaty of Misfortunes . . ."[76]

*John Astor, ca. 1815. Courtesy of Clarke Historical
Library, Central Michigan University.*

During the War of 1812, then, John Astor demonstrated a remarkable resiliency, adaptability, and decisiveness. He brilliantly
utilized every conceivable government connection and legal exception to maintain the Midwest fur trade and to keep ships and
goods moving across the Atlantic Ocean in preparation for the
postwar period. Although he lost the settlement at Astoria, lack of
effort was not the cause. Even though one can admire the qualities
that sustained his business affairs, this period in Astor's life revealed another dimension of his character and personality not
quite so flattering. Astor's dominating interest was his own busi-

ness, which he pursued tirelessly with political officials at every level, asking for favors and special treatment at every opportunity and, when necessary, peddling influence to whomever was susceptible. Despite his frequent contact with federal officals and with national issues (e.g., government loans and the bank), the financier never thought or acted like a statesman. The struggle with Great Britain, then, was not, to him, a clash of ideologies or political principles, but a threat to his business interests. This single-minded pursuit of personal goals was both his strength and, ultimately, his weakness.

CHAPTER SEVEN

Change in Postwar America, 1815–1819

IN 1815, John Astor was fifty-two years old and at the height of his business skill and political power. Despite the War of 1812, he had sustained his fur trade operations in the Midwest and had conducted a reasonably profitable trade with Europe. This chapter describes the New York financier's dramatic business expansion from 1815 to 1819, an expansion that included a revival of the American Fur Company and new initiatives in trade with Europe and China. In addition, Astor translated influence into power and became a primary force in establishing the Second Bank of the United States (BUS) and in directing its branch in New York City. But just when Astor's wealth and power rose to unprecedented levels, his mental and physical well-being collapsed after the tragic death of his grandson, John Jacob Bentzon. Unable to concentrate on his business and political affairs, Astor sailed to Europe in 1819, where he spent considerable time over the next fifteen years. The year 1819, then, was a turning point in Astor's business and personal life, ending his hard-driving, single-minded pursuit of wealth and power.

When John Astor learned of the the war's end in February 1815, he already was thinking of a comprehensive plan to link the trade with China and Europe to a fur trade conducted from coast to coast. To his nephew in Canton, George Ehninger, he wrote, "By the peace we shall have a right to the Columbia River & I rather think that I shall again engage in that business." To Thomas Wilson a financial connection in London he commented that he would pursue the China trade and "something in furs on that I have not yet fixed.[1] The hesitancy in Astor's plans had two causes. First, he was uncertain about the status of Astoria captured during the war; second, he did not know whether Canadian fur traders would be allowed in American territory around the Great Lakes. Although it would take over a year for these issues to be clarified, the New Yorker waited no longer and moved immediately to expand his commitment to the China trade.

The War of 1812 had cut off the China trade, thereby creating a demand for American furs in Canton and for Chinese teas and silks in the United States and Europe. John Astor was prepared, however: he had considerably expanded his fleet of ships during the war to full ownership of eight vessels including the *Beaver* then in Canton; the *Fingal* and *Boxer* in European ports; the *Pedler* and *Forester* in the Pacific; and the *Hannibal,* the *Enterprise,* and the *Seneca* in New York harbor. Sensing the war's end and the windfall profits awaiting the first vessel to reach Canton and return, Astor had risked a small cargo of furs and ginseng worth $30,000 on the *Macedonian,* which sailed in January 1815 for Canton. If the war ended, Astor hoped that the return cargo of teas would produce profits of approximately $300,000. He next outfitted the *Seneca,* secured one of his favorite captains, F. A. De Peyster, and paid him a bonus of $5,000 to sail on March 13 for China. In May, the *Fingal,* after returning from a voyage to Europe, also sailed for Canton.[2]

Astor's vessels arrived in Canton one after the other, along with perhaps three dozen other American ships that season, all hoping to cash in on the postwar markets. Cornelius Sowle, who had been stranded in Canton with the *Beaver* since 1812, received instructions from Astor to purchase a cargo and set out for New York. The *Macedonian, Beaver,* and *Seneca* all arrived back in New York City between January and April 1816. The *Fingal,* however, was lost at sea, and Astor immediately had another vessel, the *William and John,* built that year. By early 1816, Astor had amassed a considerable stock of black and green teas, silks, and nankeens for distribution in American and European markets.

The pace of activity continued brisk in 1817 and 1818, with usually three vessels a year traveling between Canton and New York City.[3]

The New Yorker not only expanded his postwar trade with both China and Europe but also altered its structure and organization. His first task was to find someone to assist in managing a capital of approximately $800,000, with $500,000 concentrated in the China trade and $300,000 in the fur business. This capitalization consisted of ships, furs, teas and silks. Given the number of vessels involved and the twin focus of furs and China goods, Astor plainly needed a partner who could manage part of the business and share the risks. His first choice was his close friend Albert Gallatin, who had returned from Europe after successfully negotiating the Treaty of Ghent. Gallatin was temporarily without a government position, although he had been offered an ambassador's post in France. But Gallatin was concerned about money since he earned only $2,500 per year from investments and felt that the salary for an ambassador was insufficient at $9,000 per year. Astor offered Gallatin a one-fifth share, approximately $160,000, in the combined fur and China trades. Gallatin would be able to secure his share on a loan from Astor at an interest rate of 6 or 7 percent. Astor admitted that profits fluctuated, but he told Gallatin to expect net profits on his share of $50,000 to $100,000 per year, even after paying interest on his share of the capital. Gallatin, however, finally refused the offer, preferring the ambassadorial post in France to commercial pursuits.[4]

Astor then encouraged his son, William Backhouse, to join him, even though William had been reluctant to follow a commercial career and had caused his father considerable unease with his lack of business interest. At the age of sixteen, he had gone to Heidelberg, not far from his father's first home in Walldorf, and then later studied at Göttingen. He traveled extensively throughout Europe and, during the war years, his father had fretted constantly over his safety. After the war, William had returned to New York City for a short period, only to leave once again for Europe, leading his father to make the worried comment, "I wish him to be engaged in some Honourable employment."

It is difficult to determine the exact relationship between father and son, although Astor rather caustically commented to Albert Gallatin in late 1816, "He intends to leave Europe next Spring & come home to settle himself in what way I know not— but he is steady & if he Remain so he will do well enough." With

Gallatin's refusal of a partnership, though, William was the next logical choice. By mid-1817 he was situated in his father's New York office, and the next year he became a partner in John Astor and Son. His father, though, was uncertain about his ability and commented, "My son having no employment & not wishing to be idle he is in my counting house & to make it somewhat interesting to him I made him my partner so that my business is now conducted under the firm of John Jacob Astor & Son."[5]

Astor also reorganized his China trade to provide the firm with a permanent agent in Canton. Until this time, he had depended on ship captains or accompanying business agents to purchase goods and sell his products, yet these arrangements were outmoded. Other firms such as Perkins and Company had permanent agents in Canton. These agents bought and sold in the marketplace throughout the year and took advantage of lower prices created by changes in supply and demand. On occasion, Astor paid a commission charge, usually a fixed percentage of the sale, to use the services of Perkins's agent. Eventually Astor appointed his own agent, Nicholas G. Ogden, the son of a prominent New York merchant, to act as his permanent representative in Canton for five years—in exchange for a one-fifth share in all China ventures. Ogden had represented the New Yorker on two earlier occasions, although he had acquired the dubious distinction of having been the supercargo on two vessels, the *Lark* and the *Fingal,* both of which had sunk. Ogden left New York City in early 1817 to assume his position in Canton.[6]

The New Yorker's postwar trade with Europe and the Pacific Coast also reflected significant alterations from prewar routes and products. New York City was the hub of this trade as furs from the interior of North America, Chinese teas and silks, and European manufactures, were brought there before sale or shipment elsewhere. As the China trade increased in volume and the market prices for teas and nankeens fluctuated along the East Coast, it was necessary to send more and more vessels to Europe as well as to the West Indies. Astor and his chief accountant, William Roberts, tracked prices in markets throughout the world, sending cargoes and purchasing goods based on their judgment of supply and demand in the market. Thus the cargo of a vessel would first be sold to other merchants, offered at thriving New York City auctions, or transshipped to vessels bound for European ports such as Le Havre, Hamburg, Bordeaux, Saint Petersburg, London, and Amsterdam. Although it could take up to four years to sell a ship's cargo, gross sales could amount to between $150,000 and $225,000.[7]

Vessels from Europe returned to New York City with many new products. Lead, quicksilver (mercury), and opium were then used in the voyages to Canton, thus lessening the need to carry specie in order to pay for teas and silks. In July 1815, the *Boxer* inaugurated this new trade, sailing first for Gibraltar, calling at Smyrna (now İzmir) on the Turkish coast and then returning to New York. On rare occasions, ships such as the *William and John* in 1817 left New York for Gibraltar, presumably with a partial cargo of furs and ginseng, picked up additional items such as lead and opium, and then continued on to Canton. In 1818, for example, the *William and John* carried over two hundred tons of lead from Gibraltar to Canton.[8]

The opium trade presented special problems in the Canton market. The British first imported opium from India; and since the mid-eighteenth century with the introduction of smoking, the Chinese government, conscious of its social consequences, had tried unsuccessfully, to stop its importation. Consequently, the opium trade was illegal in China, although nearly all the China traders smuggled it in. Opium was a regular, although small part of Astor's cargoes from 1815 to 1820. Occasionally, opium was sold to traders just outside Canton in exchange for silver, which was then used to purchase teas. Astor's instructions to his agent Nicholas Ogden exhibited the obvious caution needed in this trade; "I should think opium must towards the last of the season get up, in a few hands. I believe no one knows of our having any on board the *Seneca,* except Captain Clark, and its put up in casks as if furs."[9]

The constant search for new products to increase the profitability of the Canton trade also led to a further change in the pattern of voyages across the Pacific Ocean. Rather than single trips direct from New York to Canton and return, vessels now traded in several ports in the Pacific region back and forth to Canton over a period of two or three years before returning to New York. In June 1815, John Ebbets sailed from New York City in command of the *Enterprise,* bound first for the Northwest Coast. There he obtained seal skins from the Indians along the coast and, continuing westward, acquired sandalwood in the Hawaiian Islands. Sandalwood subsequently became an important cargo. It was a royal monopoly, which the native rulers cut—for a brief period lasting through the

1820s—without regard to preservation. The sandalwood was sold to Western traders headed for Canton where the Chinese used it as incense. The *Enterprise* finally arrived in Canton in December 1816 with its cargo of sandalwood and furs. It returned to the Hawaiian Islands with silks and decorative items and traded for more sandalwood; then it set out for the Latin American Coast, where it acquired copper, sealskins, and silver; returning once again to the islands for more sandalwood; and finally arrived back in Canton in November 1818. The *Enterprise* sailed back to New York City in September 1819 carrying teas, nankeens, and silk.[10]

The *Pedler* left New York in 1819, and also engaged in one of these complex voyages. By depending on his captains to call at several ports either along the Latin American Coast or the Northwest Coast to garner items for trade in Canton, Astor avoided sending large amounts of specie. The *Pedler,* for example, first went to Oahu, then to the Northwest Coast to trade with the Indians and on to New Archangel to purchase furs. After returning to the islands, the *Pedler* continued on to Canton in February 1821 only to make the circuit all over again. It did not return to New York City with teas and silks until August 1823. These vessels, then, were general traders in the Pacific region, gathering products and making profits on each voyage.[11]

The search for new markets and products for the China trade did not always prove successful. One noted example involved the *Beaver,* under Captain Richard Cleveland, which sailed from New York in July 1817 with a cargo of teas, silks, clothes, tin, and lead valued at $140,000. The intent was to explore the markets for these products in Peru and Chile, which had just rebelled against Spanish control. Undoubtedly, Astor hoped to acquire products such as silver and copper, which then could be exchanged for furs along the Northwest Coast, before heading for Hawaii and Canton. Unfortunately, the political situation was still unsettled, thus when the *Beaver* entered the port of Talcahuano, Chile, it was seized by Spanish forces. The royalists stripped the sails from the ship, removed the crew, and expropriated the cargo.

But Astor was lucky not to lose everything. His supercargo on the vessel, Francisco Ribas, was able to steal a dinghy and escape. He eventually got to Valparaiso, where he learned that an American naval vessel, the *Ontario,* under Captain James Biddle, was in port. This meeting was an amazing coincidence because Biddle was then on his way to Astoria to reassert American claims there.

Biddle delayed this mission while he conducted negotiations with the royalist forces in Chile and Peru for the return of Astor's ship as well as the property of other American merchants similarly disadvantaged. He successfully recovered the *Beaver,* whatever cargo remained unsold, and damages of approximately $15,000. The *Beaver* then traded along the coast for nearly two years before returning to New York in 1820 with a cargo of cocoa weighing 840,456 pounds.[12]

Astor's foreign trade in the years after the War of 1812 had expanded substantially. His ships traded all over the world—in Europe, Latin America, along the Pacific Coast, in the Hawaiian Islands, and in Canton. All this activity, though, was still focused on the Canton market and its demand for products such as furs, sandalwood, lead, and opium in return for teas, nankeens, and silks. But although Astor launched into this vastly expanded trade with great confidence in 1815 and 1816, he was nowhere near as certain of the other main focus of his business—the fur trade. Here, the years after the war were more difficult, and required even more substantial changes in strategy and organization.

Astor's plans for the fur trade were very uncertain both on the Pacific Coast and around the Great Lakes. The Treaty of Ghent, ending the War of 1812, did not give Astor control over the fur trade, for British traders were not barred from American territory nor was there a settled boundary from the Rocky Mountains to the Pacific Ocean. Astoria also was not specifically mentioned in the Treaty of Ghent. Because of Astor's constant pressure on American officials and his friendship with Albert Gallatin, who was one of the peace commissioners, the Americans assumed it would be returned after the war under the general clause calling for restoration of all captured properties.[13] Despite the uncertainties, there was no doubt in Robert Stuart's mind when he visited with Astor in New York in 1815 that "he is digesting a very extensive plan for establishing [controlling] all the Indian countries within the line of demarcation between Great Britain and the U.S. and the probability is that a considerable time may lapse before that object can be brought to full as he wants an exclusive grant or privilege."[14]

The meaning of Stuart's phrase should not be taken literally, for Astor was not after a government monopoly, although his long-range plan involved the federal government's assistance. He desired legislation banning British traders from American territory, thus ending foreign competition. Second, he wanted a small military force of approximately twenty-five men to reoccupy and protect the Astoria outpost. Third, he requested the abolition of government factories wherever private capital could supply the Indians. Although he presented his case before administration and congressional officials in 1815 and early 1816, Astor did not wait on government action. Instead he pursued interim plans for the trade.[15] He entered into negotiations with Canadian traders and with Americans such as Charles Gratiot, Ramsay Crooks, and Robert Stuart.

Astor first revealed his short-term plans for the fur trade to his most trusted associates, Ramsay Crooks and Robert Stuart. During the war's final year, they had traded for him in the Great Lakes, in upstate New York, and in Canada in hopes of participating in a revived American Fur Company. In February 1814, for example, Astor promised Crooks that when peace came "we shall make as much money as you want *by the Indian trade.*"[16] In February 1815, however, he summoned both Crooks and Stuart to New York City and informed them that he was reestablishing the partnership in the Great Lakes with the Canadians through the South West Company. The New Yorker indicated his hope that the partnership would be temporary and that soon Congress would exclude the Canadians. In the interim, Astor offered to supply both Ramsay Crooks and Robert Stuart with goods for an independent trade. Both men accepted and decided to trade along the upper Missouri River while awaiting the maturation of Astor's long-range plan. Robert Stuart assured Crooks that Astor would give them a larger share in the future but only "as his own *dear* interest will permit, for of that you are no doubt aware, he will never lose sight *until some kind friend will put his fingers over his eye lids.*"[17]

During the early months of 1815, Astor also expanded his involvement in the Saint Louis region by purchasing furs from Charles Gratiot. He first ordered fifteen to twenty thousand pounds of deerskin; and in July, he authorized Gratiot to expend up to $100,000 for bear and deerskins. Astor obviously intended to provide a strong competition for resident Saint Louis traders and may have even envisioned a company, similar to his plans before the war, that would eventually spread to the Rocky Mountains.[18]

In the Great Lakes region, the New Yorker revived the South West Company in which he shared the southwest trade with the

Robert Stuart, ca. 1820. Courtesy of Robert Stuart House, Mackinac Island.

Canadians. He signed a new contract in October 1815 that gave him a 50 percent share and extended the life of the South West Company for five years. His Canadian partners were the firms of Forsyth, Richardson and Company; McTavish, McGillivray and Co.; and Pierre de Rocheblave. The Canadians knew that the South West Company would have a limited existence given Astor's competitive position and close ties to the American government. Thus, the Canadians had little choice but to agree when Astor demanded the insertion of a clause that would nullify the contract, if the American government were to pass laws or regulations excluding Canadian traders from American territory. Thus Astor's strategy was to take a share of the southwest trade, while he pushed the government to legally exclude the Canadians.[19]

Astor pursued a similar dual strategy in regard to Astoria. He began discussions with the North West Company to share the Pacific Coast trade, even while urging the American government to send a military force to retake the post. Astor knew that American negotiators had argued strongly for its restoration at the peace treaty. In March 1815, Secretary of State Monroe indicated to the British Minister, Anthony St. John, that the United States intended to reoccupy the post as soon as possible. Monroe subsequently asked Astor precisely how it had been lost. The issue was important because the North West Company argued that Astoria had been purchased legally and was not a prize of war. Astor, though, maintained that the purchase was invalid because it was signed under threat of military seizure by Duncan McDougall, a British subject and traitor to Astor's interests.[20]

While he organized the fur trade on an interim basis, Astor maintained pressure on the administration throughout the later months of 1815. Albert Gallatin, who had returned from Europe after negotiating the Treaty of Ghent, was his major advocate within the government. Astor wrote Gallatin three extraordinary letters in early October spelling out precisely what he desired from the government and asking Gallatin to present these proposals to President Madison and Secretary of State James Monroe during a series of scheduled meetings later in the month. He again urged the exclusion of British traders, expressing his desire to form an American company only if the government would take some effective action. He also stressed the point that American capital would only flow into the fur trade if the government closed the government factories. He urged Gallatin to suggest to President Madison that he send a resolution to Congress recommending such action. Finally, Astor argued that the federal government should reclaim Astoria by sending both a military vessel and troops, in return for which he promised to reoccupy the settlement.[21] It is important to recall that at the same time that Gallatin presented these proposals to the administration, he was still considering Astor's offer of a partnership in the fur and China trades.[22]

Whether President Madison and Secretary of State Monroe desired to please Gallatin—they wanted him to take the post as ambassador to France—or whether they really accepted all of Astor's arguments; nevertheless, they agreed to send a military vessel and troops to reclaim Astoria. The government made two efforts to send an American ship, first in late 1815 and again in early 1816, but each time the order was canceled when military problems first with Algeria and then with Spain intruded.[23] Astor must have had a sense of déjà vu, for repeated delays also characterized the government's actions toward Astoria during the War of 1812. In early 1816, Astor still debated whether to go back to the Pacific Coast as much depended on "whether our government will act or not, if they do I think it [probable] that I shall proceed, if not I think it doubtful whether myself or any other citizen will engage. The truth is it will be discouraging unless the government takes some interest."[24]

Even though the New Yorker sought government help in pushing the British out of Astoria, he could not be sure of success. He, thus, willingly discussed some form of joint occupation with the North West Company. The North West Company had initiated the idea because the Pacific settlement proved to be a losing venture without regular supply ships, a yearly vessel to Canton, and subsidiary business with the Russian colony at New Archangel. The North West Company partners also realized that they needed an agreement with an American firm in order to market the furs. James Keith, who was in charge of the Columbia post, strongly recommended such action, and in 1815 William McGillivray of the North West Company was willing once again to negotiate with John Astor. The New York financier went to Montreal in April 1816, obviously in a commanding position and with the intention of signing a contract setting up a joint company on the Northwest Coast, similar to the South West Company in the Old Northwest. At the last moment, he suddenly refused to sign and hurriedly left Montreal to the amazement of North West Company partners, John Richardson and William McGillivray.[25]

The reason for this abrupt action is not hard to fathom. On 29 April 1816, Congress passed a law requiring that licenses to trade with the Indians could only be granted to American citizens and that foreigners violating the law would be arrested and their furs and goods confiscated. Foreign nationals who wished only to pass through the Indian territory needed a passport. Legislation the Canadians had feared since the 1780s, and which Astor had recommended and lobbied for at least since 1808, was now a reality. There was no question that American traders would now challenge Canadian control of the fur trade. Such legislation, though, was not passed as a special favor to Astor, although he certainly had an impact on its spirit and wording. Rather, the law accorded perfectly with the U.S. government's desire to completely neutralize British activities among the Indians by eliminating their participation in the fur trade.[26] As he journeyed back to New York City from Montreal, the New Yorker's paramount thought must have been that a continental fur trade organized under the umbrella of the American Fur Company was now, more than ever, close to fulfillment.

In the succeeding months, however, Astor rethought his grand design for the fur trade and changed his strategy. He abandoned all thoughts of a continental trade and settled instead for a revived American Fur Company initially limited to the Great Lakes region. What caused such a sudden change? A major factor was Astor's knowledge that he would be able to control the southwest or Great Lakes trade and acquire all the furs necessary for the Canton market. He no longer really needed the furs from the Northwest Coast or from the Russians at New Archangel, *if the risks were too great.*

By 1816, he also knew that the federal government was not committed to controlling the Pacific Coast. The president had steadily refused to send military forces there, and the American ship *Congress,* which was to sail in mid-1816 for Astoria, was rerouted to the Gulf of Mexico at the last moment. President Madison and Secretary of State Monroe obviously wished to reclaim America's post on the Pacific Coast; however, they had no wish to create an international incident by forcefully removing the British traders. Thus, when John Quincy Adams as secretary of state finally sent the *Ontario* to the Pacific Coast in October 1817, Captain James Biddle carried orders only to assert American sovereignty by some symbolic gesture, and not to disrupt or remove the North West Company traders. With so little government support, Astor was unwilling to risk more money and goods on the Pacific venture.[27]

Equally important in Astor's decision to reduce the scope of the American Fur Company was the tenuous nature of his agreement with the Russian-American Company to supply its colony. The agreement had lapsed because of the war, and it had formally expired in December 1816. The Russians were not anxious to renegotiate: they felt Astor's prices for goods were too high. A problem also arose when Wilson Price Hunt, leaving Astoria in the hands of the North West Company in February 1814, had sailed to New Archangel. There he met yet another Astor vessel, the *Forester,* under William J. Pigot. The Russian governor, Alexander Baranov, distrusted both men, believing they were trading arms and goods with the Indians in violation of their contract. By 1816, moreover, the Russians were intent on supplying their own colony as well as pushing settlements south along the coast. For his part, Astor was also disappointed with the profits. In two trips from New Archangel to Canton in 1812, Cornelius Sowle, captain of the *Beaver,* had sold furs at low prices to Perkins and Company in Canton, in direct violation of Astor's instructions to sell directly to Chinese merchants.[28]

The decision to abandon Astoria was surrounded with ironies. Had he known in time, Astor easily might have reoccupied the settlement in 1817–1818 without the aide of military forces. When the British chargé d'affaires in Washington, Charles Bagot, learned that President Monroe and John Quincy Adams had sent Captain Biddle and special envoy John Prevost to Astoria on board the *Ontario,* he assumed that America intended a military takeover. Bagot and Simon McGillivray of the North West Company urged the British government to resist the American intrusion, yet Viscount Castlereagh, British foreign secretary, decided to allow the Americans to repossess Astoria without a struggle, although insisting on British rights to remain in the territory. In essence, Castlereagh preferred to negotiate the whole issue at some future date.[29]

This decision led to rather bizarre events on the Northwest Coast. Captain Biddle had met with protracted delays in Latin America while conducting negotiations with royalist and rebel forces. He had also become separated from the American envoy, John Prevost, and thus sailed alone to the mouth of the Columbia River, arriving in August 1818. There he asserted America's claim to the region but then left the bewildered North West Company traders in possession of the fort. Two months later, John Prevost arrived on board H.M.S. Blossom. He had met the ship off the coast of Chile and sailed to Fort George (Astoria) in order to restore it to America. In October, the traders gathered for a ceremony in which the British flag was lowered and the American flag raised over Fort George—or was it now Astoria?[30] As Astor had abandoned the project by this time, the North West Company was allowed to maintain the fort and continue its business until a more formal diplomatic solution was reached. The diplomats were already at work. The Convention of 1818 avoided a head-on confrontation and produced a joint occupation of the Oregon Territory for ten years, after which the issue would be finally settled; in fact, it took much longer and nearly embroiled the two countries in yet another war during the 1840s.[31]

Astor was bitterly disappointed over the loss of Astoria: it bothered him throughout his life. American officials repeatedly sought his account of how the settlement was lost because periodic efforts to reestablish American rights to the region were partially based on the founding of the original Astoria settlement. In 1818, John Calhoun, secretary of war, briefly entertained the idea of incorporating a single company in the far western trade to drive the British from the coast. In 1820, Representative John Floyd of Virginia pushed Congress to reassert American interests in order to capture the lucrative fur trade to Canton. Floyd had talked to many former Astorians such as Ramsay Crooks and Russell Farnham. When the Americans and British resumed negotiations over the Oregon Territory in 1823, John Quincy Adams asked Astor for yet another narration of the crucial events.[32] Perhaps most galling of all was the fact that the North West Company continued to trade from there, and in 1817 Perkins and Company of Boston entered a multiyear contract to supply the post and to ship its furs to Canton. For a brief period, James Keith, the North West Company leader at Fort George, established trade with the Russians at New Archangel, although it was never a profitable venture. Eventually the post was taken over by the Hudson's Bay Company when it absorbed the North West Company in 1821. The Hudson's Bay Company was able to fully exploit the coastal trade.[33]

Astor always resisted any criticism of his role in the whole venture and blamed others for its failure. His major incentive for employing Washington Irving to write *Astoria,* published in 1836, was to applaud his own vision for conceiving the project and to justify his decision to pull out. The New Yorker was most critical of Donald McKenzie and Duncan McDougall, who originally sold the Pacific Fur Company; of his own ship captains, Jonathan Thorn and Cornelius Sowle, who disobeyed his orders; and of American policymakers who refused to more boldly assert American interests in 1815 and 1816. Astor's sense of disappointment only increased with time. In 1817 he wrote Albert Gallatin, "We have no settlement on the Columbia. The Northwest Company [sic] have it and are doing rather better than heretofore. The Russians are making extensive arrangements on the Northwest Coast. They are doing that which I wish to have & wanted to do but you know why I did not succeed. I think it was not my fault." In 1827, he wrote, "I never had but one opinion—our government ought in 1815 and 1816 taking possession placed a post of 50 men which would have been as good as 5,000—our people would have gone to trade & got the Indians with them." More to the point were his comments in 1832 to Wilson Price Hunt, leader of the overland expedition in 1810, "Had we succeeded in keeping Astoria, ere now we should all have made great fortunes there, and even more and much more than the Hudson Bay Company [sic] now do."[34]

Astor's decision in mid-1816 to abandon Astoria and the simultaneous passage of the license law that prohibited Canadian traders from crossing the border required immediate adjustments to his plans for the fur trade. To this end, he took three steps: negotiated new agreements with Saint Louis traders; formally purchased the South West Company's supplies and buildings in American territory; and reestablished the American Fur Company in the Great Lakes.

As he alone would now be responsible for capitalizing an American company, hiring traders, and purchasing goods, Astor knew that he could not, in the beginning, challenge the large fur trade interests in Saint Louis and along the Missouri River. Consequently, he established a formal relationship with Saint Louis traders such as J. P. Cabanné and Company and Berthold, Chouteau, and Company. As part of this contract, he recalled Robert Stuart and Ramsay Crooks from the Saint Louis region and promised the Saint Louis companies that he would not supply any outside traders or purchase any furs except from them. In essence, Astor became the exclusive agent for Saint Louis traders. He, thus, was guaranteed a steady supply of furs from the region without having to employ traders or risk capital. The contract, though, was not a formal partnership and apparently was only for a limited period—a year or two. One casualty of this agreement was his old friend Charles Gratiot, who was not aligned with either of the Saint Louis firms, and Astor was obliged to decline purchasing any furs from him.[35]

Astor next closed out his Canadian partnership, the South West Company. One might wonder why Astor did not simply takeover all their equipment and goods then in American territory as they could no longer legally trade. Not only was the New Yorker insistent on the ethical responsibilities inherent in contracts but he also needed the Canadian traders and access to supplies and markets in Montreal and London. Moreover, the South West Company still had goods in the interior and expected a division of profits from the current trade season.

Negotiations began when Pierre de Rocheblave, a Canadian partner, came to New York City in the winter of 1816, and they were finalized when Astor visited Montreal in September 1817. No bill of sale has survived, but accounting ledgers indicate that Astor made quarterly payments from $22,000 to $25,000, paying a total of approximately $100,000 for the South West Company's goods, buildings, and real estate at numerous locations in American territory, including Mackinac Island and Detroit. Astor was extraordinarily pleased with the arrangement and believed that he had been compensated somewhat for his losses at Astoria.[36] As he reported triumphantly to Albert Gallatin, "I have bought out all the Scotchmen at Montreal from the Indian trade and in about 2 months I will have $300,000 of property in the woods & among the Indians. How to get it out again time will tell."[37]

His next move was to create a structure—the American Fur Company—to organize the American trade. Significantly, the New Yorker did not copy the complex partnerships and diffuse leadership structure of the North West Company; instead, he returned to the notion of a stock company with managerial power vested in the president, board of directors, and salaried agents. The American Fur Company already possessed a corporate charter from the New York State legislature, and it was the legal framework that Astor had used to enter the South West Company and the partnership with the Russian-American Company. The American Fur Company, nevertheless, was a paper organization with few stockholders other than Astor and his business associates. The New Yorker had to breathe life into the organization as well as expend a considerable capital in purchasing goods and in hiring field managers and traders. Because he controlled the great majority of stock, Astor assumed all the financial burdens of the company. In return, he received a 2½ percent commission for marketing the furs in addition to yearly profits.

The New Yorker needed field managers for the American Fur Company. Ramsay Crooks and Robert Stuart, who had been waiting for Astor's call since just after the war, were appointed in early 1817. Ramsay Crooks was employed as the principal agent on a three-year contract at an annual salary of $2,000 in addition to profit or loss on five shares out of one hundred in the company. Robert Stuart had an almost identical contract, although his salary was $1,500 and he held fewer shares of stock, reflecting his subordinate position to Crooks. A third agent was William Matthews, another veteran of the Astoria expedition, who had responsibility for company business at Montreal.[38]

The most immediate tasks for Astor and his managers, in their efforts to control the Great Lakes trade, were to order goods and to hire traders. In these early years, they made slow but visible progress in creating an *American* company divorced from the Canadians. For the 1817 trade year, Ramsay Crooks purchased goods such as tobacco plugs, whiskey, and foodstuffs throughout the Midwest, whereas Astor ordered blankets and other textile products from New York suppliers. The Tariff Act of 1816 established high tariffs on the import of British goods and reinforced the policy of buy American. But Astor never completely abandoned imported goods because American products, particularly blankets, were inferior to the English product and weakened the American Fur Company's competitive position.[39] The fur trade also depended on handcrafted items such as canoes, silver earbobs, hatbands, broaches, trousers, and caps—the only source for these goods was the dozens of small craft shops in and around Montreal. Thus Crooks, along with William Matthews, spent a part of the year in Montreal visiting artisan shops to arrange for the delivery of goods the following year.[40]

The American Fur Company initially hired approximately 125 men to serve as traders, interpreters, boatmen, and clerks. The clerks were the most important as they controlled the trade within a defined area and assumed responsibility for an entire outfit's year supply of goods and furs. Ramsay Crooks often simply employed the former traders of the South West Company such as John Johnston at Saint Marys Falls (Saulte Sainte Marie) or William Morrison and James Grant at Fond du Lac. Crooks's most immediate need was for voyageurs, and although many independent traders could be found in small villages such as Chicago, Prairie de Chien, and on Mackinac Island, Montreal was still the central location of the fur-trade community. Even though the intent of the congressional legislation was to put the trade in American hands, Astor, Crooks, and Matthews all knew that there were simply not enough Americans skilled in the trade to supply the American Fur Company. They needed carpenters to build the canoes, tailors to make the traditional clothes of the trade, interpreters to communicate with the Indians, skilled canoe handlers to navigate the western lakes and rivers, and traders with the temperament to spend long months in the wilderness. In a remarkably vivid example of cultural blindness and racial stereotyping,

Crooks once tried to explain to Astor why Canadian traders were essential to their efforts:

> These people are indispensable to the successful prosecution of the trade, their places cannot be supplied by Americans, who are for the most part . . . too independent to submit quietly to a proper contract, and who can gain anywhere a subsistence much superior to a man of the interior, and although the body of the Yankee can resist as much hardship as any man, tis only in 'the Canadian we find that temper of mind,' to render him patient, docile, and preserving. In short, they are a people harmless in themselves whose habits of submission fit them peculiarly for our business.[41]

In the springs of 1817 and 1818, William Matthews and Ramsay Crooks hired over 125 traders in Montreal. In 1819 the number dropped significantly because many traders were on multiyear contracts and because the American Fur Company had established control over many independents who lived in the Great Lakes region. The American Fur Company paid wages from $100 to $150 per year for terms ranging from one to five years. Traders often received advances on wages and free equipment that included blankets, trousers, and tobacco. Crooks and Matthews thus faced a major loss when traders deserted; in 1817, the desertion rate was as high as 20 percent. No doubt, insecurity about the future of this American company contributed to the large number of desertions.[42]

The gradual alteration in routes into the interior was one observable change in the patterns of the North American fur trade with the emergence of the American Fur Company. William Matthews at first followed the traditional pattern, that is, in the spring, the traders loaded their canoes and departed for the West from Lachine below the rapids outside Montreal. From there, the brigade journeyed up the Saint Lawrence and then overland, or by river, to the Great Lakes and ultimately Mackinac Island. Ramsay Crooks and Robert Stuart, though, used an American route both for the shipment of furs to eastern markets and the movement of English and American goods inland. Even though the journey was more difficult, they wished to stay within American territory in order to avoid tariffs and abide by the license laws. Forwarding and commission firms were in their infancy, and contracts had to be established with many small firms along the way. Some goods were moved by wagon westward from Albany through Schenectady to Geneva and then Buffalo, where forwarding firms would handle shipment to Detroit and then north to Mackinac Island. On other occasions, the goods went from New York City to Albany, west on the Mohawk River through Oneida Lake, down the Oswego Creek to Oswego on Lake Ontario, and then to Buffalo, with shipment from there to Detroit or Mackinac. Usually either Ramsay Crooks or Robert Stuart accompanied the goods on the journey to assure that they reached Mackinac Island in late spring or early summer.

Within a few years, transportation routes to the Old Northwest noticeably improved, first with toll roads, then canals—especially the Erie Canal—and lake steamboats. In fact, by 1820, Ramsay Crooks had negotiated contracts for the Lake Erie Steamboat Company to carry goods and furs for the American Fur Company from Buffalo to Mackinac and return twice a year, once in late spring and again in August. An indication of the dramatic changes in fur-trade routes was that, in 1819, William Matthews sent only two canoes from Montreal with traders and goods: in each succeeding year, the American Fur Company further reduced its dependence on Montreal traders and merchants.[43]

Mackinac Island was the center of interior operations for the American Fur Company. It had been the headquarters of numerous firms that participated in the southwest trade since the early eighteenth century and a rendezvous point to which interior traders returned in early summer to sell or exchange their furs for another year's supply of goods. Traders usually left Mackinac Island in late summer or early fall for trading territories throughout the Great Lakes. The American Fur Company took over buildings that had belonged to the South West Company and employed carpenters and masons to construct a new store and residences for traders. Even though in the first few years Robert Stuart and Ramsay Crooks would return to New York City in the late fall, they realized the necessity of maintaining a permanent staff on the island. Eventually, Samuel Abbott was appointed resident manager and he, in turn, soon employed carpenters and blacksmiths throughout the year to add new buildings and to manufacture axes and animal traps for the next trade season.[44]

In organizing the fur trade and in establishing its presence throughout the Great Lakes, the American Fur Company quickly established a reputation on the frontier and among later historians as an avaricious monopoly that crushed opponents and frus-

*Detroit waterfront, 1820. Courtesy of Clarke Historical
Library, Central Michigan University.*

trated official American frontier policy. These characterizations,
though, were often inaccurate and have long-distorted our views
on Astor, the fur trade, and government policy. It is important
to recognize that, in 1816, Astor faced substantial competition.
Purchasing the interests of the South West Company was only a
first step; for several years Canadian traders continued to smuggle
goods into American territory from Drummond Island and supplied goods to the Indians who journeyed there. Independent traders at Prairie du Chien and Green Bay such as John Lawe and
Joseph Rolette, moreover, tried to maintain their traditional ties
to Canadian suppliers.[45]

The American Fur Company was also caught in the struggle
between two Canadian rivals—the Hudson's Bay Company and
the North West Company. At the very time it was being expelled
from American territory, the North West Company faced a more

serious threat from Thomas Selkirk. The Earl of Selkirk had obtained a substantial stock interest in the Hudson's Bay Company in 1808 and then subsequently acquired 116,000 acres of company lands in the Red River valley, embracing parts of northwestern Minnesota and eastern North Dakota. Selkirk's intent was to establish an agricultural colony of emigrants from his native Scotland and Ireland. This plan threatened to block the North West Company's expansion to the north and west. In 1816, the North West Company traders launched an attack on Selkirk's colony, only to see Selkirk retaliate and capture Fort William in addition to posts at Saulte Sainte Marie, Sandy Lake, and Fond du Lac. Other than Fort William, these posts were in American territory and the property of the American Fur Company. Astor protested these seizures to the American government. Although the federal

American Fur Company warehouse, ca. 1903. Courtesy of Clarke Historical Library, Central Michigan University.

government took no direct action, local officials allowed American Fur Company traders to confiscate the goods of Selkirk's agents found in American territory.[46]

Competition also came from American firms such as Conant and Mack of Detroit and David Stone from Boston. There were many other independent traders who pushed up the Mississippi River and its tributaries from Saint Louis. All the traders and merchants arrived on Mackinac Island in the summer to bid on the furs coming from the interior. In the summer of 1817, the American Fur Company was only able to purchase a large share of the furs not previously contracted for; thus the year's trade yielded only a small profit.[47] The American Fur Company, then, did not enjoy a *monopoly*. From the beginning, it had to compete for control of the fur harvest; a competition that, Astor believed, only a large, well-organized company could win.

In addition to misunderstandings about the American Fur Company's "monopoly," historians, as well as some government officials, at the time failed to appreciate the convergence between the goals of the American Fur Company and the government's western policy. John Astor had an uncommon ability to influence policy, but this influence was not alone the product of his skill as a lobbyist. From the beginning of the nineteenth century, federal officials believed that if American capitalists controlled the fur trade, then British influence over the Indians and frontier settlers would dissipate. Since 1808, Astor's name was synonymous with American interests, and federal officials such as James Madison, James Monroe, Albert Gallatin, and John Calhoun believed that the American Fur Company's success was an important ingredient of American control of the West. Astor knew this and never missed an opportunity to alert legislators and administrators to the most efficient methods for assisting private capitalists.

The 1816 trade law, for example, which prohibited foreign traders from entering American territory, was not meant to be rigidly enforced. Federal officials, including newly elected President Monroe, knew that if they wished to break the Canadians' control of the Indians, American capitalists, like Astor, would need to employ Canadian traders to move goods into the interior. Consequently, licenses were to be given to foreigners, at the discretion of the Indian agents, in the trading areas. The immediate effect of the 1818 trade law, then, was not to bar Canadian traders from American territory; rather, the law excluded Canadian companies, particularly Astor's former partners in the South West Company.[48]

Before Astor understood precisely how President Monroe intended to implement the law, he asked for six to nine blank licenses that could be filled in by local authorities at Mackinac. Secretary of War George Crawford responded immediately. He sent Astor a copy of the 1816 law along with his instructions to Lewis Cass, governor of the Michigan Territory and superintendent of Indian affairs. These instructions explicitly approved the licensing of foreigners. Crawford, thus, assured the New Yorker that frontier officials were fully cognizant of the law's intent. In June 1816, his deputy, George Graham, wrote to the Indian agent and military commander at Fort Mackinac a far more explicit statement that mentioned specifically that Astor and his agents had a very substantial investment in the trade and "I am directed by the Secretary of War to request that you will give to these gentlemen every possible facility and aid in the prosecution of their business that may be compatible with your public duties."[49] Governor Lewis Cass, who as superintendent of Indian affairs was directly responsible for the implementation of government policy, also wrote to his Indian agent at Mackinac, "From all the information, which has reached [me] I have no doubt but the Government expect that the Country North & West of us will be supplied with goods by the Capital and enterprize of this Company."[50]

Astor's influence was apparent again in 1816 and 1817. When he completed the purchase of all South West Company interests, he wrote to President Monroe and suggested that a more rigid enforcement of license laws against British interests would not be acceptable, although cautioning he would still need to employ Canadian boatmen and interpreters.[51] In late 1817, following a tour of the Old Northwest, President Monroe went ahead with a total exclusion of foreign traders only to quickly soften the order when Astor objected that he still needed the assistance of some Canadian personnel.[52]

Although Astor clearly received assistance from the national government, he was not alone the beneficiary of policies designed to encourage American capital in the fur trade. The American Fur Company was simply the largest and most well-known firm. Governor Cass in 1817 was equally helpful to David Stone and the Detroit firm of Conant and Mack, who were anxious to receive licenses for their foreign traders. Cass wrote to William Puthuff, the

Lewis Cass, ca. 1830s. Courtesy of Clarke Historical Library, Central Michigan University.

Mackinac Indian agent, "When American capital & enterprise are embarked in this trade it is polite to encourage it by all proper means." David Stone thus was able to inform his traders in the Great Lakes region that his Washington contacts assured the availability of licences for foreign traders.[53]

Despite the intentions of federal policy, the American Fur Company experienced innumerable problems in securing licenses and was constantly at odds with government officials on the frontier, leading inevitably to its not undeserved reputation for attacking uncooperative Indian agents and military commanders. Such conflicts were not totally the fault of the American Fur Company, but they often resulted from two causes: the contradictions in government policy and the hostility of frontier officials.

First, government policy toward the West was quite complex and often one government agency worked at cross-purposes to the others, with private enterprise trapped in between. Overall, the federal government sought to establish American control over the Great Lakes, the Mississippi River, and the Missouri River regions. In order to dispel British influence and control the Indian population, the government maintained and constructed new military posts at key locations, like those at Chicago (Fort Dearborn), Green Bay (Fort Howard), Mackinac (Fort Mackinac), Prairie due Chien (Fort Crawford), and Saint Paul (Fort Snelling).

The secretary of war also had direct responsibility for Indian policy and established Indian agencies to separate Indians from British influence, essentially through trade laws such as the license law of 1816, which gave Indian agents the power to distribute licenses to respectable traders. Indian agencies also encouraged the Indians to abandon the fur trade and take up commercial farming. Finally, the government decided after the war to continue the factory system. Its goal was to end British influence over the Indians by establishing government trading houses that directly competed with the supposedly unscrupulous traders.

The ironic fact about these policies was that most American officials both at the national and local level had completely misinterpreted British intentions. The British government had abandoned its Indian allies and had ignored the Canadian fur-trade lobby. The fur-trade industry had simply become less important to Great Britain's economic plans.[54]

Although Washington policymakers may have believed that the presence of all these agencies would produce the desired peace and security on the frontier, the contradictions were readily apparent. Indian agents were sent to end British influence, yet they were required by law and presidential directive to license foreign traders when the needs of Indian and American interests so dictated. These traders subsequently provided the competition that made it nearly impossible for the factory system to compete with the private sector. Such enterprises, particularly the American Fur Company, were equally confused. The federal government, on the one hand, encouraged the movement of American capital into the trade; on the other hand, it established factories at Green Bay, Chicago, and Prairie du Chien that competed with individual ventures.

Alongside the inherent inconsistencies of American policy, the American Fur Company also daily encountered many American officials, particularly local Indian agents and military officers, who were veterans of the War of 1812 and found it difficult to allow fur traders, many of whom had actively fought against the United States, to move freely about the Great Lakes region. These officials, moreover, were insensitive, if now Draconian, in handling British and French Canadians, who were long-term residents of the region but were now subject to American rule. Governor Ninian Edwards of the Illinois Territory saw the British traders at Green Bay and Prairie du Chien as agents of the British government and recommended to Secretary of State James Monroe that all of them be forcibly driven from the territory and the communities then be resettled with "good American citizens." William Puthuff, Indian agent at Mackinac referred to the traders as "reptiles" whose only aim was to carry out a British policy that "has one primary motive, one leading principle, one great & never to be forgotten design. It always has been thus actuated & influenced to alienate the Indians from the American government & people, to attach them to the British interests by every & by any of the most insidious means."[55] Understanding and respect for the rights of foreign nationals in American territory was not a high priority among American officials. They were unable to separate fur traders of British and French extraction from the government under which they had previously lived.

Frontier hostilities were exaggerated because national officials never told local Indian agents and military officers of the subtle rationale that distinguished between British and American capital employed in the trade and which equated American Fur Company business objectives with national policy. No one on the frontier would have known of Astor's plan to buy out Canadian interests in the South West Company in 1815. To many frontier officials the American Fur Company was a cover for the South West Company because the majority of its traders either came from Montreal or were British citizens living at Green Bay and Prairie du Chien. Even Lewis Cass, a strong supporter of government policy, must have been slightly bemused by the fact that in 1818 Ramsay Crooks was still a British citizen and needed a special pass to travel freely throughout American territory.

Astor's ties to the South West and North West companies also were well known, and his interest in American policy continually questioned. An article in the *Philadelphia Aurora* of December 1815, for example, urged exclusion of all British traders and suggested that both Gallatin and Astor were connected to these Canadian firms.[56] William Puthuff, Indian agent at Mackinac, referred to Astor and the American Fur Company as "deeply self-interested mercenary enemies." He warned his superior, Lewis Cass, that Astor has assured his British friends that he would get everyone licenses, despite the 1816 law. "I wish to God the President knew this man Astor as well as he is known here," Puthuff exclaimed. "Licenses would not be placed at his discretion to be distributed among British subjects Agents or Pensioners. I hope in God no such license will be granted, . . . and should they succeed incalculable evil will assuredly grow out of the measure."[57]

Although in hindsight one can sympathize with the frustrations of government Indian agents and military officers, they were often wrongheaded in their interpretation of government policy. When they threatened the American Fur Company, Astor quickly responded. Two rather famous incidents, one with Major Puthuff, Indian agent at Mackinac, and the second with Colonel Talbott Chambers at Prairie du Chien, exhibited the New Yorker's none-too-subtle means for protecting his company.

Major Puthuff was extremely supportive of the 1816 license law. In the early summer of 1816, he arrested traders as they brought furs to Mackinac Island from the interior because none had licenses to trade. Of course, there was no way that they could have complied with the law as they were in the interior when the law was passed in April 1816. Puthuff had four boats patrolling the Straits of Mackinac to prevent any traders from slipping through and, in accordance with the law, he promised military personnel and informers 50 percent of the seizure. Puthuff also strictly interpreted the law against foreign traders, thus ignoring government directions to use discretion and to assist American interests. Puthuff complicated matters even further by unilaterally increasing the fees for licenses from $5 to $50. American Fur Company traders had so much difficulty in securing licenses that Ramsay Crooks went to Detroit and complained to Lewis Cass, superintendent of Indian affairs. Cass subsequently ordered Puthuff to issue the necessary licenses. The American Fur Company and Major Puthuff were at virtual war throughout the 1816 and 1817 trade seasons; and, despite repeated warnings from his superiors, especially Governor Cass and the secretary of war, Puthuff continued his private vendetta against British traders.[58]

Finally, Astor decided to strike back. After the 1817 trade season, he asked Ramsay Crooks and Robert Stuart to compile a bill of particulars against Puthuff that he would personally take to Washington. The New York financier spoke with many officials and left a long memorandum for Secretary of War John Calhoun. The latter subsequently ordered Governor Cass to investigate the charges; Cass, in turn, reported that the situation on the island was out of control. Robert Stuart returned to Mackinac Island with considerable unease in the summer of 1818 because Puthuff had learned of the American Fur Company's attack against him. "I expect nothing short of the major's saluting us with the butt end of a pistol," Stuart commented.[59] But Puthuff was no longer a threat, for Calhoun removed him from office in 1818.[60]

Colonel Talbot Chambers, military commander at Prairie du Chien's Fort Crawford, also found himself on the losing end of a confrontation with the American Fur Company. The facts of the case were clear, but the motives of the participants were not. In the fall of 1817, Ramsay Crooks sent two American citizens, Russell Farnham and Daniel Darling, to trade south of Prairie du Chien and north of Saint Louis on both sides of the Mississippi River. Colonel Chambers had stopped the men on the grounds that the licenses they carried from Colonel Puthuff at Mackinac were not valid in the Missouri Territory. He then sent them to Saint Louis to obtain licenses from Governor Clark. When they engaged in trade in violation of Chambers's orders, they were arrested and sent, under guard, to Saint Louis.

Crooks and Astor were furious. If the Chambers decision was left unchallenged, the American Fur Company would have to obtain trading licenses from many different Indian agents, depending on the region. They also believed that Chambers and Governor Clark wished to protect the interests of Saint Louis fur traders from the American Fur Company's competition. There was probably some merit to this argument as Chambers had licensed traders employed by Astor's competitor, David Stone and Company. Chambers, moreover, was not a model government official. He was often criticized for his harsh application of military rule in the Prairie du Chien community. Not only had he conducted public floggings but he had also banished a local trader, Joseph Rolette, in punishment for his British sympathies and confiscated his property without due process.[61]

The American Fur Company again showed how rapidly its power and influence could be applied. Ramsay Crooks and Robert Stuart complained to Lewis Cass and together wrote a strong letter to John Astor, which he then presented to John Calhoun, secretary of war. Crooks and Stuart argued that Colonel Chambers should be taught

> that though he may command at a station, beyond the immediate Controul of the Civil law, he has not the power to abridge the right of any Citizen. . . . It is high time the trade should be relieved from the persecution of such petty tyrants, and the War Department ought to make it a rule, that Officers at frontier posts have *simply,* the right to ascertain whether the trader is licenced, not to constitute themselves judges, of the power Indian Agents possess to grant these permissions.[62]

There was little doubt that Chambers had exceeded his authority, and Calhoun assured Astor that the American government had not approved such actions. Governor William Clark, though, continued to harass American Fur Company traders along the Mississippi River and its tributaries. New complaints from the American Fur Company resulted in immediate and explicit instructions from John Calhoun to Governor Clark to respect all licenses issued to the American Fur Company by Indian agents at Chicago, Mackinac, and Green Bay.[63]

Ramsay Crooks and John Astor, though, wanted to push the case further. Calhoun had admitted that Chambers had acted illegally, thus the American Fur Company sued him for damages resulting from the loss of trade. Crooks never left any doubt about the rationale behind the suit, which was to make an example of Chambers and to deter other government officials from arbitrary application of existing laws and regulations. A gloating Crooks reported to Astor in 1820 that the suit against Chambers had already had a good effect, "Our traders pursue their business now without interruption; indeed I am told the officers generally take some pains to appear uncommonly civil."[64] One might well argue that the American Fur Company abused its power, but Chambers also had violated the law. By 1825, the War Department court-martialled him for alcoholism and repeated abuses of his military office.[65]

By early 1819, the American Fur Company had made an impressive start. Although it did not have a monopoly of the trade, it was the largest and most efficient company. The New Yorker had extraordinary advantages over the competition owing to his years of experience with the Canadians, knowledge of the markets, and formidable influence on policy and government personnel in Washington. He insisted on fair application of existing laws regarding licenses (the intent of which laws he often knew better than frontier officials); and, if necessary, he was not hesitant to use his power and influence.

But why did Astor have such substantial power and influence in Washington during the postwar period? His ability to move easily among the Washington policymakers was partly personal. James Monroe and Henry Clay had borrowed money from him for their personal use. Astor also was Albert Gallatin's financial advisor, maintaining and investing his money during Gallatin's frequent absences from the country, first as a peace commissioner and later as ambassador to France. Astor, thus, corresponded with many politicians and demonstrated no hesitancy in expressing his views on economic policy or in recommending friends for government appointments.[66] Yet there was nothing improper in Astor's conduct nor that of government policymakers, rather his career was a vivid example of the close ties that existed between businessmen and politicians in a developing capitalist economy.

But Astor's main source of power and influence was his continued involvement with postwar government finances. During the war, Astor, Stephen Girard, and David Parish had been major contractors for government loans, and in 1814 they had made an effort to establish a national bank that would have forced specie redemption and allowed for additional government borrowing through the bank itself. Yet the financiers had been unsuccessful because some politicians suspected that the bank advocates were primarily interested in security for their government bonds. By late 1815, however, deteriorating economic conditions reduced the political differences and politicans came to understand the advantages of a uniform currency and the resumption of specie payments. Secretary of the Treasury Alexander Dallas and Congressman John Calhoun prepared a bank bill and guided it through the Congress, and on 10 April 1816, Madison signed the bill creating the second BUS. Although Girard and Astor remained aloof from the political process so as not to incite political opposition to the role of government bondholders, nevertheless, they communicated their support directly to Secretary Dallas and President Madison.[67]

The influence of Astor, Girard, and many other financiers was clearly evident in the structure and organization of the bank. The charter was very similar to the first BUS. Its capital was larger, $35 million, but, as before, the government owned one-fifth of the stock and the BUS served as a government depository. Its main office was located in Philadelphia, with branches established throughout the country. Most important, businessmen were allowed to purchase bank stock by using only ⅕ specie and the rest in government debts. Thus Astor, Girard, and many other capitalists who held government bonds automatically became important in the bank's management. To assure a leadership role for the government's financiers and the Republican administration, the bank was to have twenty-five directors, five of whom were to be appointed by the president and the rest selected by the stockholders. John Astor was among the appointed directors along with William Jones, Stephen Girard, Pierce Butler from Philadelphia, and James Buchanan from Baltimore. Astor was also appointed one of the commissioners for receiving stock subscriptions in New York City.[68]

The conservative financial faction, represented by Astor and Girard, who wished to return the country to specie payment and slow, controlled growth, could not so easily control the BUS's operations. The BUS was a battleground of opposing views on the role of banks in the economy. More liberal businessmen, many of whom were Republican politicans, counseled liberal credit policies that allowed the bank to use its notes and loans to stimulate economic development. Baltimore entrepreneurs such as James Buchanan, James McCullough, and Dennis Smith were the major proponents of this view and formed a well-organized syndicate to purchase bank stock. At the same time, Astor and Girard brought together more conservative Republican and Federalist businessmen.

Astor and Girard subscribed up to the limit of 3,000 shares allowed for an individual. When stock subscriptions were lagging in New York City, Astor considered forming a company of his business friends to subscribe for the remainder. The New Yorker worked closely with other directors such as William Jones, Pierce Butler, and Stephen Girard to assure that the right people bought stock. In July and August 1816, Astor sent personal representatives to Philadelphia to discuss strategy with William Jones and Stephen Girard. When stock subscriptions were nearly $3 million short after the books were closed on 23 July 1816, Astor and Girard immediately formed a syndicate to make up the differences. On 23 August, when the subscription books reopened in Philadelphia, Stephen Girard stepped in and took all the remaining stock, 29,736 shares.

While Astor received an additional 1,000 shares for distribution, most went to Philadelphia and Baltimore capitalists.[69]

Astor and Girard further wished to select the officers and directors of the second BUS. Their most important objectives were to maintain Republican and personal control and to secure Federalist representatives, whose banking views were compatible with their own. Again letters and personal representatives were constantly on the move between New York and Philadelphia so that all agreed on a slate of candidates for board seats. Astor communicated with Boston stockholders and supported James Lloyd, a well-known Federalist there for a seat on the board.

Despite their efforts, Astor and Girard were outsmarted by Baltimore capitalists at the stockholders' election of a board of directors. Astor and Girard had not considered a bank rule that stated no person, no matter how much stock under their control, could vote more than 30 shares. When the Baltimore capitalists subscribed to the stock, however, they had shrewdly listed it in many different names, even though only one person actually controlled the stock. George Williams, a Baltimore merchant, for example, took 1,172 shares of stock but placed it under 1,172 separate names and then voted the proxies for each. Even though Astor and Girard were able to secure some seats on the board for people like Brockholst Livingston of New York City, James Lloyd of Boston, and Thomas Willing of Philadelphia, the Baltimore contingent, with their greater voting leverage, was far more powerful. Consequently, they controlled the appointment of William Jones as president, a choice that Girard strongly opposed and Astor accepted as unavoidable. Jones was already beset by personal financial problems and was known as an inept administrator during his short stints as secretary of the treasury and secretary of the navy.[70]

Astor may have decided to play down his opposition, choosing instead to concentrate on other important issues such as the location and control of branches. The New York branch of the Second BUS, in particular, would be one of the most crucial because New York was the country's commercial capital. Astor was given the responsibility of organizing this branch and was named its president. His duties included renting a private home to house the bank, having vaults constructed, handpicking its directors as well as its cashier, who was responsible for the day-to-day operation. By early January 1817, Astor reported to President Jones that the branch was ready to begin operations.[71]

Astor's stewardship of the New York branch was an active one, and he often clashed with the liberal policies of the bank's president, William Jones. Astor warned others about the needless speculation in the bank's stock that was engineered by the Baltimore faction and urged caution in the issue of notes. He also opposed the central bank's policy of redeeming notes at any branch. The natural paths of commerce, Astor argued, brought notes of seventeen branches, located throughout the United States, to New York City and placed a disproportionate burden on the New York branch. Finally Astor was uneasy when branch banks lent money, not on the basis of goods or commercial transactions, but on the basis of personality. He was particularly upset when U.S. Vice President Daniel Tompkins, then close to bankruptcy, requested a personal loan of $7,500 from the New York branch. He had first visited William Jones in Philadelphia and secured his approval. Astor wrote Jones wondering if "you see nothing inconsistent with your general system of operations." By March 1818, Astor was openly critical of Jones and the national bank's policies and felt that the institution could not sustain specie payments. The New York financier predicted a general financial collapse.[72]

Astor was correct as both the Second BUS and the entire economy were in serious trouble. Although Jones has probably taken an unfair amount of blame for the depression of 1819, he did refuse to control the often illegal stock speculation by Baltimore merchants and failed to monitor carefully the bank's note and loan policies. The unregulated issue of credit by the Second BUS and by the state banks had fueled a tremendous inflation in the postwar period. Foreign markets at first expanded and received American agricultural products but then declined as demands were met. In 1818, the Second BUS tried to establish control. It tightened credit by withdrawing notes from circulation and requiring each branch to redeem its own notes. The entire economy felt the shockwaves as the country careened toward the depression of 1819. Ultimately, there was a congressional investigation that forced Jones's resignation as president. Yet all these events meant little to John Astor who had abruptly withdrawn from nearly all business affairs in 1818.[73]

The precipitating event for this sudden action was the death of his grandson and namesake, John Jacob Bentzon, the child of Adrian Bentzon and Astor's eldest daughter Magdalen. In January 1818, Astor had set out on a business trip to Baltimore, Philadelphia, and Washington with his daughter Eliza and the boy, John

Jacob, who was seven years old. While the elder Astor changed for dinner one evening in Washington, the boy sat outside. There he met an older boy, and the two left for the Tyber Creek with their ice skates. When he discovered the boy had left, Astor followed only to discover that both boys had apparently broken through the ice and drowned. Astor was devastated and felt responsible for the boy's death. By early March 1818, when he wrote to Albert Gallatin describing the tragedy, Astor commented "I am lessening my business & am endeavoring to bring my concerns more to a point. I know I have money enough & perhaps as much as can do good & being no longer ambitious & see no use in doing more than enough." Shortly thereafter he spoke of the "great misfortune which had befallen me . . . and that I assure you it has & does continue to grief me beyond expression."[74]

The financier exhibited signs of depression as he found it increasingly difficult to concentrate on business. At the same time, his health began to fail. For the first time, his correspondence became more philosophical and on occasion reflected his depression. He wrote to his old friend and partner Peter Smith, "Many things must not you & me leave undone & what of it. Have we not done enough already for others, now let us act for ourselves. Let us prepare for a better world and endeavor to be tranquil & happy here, this is what I am daily endeavoring to do & I trust you are not doing less."[75]

By 1819, Astor hit upon a solution to his personal problems— he would journey to Europe where the diversion of constant travel on the Continent might relieve his mind. He left all his business affairs in the hands of his son, William, who only recently had become a partner. Although Astor was clearly withdrawing from business, he, nevertheless, gave detailed instructions to his son concerning strategy and policies in regard to both the fur and China trades. Astor also indicated that he would still control the sale of all furs and teas from his European residence.

But this was a changed John Astor who sailed for Europe in June 1819 in the company of his daughter Eliza and his eldest, but mentally ill son, John Jacob. Interesting, too, was the fact that Astor, who would spend many years in Europe in the next decade, was not accompanied by his wife. Although the sources do not reveal any reason for the separation, Astor was estranged from his wife from 1819 until her death in 1834. For the next two years, he wandered restlessly around Europe, staying several weeks and

months first in Paris with his friend Albert Gallatin, then to
Geneva, Rome, and Naples. He also visited relatives in Germany
before returning again to Paris. Astor admitted that travel and
new scenes were the only cures for his depression. He did not return to the United States until the fall of 1821, only to depart
once again in 1823 for another three years on the Continent.[76]

Unquestionably, then, 1819 was a seminal year in the life of
John Jacob Astor. After developing one of the largest merchant
businesses in the country and cultivating political influence
matched by few other financiers, the New Yorker put everything in
the hands of his son, William, whose business abilities even he
doubted. From this point forward Astor only rarely showed the
daring entrepreneurial energies that marked his earlier career.
Nevertheless, he did not become an absentee manager. With the
passage of time, he regained an interest in business and watched
carefully the business entrusted to his son and to his chief lieuten-
ants, Ramsay Crooks and Robert Stuart. No one who worked for
him or competed with him doubted that John Jacob Astor made
the major decisions regarding policy and strategy in the fur and
China trades. It may be that the strength of Astor's organization
and administration was even more apparent in the 1820s as he
guided the fur and China trades through booms and depressions
until he eventually withdrew from both endeavors in the 1830s.

CHAPTER EIGHT

The Corporate Manager

The American Fur Company, 1819–1834

THIS CHAPTER describes John Astor's management of the American Fur Company from the point of his departure for Europe in 1819 to the sale of the company in 1834. My purpose is not to provide a detailed history of the company—a worthy project that surprisingly no historian has yet attempted—but to correct historical inaccuracies about Astor and the company that prevent a proper appraisal of his business career. Chief among these mistaken notions is that Astor left the decision making within the company to his subordinates, particularly to Ramsay Crooks, partly because of his frequent absences in Europe and partly because of his lack of interest. On the contrary, whether he was in Paris, Geneva, London, or New York, Astor was in frequent contact with his field managers and made all the major policy decisions related to finances, markets, expansion, and contraction.

Historians also have incorrectly analyzed the American Fur Company's corporate organization and strategy. This firm was a stock company in which Astor continually expanded the number of people involved not only to reduce the risk but also to expand its market control. Employing more than seven hundred people, involved in both domestic and foreign markets, and utilizing business strategies such as buyout and mergers to reduce competition,

the American Fur Company operated in a manner similar to railroad and manufacturing corporations of the industrial age. The
American Fur Company, under John Astor's direction, become one
of the first modern corporations in American history.[1]

When John Astor departed for Europe in the spring of 1819,
the American Fur Company had a coherent organizational structure that provided effective management and allowed continued
expansion throughout the Great Lakes region. Ramsay Crooks was
the chief lieutenant. He lived in New York City and worked closely
with Astor's son William Backhouse and with William Roberts, the
chief clerk and bookkeeper. In the spring, Crooks would leave New
York City and journey to Mackinac Island to supervise the exchange of goods for the winter's harvest of furs and visit company
posts throughout the territory. Robert Stuart, on the other hand,
functioned as the primary field manager and lived permanently
on Mackinac Island, interacting daily with traders, Indians, and
government officials. John Astor handled all orders for manufactured goods from his base in Europe and determined which, how
many, and where furs were to be shipped.

Astor had slowly expanded the number of people involved in
the company. He formed an agreement with his chief competition
on Mackinac Island, David Stone and Company, that allowed Stone a
share in the American Fur Company in exchange for Stone's promise to move his operation into the Saint Louis region. In addition,
the New Yorker allowed Michael Dousman, a Mackinac merchant
to purchase shares in the firm. At minimum, American Fur Company partners by 1819 included Ramsay Crooks, Robert Stuart,
Stone and Company, Michael Dousman, and William B. Astor. But
there was no doubt that John Astor alone determined policy.
Crooks continually assured Astor in long and detailed letters that
all instructions as to the shipment of furs were being strictly followed. Crooks bristled at the constant scrutiny; in one letter, he
complained to William Matthews, the company's Montreal agent,
that they dare not purchase a lake steamboat, knowing Astor's reluctance to authorize such expenditures.[2]

Astor's hesitancy was born of his own doubts about whether to
continue in the fur business. His original contracts with Crooks and
Stuart were for three years and were due to expire in 1821. When
he departed for Europe, the company's profitability was still questionable. There was substantial competition from the North West

Company, the American factory system, and independent traders. Also, there had been few returns on outfits from 1816 to 1818, so that no clear pattern was evident. William B. Astor and Ramsay Crooks queried Berthold and Chouteau of Saint Louis as to whether they would be interested in purchasing Astor's share of the American Fur Company. Although John Astor indicated a willingness to entertain offers for his interest in late 1819 and early 1820, he had changed his mind by late 1820.[3]

Astor's decision was at least partly related to his recovery from the depression that followed the death of his grandson—the reason he had abruptly journeyed to Europe. Since his arrival in Europe, he had traveled from Le Havre to Paris to Geneva in September 1819; in November and December, he was in Rome and Naples. In 1820, he again was in Paris with his old friend, Albert Gallatin. During this period, Astor and his daughter, Eliza, visited his hometown of Walldorf, Germany, and stayed several weeks with Astor's brother, John Melchior, in the Moravian village of Neuwied on the Rhine.[4] As his mental outlook brightened, Astor received optimistic reports from Ramsay Crooks concerning their ability to capture a significant share of the fur business in the Great Lakes. Most important, by 1821 Crooks reported that Congress would soon end government factories, a system Astor had considered the major stumbling block to private enterprise in the fur trade.[5]

The federal government had established the factory system in 1796 primarily to protect the Indians from fur traders. The federal government also hoped to directly challenge British fur-trade companies—in the absence of American private enterprise—for the allegiance of the Indians, thus strengthening American control on the frontier. Indeed, Congress expanded the system immediately after the war with new or reestablished factories in the Midwest at Chicago, Green Bay, and Prairie du Chien as well as in the South and West. These factories offered goods in exchange for Indians' furs and so competed directly with British and American traders. Throughout its history, legislation had expanded the system, but always with the belief that eventually the government would abandon the factories either when the British threat no longer existed or when American enterprise was sufficiently well established to challenge the British. Yet as the system evolved, it gained a full-time administrator, the superintendent of the Indian trade, a position that was held after 1816 by Thomas L. McKenney. In the years after the war, McKenney was an articulate and passionate spokesman for the system's humanitarian goals of protecting the Indians from all traders, whether British or American, and of educating and civilizing the Indians for productive lives as agriculturalists.[6]

Yet the factory system faced growing opposition not only from those with justifiable criticisms of its operations but also from private capitalists anxious to secure profits in the fur trade. No one more consistently and effectively opposed the factories than John Astor. Astor was single-minded in his viewpoint: the factories were an arm of the government's diplomatic and Indian policies established in the absence of private enterprise to challenge the British along the border. If American capital was sufficient to prosecute the fur trade, Astor argued, then the government should withdraw. In 1808, when Astor first negotiated with Thomas Jefferson concerning his intention to launch an American company in the Great Lakes and Missouri River region, he believed that the government would eventually end the factory system. After the war, he cautioned Secretary of State Monroe, through the aegis of Albert Gallatin, that American capital would be reluctant to enter the fur trade unless the factory system was abolished.[7]

As the American Fur Company spread its agents over the Midwest, it directly competed with factories at Green Bay, Chicago, and Prairie du Chien. These confrontations often led to open hostility between government factors and the employees of the American Fur Company. Although numerous historians have stressed that Astor personally destroyed the system; the fact is that in the years after 1815 the factories never had a real chance of success.

The government's frontier policy was in striking disorder wherever factories were located: Indian agents licensed traders while factories competed with them for the Indians' furs. The entire factory system was capitalized at $300,000 but competed with the far more extensive capital of the American Fur Company, the Missouri Fur Company, and hundreds of independent traders supplied by smaller operators such as David Stone and Company. Government factors also challenged an existing trading society supported by credit relationships, gift giving, and intermarriage between traders and Indians. Governments factors could not advance credits nor could they provide the same quality of foreign goods as Astor's American Fur Company. On the frontier, the competition between the traders and factors quickly deteriorated, and undoubtedly the American Fur Company occasionally used liquor or lowered the price of their manufactured items to gain the upper hand. The factories simply could not compete, and after the War of 1812, they were a financial failure. Moreover, their *raison d'être*—to neutralize British control of the Indians along the border—was no longer an issue with the emergence of American companies in the fur trade.[8] When their failure became obvious a few years after the war, it was left to Congress to abolish the factory system.

Undoubtedly, Astor's agents and other fur-trading interests were ultimately responsible for the demise of the failing system, but it was proceeded by a long and bitter process that took four years and produced intense lobbying and political mudslinging. In January 1818, Robert Stuart and Ramsay Crooks, struggling to get a toehold against competition in the Old Northwest, urged Astor to use his influence in Washington against the factories because they "have become so numerous, and are of late provided with such extensive means, as threatens in a very few years more, to annihilate private competition, and throw the whole trade into the hands of the Government."[9] Astor and Crooks carried this message to Washington in 1818 and personally spoke with lawmakers. Conscious of the federal government's desire to reduce British control over the Indians, Astor threatened to withdraw from the fur trade unless Congress ended the factory system.

In a rather ironic twist, Astor discovered at this time that John Johnson, the Prairie du Chien factor, was using a building that belonged to the American Fur Company. To indicate his general unhappiness with government factories, Astor ordered Johnson either to pay rent or abandon the building. When Johnson and the government refused, Astor and Crooks took the case to court.[10]

The American Fur Company's lobbying efforts against the factory system had its first major success in spring 1818. Congress temporarily extended the system for another year, but directed Secretary of War Calhoun to report on a system for breaking up the factories. Calhoun solicited opinions from several people, including Thomas L. McKenney, superintendent of the Indian trade, and Lewis Cass, governor of the Michigan Territory. Of course, McKenney defended the system and warned that without government factories the American Fur Company would become "one vast engine of monopoly." Cass, though, was more reasoned and pointed out that, unlike the prewar period, American firms were now quite capable of providing goods for the fur trade. Cass favored an end to the factories, with strict new laws in regard to licenses and the use of liquor in the trade.

Calhoun's subsequent report recommended a compromise plan. He suggested that factories should be abolished east of the Mississippi River, where the Indians, protected by government laws, were prepared to deal with competing private traders. West of the Mississippi River, though, Calhoun wanted a single, chartered company (along the lines of the Hudson's Bay Company) that would be able to compete with the British for the Indians' allegiance. The secretary's plan was not popular; indeed, it caused further controversy. Although fur-trade interests wanted the factories ended, they were not anxious to see strict new laws on licenses or a government monopoly in the Far West. Congress failed to resolve the issues and once again continued the system from March 1819 to March 1820.[11]

With John Astor now in Europe, Ramsay Crooks was the American Fur Company's principal lobbyist during successive sessions of Congress. As each year passed, the debate became more heated. Thomas L. McKenney gathered support from religious and humanitarian groups and regularly used the columns of the *National Intelligencer* to portray the private traders as inhumane scoundrels out to destroy Indian cultures. On occasion, an anonymous pamphleteer (who may well have been Ramsay Crooks) attacked McKenney's motives and his facts. Congress meanwhile continued to argue over the wisdom of abolishing the system. In the spring of 1820, a bill (along the lines of Calhoun's earlier report), that proposed to raise the price of trading licenses and to require a $10,000 bond from each trader, was introduced and passed in the Senate and referred to the House. Crooks fought desperately against the bill, along with another field manager, Samuel Abbott, and Congressman William Woodbridge from Michigan. If licenses became too expensive, Crooks feared that there would be fewer traders. The factories, then, would gain an enormous advantage against the private traders.[12]

Crooks reported to Astor in May 1820 that they had defeated the bill, but he bemoaned the fact that Congress still lacked the nerve to abolish the system. The threat of new laws highly detrimental to private enterprise led Astor in January 1821 to write President Monroe from Paris. Astor reminded Monroe that, as Congress considered new laws for the trade, it must remember

Ramsay Crooks. Courtesy of State Historical Society of Wisconsin.

that the American Fur Company had over $400,000 invested in personnel and supplies for the trade. The message was clear; Monroe should control the political forces that might take precipitous action harmful to private enterprise.[13] Throughout this struggle, neither Crooks nor Astor demonstrated the least concern for the Indians. In their minds, the factory system was simply a government-subsidized business competitor.

Congress again renewed the factory system from 1820 to 1821, but this time Crooks knew that they were close to victory. He thus began careful preparations for the final struggle in late 1821. In November 1821, he told Astor that success was assured but that the cost would be high. "Great efforts will be made by Mr. McKenney, & his friends to save the Factories. His official reports to the

Indian Committee will villify the Traders, and whine over the unfortunate & helpless conditions of the poor Indians." Crooks, however, promised to contest McKenney's every statement "for I cannot, and will not tamely submit to his scurrilous abuse."[14]

Crooks also had plenty of assistance for this final assault from Jedidiah Morse, a respected writer and supporter of humanitarian Indian policies. At the behest of Secretary of War John Calhoun, Morse had undertaken a thorough investigation of the factory system, including visits to several factories in the Old Northwest. His report, issued in 1821, provided ample testimony and statistical evidence to support his unequivocal recommendation that the factory system be "readily" abandoned.

Crooks found another powerful ally in the newly elected Senator from Missouri, Thomas Hart Benton, a dedicated expansionist with close ties to the Saint Louis fur-trade community. Benton previously had represented the American Fur Company in a legal action against Colonel Talbot Chambers, when Chambers had arrested its traders. Benton was joined by John Floyd, congressman from Virginia, who had argued in Congress for the reoccupation of the Columbia River region and the pursuit of the Far West fur trade. Churchill Cambreling, a former business agent of John Astor, was the congressman from New York at this time. This group—Crooks, Floyd, Cambreling, and Benton plus Russell Farnham, another American Fur Company trader and former Astorian, all stayed at Brown's Hotel in Washington, where they talked of the Far West, Astoria, and the need for the government to turn the fur trade over to private enterprise.[15]

The opening of the congressional session in December 1821 marked the beginning of the end for the factory system. Congressman Floyd introduced a curious resolution that linked his favorite project of reoccupation of the Columbia River with the ending of the factory system. While Floyd chaired a committee to investigate these goals, Benton served as a member of the Senate Committee on Indian Affairs, which also began hearings on the system of government trade. By the end of January 1822, Crooks felt confident enough to leave Washington. In May 1822, Congress abolished the factory system and managed to do so without being completely in the service of private fur-trade interests. The bill included new regulations that strengthened the government's hand in eliminating liquor and in licensing traders. The liquor law was especially stringent because it allowed Indian agents and military officers to search the goods and personal belongings of any trader suspected of carrying liquor into the Indian country.[16]

As Congress moved to end the factory system, Astor decided to continue operation of the American Fur Company. He summoned Crooks to Paris in March 1821, and a tentative agreement was reached to extend the life of the company for an additional five years to the summer of 1826. For his services as the principal company manager, Astor increased Crook's share in the company from five to twenty shares. Crooks then negotiated contracts for the other agents, including Robert Stuart, William Matthews, and former Astorian Benjamin Clapp. Crooks carried these new contracts back to the United States and then offered Stuart and Clapp ten days to decide whether to accept the terms. Clapp refused a contract for five shares and a salary of $1,200. Instead, he and George Ehninger, Astor's nephew, opened a mercantile firm in New York City. Robert Stuart was also disgusted, but reluctantly accepted a contract at an annual salary of $1,500 and a small increase in shares from two and one-half to five. The growing disparity in shareholding between Crooks and Stuart reflected Crook's level of responsibility and Astor's concern about Stuart's reputation as a hard-living frontiersman.[17]

In Paris, Crooks and Astor also discussed plans for expansion of the firm into the Saint Louis region. Both men had an intimate knowledge of the trade on both the Mississippi and Missouri rivers. Astor's interest in the region dated from 1803 when he first approached Charles Gratiot and Auguste Chouteau with an offer to supply goods in exchange for furs. He had envisioned Saint Louis as a major depot in the western fur trade in his original plans for Astoria; and even after its failure, Astor had maintained protective agreements with Saint Louis traders such as Berthold and Chouteau to purchase their furs but to refrain from sending his own traders to the region.[18]

Crook's ties to Saint Louis were also substantial. He had traded along the Missouri River in 1807 and 1808 before signing on for the Astoria venture, and now he wanted to reenter this region. In 1818, he stopped in Saint Louis on a journey to visit American Fur Company posts throughout the Old Northwest. He left trade goods with former Astorian, Wilson Price Hunt, for distribution to traders, and he revealed his desire to establish a branch of the American Fur Company there. Astor gave Crooks permission to

move forward after their meeting in Paris in spring 1821, and
Crooks confirmed that arrangement in July, "I still intend going
to St. Louis with a branch of our concern, and will draw from the
outfits usually made at this place [Mackinac]."[19]

His major competition in Saint Louis was Stone, Bostwick and
Company, who, after agreeing to leave Mackinac and the northern
Great Lakes to the American Fur Company, had gone to Saint
Louis. From there, they supplied firms on the Missouri River,
along the Illinois River, and in modern-day Indiana. Basically,
Crooks was an aggressive manager who wanted to confront the
competition directly and wherever possible to expand the firm.[20]
In early 1822, Astor consented to a planned and cautious expan-
sion at Saint Louis, allowing Crooks to establish an American Fur
Company post under Samuel Abbott.[21]

Crooks's desire for open competition was not the strategy that
John Astor wished to follow; and despite historical accounts that
suggest Crooks determined strategy, nothing could be farther from
reality. Astor was far more cautious, but then it was his money
that bankrolled the company. Moreover, Astor had observed the
bitter trade rivalries in Canada since the late eighteenth century,
and he feared the wastefulness of unrestricted competition.
Throughout their long association, Astor constantly lectured
Crooks about the need for economy and caution, and Astor never
let him make the principal strategic decisions. Exasperated at one
point over the Saint Louis expansion, Astor bluntly revealed his
view of Crooks:

> "Mr. Crooks is clever as an Indian trader & for making the general
> arrangement for prosecuting the trade but he is not a merchant &
> I have no hesitation to say to you as I would to him that . . . let
> him have the means [he] will lose ten fortunes before he can gain one.
> The fact is that I have ever since these four years recommended to
> curtail our trade but he has been pushing on & would do so still more
> if he were let alone. His ideas as before as to the trade are fallacious
> & extravagant."[22]

What, then, was Astor's strategy? With the reestablishment
of the American Fur Company in 1817, he had decided to build
an integrated firm employing its own traders and concentrating
on an area from the Old Northwest to the Mississippi River. Any

expansion or contraction would be dictated by markets and fur harvests. Not only was Astor acutely conscious of costs but also he feared the competition of government factories and fur-trade firms in Saint Louis. By 1820, these firms included the Missouri Fur Company under Joshua Pilcher, which had pushed steadily up the Missouri River, and the French Fur Company composed of Bartholomew Berthold and Pierre Chouteau, Jr. In addition, William Ashley and Andrew Henry, who possessed strong political and economic ties in the East, planned to enter the Far West trade. These firms received a large portion of their goods and marketed their furs through Stone, Bostwick and Company. With so many firms already in the field, Astor decided that it was too risky to hire his own traders and supply outfits at Saint Louis. His strategy was to unite with a few of the existing firms and thereby avoid competition. In April 1822, Astor, accompanied by his daughter Eliza, arrived in New York City from his extensive sojourn in Europe to handle the complex business negotiations that such a plan entailed. "The old gentlemen looks well," Crooks commented on meeting with the boss on his arrival, "and Miss Eliza has the wholesome strait [*sic*] appearance of an Englishwoman."[23]

Astor's goal was to enter the trade on the Missouri River at minimal risk, that is, without the burden of hiring more traders and establishing new posts. Like the great Montreal merchants of the eighteenth century, the New Yorker wished to supply other firms with goods and market their fur harvest on commission. Consequently, Ramsay Crooks, now operating under direct orders from Astor, went to Saint Louis during the summer of 1822. He first approached the Missouri Fur Company proposing a partnership in which the American Fur Company would supply the goods and be the exclusive agent for marketing furs. The Missouri Fur Company, already heavily in debt to its supplier, Stone, Bostwick and Company, refused the offer, preferring to remain both small and independent. Next, Astor tried Berthold and Chouteau, who already received their goods from Stone, Bostwick and Co. as well as the American Fur Company. Astor, though, wanted an exclusive agreement; he would be the only broker, an exclusive agent for goods and furs. But Berthold and Chouteau also were reluctant to surrender their autonomy to Astor and proposed instead a limited contract to purchase selected goods and sell some furs on condition that the American Fur Company stay off the Missouri River. This proposal Astor found unacceptable.[24]

Failing to arrive at a form of agency agreement with Saint Louis companies, Astor adopted a new strategy—a merger or horizontal combination with the other major broker in the region, Stone, Bostwick and Company. By 1822, Stone provided bothersome competition along the Mississippi River, was very strong on the Missouri River, and had even pushed into areas around Detroit and Chicago. Resisting all efforts and the advice of Ramsay Crooks and Robert Stuart to unilaterally expand the American Fur Company, Astor informed his managers in November 1822 that he was holding conversations in New York City to unite the two firms.[25] By January 1823, the agreement was complete. Stone, Bostwick and Company was to become a shareholder in the American Fur Company for a term of three and a half years, beginning 1 April 1823, and ending 1 October 1826. The stock split was approximately one-quarter for Stone, Bostwick and Company and three-quarters for the American Fur Company. All business would be conducted under the name of the American Fur Company. This agreement allowed Astor into the Saint Louis and Missouri River trades as a supplier of other companies. He also concluded a supplementary contract with Berthold and Chouteau, now Bernard Pratte and Company. The American Fur Company promised not to send new outfits into the Saint Louis and Missouri River trade in exchange for the right to supply all their goods and to market their furs.[26]

Putting these agreements into operation required a complex series of negotiations with agents and traders. Ramsay Crooks, who had no part in the negotiations, was informed in January 1823 that his contract as agent would run the same term as the Stone agreement and involve a one-fifth share of the profits of Astor's share. Astor, though, indicated that Crooks would be allowed to come in for one-fifth of the whole if he desired. When Robert Stuart learned of the agreement in February 1823, he was informed that David Stone would soon arrive to complete an inventory of all goods at Mackinac in order to determine the concern's total capital. Oliver Bostwick, Stone's partner, was to join Ramsay Crooks and Samuel Abbott at Saint Louis, where the goods and furs of both companies would be inventoried and valued. Eventually the American Fur Company took over the building formerly occupied by Stone and Bostwick.[27]

The union of the two companies also meant substantial personnel changes. Samuel Abbott, for example, was informed that he was Oliver Bostwick's assistant at Saint Louis, where formerly he had headed the American Fur Company's post. The American Fur Company's bookkeeper at Saint Louis was displaced by Bostwick's man, but Crooks promised to find him a place in the store at Mackinac. There were changes in top management and the basic organizational structure as well. William B. Astor was elected company president and assumed responsibility for ordering goods and sending furs to market. Robert Stuart was to remain in charge at Mackinac, although Astor cautioned his longtime friend that profits would be smaller than earlier expectations. David Stone was given control of the Detroit region, and Oliver Bostwick was to manage at Saint Louis. For the next several years, then, the American Fur Company had three departments: Mackinac, or the Northern Department; Detroit; and Saint Louis, or the Western Department. Ramsay Crooks, who appeared confused in spring 1823 about his role, remained overall manager who controlled the three departments and provided coordination with the New York office.

Having set the whole process in motion, John Astor returned to Europe in June 1823. In 1824, he purchased a permanent home, Genthod, which was approximately three miles from Geneva, Switzerland, on the shore of Lake Geneva. From this idyllic setting, he followed the swings in international fur markets and the performance of his principal managers.[28]

The merger produced organizational changes that were part of John Astor's strategy to reduce competition and control costs. The basic idea was to divide supply and markets with the opposition, thus enabling the American Fur Company to compete effectively with the remaining companies in the field. Consequently, the organizational changes were extended from central management into the field so that each department had a defined geographic area for operation. Each trader or outfit within a department was further proscribed in terms of the areas in which they could trade. David Stone's Detroit Department controlled traders south into Indiana and Ohio (formerly these traders reported to Stuart at Mackinac). Oliver Bostwick's Western Department at Saint Louis not only handled arrangements for the supply of Missouri River companies but also sent outfits into southern Illinois. Robert Stuart at Mackinac controlled the largest number of traders. In 1823, Stuart sent major outfits to these carefully defined regions: Fond du Lac (Wisconsin), Lac du Flambeau (Wisconsin), Grand River

*American Fur Company Post, Fond du Lac. Courtesy
of Clarke Historical Library, Central Michigan
University.*

(Michigan), Chicago, upper Mississippi, Follesavoines (northwestern Wisconsin), Ance Quivinan (Keweenaw, Michigan), and Saint Joseph (Michigan).[29]

Dividing these territories was the subject of considerable discussion among field managers. Stone, Crooks, Bostwick, and Stuart fought constantly over jurisdiction; and clerks and principal traders in the field continually impinged on neighboring territories. Part of the reason for the confusion was that neither Stuart nor Crooks were privy to the negotiations and specific details of the contract between Astor and Stone. With Astor in Europe, Crooks and Stuart felt Stone often violated the contract's spirit. Stone, for example, sent traders into the Chicago region, where local traders, John Crafts and John Kinzie, reported to Robert Stuart. Crafts was also a problem as he sent traders down the Illinois River and invaded territories now assigned to the Western Department. Joseph Rolette, who controlled the Upper Mississippi

Outfit from Prairie du Chien, had to limit his territory to avoid conflicts with outfits coming from Saint Louis and from Green Bay. Often, heads of outfits violated the boundaries, bringing quick reprimands from Crooks and William B. Astor.[30] A rather vivid example of these territorial and personnel problems was the following letter from Crooks to the rapacious Joseph Rolette, who engaged in virtual open warfare with other Wisconsin traders:

> I am perfectly aware that the capital placed in your hands by the Company gives you the power to injure all your competitors, if not destroy their business altogether, and I am not ignorant of the advantages which such a result would secure nor have I the smallest doubt that such is your aim. Still however obvious the benefit, moderation toward those who derive their supplies from us, must be the governing principle.[31]

Astor knew that a leaner, more efficient organization would be more likely to control the costs of operation and personnel. With the merger, the American Fur Company instituted money-saving measures such as cutting back the number of traders and reducing the supply of goods for each outfit. An April 1823 memorandum from Astor, for example, instructed all field managers "not to give credit on any goods to any person but such as are deemed to be perfectly safe."[32] Astor's intent was to reduce the credit system whereby the company gave trader's goods over and above what might be normally allocated to an outfit. Astor continually insisted that fur markets were unstable and, in the long run, "furs of this country are going & have been for many years past going out of use."[33]

Astor did not want to sell goods to any traders who were not already on salary agreement with the company. The company would, thereby, avoid risking any additional capital in the interior. In essence, Astor wished to eliminate many traders and force them either to leave the trade or to secure their goods elsewhere. As the word passed from Astor to the field managers and finally to the heads of outfits, its brutal impact was felt keenly. As Robert Stuart translated the order to one clerk, "I have also to beg that you will not allow the men to take much over their wages, and such men as are not desirable in the Country, be sure to bring out, entirely clear of debts, that we may get rid of them. . . . It is only by economy and good management that the trade can be at all sustained." Neither Crooks nor Stuart agreed with Astor's austere and hard-nosed approach. Eventually, Astor reluctantly allowed them some discretionary authority to risk goods with independent traders.[34]

These organizational strategies were, in effect, also competitive strategies. Despite assertions that the American Fur Company routinely mistreated traders and simply desired to crush its opposition (although such practices did occur), the company actually had a far more sophisticated view of its regions and personnel. In some areas, the company committed extensive resources knowing that the fur harvest would be large, or that the head of the outfit or particular traders were unusually skilled, or that little competition existed. Joseph Rolette at Prairie du Chien was given more goods and a large trade area, plus a salary and profit sharing, in recognition of the fact that his outfit regularly returned large profits.[35]

However, at Green Bay, the American Fur Company slowly reduced the size of the outfit and the number of traders. Where formerly the company sent goods to several traders united in a copartnership known as the Green Bay Company, Crooks and Stuart disbanded this partnership in 1824 and thereafter supplied only a few men. Green Bay contained a settled Yankee community with numerous independent traders plying the Indians with goods and liquor. The American Fur Company realized that it would never be able to overtake the competition. Consequently, they tried to create a stalemate in the region, thus ensuring that the competition could not gain so large a profit that it would threaten more profitable trade areas elsewhere. Crooks once described this strategy as follows, "The number of houses we have now in the Indian country are it is true by no means necessary for the collection of all the skins, did not competition exist . . . ; [but] the abandonment of any tract of country or even a solitary fort will secure to our rivals a certain profit there, to annoy us more effectively elsewhere."[36] When one of the Yankee traders at Green Bay offered to sell out to the American Fur Company, Robert Stuart recommended against such an action because "I would rather he should supply some of the people, than we; for whether there is opposition or not, no money is to be made there." The strategy was not lost on the traders. John Lawe, a leader in the community, once commented that "they [the company] don't wish I believe to ruin us for fear an opposition might form and come into the country."[37]

At Chicago, where the American Fur Company had profitable outfits throughout the 1820s, Crooks and Stuart consistently maintained well-paid and loyal local managers. In 1823, John Crafts was offered either a share of profits in the outfit or a salary of $1,000 per year. A trader such as Gurdon Hubbard, who had started with the company at $150 a year as a member of the Illinois Outfit, received a raise to $500 per year and eventually a share of the outfit. Like good managers throughout history, they considered good personnel crucial to success. As Astor once crassly phrased it, "as with skins for good men we can not pay too dear & indifferent *ones are at any price too dear.*"[38]

In essence, this pattern demonstrates that the American Fur Company was never a monopoly anywhere it operated. Other firms and independent traders were always a problem for the American Fur Company. Where rivals posed a major threat, the company tried to buy them out or compete head to head; but, at other sites, the company simply coexisted with the competition knowing its outfit was strong enough to secure a share of the furs. The strength of the competition and the strategy employed varied in each department. In some areas, Astor's firm was perhaps smaller than the total opposition. At Green Bay, for example, as the years passed the company supplied a small percentage of the total capital in the trade and employed only about half the registered traders. At Chicago, on the other hand, the American Fur Company was the dominant firm. In the Western Department, the American Fur Company refrained from employing its own traders and instead formed agreements with other companies such as Bernard Pratte and Company to supply them with goods for a share of their fur harvest.[39] The American Fur Company, then, was a national firm that attempted—and not always successfully—to create a condition of oligopoly in which it was the largest firm with better control of markets and supply than any of its competitors.

But competitors there were, and nowhere did Astor's company receive more challenges than from companies pushing westward along the Missouri River. Astor had agreed to stay off the Missouri River. Instead, he merged with Stone, Bostwick and Company and supplied firms with goods for the trade in return for furs. When Astor returned to Europe in 1823, he was perhaps overconfident of his ability to secure a major share of the Missouri River harvest. Two competitors, William Ashley and Kenneth McKenzie, threatened the American Fur Company's Western Department. Between them, William Ashley was the more serious threat. Ashley, who was then serving as lieutenant governor of Missouri, also had been a successful lead miner and land speculator. In 1821, he joined in a business partnership with Andrew Henry, a longtime Missouri River trader who had crossed the Rocky Mountains nearly a decade earlier. In 1822, they advertised for a force of one hundred men to go up the Missouri River to its source and to remain in the western country for several years. Ashley realized that the great distances and difficulties of travel to the Rocky Mountains precluded an annual return to Saint Louis. In addition, he knew that Missouri River tribes such as the Blackfeet and the Arikara were hostile to the American invasion; thus he did not employ or trade with the Indians.

But Ashley and Henry were unable to avoid the hostile tribes; in 1823, Indian unrest all along the upper Missouri River forced Ashley to innovate once again. He now decided to abandon the Missouri River route and set out overland to the eastern slopes of the Rocky Mountains. He avoided the custom of establishing fur-trade posts; instead, his trappers roamed the mountains and streams through the winter trapping furs more or less as independents. For the first time, in the spring of 1825, they returned to a previously determined spot, Henry's Fork on the Green River. Here they sold or traded furs with Ashley's representatives, who resupplied them with goods.[40] This first rendezvous further revolutionized the fur trade. Ashley had bypassed the Indians as trappers and abandoned fixed posts. Each year the location of the rendezvous changed as traders found plentiful fur supplies along the streams on the eastern and western slopes of the Rocky Mountains.

To the American Fur Company the challenge was quite real. Ashley produced a substantial supply of furs that disrupted the prices (Astor had previously controlled them) in fur markets in New York City and elsewhere. Astor's more traditional mode of trade in the Great Lakes and on the Missouri River, moreover, required larger supplies of goods than Ashley in order to exchange for the Indians' furs, thus adding to the cost and risk of the trade. When Ashley did need goods, he tried, whenever possible, to buy from eastern suppliers other than the American Fur Company, thereby remaining quite independent of Astor's firm.[41]

The American Fur Company also faced direct competition on the Missouri River from Kenneth McKenzie. He headed the Columbia Fur Company, a group of Canadian traders forced south into American territory after the Hudson's Bay Company and the

North West Company merged in 1821. McKenzie had strength along the Missouri River from Council Bluffs west; he also traded along the Upper Mississippi River, thus threatening the lucrative outfits of Joseph Rolette. As early as 1824, William B. Astor assured his new partner, David Stone, "everything that is practical and proper, shall be done to avert the injurious consequences of the threatened opposition [Kenneth McKenzie] along the line of the Mississippi and country adjacent."[42]

Despite the increased competition, the years from 1823 to 1826 were profitable for the American Fur Company. In 1826, John Astor pointed with pride to the company's success in a letter to Albert Gallatin, "Our trade now extends all over the south Shore of Lake Superior & along our northern boundary line to the Lake of the Woods over the whole Arkansas, Missouri, & Mississippi country above St. Louis & also the Illinois & Wabash & Lake Michigan country."[43]

With his merger agreement about to expire and conscious of the new competition, Astor returned to the United States from Europe in the spring of 1826 to undertake yet another company reorganization and expansion in order to control the new competition. Astor's contracts with Crooks and Stuart were due to expire in October 1826, so that the first step was to reemploy his experienced managers. As usual Astor preceded his negotiations with vague threats of retiring from the trade, but these statements were bargaining ploys as he already had decided to expand the firm and to extend the company's life. Both Ramsay Crooks and Robert Stuart visited Astor in New York City in May 1826. Stuart settled first on a new contract. He would now receive a five-year contract with an annual salary of $2,500 and a 15 percent share of the profits. The negotiations with Crooks were more difficult. Although no records exist concerning the final settlement, Crooks must have received a substantial increase over his earlier contract, with a salary in excess of $2,500 and approximately a 30 percent share of the profits.[44]

But there was evidently much more than salary to the discussion in New York City, for Astor now believed it was time to secure a greater share of the Missouri River trade and to make a substantial change in structure and personnel. The relationship with Stone, Bostwick and Company had always been uneasy, and Astor had only extended their contract for one year until October 1827. Bostwick, in particular, proved to be an inept manager. He routinely was late in ordering goods and maintained sloppy accounts—a major trans-gression in Astor's organization. Bostwick's Western Department, moreover, had compiled a $55,000 debt, largely through grant-ing credit to traders. By 1826, Astor wished to dump Stone and Bostwick in favor of Bernard Pratte and Company. The two prin-cipal partners of this firm were Bernard Pratte and Pierre Chou-teau, Jr. In 1825, Crooks had brought the two firms closer when he married Pratte's daughter, Emilie. Astor thus signed a contract in 1826 with Bernard Pratte and Company, and it now became the American Fur Company's Western Department. But Astor wished to avoid open warfare, so he simultaneously bought out Stone and Bostwick; although he urged Crooks to recheck their books, feeling that his former partners were not altogether honest.

Even though part of the American Fur Company, Pratte and Company, were considerably more independent than had been the case with Stone, Bostwick and Company. Their agreement was not a merger but a pooling arrangement. Astor supplied the trade goods at a 5 percent commission and received 7 percent on all money advanced for the trade. He had the exclusive right each year to bid for all Pratte and Company's furs, but they could refuse his offer and opt instead to pay Astor a 2½ percent commission for marketing the furs. The firms agreed to share the profits and losses on trade on the Mississippi River below Prairie du Chien and all along the Missouri River. As relatively independent firms, dual sets of books were maintained with an American Fur Com-pany accountant working alongside Pierre Chouteau, Jr., in Saint Louis. There was an additional bonus for the American Fur Com-pany in these new arrangements. As it was now the most impor-tant source of trade goods in Saint Louis, the American Fur Company also secured a one-half interest in Ashley's outfit for the rendezvous of 1827. For the first time, then, Astor had become a more active participant not only on the Missouri River but also in the Rocky Mountain trade.[45]

But Astor was not yet finished with the reorganization. He had decided that further competition with Kenneth McKenzie's Columbia Fur Company along the upper Missouri River was un-productive. McKenzie was far more active and successful trading with the Blackfeet and Crows and had a large quantity of muskrat pelts and buffalo robes to challenge Astor's market strategies. Crooks came West in 1827 knowing that McKenzie's contracts with suppliers were due to expire. "To secure even Mr. McKenzie would be very desirable for he is certainly the soul of his concern,"

Pierre Chouteau, Jr. Courtesy of Missouri Historical Society.

Crooks wrote to Astor, "but I would prefer taking with, such of his partners as are efficient traders and might continue to annoy us; so as to annihilate their opposition entirely, for it is the only sure mode of improving our affairs."[46]

After considerable bargaining, the two sides reached an agreement. In late July, the Columbia Fur Company merged with the American Fur Company and became its Upper Missouri Outfit. This outfit was restricted to the Missouri River locations, leaving areas to the south and the Mississippi River trade to other American fur company traders. In a brief period, then, John Astor again had reorganized the trade to end competition, to specify trading territories, and to shift personnel in order to acquire greater control of fur supplies and ultimately advantages in the marketplace.[47]

From 1827 until its sale in 1834, the American Fur Company settled into a predictable trade pattern. At the head were the company's central offices in New York City composed of John Jacob and William B. Astor. Despite occasional thoughts of retiring from the trade—a discussion tactic Astor probably used to gain some advantage from his managers and competitors—he managed the trade from his New York office until returning to Europe in 1832. Robert Stuart remained in charge at Mackinac to oversee the

Northern Department and Pierre Chouteau, Jr., controlled the Western Department and the Upper Missouri outfit. As usual, Ramsay Crooks functioned as a general manager. Even at this late date, the company maintained an agent in Montreal, the former Astorian, Gabriel Franchére. The American Fur Company was now larger than any of its competitors, with a capital of perhaps $1 million and a work force in excess of 750 men. Annual supplies sent to the traders were approximately $400,000, and the fur harvest had an average value of $500,000. These figures can only be approximations because complete account books have not survived and because the American Fur Company both imported goods and exported furs from many locations.[48]

The management of this firm required extraordinary flexibility and organization. With Mackinac as the central depot for the collection of furs and disbursement of goods, transportation was reliable as steamboats plied the lakes and rivers. The Erie Canal provided fast and dependable service to New York City. The Northern Department had an increasingly more settled business with traders located at fixed locations, often these were now small towns, like Green Bay or Chicago. The trade depended on the primarily agricultural tribes in the Great Lakes region and upper Mississippi River.

The fur trade in the Western Department was considerably different from the Great Lakes trade. Here expansion was still the motif. Kenneth McKenzie pushed up the Missouri River and established key posts such as Fort Pierre, near the junction of the Teton and Missouri rivers, and Fort Union, at the confluence of the Yellowstone and Missouri rivers. These posts flourished despite the absence of agricultural settlement, and they were the foci of all exchanges between trappers and Indians. To complicate the trade, the Indian tribes here were nomadic and often hostile. The fur harvest on the upper Missouri River included beaver and muskrat, but bison robes were also a major trade item. These furs and robes were then shipped down the Missouri River to the hub at Saint Louis where they were sent to New York City either by way of the Mississippi River to New Orleans or by the Ohio River or Great Lakes.[49]

Until the 1830s, the distance of one thousand miles from the center at Saint Louis to Fort Union on the Yellowstone River was a great hindrance to trade. The Missouri River was difficult to navigate and provided easy passage only for a brief interlude from the spring snowmelt in the mountains to late June or early July. In that time period, flatboats were poled upriver with goods and then quickly returned with furs downriver to Saint Louis. The introduction of the steamboat on the Mississippi River and lower Missouri River saved time and effort in the 1820s. Kenneth McKenzie, though, urged construction of a vessel, the *Yellow Stone,* that could navigate all the way to the upper Missouri River. The Astors agreed to the project, and the *Yellow Stone* undertook its first trip in 1831, making it to Fort Tecumseh; in 1832 it reached Fort Union. Even with these successes, Pierre Chouteau, Jr., of the company's Western Department realized that they needed a boat with even shallower draft and a more powerful engine. Thus he gained authorization from the New York office for its construction. Always conscious of the costs and knowing that business would not justify two vessels, the Astors then ordered the sale of the *Yellow Stone.* Overall, the steamboats revolutionized Far Western trade; they required fewer employees and were faster and more dependable.[50]

Although thousands of miles and often an ocean separated John Astor from traders he had never met, places he had never seen, and events he had only read about, his personal direction was always apparent. Corporate reorganizations were a highly visible demonstration of Astor's executive abilities, but his supply and marketing skills were equally important. Although this side of the fur trade possessed none of the romanticism of the *Yellow Stone's* first voyage or the annual gathering of traders on Mackinac Island, it was the "nuts and bolts" of the business and a primary reason for the American Fur Company's success.

From his earliest days as a fur broker, Astor's goal was to buy and sell furs in markets where he had an advantage. He never depended solely on the furs gathered by his own firm. He had purchase relationships throughout the decades with independents such as William Ashley of Saint Louis; Menard and Valle in Illinois; Gillespies, Moffatt, Finlay and Company in London; and Gillespies, Moffatt and Company in Montreal. On occasion, Stuart, Crooks, and Chouteau purchased furs outright from small traders and merchants at Mackinac or Saint Louis. Although never outfitting traders for the southwest, Crooks and Chouteau on occasion purchased furs in Saint Louis. Through his Montreal and London connections, Astor also bought beaver, muskrat, and otter furs from the Hudson's Bay Company.[51]

The year's fur harvest usually was shipped from Mackinac and Saint Louis to the company's warehouses in New York City, although Astor also sent furs directly from New Orleans to Europe or from Mackinac to Montreal. Furs were packed by type—bison robes, muskrat, deer, and beaver. But within these packs good and bad furs would be mixed so that eventual buyers would be obliged to accept a mixed lot. Often packs would be further designated by the area from which they came—the Illinois River, upper Missouri River, and Lake Superior. At each stage of shipment, Astor demanded a precise count of the number of packs and animal pelts. Thus Stuart or Chouteau would send an inventory that indicated the precise number of beaver, bear, fisher, marten and otter skins. In New York, Astor's clerks reexamined all packs and compared them to the inventories. If the figures did not correlate, the clerks would check to see if the furs had been stolen or mislaid in shipment. Having received these detailed inventories, Astor checked the production of each department and outfit, and often sent letters expressing his satisfaction or displeasure with the harvest. Depending on orders and market conditions, some furs would be repacked in New York for shipment elsewhere.[52]

The purpose of Astor's worldwide fur purchases was to control prices as best he could in the markets. His distinguishing business characteristic, over most competitors, was that he sold in international markets and was never forced to flood a particular market with specific furs from one year to the next. From his earliest days in the fur trade, Astor had developed a personal knowledge of these markets unsurpassed in the industry. His long contact with the China trade, knowledge of the Russian trade, and extensive travels in France, Germany, and England informed his decision making at every juncture. On occasion, particularly in the 1820s, when he spent so much time in Europe, he attended the great auctions in London, where American furs were auctioned off against those of the Hudson's Bay Company; or he traveled to various fairs such as those at Leipzig and Hamburg.

Surviving American Fur Company accounts from the years 1818 to 1829, indicate that the distribution of fur shipments was approximately 48 percent to London, 25 percent to Hamburg, and 10 percent to Canton. The remaining furs were sent to locations such as Marseille, Smyrna, and Le Havre. Equally important to the American Fur Company were North American markets. Here furs were sold either directly to hatters or through retail and wholesale agents in Boston, Philadelphia, Baltimore, Albany, and Montreal.[53]

Auctions in New York City, though, were among the most important devices for initial sale. Often these were conducted at the company's warehouse, although many sales were conducted by the city's auction houses. Sales were not held every year as their timing was determined by word from Astor or one of his agents about prices in Europe. Usually, buyers would bid on lots; and if the bidding threatened to dip below what Astor called a "fair" price, he would purchase his own furs to stabilize the price. Reporting on an auction to Bernard Pratte and Company in 1834, he commented, "as usual, I bid them up to such prices as I deemed a fair one to sell at. To keep them up I had many of them struck off to me . . . and I will keep them . . . until our September sale."[54]

These auctions attracted many buyers and involved thousands of dollars and skins. At a large fur auction in America in 1824, the American Fur Company sold 12,500 pounds of beaver, 120,000 muskrat skins, 72,000 raccoon, 60,000 hare and nutria, and 10,000 buffalo skins. A sale in 1826 increased those totals substantially, and in 1827, Astor estimated that he had sold 200,000 muskrat pelts at public auction and 550,000 at a private sale in one week.

Many furs were not sold at New York auctions because Astor projected that they would bring higher prices in Montreal, London, Hamburg, or Saint Petersburg. The financier studied the yearly prices and sales in various world markets, estimated the supply of furs in each market, and then predicted, with remarkable accuracy, that deer would sell higher in Hamburg but that bear and muskrat would bring better prices in Saint Petersburg, Philadelphia, or Canton. When markets were glutted, Astor simply withdrew particular pelts from the market for a year or two, stored them in New York City, Paris, or Canton, and then released them for sale when demand renewed and prices rose. Although few reliable statistics have survived concerning the American Fur Company's yearly sales volume, there are occasional indications. From 1818 to 1823, for example, furs valued at $842,419 were sold in New York City, another $500,000 exported to Europe, and $250,000 sent to markets in Canton and elsewhere. Since Astor typically received a 2½ percent commission on fur sales from both the American Fur Company and independents, his great care in selecting markets was obviously a major ingredient in the company's profitability.[55]

The determination of the sale price and the best market location were based both on an analysis of previous experiences as well as on a projection of future trends. Astor monitored market sales one year and then predicted the demand for deer, muskrat, or raccoon the next. In 1830, for example, he reported to Robert Stuart that bear skins sold well in London because of the French demand for military uniforms but that raccoons were lower than expected. On the basis of such information, interior traders were directed to collect only certain pelts the following year. Reasonably precise prices were established to guide Crooks, Stuart, and Chouteau in the purchase of pelts. In a letter to Crooks in 1830, Astor revealed his business philosophy, "It is our business to give them [traders] a fair price taking care however not to expose us to any heavy loss."[56]

Field managers such as Robert Stuart or Pierre Chouteau did not have much latitude once Astor established the prices that would be allowed for particular furs. In 1825, William B. Astor, sent Robert Stuart a long list of prices that could be paid for various furs with the following note attached, "At foot [of letter] you have note of the prices I think you ought to pay next season, predicated upon the present state of the market; in conjunction with well-founded prospects; and should any material alteration occur, you will be duly informed."[57] Astor's understanding of the laws of supply and demand was apparent in the following cautionary note to Robert Stuart after a particularly good fur sale in New York City, "If skins take any advances there will be buyers and traders and we must then be careful that we do not exceed the bounds of prudence, for whenever trade is good, there becomes danger of its being overdone and the article which is thriving beyond its true value falls and gives heavy losses. No doubt in a year or two this will be the case with muskrat skins and I hope all our people will be prudent."[58]

Market forecasts were extraordinarily important in radically changing Astor's business in the mid-1820s, at which time he decided to withdraw from the China trade. Since the loss of Astoria and the connection with the Russians, Astor no longer had easy access to furs along the Northwest Coast. He had continued the trade in the Pacific region by having ships gather furs at many stops along the Northwest Coast in addition to sandalwood from the Hawaiian Islands. Gradually, however, the supply of sandalwood was exhausted and the market for furs in Canton declined. The China trade always had depended on the exchange of furs and sandalwood for teas and silks, and the decline of these markets necessitated a change of direction.

Trade statistics support the wisdom of Astor's decision to pull out. The high point of the fur trade in Canton was in 1811 when Americans imported 367,215 furs; but after the War of 1812 such numbers were never equaled again, and the market fluctuated wildly from a low in 1820–1821 of 38,055 to a high of 160,009 in 1821–1822; and then dropped to 79,932 in 1822–1823. The secretary of the treasury reported that the dollar value of the fur trade with Canton from 1821 to 1826 was equally volatile: 1821, $142,399; 1822, $78,158; 1823, $100,910; 1824, $89,839; 1825, $33,130; and 1826, $45,110.[59]

Broader changes across the American economy also influenced Astor's decision. In general, both in trade with Europe and China, Astor had less need to own ships and to incur the capital expense and risk because specialized shipping lines had multiplied in the years after the war. The Blackball Line, established in 1818 to run on a schedule between New York City and Liverpool, was the first, but within a decade additional shipping lines crisscrossed the ocean to Le Havre, Hamburg, and London. Government trade policy, moreover, which had encouraged the China trade before the War of 1812, now protected the emerging American textile manufactures and placed high tariffs on the import of silk and nankeens. Astor's American competition also became more organized and specialized. Resident agents in Canton were replaced by large commercial houses such as Perkins and Company of Boston and Thomas H. Smith of New York. In the early 1820s, the rampant speculation of American firms in teas and the difficulty of making a profit especially disturbed Astor. In 1826, the speculation produced a tremendous glut in the American market and brought a precipitous decline in price. Several New York and Philadelphia China traders were ruined; but, by this time, Astor has already extricated himself from the China trade.[60]

Astor's withdrawal from shipping and from concentration on the Canton market was gradual, but largely completed by 1825. As early as 1820 his agent in Canton, Nicholas Ogden, reported great difficulty in returning a profit, and in 1823 William Astor reported that his father had decided to withdraw. In 1824, Benjamin Clapp was sent to Canton to close up the business after the death of Ogden. In the 1823–1824 season, four Astor vessels called at Canton; one in 1824–1825; two in 1825–1826; and none in 1826–1827. By this date, Astor has sold all his ships.

From the mid-1820s until his sale of the American Fur Company in 1834, though, the financier continued to ship furs to Canton and receive teas in return; but he now had the luxury of being able to utilize this market only when he judged that the prices would be satisfactory. For example, in the early 1830s, the Astors sent casks of otter and beaver to Canton through James P. Sturgis and Company of Boston. They also established a credit line of $25,000 with another Canton trader, Charles Talbot.[61] Astor's trade had finally come full circle. He started in the China trade in the 1790s by shipping furs through other merchants, built his own vessels when it seemed the markets and necessity demanded, and then withdrew as markets declined and the risks were no longer justified. It may be that Astor's strongest asset as a businessman was the ability to understand the economic changes of his era and to adapt his strategies, markets, and products to fit new circumstances.

In addition to his control over the supply and marketing of furs, Astor also monitored the cost and quality of trade goods supplied to the Northern and Western departments and to individual outfits and traders within the departments. The American Fur Company's central office in New York City had primary responsibility for purchasing goods such as heavy woolen blankets, silver earbobs and brooches, traders' clothes, animal traps, mirrors, tobacco, and yarn. By the late 1820s, a year's supply of goods for the Northern and Western departments totaled approximately $65,000 each. The purchase of these items entailed substantial effort: William B. Astor and Ramsay Crooks had to contact numerous suppliers in order to secure the most competitive prices. Often traders' clothes and silverwork were purchased in Montreal; mirrors and beads came from Europe; woolen blankets were imported from England; and tobacco was purchased from wholesalers in Ohio and Kentucky.

By the early 1820s, the American Fur Company had instituted a careful process for determining the type and quantity of yearly purchases. In early fall, each clerk heading an outfit submitted his request for goods to department heads, like Robert Stuart and Pierre Chouteau. Based on the previous year's trade and existing inventories, department heads immediately sent the orders to the American Fur Company's central office in New York City, where inventories and account books were again checked. Ramsay Crooks and William B. Astor eventually chose the appropriate suppliers in Canada and England and insisted that all goods must reach New York City no later than March and arrive at Mackinac and Saint Louis by early June. Timing was crucial. At Mackinac and Saint Louis, department heads assembled outfits before traders started for the interior in late June or early July. But the ideal was hard to achieve. American Fur Company letterbooks were filled with complaints from department heads and traders when supplies were late, damaged, or destroyed in transit. In July 1823, Robert Stuart fumed when he still had not received trade goods, predicting that the delays would affect the profitability of the entire season. In 1832, William Astor assured Pierre Chouteau, Jr., that the company would try to replace his supplies lost in a steamboat accident.[62]

For John Astor and Ramsay Crooks, securing quality goods at reasonable cost was an essential element in a highly competitive business. In 1822, Astor ordered Crooks and Stuart to send him samples of their current stock so he could contact European suppliers in hopes of reducing costs by 5 percent. In 1823, Crooks considered making annual trips to England to purchase blankets and other woolen goods to avoid the high prices and commission charges of English wholesalers.

Despite charges by some historians that the American Fur Company routinely overcharged traders and Indians for poor quality goods, in fact, business and economic conditions were responsible for what appeared as exorbitant prices. In the mid-1820s, Astor usually supplied goods at cost to departments and outfits or charged a commission or no more than 5 percent. Yet his price also included a standard markup for transportation. Seventy-five percent over cost was a standard markup for goods purchased in England and transported to Mackinac or Saint Louis, whereas the figure was set at 25 percent for goods purchased in the United States. Like other products in the early nineteenth century, furs and goods moved great distances along a slow and unintegrated transportation system that left profit margins very small. Thus a blanket purchased for $3.65 in England might legitimately sell for $8 or $9 in the interior. Not only was ocean travel expensive but goods, particularly blankets, faced increasingly higher tariffs in the nineteenth century as Congress sought to protect home manufacturers.[63]

In evaluating the American Fur Company's business practices, it is important to recognize that the Indians were knowledgeable consumers; in some areas they were able to bargain between American traders and the Hudson's Bay Company. On several occasions, the American Fur Company marketed cheaper American blankets to cut costs, but such efforts failed because the Indians and traders demanded the higher-quality English blankets. I am not arguing that Astor treated the Indians fairly. In the longer view, the fur trade, over several hundred years, was a prime element in the destruction of Indian cultures. But, in the American fur trade, the Indians were generally very hard bargainers in an economic world of few alternatives. Astor set prices and offered goods that reflected the demands and costs of the fur industry. Lewis Cass and William Clark, both regional superintendents of Indian Affairs, perhaps phrased it best in reporting to a congressional committee investigating the economic state of the fur trade:

> Contrary to the opinion generally entertained, they [the Indians] are good judges of the articles which are offered to them. The trade is not that system of fraud which many suppose. The competition is generally sufficient to reduce the profits to very reasonable amount, and the Indian easily knows the value of the furs in his possession; he knows also the quality of the goods offered to him, and experience has taught him which are best adapted to his wants.[64]

Like his counterparts in the industrial world later in the century and unlike merchants of the early eighteenth century, Astor maintained increasingly complex accounts that aided in controlling costs and producing acceptable profit margins. Clerks, who headed outfits, reported to department heads the precise figures on the quantity of goods advanced, wages of traders and interpreters, number and cost of furs, and the cost of transportation. These figures were reported to the New York office, where journals of the daily accounts and ledgers bringing together separate accounts, lists of outstanding inventories, and debts provided at a glance the status of each outfit, trader, and department on an annual basis. Astor also kept separate accounts that detailed market prices received for the sale of furs and the profit and loss statement for each year. All these accounts carried over for many years as it might take several years for furs or China goods to reach the retail marketplace. Separate accounts were maintained for each ship and its cargo involved in the China and European trade. Astor, though, could easily look across all the separate accounts and estimate each year costs, debts, inventories, and sales.[65]

Astor used the information gleaned from the account books to reduce costs and to increase profits. This ability to act on information contained in the account books was a significant advance over standard business practices in the eighteenth century and a hallmark of later industrial giants. Astor's correspondence with his department managers was filled with specific orders on cost control measures. These letters often produced fairly hostile reactions on the part of managers, who rarely concerned themselves with the mundane statistical analysis of the trade. Based on fur prices a year earlier, for example, Astor ordered a 10 percent reduction in goods purchased for 1826. This directive brought a harsh reply from Robert Stuart, who believed that more goods produced more profits. But Stuart also knew who was boss, "You will, of course, act your pleasure. I have now repeatedly urged my views . . . and will no longer importune you." In 1823, John Astor's check of Stuart's expenses resulted in the following note, "I have been vexed and I am not pleased with the expense the company has been put to in buildings." In 1824 and 1825 the volume of trade goods sent to posts at Mackinac and Saint Louis was reduced because Astor's check of the account books revealed that their inventories, $37,818 and $59,603, respectively, were excessive, resulting in carryover debts from one year to the next.[66]

By the mid-1820s, Astor also restricted the amount of goods that could be advanced on credit to either traders or Indians. "The more I see of it the more I am convinced that we have ever imported too many goods & been induced to give them too freely to people who are not able to pay for them less so when skins and furs are so very cheap."[67] When he determined that a trader's debt was too large, Astor moved quickly to correct the situation. Oliver Bostwick was removed from the Saint Louis department for compiling excessive debts. Astor ordered Robert Stuart in 1828 to personally visit Joseph Rolette, head of the company's Upper Mississippi Outfit, when the accounts revealed that he was in debt for $8,000. The traders at Green Bay eventually used their land claims and titles to settle a large debt to the American Fur Company.[68] Although the trade in the interior operated at times on rules of barter and the cultural traditions of gift giving, the bottom line was in the account books; and they were monitored continually by John Astor.

Despite his success in the fur industry, John Astor decided to sell the American Fur Company in 1834. This decision emanated from a series of complex political and economic factors. The fur industry itself underwent substantial changes owing to the Industrial Revolution. Cheap, machine-produced clothing cut into the markets formerly dominated by furs. As early as 1823, Astor foresaw the change, "These articles [furs] seem really to get out of use. The people on this continent are everywhere & everyday getting poorer, & as many articles of manufacture which are now very low, can be used in place of deer skins & furs, they receive of course the preference." In 1832, Astor reported from Paris that beaver, which had been used extensively in hat manufacture, would no longer yield large sales, "I very much fear Beaver will not sell well very soon unless very fine, it appears that they make hats of silk in place of Beaver."[69]

Throughout the 1820s, the American Fur Company as well as other American fur-trade companies had increasing difficulty competing in world markets. Two congressional investigations of the American fur trade, in 1828 and in 1832, reached a similar conclusion, "The fur trade of the United States is in a state of great depression, and carried on at a great loss in lives and property, and with uncertain and precarious profit."[70] Both committees agreed with numerous letters they received from Astor and others about the causes for the decline. The Industrial Revolution was partly responsible as Congress, seeking to protect home manufactures, established higher duties on imported textiles, especially blankets. Astor depended on British textiles for the fur trade and had to compete with Canadian traders who paid no duties. Equally discriminatory was the fact that foreign countries could export furs to the United States without tariffs. From 1822 to 1827, annual foreign shipments were valued at approximately $300,000. Americans such as Astor, though, were obliged to pay duties to ship into Europe and were totally excluded from the Russian markets. Thus the Hudson's Bay Company was able to undersell the American Fur Company both in Europe and in the United States. Despite his efforts to lobby Congress, Astor expected little help, once remarking to Robert Stuart, "We must never expect anything from the government or congress. It is time and money lost to attend to them."[71]

Perhaps more important than changing fashion and unfriendly markets, Astor's decision to quit the trade was linked to America's westward expansion, which altered the nature of fur production. In the Great Lakes region, Indian tribes had ceded their lands to the federal government and agreed to live on reservations or to move west of the Mississippi River. The Indians' departure meant the loss of a "cheap" labor supply and an increase in the cost of gathering furs. In addition, the growing farm and city populations furthered altered the numbers and habitats of animals. In the early 1830s, the American Fur Company continued to make profits, but it was now a money trade. The company sold goods for cash to white settlers and to Indians at treaty cessions. The American Fur Company also made large claims against the Indians for losses incurred in the fur trade, and these money claims became a standard clause in treaties negotiated with the Indians. In 1833 at Chicago, for example, the American Fur Company's claim was $17,000. As cities such as Chicago, Milwaukee, and Green Bay developed commercial economies in the 1830s, fur trading became largely a part-time occupation of farmers and city residents. The era of the specialized fur trade that had dominated the frontier economy was over in the Great lakes.[72]

In the Far West, rapid expansion and competition were the American Fur Company's chief problems. The company's reorganization in 1827–1828, which brought it into close alliance with Bernard Pratte and Company in Saint Louis and Kenneth McKenzie as head of the Upper Missouri Outfit, successfully strengthened control of the fur harvest on the Missouri River. However, the company was unable to monopolize the fur supply coming into Saint Louis. William Ashley's rendezvous system in the Rocky Mountains was so successful that he was able to sell his interest to others in 1826 and specialize in the supply of traders. By 1830, Astor faced a strong competitor in the Rocky Mountain Fur Company. In addition, many independent traders and suppliers, including Captain Benjamin Bonneville, backed by New York capitalists, and Nathaniel Wyeth from New England, participated in the annual rendezvous.

From this activity, both on the Missouri River and in the mountains, furs flooded markets and depressed prices. Although the number of furs reaching market increased for a time, traders had to push deeper into the mountains and farther into the Great Plains as they depleted the supply of beaver and buffalo. During a congressional investigation of the fur trade in 1831–1832, Governor Lewis Cass clearly explained the dilemma of the western fur trade, "In a general view the fur trade is declining. This result is . . . owing to the rapid diminution of the animals which supply the most valuable furs. Increased activity and enterprize, however, by pushing adventurers into more remote regions, and opening new districts . . . will . . . counteract this diminution—at a greater expense indeed, but still, for a time, with considerable effect."[73]

Not surprisingly, these conditions forced Astor into more direct competition in the early 1830s; a situation he had always sought to avoid. Kenneth McKenzie, head of the American Fur Company's Upper Missouri Outfit, and Bernard Pratte and Company had not been ignorant of the valuable fur harvest in the Rocky Mountains and for several years had sent outfits to the rendezvous. In the early 1830s, the American Furs Company decided to challenge its competition directly and sent large outfits to the Rocky Mountains under the direction of Lucien Fontenelle, Henry Vanderburgh, and Andrew Dripps. Simultaneously Robert Campbell and William Sublette from Saint Louis, with the backing of William Ashley who was now in Congress, chose to invade the upper Missouri River territories of the American Fur Company. For a short period, the competition was intense both in the mountains and along the Missouri River. It was not unusual for competing trading posts to be located in the same region and for traders, such as McKenzie, to offer high prices for furs merely to drive the competition from the field. Substantial violence, both by the Indians and by competing traders, characterized this period. Stories of this violence drifted eastward, where Congress and the public developed a critical view of traders and the American Fur Company.[74]

At this same time, Congress was examining the laws affecting the Indian trade, particularly those laws relating to liquor. The federal government's desire to completely ban liquor from the Indian trade resulted from its inability to enforce existing policies. The basic legislation, dating from 1802, gave the president the power to prevent the use of alcohol among Indian tribes. This legislation was strengthened in 1822 when Congress authorized Indian agents to search the goods of traders headed for the Indian country and to confiscate liquor. In 1824, Congress required traders to locate at a specific post, determined by the Indian agent, thus enabling government officials to regulate trading practices. The American Fur Company initially supported efforts to control the liquor traffic because its competitors—independents and Canadian traders—were the major offenders. When government initiatives failed, the company itself resorted to the use of liquor in order to meet the competition. Ramsay Crooks early stated the company's rationale, "If the Government permit the sale of this pernicious liquid we can have no hesitation in availing ourselves of the privilege, though we are convinced its total prohibition would benefit both the country at large and the natives who are its victims."[75]

Throughout the 1820s, the American Fur Company was involved in numerous controversies with frontier officials over the vagueness and inconsistency of federal laws. These incidents led to a somewhat unfair portrait of the company as more venal than any of its competitors. In fact, the issue was extraordinarily complex. Federal legislation outlawed liquor only in Indian country. But what was Indian country and who was to determine the boundaries? In one famous case, an American Fur Company trader, William Wallace, was stopped by an Indian agent for transporting liquor into Indian country and was convicted by a local jury. The judgment was reversed after Astor demonstrated to the Supreme Court that Wallace was not in Indian country.

Federal laws also proved impossible to enforce because traders were entitled to liquor and considered their daily ration an inalienable right. Consequently the American Fur Company's shipping ledgers revealed that every year large shipments of liquor made their way, quite legally, to Mackinac and Saint Louis. Frontier officials such as Colonel Josiah Snelling and Indian agent Lawrence Taliaferro at Fort Snelling on the Mississippi River continually attacked the company because its traders carried liquor and used it openly in towns such as Prairie du Chien and Green Bay.[76] Astor defended his traders from government attacks, but he knew that abuses occurred and often wrote warning notes to his agents. "I presume it not necessary to caution you," he wrote to Oliver Bostwick in 1826, "against sending or permitting any liquors to go direct or indirect with any outfits made by you." But Astor and his agents never gave in on the notion that traders were entitled to liquor and that the company could sell it everywhere but in Indian country. Appearing before Congress in 1826, Robert Stuart frankly admitted that the company imported massive amounts of alcohol to Mackinac for the use of the traders. In 1830, Astor even encouraged Robert Stuart to increase the sale of liquor in the company's retail store at Mackinac.[77]

Astor was particularly worried over Congress's proposed legislation in 1832 because of its effects on the company's ability to compete with the Hudson's Bay Company along the northern border. Since the 1820s, the American Fur Company had government permission to use liquor in this region in order to break the Indians' attachment to the British. Sensing the American government's changing attitudes, Astor opened discussion with the Hudson's Bay Company to mutually exclude all liquor from the trade. John Astor and George Simpson of the Hudson's Bay Company met in New York City and agreed in principle that liquor use should be curtailed, but a binding agreement never ensued.[78]

When congressional reform threatened an absolute ban on the transportation of any liquor into the Indian country, Astor launched a major effort to defeat it. He wrote Governor Cass and Congressman William Ashley, his occasional competitor in the trade. Ashley, who well knew the importance of liquor, refused to help, either out of personal conviction or because, as Astor's competitor, he sensed an advantage. Astor was unable to sway Congress, and the new law was unequivocal in its intent, "No ardent spirits shall be hereafter introduced under any pretence, into the Indian country." William P. Astor, Pierre Chouteau, Jr., and others attempted to secure an amendment to the bill to provide for exceptions in competition with the Hudson's Bay Company, but all such efforts were futile.[79]

By the summer of 1832, then, Astor had suffered numerous setbacks. Not only was he disappointed concerning the new legislation but fur trade markets were everywhere depressed, particularly owing to the competition of the Hudson's Bay Company. In addition, Astor's own health was poor. As he left the United States for Paris in June 1832, Astor mentioned his desire to retire from the trade. It was an opportune moment. One year hence, the American Fur Company's charter in the state of New York would expire, and his arrangements with Bernard Pratte and Company would also end in 1834.[80] Between 1832 and 1834, two incidents placed the American Fur Company under heavier public scrutiny and probably ended any doubts in the New Yorker's mind about retiring from the trade.

Before receiving word of the passage of the new liquor law, Indian Superintendent William Clark gave Pierre Chouteau, Jr., the usual permission to carry a large quantity of liquor (one thousand gallons) into the Indian country. By the time the shipment reached Fort Leavenworth, the new law was in place and zealous frontier officials immediately confiscated the liquor and reported the company's transgression. The traders were furious; one in particular, J. P. Cabanné, was determined that if the American Fur

Company could not use liquor, neither would the competition. Cabanné then sent an armed contingent against an independent trader, P. N. Leclerc, confiscating his liquor in the name of the government. When reports of the incident reached the East, both the public and Commissioner of Indian Affairs Elbert Herring were convinced that the American Fur Company considered itself above the law.

Kenneth McKenzie on the upper Missouri River now further exacerbated public hostility toward the American Fur Company. He felt that he had found a way to avoid the liquor law and have sufficient liquor in the interior to challenge the competition. The law only forbad transporting liquor into the Indian country, McKenzie reasoned, but it said nothing about setting up a still. About the same time, the public also became aware of a plan (first devised by Kenneth McKenzie) to make medals with the likeness of John Astor that were to be used in the Indian trade. William B. Astor and apparently some government officials, exercising lamentable judgment, assented to the idea, but the effect was to arouse widespread indignation. Astor's American Fur Company had overstepped its bounds. Presidents and kings might appear on medals, not the president of a fur company.[81]

In the middle of these political and economic difficulties, John Astor sent word from Paris in March 1833 that he was ready to sell. Undoubtedly, Astor's decision was affected by the changing fur trade and the disturbing news of runaway events on the Missouri River and in Washington. Crooks did not at first believe the news commenting, "He may or he may not come, and though he has arrived near a termination of his endless association, the business seems to him like an *only* child which he cannot muster courage to part with."[82]

Despite his misgivings about Astor's intent, Crooks made immediate plans to replace Astor in the American Fur Company. He first contacted capitalists and concerns, especially Bernard Pratte and Company, who might be willing jointly to purchase Astor's stock interest. Crooks had no difficulty finding partners, although Chouteau preferred independence. Nevertheless, Chouteau and Crooks agreed that they had to resolve existing problems in Washington and on the Missouri River before any purchase of the company could be contemplated. Consequently, they first banished the unpredictable McKenzie from the upper Missouri River. Next they assured Commissioner of Indian Affairs Elbert Herring that the company was moving to control company traders. Finally, they approached William Sublette and James Campbell—the principal competition on the Missouri River and in the mountains—about the possibility of cooperation rather than competition. Ramsay Crooks and Pierre Chouteau, Jr., had learned their lessons well from John Astor—avoid destructive competition at all costs. At a meeting in New York City in January 1834, the American Fur Company bought out the interests of Sublette and Campbell in the upper Missouri River country and agreed to stay out of the mountains for one year.[83]

With political and competitive problems controlled, Crooks and Chouteau were prepared to talk with John Astor, who returned from Europe in April 1834. Apparently, negotiations went smoothly because, in his extreme depression, he was more determined than ever to pull out. Most troubling were the deaths of several relatives and that of his wife a week before he returned. His state of mind was reflected in a note to his old friend and employee, Wilson Price Hunt, in May 1834, "I hope . . . you are well. . . . As to me, while absent, I lost my wife, brother, daughter, sister, grandchildren & many friends & I expect to follow very soon. I often wish you were near me. I should find much in your society which I am in need of being no longer disposed to business or rather not able to attend to it, you know that I gave up a good part, & am about to dispose of the rest." However, Crooks was less moved and commented, "Son Cher fils is as amiable as ever, and always very poor when anybody wants money and he does not wish to part with it."[84]

Although Astor was depressed and ill, neither was a prime cause for his action. He had made a calculated business decision based on his knowledge of the changing worldwide fur markets and the effects of both the Industrial Revolution and westward expansion. The fur trade, as he had known it for forty years, was no longer an industry totally dependent on Indians and traders. Furs remained a viable product for both internal and external markets, but their economic and political importance was on the wane. Similar to his departure from the China trade, Astor had an uncanny sense of timing and a willingness to change.

The exact terms of the American Fur Company's sale are not entirely clear. Essentially, it was a two-part deal. Crooks and other capitalists bought the Northern Department and retained the name of the American Fur Company. The sale price was approximately $300,000. The new company had one thousand shares, nearly half of which were to be controlled by Ramsay Crooks. All the purchasers had to borrow capital from Astor to complete the purchase, so they mortgaged their shares to Astor until their debts were paid. For example, Crooks paid only $20,000 in cash and borrowed $120,000. Not until 1841 was Crooks able to extinguish this debt. Even though Astor initially controlled over eight hundred shares of stock in the new firm, he was totally divorced from any managerial decisions.

Having completed the sale of the Northern Department, Pratte, Chouteau, and Company, which succeeded Bernard Pratte & Company, purchased Astor's interests in the Western Department and the company's inventories there. Soon after the company's sale, both Crooks and Chouteau, realizing the advantages of cooperation in the trade, agreed not to intrude on the other's territory and to jointly market furs. As Crooks phrased it, "Competition can now be avoided between the West and the North."[85]

The sale of the American Fur Company apparently did not adversely affect Astor emotionally. Although he was now seventy-one years old, Ramsay Crooks reported to Pierre Chouteau in January 1835 that the financier had recovered from the deaths of close family members:

> Your old friend Mr. Astor has improved wonderfully in health since his return to America, & looks as if he would last 20 years yet. He has been suspected of an inclination to try whether he would not be more fortunate in a *second* attempt, than he was in his first matrimonial connexion: but I think the report groundless—not that his still good looks, & great fortune, would not procure him a tolerably young helpmate.[86]

Indeed in the early 1830s, Astor was still active in business affairs, although now his energies were concentrated on activities central to the new industrial nation—urban development and promotion. Since his first years in New York City, Astor had invested capital in city and surrounding agricultural lands; and these activities alongside his organization of the fur industry suggest that he was a businessman thoroughly comfortable in modern industrial society. To this story, we will turn next.

CHAPTER NINE

Financier, Speculator, and Developer, 1815–1848

WHEN JOHN Astor sold the American Fur Company in 1834, he did not lack for business interests, for throughout his long career he speculated and invested in agricultural and urban lands, lent money on bonds and mortgages, and purchased stock in banks, canals, and railroads. The enormous profits that resulted from the fur and China trades created a need for a diversified use of capital, necessitating that Astor gradually evolve a second business, that of acquiring and managing diverse investments and speculations. At first he speculated on a small scale in New York State agricultural lands, but by 1810 he was both lending money and purchasing New York City real estate on a large and complex scale. He devoted equal care and evolved business strategies for these investments as he had for the fur and China trades. His portfolio was a mixture of speculative endeavors and conservative, long-term investments that reflected an internal logic. For example, along with the purchase of New York City lots he also lent money to encourage house construction, financed the building of hotels, and purchased stock in railroads and banks. These investments, particularly in land, were far from being haphazard or unrelated to broader patterns of economic development; indeed, Astor's other business provided the most striking example of his modern business mentality.

Initially the New Yorker's land purchases were almost entirely speculative. In the 1790s, he joined with Canadian fur traders such as Alexander Henry the Elder in the purchase of undeveloped lands in Canada situated along the border with the United States. The plan was to acquire the lands at a low price from the government, spend a small amount in survey and development, and then quickly sell to farmers. He spent little time in managing these purchases and soon sold his share to other investors. One tract of over 1,000 acres he sold in 1803 to his brother, George.[1]

Astor also speculated in New York State agricultural lands in the late eighteenth century. He bankrolled a $25,000 investment in 37,000 acres in the Mohawk Valley, known as the Charlotte River and Byrnes Patent lands. His fur-trading associates, including William Laight of New York City and Peter Smith of Utica, assumed the majority shares, although they borrowed the capital from Astor. Smith, who lived in the region, was the agent for the land's sale and development.[2]

With Astor and Laight as reasonably silent partners, Smith's task included selling lands to settlers, arranging mortgage and interest payments, and leasing land to farmers who then returned a portion of the wheat or other crops to the owners. Historian David Ellis's extensive study of landlords in New York State showed that the Smith–Laight–Astor combination sold the land on reasonable terms and often extended mortgage and interest payments up to seven years. In comparison, other New York and foreign capitalists such as the Holland Land Company opted for leasehold systems in which the majority of farmers were tenants with little hope of ever acquiring clear title.

Astor was satisfied with occasional sales for cash and in-kind returns, with only minor grousing about poor returns. From 1810 to 1813, for example, he demanded a closer accounting of his share and urged Peter Smith to secure an increase in produce from tenants. Undoubtedly, Astor's demands were stimulated by his expenditures on Astoria and the reduced trade because of the War of 1812. But Smith resisted these pressures, sending the New Yorker detailed information about the depressed prices for grain, his attempts to introduce new crops, and plans to quarry stone off certain parcels.[3]

Even though these lands were originally a speculative purchase, they ultimately became a safe haven for Astor's capital until his decision to sell in 1829. Astor exerted little oversight but
trusted the judgment of his agent and partner, Peter Smith. Land
sales were not brisk, only 13,167 of 37,000 acres were sold. Peter
Smith's sudden desire for compensation in his role as agent rather
than slow sales, however, accounted for Astor's decision to sell.
Smith originally had agreed to serve as manager without compensation because Astor had lent him the money for his share. Astor
considered Smith's belated request unfair and retaliated by presenting him with a bill for his share of expenses encountered
nearly twenty years earlier. After a friendship of forty years, the
two men exchanged nasty letters until Smith purchased both Astor and Laight's share in the remaining lands for $29,000. Astor
once again lent Smith the capital for the purchase. The sale ended
the dispute and restored a long-standing friendship.[4]

The Charlotte River and Byrnes Patent lands demonstrated
an important characteristic of Astor's landholding strategy: although his early purchases were speculative, he later viewed agricultural lands as a secure, long-term investment. Over the years,
he owned many New York State tracts from a few hundred to several thousand acres. For example, in 1813 and 1814 he owned
6,000 acres both in Tioga and Chenango counties. Either he or
his son William watched these lands carefully so that taxes were
paid and when prices were acceptable, sales were concluded. At
Astor's death some of these early purchases were still part of the
estate, although none ever approached the value of his New York
City real estate.[5]

The New Yorker's speculation in Putnam and Dutchess counties must be treated separately, however, for this purchase, although legal, revealed his crass opportunism. In 1779, New York
State had legally confiscated the fifty thousand-acre estate of
Roger and Mary Morris because of their allegiance to the British
cause. Like many other states during the Confederation, New York
was in dire need of capital and sold the land to farmers for
$59,784. Yet states could not legally confiscate land encumbered
by debt or prior claim, and individuals had the right to seek redress in the courts or through the legislature. In 1809, Astor
learned from a London correspondent that Roger and Mary Morris
had possessed only a life interest in the property and had deeded
the land to their children. Consequently, the state had mistakenly

sold the Morris lands without compensating the children. In 1802, New York State officials admitted the possibility of error and indicated that the courts were open to a settlement. Yet the Morris heirs, all of whom lived in England, never pressed the claim, perhaps unwilling to spend the money for legal fees. When approached by John Astor's agent in 1809, they were quite willing to sell their claim for $50,000; a return they probably never expected in any case, especially with a war between England and the United States on the horizon.

The financier had no desire to settle the land or disrupt the occupants. Instead, he perceived the opportunity for a tremendous return if the state were to recognize his title and compensate him at the land's market value. Given the time, 1809–1810, Astor probably hoped a quick settlement would provide needed capital for the Astoria venture. To pressure the state, he sent an agent, Henry Livingston, to Putnam County to inform farmers and townspeople that their land titles were defective. Astor also sold part of the claim to other capitalists, thereby recovering immediately his initial investment.

When the state took no immediate action, Astor offered to settle in 1813 for $415,000, a figure he claimed was the value of the land plus interest from the date of confiscation. He argued that quick action would avoid further confusion over clear title. The state, though, was in no hurry because the original titleholder, Mary Morris, was still alive, and thus the heirs' claim was not legally enforceable until the woman's death.[6]

In 1819, Astor again suggested a settlement to the state legislature, perhaps with the hope that his friend, De Witt Clinton, who was governor, might facilitate the process. To investigate the claim, the legislature appointed a commission composed of Martin Van Buren, Nathan Williams, and Thomas J. Oakley. They acknowledged the claim's validity and urged the legislature to settle, particularly as Astor offered the same terms as in 1813. Yet Astor also threatened that if a settlement was not reached, "I will feel myself at liberty to bring suits against the occupants" upon Mrs. Morris's death. But the state again refused to act unless Astor paid the landholders for improvements, and he refused any settlement that reduced the claim's value.[7]

The death of Mary Morris in 1825 finally forced a resolution. The New Yorker was again before the legislature asking for $450,000, but the state insisted on a court test of the claim's validity. Both

sides agreed to a lengthy procedure in which Astor brought eject-
ment suits against landholders at least three times, and even
though he won in the lower courts, the state appealed to the Supreme Court of the United States. In one case, Daniel Webster
represented the state of New York and attacked Astor's supposedly
"unprincipled" speculation. The state dragged one case after another through the court system hoping perhaps that either Astor
might expire or that the courts might reduce the settlement. Despite Webster's splendid rhetoric, the U.S. Supreme Court repeatedly decided in Astor's favor and finally admonished the state's
lawyers for nitpicking over small points. It firmly upheld the lower
courts' support of the claim, "We have seen no reason, upon the
present argument, to be dissatisfied with the opinion thus expressed. It appears to us to be founded in principles of law, which
cannot be shaken without undermining the great security of titles
to estates."[8]

In 1832, twenty-three years after purchasing the claim, Astor
received a settlement of $45,000 plus $100,000 interest payable in
5 percent state stock. Although he stated that the whole affair had
netted little profit, the return on a $50,000 investment was quite
substantial, even after subtracting legal fees and the endless personal frustration. Yet Astor also lost something. The public had
followed the case with great interest: by 1832, the questionable nature of the claim permanently damaged the financier's reputation
with his contemporaries.[9]

Although one would be hard-pressed to discover any business
or social utility in Astor's land dealings in western New York, his
New York City real estate operations were quite different. He was
one of the early urban developers in the new nation, operating a
land-management business every bit as complex as the fur or
China trade. The increase in the size and number of cities was a
significant element in the economic transformation of the early
Republic, and this growth was especially striking in the principal
commercial centers such as New York, Boston, and Philadelphia.
New York City, for example, grew from a population of 33,131 in
1790, to 60,489 in 1800, to 96,373 in 1810, to 123,706 in 1820, to
202,589 in 1830, and 312,710 in 1840.

Historians have analyzed various aspects of the process of urban development such as the emergence of business and laboring
classes, the patterns of trade, the building of canals and overseas
shipping lines, and the formation of banks and trust companies to

finance trade and transportation.[10] But we know far less about the physical growth of these cities, especially about the real estate business, which involved the buying and selling of city lots and the financing and constructing of houses, stores, and commercial buildings.[11]

Astor's New York City real estate business suggests two unexpected but clear hypotheses. First, Astor helped increase the number of houses, stores, offices, and public buildings through a highly efficient and profitable development strategy in an era when private financiers alone built the city. Although Astor was certainly not a philanthropist nor a social reformer in his approach to rents and mortgage contracts, neither was he the "drooling capitalist" of popular literature. Second, Astor's real estate speculation and promotion was a carefully organized business requiring constant oversight; sophisticated business strategies in relation to market, location, and price; and careful accounting procedures. Contrary to the notion that urban land purchases reflected a wild scramble for quick profit, Astor's land business reflected the more sophisticated business methods and strategies characteristic of commerce and trade during the business revolution in the new Republic.[12]

The argument presented here contrasts sharply with much of the existing historiography on land development, whose focus has been the agricultural and urban development of the American West. Historians have argued that agricultural real estate investment is not a business but a speculative activity that extracted profits without simultaneously contributing to the land's improvement. Even though Allan Bogue, Robert Swierenga, and many other historians have established the positive effects of land speculation and investment on economic growth, yet, except among economic and business historians, the "speculator" still remains an authentic villain.[13]

Recent studies of urban development on the East Coast also have embraced the antispeculator tradition. They have suggested that the old wealth of seaport cities dominated the ranks of city speculators. These urban aristocrats supposedly fled the world of commerce and manufacturing that dominated the seaport economies from 1789 to 1840. Fearful of investing in new businesses, they purchased or speculated in city lots. These landed aristocrats rarely improved the property but garnered fabulous profits from the natural increase in the value of city property as trade and commerce flourished. Urban real estate speculation, according to this interpretation, was an unproductive activity that delayed rather than advanced economic development.[14] In the current literature, no individual more thoroughly symbolizes these urban landlords than John Jacob Astor. Despite the careful work of Kenneth Wiggins Porter, Astor has remained the quintessential urban speculator and landlord first depicted in the works of social reformers such as Gustavus Myers and Burton Hendrick at the turn of the century.[15]

A reassessment of Astor's role in urban development begins logically with his acquisition of city property. Even though Astor bought a few lots in New York City in the early 1790s, he did not begin an organized real estate business until the early 1800s. In 1801, he made five purchases in New York City. In 1801–1802, he spent in excess of $125,000; by 1809, he had invested over $400,000 in Manhattan real estate. The timing of these initial purchases was linked to his successful expansion in the China trade and his increasing control over the American fur trade. In addition, in the period from the late 1780s until 1815, New York City's population had tripled and land values exploded; one historian has estimated a 750 percent increase.[16]

Astor was generally a conservative merchant, thus he employed a fixed amount of capital—usually around $1 million in the fur trade and China trade. As his mercantile business grew more profitable, Astor continually used these profits to purchase urban real estate, which, in time, also began to yield substantial returns. Between 1800 and 1819, Porter estimated that Astor invested nearly $700,000 in Manhattan property and added another $500,000 from 1820 to 1834; then he increased the outlay another $800,000 from 1834 until his death in 1848. Total expenditures just for land, then, from 1800 to 1848 were over $2 million. During the 1830s, Astor regularly plowed profits from rents and sales into new purchases, and in some years his total capital outlay for property and improvements exceeded $200,000. If one had assessed the value of his city lots in any year after 1810, it would have exceeded $1 million.[17]

Before his death in 1848, Astor and his son, William, separately inventoried their joint real estate holdings; in a surely understated estimate, they fixed the total value at over $5 million. This inventory also revealed an extraordinary diversity in terms of the land's location, value, and use. Not only did they list undeveloped lots and blocks but also lots with houses, multifamily apartment buildings, retail stores, business offices, hotels and a theater.[18] The inventory alone demonstrates that Astor was involved in the business of urban real estate development.

The New Yorker's real estate business was conducted over nearly a half century and his investment strategy was quite varied. On occasion, he speculated, that is, purchased land in expectation of its value increasing and a quick sale. At other times, he purchased land on the city's periphery, conscious that the capital was secure and that the land would increase moderately in value. But he was also a modern developer, for he spent large sums for improvements to increase the land's value.[19]

This mix of investment techniques was evident in Astor's earliest purchases. He understood that Manhattan's inevitable expansion must be to the north and that property only a quarter or half mile from Wall Street or Pearl Street would eventually increase in value. The land much farther north also was of interest, even though it was already owned by wealthy merchants who had purchased agricultural estates in the eighteenth century. When population pressures and increased property values first drove artisans and laborers away from the docks and commercial centers at the tip of Manhattan, they purchased or leased small tracts from the estates of these country gentlemen. Astor watched the land market and acquired several large estates situated well beyond the city's border of the early nineteenth century. For example, he bought farms belonging to John Cosine and Medcef Eden, whose properties were located, respectively, between Fifty-third and Fifty-seventh streets from Broadway west to the Hudson River, and from Forty-second to Forty-sixth street along Broadway and northwest to the Hudson River. These large parcels were then subdivided into blocks and lots before their development and sale. Some lands were not brought into the marketplace for several decades, not until Manhattan's population moving north reached Fourteenth Street in 1820. By 1860, the settled area had reached as far as Forty-second Street.[20]

Astor not only purchased undeveloped parcels on the city's periphery but also diversified his interests throughout the city. He acquired many lots in major business districts along Pearl and Wall streets and on lower Broadway. These lots were initially more expensive because of their location, yet they returned more substantial rentals over the years. Although there was some residential and business segregation even before the Revolution, this trend accelerated in the early nineteenth century. The land in the old commercial centers along Pearl and Wall streets increasingly accommodated retail businesses, thus forcing the artisans to seek housing elsewhere. Even the established neighborhood of the wealthy along lower Broadway slowly was invaded with shops and stores. Indeed, the old commercial center of Manhattan actually lost population in the period from 1820 to 1860, even as land values rose because of increased commerce.[21]

Astor also leased water lots from the city government. These lands were usually underwater and located along the East and Hudson rivers. The city government leased these lands for a nominal sum to the adjacent property holders who agreed, either alone or in partnership with the city, to drain the land and finance improvements such as bulkheads and roads. In return for these improvements, the city allowed Astor to sublet the lot. Of course, the value of his adjoining property also increased in value.

Undoubtedly, Astor had used his social and economic position in order to receive valuable water lots at a fraction of their value. Yet recent research has shown that the city government commonly used the lease system to accomplish necessary public projects— the draining of usable land, opening of streets, expansion of wharf facilities, and the protection of citizens from disease-breeding stagnant pools. The lease of water lots, therefore, benefited both the city and the private investor. The city, moreover, was especially vigilant and continually pushed leaseholders to complete the necessary improvements on time and to the city government's satisfaction. In these cases, then, Astor's private interest and the public good nicely dovetailed.[22]

New York City's physical and commercial expansion in the early nineteenth century was an enormously complex economic process, but Astor's participation provides a glimpse into the movement's dynamics. The need for housing and commercial buildings was virtually insatiable due to tremendous increases in population and the spread of small industry and retail businesses. In 1824, for example, 1,624 new buildings, mostly two and three story, were constructed in Manhattan. The *Niles Weekly Register* estimated that 2,000 houses were built in 1828 at a total cost of $5 million. The city government had adopted a gridiron plan to order city streets and regularize land titles in 1811, but government intervention to control land prices and to oversee land use was virtually nonexistent. The city's physical development, then, was left to land developers responding to market considerations.

Astor had numerous strategies for profiting from this land and building boom; and his efforts had the residual effect of contributing to the property's improvement and the city's growth. Typically, he owned a number of lots within a neighborhood, a series of perhaps five or six contiguous blocks. On each block, he would improve a few lots by building houses, digging wells, and putting through streets. Then these lots and buildings were sold; and as the neighborhood gained population, the value of Astor's remaining lots rose in value. Astor continued to improve the remaining lots but at a much slower pace, preferring to sell or simply to sit on the undeveloped parcels for years.

In his real estate books, he noted several examples of such strategies. A single lot on Broadway between Spring and Broome streets cost him $750 in 1804. In 1818, he added a well; in 1833, he leased the property after building a house for $2,770. In 1836, he spent over $11,000 to build a store on a lot he owned at the corner of Pine and Pearl streets, obviously intended for lease to retail businesses. In the same year, he constructed three residences on Broadway above Pine Street for $12,600. Yet other parcels received no improvements. In July 1811, he acquired lots on Lombardy and Madison streets for $13,511. He purchased additional lots on the same streets in 1814 for $14,000; yet he held all parcels until 1827, when he sold them for double and triple their original price. In 1803, on the other hand, he purchased thirty-two lots for $12,500 near Bowery and Elizabeth streets. In 1806 and 1813, he acquired an additional six lots for $5,500; then from 1815 to 1840, he built several houses and opened a street while selling lots whenever possible. In 1845, Astor calculated that he had spent nearly $29,707 on the tract and had received only $17,740 in sale and rental income. Of course, he still held the majority of lots, which by now had appreciated in value.[23]

The central characteristic of Astor business, then, was its long-term, selective-development pattern. With an enormous capital reserve, the financier did not have to buy, sell, or improve except at the most advantageous moment for securing a large profit. New York's physical development was essentially a product of hundreds of such isolated business decisions in which each developer pursued his own best advantage. Profit, then, drove the housing and land market rather than any conception of providing good housing for all the city's residents.

Residential housing was New York City's most pressing need throughout the years of Astor's real estate operations. His decision to invest, speculate, or improve a particular parcel was one of a complex set of factors that contributed to the character of city neighborhoods and led to wealth and occupational segregation. The construction of houses was the most often cited improvement in Astor's real estate books. As housing costs varied with size and with brick or wood building materials, these factors determined the socioeconomic level of buyers in a particular neighborhood.

Astor's formation of Vauxhall Garden provides one example of the conscious development of an upper-class neighborhood. In the late eighteenth century, it had been a favorite garden spot for New Yorkers. Astor purchased the tract in 1804 when it was on the city's periphery, and he then leased part of the tract with the understanding that the tenant would turn it into a formal park with statues and marked paths. Here New Yorkers came to enjoy contact with nature, to listen to music, and to watch theatre in the open air during the summer months. Upper-class New Yorkers built homes in the area in the 1820s. Astor, then, cut a street through Vauxhall Garden and formed a residential enclave for the wealthy known as Lafayette Place. His son, William, eventually built a magnificent home there alongside the cream of New York's aristocracy. As late as 1847, the Astors valued their remaining lots in this neighborhood at $821,000, with each lot worth between $10,000 and $12,000.[24]

John Astor's real estate business thrived, despite substantial difficulties in financing property exchanges. At the opening of the nineteenth century, the financial system was short of capital and capitalists worried over the volatility in city property values. New York City had only three banks in 1803, and these institutions served the interests of merchants involved in trade. Although loans on personal credit were common, these loans usually went to merchants for short-term business needs. New York soon became the new nation's financial capital and the number of commercial banks, savings and loans and insurance companies increased rapidly. But even as late as 1828, New York State severely restricted the banks from mortgage lending on either agricultural or urban land. The prevailing philosophy was that land values were too susceptible to fluctuation. As late as 1832, the New York Life Insurance and Trust Company would lend funds on urban property for only one-half the assessed valuation. In 1833, financial institutions lent only $1,966,458 on mortgages on city property, whereas private investors lent a total of $4,136,222.[25] In the absence of fi-

nancial institutions willing to support urban mortgages and building projects on a broad basis, many private capitalists, like Astor,
had both to develop city lots and to personally finance their sale,
lease, or improvement.

The New Yorker closely linked his real estate and moneylend-
ing businesses because the sale of property often required him to
accept bonds and mortgages. Unfortunately, we have only fragmentary records, but these include a few "Lists of Bondholders"
from the 1820s. In the majority of cases, Astor's bondholders had
also purchased property from him in New York City.

Typically, he sold a lot on a bond and mortgage contract of five
years at the legal interest rate of approximately 7 percent. In
1816, for example, he sold a lot and improvements on Broadway
and Spring Street for $4,500, requiring $1,000 down and the remainder by 1819 at 6 percent. Depending on the size of the debt
and the individual involved, Astor staggered the payment schedule
so that his agent collected either quarterly, semianually, or annually. The debtor usually had clear title after five years, but if he
failed to pay, Astor then had the right to sell the property at auction. In addition, the mortgagor's personal bond ensured Astor
some recompense in case the land could not be sold for its original
sale price or brought a fraction of its market value at auction. The
debtor's personal bond helped guarantee fulfillment of the contract. Astor would get either the land or the money or some combination of the two.[26]

Occasionally, the financier simply lent money to merchants
taking mortgages on city property as security. For example, Philip
Brusher borrowed $5,000 in 1827 for one year, transfering a bond
and mortgage on five lots between Prince and Columbia streets. In
1835, Astor lent Alexander Bruen $40,000, taking a mortgage on
an entire block near First Avenue and Fourteenth Street.

Astor also had numerous sale and lease arrangements that encouraged improvements to his property. He sold or leased lots below the market price with the understanding that the buyer would
build a house or store. At other times, he sold lots and then in a
separate contract lent $3,000 to $4,000 so that the purchaser
could build a house. Bonds as well as mortgages, then, were a permanent part of Astor's real estate business. In 1826, for example,
thirty-six people owed him a total of $89,769, generally at 7 per-
cent interest, with the average loan ranging between $1,000 and
$2,000. In 1827, the number of bondholders increased to fifty-eight,

and the total debt was \$161,895; by 1828, ninety-one people owed him a total of \$293,029.[27]

Given the fluctuations of the business cycle in antebellum America, Astor's role as moneylender and mortgagee inevitably led to Chancery Court, where he either foreclosed notes or purchased lots at auction. No doubt, his presence or that of his lawyers helped solidfy the popular notion that he profited from the misfortune of others and added to his landholdings through distress sales. Gustavus Myers, a socialist writer, penned the following melodramatic account of Astor during the 1837 depression, "To lot after lot, property after property, he took full title. The anguish of families, the sorrow and suffering of the community, the blank despair and ruination which drove many to beggary and prostitution, others to suicide, all had no other effect upon him than to make him more eagerly energetic in availing himself of the misfortune and tragedies of others."[28]

Myers, though, had made no effort to substantiate his charges. Years ago Kenneth Wiggins Porter counted only eight Chancery Court appearances by Astor between 1800 and 1820, a small number given his large investments. During his entire career, he was mortgagee in five hundred separate transactions and became owner by foreclosure in seventy parcels. Of these seventy parcels, many were lands not purchased from Astor but offered as security for a cash loan. Porter's judgment was that the facts simply did not support the contention that Astor had acquired the bulk of his real estate by preying on other's misfortune.[29]

Chancery Court records, which include original contracts, lawyers' briefs, and the court's decisions, moreover, further demonstrate the correctness of Porter's judgment and demonstrate that the financier had legitimate reason to seek the court's intercession. In an intensive analysis of twenty-six cases, selected at random, in the period from 1800 to 1847, Astor never purchased land at auction that was not connected with one of his own mortgages or bonds. In most cases, Astor bought land at auction in order to recover lots pledged as security for a cash note. In 1812, for example, he foreclosed on a debt of \$2,000 from John Batchelor, a blacksmith, which had remained unpaid since 1808. In 1831, he foreclosed on John Fraser, a blindmaker whose \$1,875 debt was four years overdue. In 1843, Peter Vandervoort's estate surrendered a valuable lot with a warehouse on Pearl Street after Vandervoort had defaulted on a \$30,000 note. In 1839, the Chancery

Court sold land belonging to Henry Coghill to satisfy his $9,000 debt to John Astor. Astor attended the auction and purchased the land to maintain title. He was aware that in a depression period the auction sale would not yield $9,000 and that the land might conceivably be sold for a fraction of its real value.

The court files, moreover, revealed that Astor tried to avoid the Chancery Court because it was an expensive step for both creditor and debtor. The financier, thus, frequently reduced or delayed the payment of principal on a note. Samuel Swartout, for example, borrowed $14,000 from Astor in April 1835, giving a mortgage on a lot and a brick building on Greenwich Street. The original note had been for one year, but Swartout was unable to pay and Astor allowed him to extend the note so long as the interest was paid. When Swartout failed to make interest payments in 1841 and 1842, Astor finally appealed to the Chancery Court and the security was ordered sold in order to repay the note. Chancery Court records, then, confirm the relationship between Astor's moneylending and his real estate business, and they testify to his tough, yet legal, business conduct.[30]

Because of the shortage of capital and nearly prohibitive cost of city lots, the New Yorker's real estate business also depended on short- and long-term leases. These legal instruments must have been frequently used in all seaport cities in the early nineteenth century as a response to escalating land values. The lease system had a long history in New York City. Wealthy merchants who held agricultural estates on the city's periphery in the eighteenth century usually leased small parcels for extended terms of from twenty-one to ninety-nine years to artisans forced out of the city center by the high price of land. These landowners also imitated the lifestyle of the English landed gentry, who lived on estates with imposing homes while tenants farmed the land.[31]

In the early nineteenth century, Astor acquired several long-term leases, subdivided the land, and then sublet lots to tenants. The financier's most famous lease was acquired from Aaron Burr who had purchased the lease earlier from Trinity Church, which controlled an enormous amount of land outside the city's business district. When Burr's political and financial career crumbled in the early nineteenth century, he was forced to sell his Trinity Church leases on 241 lots. Astor purchased these leases as well as additional ones from the church for a total investment of over $175,000.

Subsequently, Astor sublet the lots for any number of years up to the expiration date (1867) of the original lease from Trinity Church. Astor initially preferred to sublet for an extended term of sixty-two years on single lots, with tenants paying a lump sum ranging from $375 to $700. Later he shortened the duration of leases to twenty years and then to three and four years, with annual rental fees as opposed to a single cash payment. Two factors probably caused this change. First, he desired to regularize all his leases so that final expiration dates were keyed to 1867. Second, he realized that rising land prices made leases more valuable and thus fewer people could afford to purchase an extended lease outright. More important, Astor wanted to reserve the right to adjust periodically the annual fee for a lease depending on the market price.[32]

The lease system was unquestionably a good arrangement. Astor benefited from the property's improvement, escaped the tax burden, and received an annual rent or lump-sum payment. In addition to the payment of rent, tenants usually had to pay all taxes and assessments on the property and often agreed to build homes and stores. On occasion, Astor even specified the building's size and the construction materials. Moreover, with appropriate legal remedies written into each contract, Astor protected his legal rights should the tenant fail to pay rent.[33] Despite the fact that the lease system increased the profits of land developers, it must also be viewed as a system that, even though imperfect and subject to abuse by landlords, facilitated the exchange and development of property.

Many of Astor's tenants were artisans and small merchants; for them, the lease system was an opportunity to acquire an interest in property—even though not full ownership—for a fixed price and term. Christopher Delano, a grocer, purchased a city lot from Astor on a lease for a single payment of $750. Even though it required him to build a house and pay taxes and assessments, Delano had title to the land for forty years. Delano also had borrowed the capital from Astor in order to purchase the lease. Cornelius De Groat, a stonecutter, purchased a twenty-one year lease with an annual rent of only $70, although he had to construct a two-story brick building. David Jacques similarly obtained a lease for seventeen years at only $70 rent per year; within two years, he agreed to build a "good and substantial dwelling house" with a brick front. Astor's leaseholders could pay their rents in three installments spaced evenly throughout the year, thus further reducing the effects of capital scarcity and high land prices.[34]

Tenants also possessed and used legal rights reserved in their leases. For example, they often held the option to renew their lease after its expiration. They could protect their equity in buildings either by reserving the right to remove it from the property or by requiring the landlord, like Astor, to purchase the improvement at a price set by independent appraisers. Finally, the lease itself had an exchange value. In a society where banks were few and artisans and small businessmen lacked easy credit, a long-term lease at a low, yearly rent was valuable collateral for a loan. Astor often lent money to tenants accepting the lease as security. Tenants thus had access to cash to make further improvements to the property or perhaps to expand a business. The leasee also might sell the lease to another party charging a sum over its original cost. Thus Robert Sedgwick in 1833 renewed a lease for twenty-one years at $220 per year on a lot with a building on the east side of Broadway, but he immediately sold the lease with the building to a merchant for $2,250.[35]

In the 1820s, Astor increasingly utilized both long- and short-term leases. Usually, short-term leases, one or two years, differed in that renters or tenants had no residual interest in the property's improvements. The size of the financier's rental business was reflected in two "Rent Rolls," one for the years from 1826 to 1831 and the other from 1840 to 1848. In 1826–1827, Astor had 174 tenants who paid total rents of $19,194. These rents ranged from $30 per year to a high of $800. In 1827–1828, his rental income climbed to $26,945 with 208 tenants; and in 1830–1831, the income was $30,360 from 244 tenants. The number of tenants and total income from 1840 to 1848 was:[36]

Year	Tenants	Income
1840–1841	355	$128,767
1841–1842	354	$132,029
1842–1843	365	$131,458
1843–1844	383	$137,324
1844–1845	416	$147,319
1845–1846	436	$162,158
1846–1847	430	$182,000
1847–1848	450	$194,000

These rental books suggest other characteristics of the land business. First, Astor's tenants were remarkably diverse, composed of businesses and householders from all economic classes. Well-known New Yorkers such as Isaac Lawrence, William P. Van Ness, Joseph Coster, and Albert Gallatin payed rents from $300 to $800 per year. Many lived in the city's wealthiest neighborhoods, particularly along Broadway.

Astor also rented lots and houses on Spring and Vandam streets, where the number of tenants and the rents, which ranged from $50 to $100 per year, characterized a lower-middle-class residential neighborhood. In 1826–1827, he listed houses on Vandam Street where there were four tenants per dwelling. If each tenant represented a family, then even as early as 1826–1827, the financier's rental properties were filled to capacity. Yet I found few indications of overcrowding. The overwhelming majority of listings were for individuals or families at each location. Moreover, the number of tenants did not increase substantially over the years considering the increase in the number of rental properties. His tenants also remained remarkably stable with the same names appearing year after year. These patterns were not characteristic of the New York housing market as a whole from 1810 to 1840, when laborers and artisans constantly changed dwellings as rents soared. May 1 was the traditional date for leases to expire, and contemporary observers described New York City streets jammed with people searching anew for cheaper housing.[37]

Astor's mortgage and lease contracts also appeared to be in accord with the law and market conditions of the period. He charged the market price for lands and rented and sold to citizens who could pay his price. The financier made enormous profits from a land and housing business operated under raw market capitalism. As New York City lands increased in value and the amount of housing available was insufficient to meet the demand, many citizens were priced out of the market and driven into overcrowded tenements and slums. Although Astor may not have created New York City's overpriced housing market, he also did little to change it. At least one social reformer in the 1840s, Mike Walsh, charged that New York City landlords, particularly John Astor, were involved in "legalized plunder" because so much of the laborer's money went for housing costs. James Parton's 1865 biography offered a more reasonable evaluation. He chided the Astor family for their reluctance to help resolve New York City's continuing housing dilemma, although praising the Astors as among the city's most respectable landlords.[38]

Astor most clearly exemplified the modern promoter in the development of commercial property. These efforts included the building and leasing of stores as well as hotels. As population grew and land prices soared, urban residents increasingly separated their place of work from their residence. Small merchants, retailers, and artisans thus leased business addresses in the city while establishing homes in quieter and less expensive neighborhoods. Astor, and many entrepreneurs like him, used their capital to construct commercial buildings that were then rented to one or more businesses. In an 1847 inventory of property, for example, Astor listed the following commercial buildings and their market value: 277 Pearl Street, $17,000; corner of Pine and Pearl streets, $40,000; 153 Greenwich Street, $11,000; and 187–189 Pearl Street, $45,000.[39]

The financier, not unlike modern promoters, often reflected his cultural predilections in his business endeavors. Throughout his life Astor enjoyed the theater, often attending the Park Theatre. Although it had been built in 1798 by William Dunlap at a cost of $130,000, sat over two thousand people, and was clearly the city's best, Dunlap was unable to succeed financially. In 1805, Astor joined with another merchant, John Beekman, in purchasing the Park Theatre for $100,000. As equal partners, they maintained its reputation as an upper-class theater for forty years. When it was destroyed by fire in 1820, Astor and Beekman rebuilt on even a grander scale.

The theater was also a business proposition whose value was in the lease. Neither Astor nor Beekman wished to supervise the theater, so they leased it to a manager who paid a yearly rent, which from 1813 to the 1830s grew from $8,000 to $16,000 per year. The leaseholder staged the plays and paid the actors, receiving profits from the sale of tickets. In 1846, Astor estimated his share was still worth $50,000, although by then it was no longer the city's best. The theater burned a second time in 1848, and the land was then leased to merchants for the construction of a row of brownstone stores.[40]

No other structure more vividly dramatized the changing American city than the hotel, and Astor soon integrated it into his real estate business. By the first decade of the nineteenth century, boardinghouses and taverns were no longer able to house the immense numbers of people visiting cities for social and business purposes. The hotel evolved, which was larger than the boarding-houses, and provided lodging and meals for transients. The New York City Hotel, opened in 1794, was one of the first such establishments. With five stories and 137 rooms and it was located on Broadway near Trinity Church. By 1818, the city had eight hotels and in 1836, the number was twenty-eight. In 1835, there were 59,970 guests at the city's hotels over a 207-day period.[41]

American hotels became centers of social, cultural, political, and business life within the city. They were often the most important "public" buildings and showplaces of cultural, architectural, and technological sophistication. The City Hotel, for example, not only boasted several stories but also had ground flour shops, a bar, coffee room, and elegant halls for concerts and dress balls. In the 1820s, James Fenimore Cooper met here with literary friends.

But even though the New York City Hotel held its place among the premier hotels in the city, other metropolises built even grander establishments as first-class hotels became part of the commercial rivalry among cities. Two early examples were the Baltimore City Hotel built in 1826 and the Tremont Hotel in Boston constructed in 1829. The latter hotel was arguably the most famous. It was financed by Boston merchants, who hired the architect Isaiah Rogers to develop an elegant and innovative structure. Rogers built the Tremont as a public edifice in the Greek revival style, with large public rooms, a formal dining hall, and a central lobby. In addition, Rogers included new technologies such as gas-light in the public rooms and a plumbing system that consisted of eight water closets on the ground floor.[42]

John Astor first entered the hotel business in 1828 when he purchased the well-established City Hotel for $101,000. This investment was solely a money-making venture. It was located in a neighborhood where Astor had many other lots and buildings. He received a yearly return on his capital by leasing the hotel to a professional manager, Chester Jennings, for $12,000 to $15,000 per annum. By the late 1820s, the City Hotel had many competitors, and Astor knew this older structure was no longer the best hotel in the city. In 1833, when a faulty chimney caused extensive fire damage, Astor informed the manager that he would pay only for necessary repairs and that any efforts to modernize were at the manager's own expense. The financier continued to collect rent; and in his inventory of property in 1847, the hotel was still estimated to be worth $150,000.[43]

The financier's reluctance to refurbish the City Hotel in 1833 resulted from his plans to build a new and more elaborate structure. This project had a significance well beyond its profit potential and reflected Astor's desire to place his personal stamp—a monument to his career—on the nation's leading commercial city.

His hotel project of the 1830s was part of an important passage in Astor's life, a time in the early part of the decade when he refocused his energies and interests. He had decided first to sell out his interests in the fur trade. He also took a final trip to Paris and his home in Genthod, near Geneva, where he had lived for long periods in the 1820s. The trip itself was somewhat of a nightmare. He suffered a fall while there; underwent a painful fistula operation; and returned in April 1834 to learn of the death of his wife, his brother, Henry, and a daughter, Magdalen. The death of his wife was certainly a sad occasion but not by itself one that plunged him into despair. He and his wife were long-rumored to have had marital difficulties and his frequent absences in Europe were testimony to that reality. Yet the combination of these events, exacerbated by Astor's chronic depression, led many of his friends, such as Philip Hone, to worry about the financier's health. In April 1834, Hone visited with Astor and somewhat later commented, "He appears feeble and sickly, and I have some doubt if he will live to witness the completion of his splendid edifice."[44]

But Astor possessed untapped reserves of energy and character and soon recovered from the despair of 1834 to rededicate his energies to the land business in New York City, the hotel, and an active social life. He reentered New York City's society. Family members recalled dinner parties during the late 1830s at the financier's home in which he engaged a professional pianist and joined in singing German songs. He spent increasingly more time at his summer estate, Hell Gate, on the East River. Here he was joined by a teenage grandson, Charles Bristed, the son of his recently deceased daughter, Magdalen. Fitz-Greene Halleck, a well-known poet, who had accepted employment as the financier's private secretary shortly before his departure for Europe in 1832, also took up residence at Hell Gate. Washington Irving was hired at this time to present Astor's interpretation of the Astoria venture. Irving and his nephew Pierre also resided at Hell Gate for nine months while they studied the numerous manuscripts in Astor's possession and interviewed a stream of visitors who reminisced about the halcyon days of the fur trade. Irving described the setting:

I have not had so quiet and delightful a nest since I have been in America. He has a spacious and well-built house, with a lawn in front of it, and a garden in the rear. The lawn sweeps down to the water's edge, and full in front of the house is the little strait of Hellgate [sic], which forms a constantly moving picture. Here the old gentleman keeps a kind of bachelor hall.[45]

The building of a great hotel that would become an architectural and technological first was for Astor the project that most occupied his energies as his business and personal life underwent wrenching alteration. The idea of the hotel most likely began in 1831, and it was a joint undertaking of Astor and his son William. They decided to build the structure on Broadway between Vesey and Barclay, where Astor's own residence was then located, across from City Hall Park. In 1831 and 1832, he purchased several houses, which then had to be demolished in preparation for the new construction. Shortly before his departure for Europe in June 1832, Astor went to Boston to confer with the architect, Isaiah Rogers, and to inspect Roger's most well-known structure, the Tremont Hotel.

Despite Astor's absence in Europe, his son, William, consulted with him on every detail. Throughout the later part of 1833, William constantly pushed Rogers for the final architectural plans and specifications, suggesting changes in stairways, courtyards, and in the facade. By December 1833, William Astor was satisfied but cautioned Rogers that his father, who was in Europe, must review all plans. Astor redrew the design of the hotel's front. He also insisted on using special materials such as granite from Massachusetts and marble mined at Sing Sing Prison.[46]

By the time of his return from Europe in April 1834, materials had been selected and contractors employed. Befitting a project of this scope and public importance, the cornerstone was laid on 4 July 1834. Construction then occupied nearly two years, with both Astors carefully overseeing every step. At one point, they fired the masons and hired new ones, then threatened lawsuits when cisterns were installed incorrectly, and demanded that the contractors redo the roof, because it lacked the required number of rafters and braces. The meticulous care given to this project was clear testimony that this was Astor's monument. Nonetheless, perhaps as a mark of fondness for his son, John Astor conveyed the land title and hotel to his son William in 1834.[47]

The Park Hotel, as it was originally known, opened for business in 1836. It met all the financier's expectations and quickly became the nation's most famous hotel. The elderly financier did not resist when it was renamed the Astor House. It was an ostentatious symbol of wealth and elegance. The structure had six stories: a massive pile of granite that encircled a courtyard. There were over three hundred rooms and six hundred beds in addition to private apartments for permanent residents. The structure reflected the financier's love of European classical style, with an entrance flanked by massive Doric columns, a lobby with a floor of inlaid marble, and the rooms furnished with black walnut furniture. The architect included several technological innovations such as several bathrooms on each floor, the water piped by steam pump to a roof tank. There was literally an army of servants to care for the guests' luggage, cater to their personal needs, and also to serve meals, all in near-military precision.[48]

Although the Astor House had a symbolic value, it also cost over $400,000, and Astor planned to recover his capital. He immediately leased the hotel to the Boyden family (who had earlier managed the Tremont House) for seven years at an annual rental of from $16,000 to $20,000. Yet Astor remained connected with the hotel because the lease required him to split the cost of additional furniture, pay three-eighths of the taxes, finance all repairs owing to fire, and reduce the rent in case cholera or yellow fever affected business.

The Astors, however, hardly faced financial loss. They retained ownership and received annual rent. They also partitioned the hotel's first floor facing the street and leased this space to a number of small businesses that included a jeweler, tailor, hairdresser, haberdashery, music and piano store, drugstore, and bookstore. Rental fees from these businesses were $15,000 per year. As the years passed, Astor steadily raised the lease and rental fees as both property and business appreciated in value.[49]

The Astor House was a good example of the size and complexity of Astor's real estate business. In the 1820s and 1830s, he had invested at least $100,000 per year in New York City real estate in addition to plowing back money received in rentals and sales. His bookkeeper maintained a detailed "House and Land Book" throughout the 1830s, which revealed the strategy of keeping approximately $500,000 actively employed in the business. This figure does not include the value of city lots and improvements but

Astor's Home on the East River, Hell Gate, ca. 1860.
Courtesy of Museum of City of New York.

only the rental and sale monies received in any year plus new capital. Given the increasing value of land in the 1830s, the Astor real estate business must have had a total value of approximately $3 million to $4 million by 1830.[50]

To control and manage a business of this complexity Astor had numerous partners and employees plus a sophisticated accounting system. In New York City, his son William was the principal manager who directed numerous rental agents and oversaw the work of contractors, accountants, and bookkeepers. He also kept several New York lawyers quite busy with title searches and appearances before the Common Council and Chancery Court.

No facet of John Astor's managerial control was more important than his account books, for they exhibited his extraordinary concern with costs and his ability to assess profitability. His agents and bookkeepers maintained "Rent Rolls" that detailed the names, type of lease, and amounts collected and overdue. In a "House and Land Book," the costs of all improvements, purchases, and sales for each parcel were tracked together with the totals from his

The Astor House (far right) on Broadway, ca. 1850.
Courtesy of Museum of City of New York.

rental business. In addition to the general overview of income and expenditures each year, the account books also grouped contiguous parcels of land and considered them a separate venture or "Schedule." Then the bookkeepers noted the original purchase price of a lot or group of lots, some dating back to 1800, and the various improvements and their cost. The "Schedules" also included the money received from sales so that Astor could view the profit or loss on specific parcels from date of purchase to date of sale. These accounts, however, were not as sophisticated as one might find in 1890, for they did not account for the land's increase in value or the depreciation on buildings. Yet they were remarkably detailed and exhibited Astor's understanding of the link between cost and profit for individual lots as well as the business as a whole. Moreover, Astor used these accounts both as a record of expenses and holdings and as a guide to future business decisions such as whether to hold, improve, or sell particular parcels.[51]

But Astor's construction of buildings both for housing and for retail business always possessed another dimension characteristic of urban promoters both then and now. Astor perceived himself as a builder or creator; that physical structures such as the Astor House Hotel were acts of great social utility or benefit. Such introspection was definitely self-serving and perhaps most evident in one of Astor's last major projects, the planning for what eventually became the Astor Library. The library brought together two of the financier's avocations, his interest in literature and culture, particularly German literature, and his desire for a great monument or project. The idea first surfaced in 1837 in conversations with Joseph Cogswell, a well-known writer and advocate of German literature and culture. Cogswell was then employed by Samuel Ward, who was married to Astor's grandaughter, Emily.

Cogswell and Astor became close friends because of their similar interests. Cogswell had graduated from Harvard in 1806, studied law, and then in 1816 he joined the migration of American intellectuals (e.g., George Bancroft, George Ticknor, and Edward Everett) who journeyed to the preeminent German university at Göttingen. John Astor sent his son, William to be educated there at about the same time. While at Göttingen, Cogswell studied under librarian George Beinecke, who convinced him of the importance of scholarly libraries. He returned to teach mineralogy and work as an assistant librarian at Harvard University. While there he changed the library's system of classification to that used at Göttingen, a system he later established at the Astor Library. Cogswell left Harvard along with George Bancroft and, in 1823, they opened the Round Hill School in Massachusetts. By 1834, Cogswell had moved to New York City where he was working for Samuel Ward and practicing law. Yet he was most interested in the scholarly world. In 1838, he purchased an interest in the *New York Review* and served as its editor until 1842. Through its pages, he continued to champion German literature and education.[52]

In Cogswell, Astor had discovered a real friend; when Cogswell proposed a scholarly library, the financier expressed immediate interest. At that time, there were no public scholarly libraries available in the United States, although there were institutions such as the Library of Congress, the libraries at Harvard and Yale, and the subscription libraries such as the Library Company of Philadelphia. In 1839, Astor assured Cogswell that plans for a library in New York would begin immediately. To solidify the commitment, he wrote a codicil to his will in August 1839 guaranteeing $400,000 from his estate for a scholarly library in New York City. Cogswell was simultaneously given a blank check to purchase books whenever they came on the market. He went to Europe in the winter of 1839 with $60,000 for this purpose; when he returned to New York in the spring of 1840, he spent a portion of each day preparing a catalog of the one hundred thousand volumes that formed the collection's core. At this time, Cogswell resided next door to his benefactor and received an annual salary of $1,500.[53]

Although Astor discussed the library building, he failed to commit to a particular size or design. Cogswell soon grew frustrated with the elderly financier's indecision. In early 1842, Washington Irving, newly appointed ambassador to Spain, offered Cogswell a position as secretary to the legation, but Astor countered this proposition immediately. He now promised his friend the position of librarian at the Astor Library, immediate progress with the building, and a salary of $2,000 as he completed the purchase of books and the catalog. Cogswell subsequently moved into his benefactor's home and was the financier's constant companion for the next six years until Astor's death.

Astor was now in failing health and seized with indecision. Cogswell's acquaintances often criticized him for staying with the old man merely to get a library building. Philip Hone rather unkindly described Cogswell as Astor's "train-bearer and prime minister [who] knows when he has a good thing."[54] But Astor's will guaranteed the legacy and immediately after the financier's death in 1848, Cogswell again went to Europe to purchase additional volumes as construction began on the building. The Astor Library, located on Lafayette Place, near the homes of members of the Astor family, opened to the public in 1854 with eighty thousand volumes.[55] Alongside the Astor House Hotel, it succeeded in reminding New Yorkers of Astor's tremendous wealth. An added benefit was the establishment of one of the world's great research libraries.

In the 1830s, New Yorkers marveled at the size of their city and surely its physical creation must rank as one of the most important economic developments of the period. This brief look at John Jacob Astor's techniques and strategies in the real estate business suggests at least that he was a key figure in the city's urban expansion. Was he typical and did he reflect patterns and operations in other seaport cities? I suspect that he did, yet

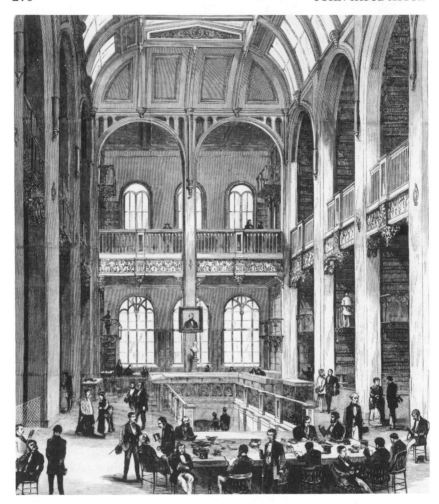

*Inside the Astor Library, ca. 1864. Courtesy of Park
Library, Central Michigan University.*

historians need to know more about other antebellum real estate
developers and about the social and economic costs of their individual and unregulated market decisions before generalizing beyond
this single case study. There seems little doubt, however, that in
Astor's case, the buying, selling, and developing of city properties
was a business every bit as complex and important as the fur and
China trades.

On a smaller scale, Astor also took one rather unsuccesful attempt in the 1830s at urban development in the American West. Because of his long contact with fur traders, Astor had gained possession of numerous tracts of land in the Old Northwest, usually to cancel the debts of fur traders. For example, when Astor withdrew from the trade in 1834, Joseph Rolette from Prairie du Chien still owed the American Fur Company approximately $10,000, which he partially paid by giving Astor title to 160 acres. Similarly, the American Fur Company extinguished the debts of Green Bay traders by taking title to lands at the juncture of the Fox River with Lake Michigan.

In 1834, Ramsay Crooks, who had purchased the American Fur Company's interest in the Old Northwest and still possessed a trade interest at the Bay as well as a share in the Green Bay lands, convinced John Astor of the economic potential of establishing towns on these lands. The Old Northwest was then alive with agricultural and townsite speculation. At Chicago, Milwaukee, Detroit, and scores of interior locations, eastern capitalists sought to cash in on the commercial boom of the 1830s. Given Astor's simultaneous interest in New York City real estate, particularly his great project, the Astor House Hotel, it is little wonder that he saw a chance to immortalize his connection to the American West. One suspects a feigned modesty when Astor was approached by the western partners who wished to name a town Astor. The financier replied, "With respect to the name to be given to the town, I can have no objection to mine being used, if it be agreeable to you and the people of the County, I consider it a compliment paid me."[56]

The town of Astor began in March 1835 when Astor, Robert Stuart, and Ramsay Crooks formed a partnership and valued their plat at $10,000, each holding a share equivalent to their former interest in the American Fur Company: Astor, 75 percent; Crooks, 20 percent, and Stuart, 5 percent. However, the partners immediately appointed a local agent, James Duane Doty, who was to be given a quarter-share of the plat for a $2,500 investment.[57]

From the beginning, there was little doubt that John Astor took a personal interest and utilized his knowledge of urban development in fashioning a promotional and financial strategy. Astor was aware that his was one of several townsites on the Fox River approaching Lake Michigan adjacent to the Navarino site promoted by local businessman, Daniel Whitney. He was also cognizant that townsites dotted the western shore of Lake Michigan, all competing for commercial dominance. Astor thus sent instructions to local agent James Doty to prepare a plat that envisioned a town of substance with main streets eighty-feet wide and minor streets sixty-feet wide. He also specified that a maximum number of lots must be located along the Fox River because of their marketability, that low prices for lots be given to artisans and professional people so that they would locate at the site, and that wherever possible purchasers be required to erect buildings on their lands in exchange for low prices. Astor also insisted that only a few lots should be sold to speculators because they contributed nothing to the town's economic foundation. He did acknowledge, though, that lots must be donated for certain public offices such as those for county government, the post office, and the federal land office.[58]

The promotion of the town of Astor never quite proceeded according to plan. The site had difficulty attracting settlers because there were already so many other townsites in the region. Many competing towns had started as early as 1833 and now possessed more improvements such as canals and steamboats. Many were also located to the south where there was better farmland and more population. Perhaps the financier had not appreciated the significant difference between the development of New York City and a western townsite. There was no ready pool of capital and commerce in the West, and thus the promoters had to create a commercial base.

By mid-1836, Astor realized that the project required additional capital, and he began to recruit partners by selling shares in the townsite at the inflated values common in western townsites in 1836. Samuel Stocking, for example, who owned a retail hat business in New York and had purchased furs from Astor, bought a 5/16 share for over $58,000. Charles Butler, president of the American Land Company and promoter of other towns in the West paid $37,500, and Norris Woodruff, a wealthy businessmen from Watertown, New York, purchased shares valued at $13,000. Astor's friend, Washington Irving, took a few shares as did Chester Jennings, the manager of the City Hotel. These new partners were important because they shared the risk, provided an immediate infusion of capital, and served as partners who could be assessed for future improvements.[59]

Throughout 1836 and 1837, John Astor was deluged with requests for capital from James Doty to improve the townsite. Astor, however, carefully evaluated each request, and this review pro-

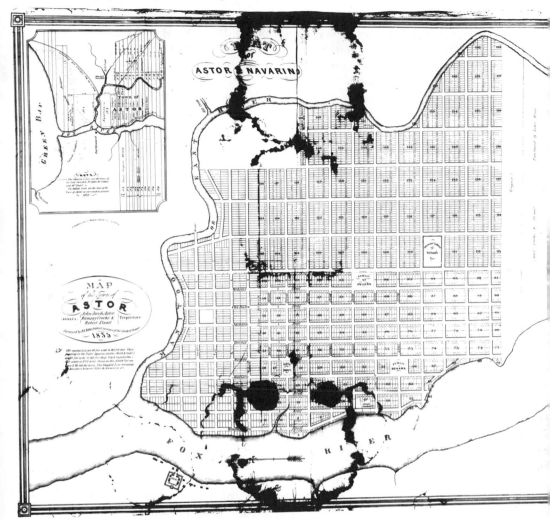

*Plat of Astor, 1835. Courtesy of Neville Public Museum
of Brown County, Wisconsin.*

duced considerable tension between agent and financier. He reluctantly consented to construct a hotel for approximately $20,000, which Doty argued was a necessity to attract visitors and new residents. The financier also advanced $10,000 for the purchase of stock in the Bank of Wisconsin and donated two lots in order to secure its location at his townsite. He agreed, along with the other shareholders, to pay for construction of a steamboat that would include Astor on its regular schedule from Buffalo around the lakes. But John Astor also said no: he refused to donate lots to several churches and to approve a major scheme for building bridges and roads.[60]

The depression of 1837 struck the Astor townsite particularly hard. The proprietors were unable to sell lots for cash and often had to extend credit to purchasers with payment required at some future date. Astor also tried the strategy used in New York City, where high prices and capital shortages were common. He leased lots at low rents for extended periods if leaseholders agreed to construct buildings and pay taxes. The proprietors of both Astor and Navarino recognized the folly of further competition and joined in 1838 to form the town of Green Bay.

Yet these efforts had no effect on the worsening financial situation. In 1838, the local newspaper was filled with notices of lots offered for public sale because of tax delinquency. Travelers to the region slowed to a trickle. The Astor House had so little business that its manager just packed up and left. To attract a new manager, James Doty required no rent on the new lease. In 1839, the Bank of Wisconsin failed, and the state revoked its charter. Eastern capitalists such as Norris Woodruff, Samuel Stocking, and Charles Butler—so carefully recruited to help with improvements—defaulted on payments for their shares. Astor purchased Washington Irving's $4,000 share for $2,000, a substantial kindness to his friend as it was practically worthless.[61]

Astor's western agent, James Doty, presented a more difficult problem. Astor had been displeased with Doty for several years because of his involvement in territorial politics, speculation in other locations, and frequent absences from the townsite. Doty was among the more freewheeling and now overextended western speculators. In 1840, he informed his boss that his financial difficulties also included questions of impropriety in administering territorial funds while commissioner of public buildings. Doty requested a loan of $12,000 to repay the territory and to protect his reputation. Astor asked his former fur-trade partner, Robert Stuart, to investigate the case, and he confirmed that Doty was culpable. Stuart, however, urged Astor to make the loan because Doty was a major territorial politician, and "thro his influence and management, Govt. is induced to make large expenditures in that region, for improvements of Rivers, Roads etc." Astor bowed to expediency and lent the money. Later Doty was appointed Wisconsin's territorial governor. He eventually paid his debt by deeding his entire interest in the townsite to John Astor.[62]

Doty's departure led Astor to appoint Nathan Goodell as agent in 1842. Goodell had little success in reversing the decline. Green Bay was remote from the main lines of commerce and emigration. Although it had been a favorable fur-trade area, it was too far North to attract farmers. Yet, the Astors still tried to protect the investment for the future. They continued to pay taxes and resisted efforts to sell off the silverware and furniture in the hotel. In 1845, Goodell and a local citizens' committee came to New York and secured from the Astors $15,000 to build a steamboat that would run regularly from Green Bay to Buffalo. The Astors also promised to direct the great tide of German emigrants to the region. Only a year before his death, John Astor castigated the local agent for the failure of the steamboat project, yet indicated that his son William had invested in yet another attempt with the Mississippi and Lake Erie Navigation Company.[63]

Although the Green Bay investment was a failure, Astor did not loose a significant amount of money. The land itself had cost very little because it came in settlement of the debts of fur traders. Moreover, he had shared some costs with other investors. The Green Bay project also demonstrated the advantages of great wealth. Astor did not abandon the townsite but surprisingly continued to throw good money after bad in the late 1830s. When all these efforts failed, he could afford to just suspend operations and await an economic resurgence. The Astor estate maintained ownership of the site and continued to sell and lease lots into the 1860s. By then population, commerce, and manufacturing had come to Green Bay and compensated for earlier financial losses.[64]

Although the development of New York City real estate and occasional ventures such as the Astor townsite occupied the financier in the 1820s and 1830s, he also diversified investments so that his excess capital was both protected and productive. Like many wealthy men during this period, Astor was a private banker. He lent money to friends and businessmen throughout the country with security based on personal bonds and mortgages. He was especially active in the boom economy of the 1830s. He preferred short-term investments and funded individuals with established business or political reputations. For example, in 1826, Governor

Thomas Worthington of Ohio borrowed $11,500 for six years at 7 percent interest. Businessmen, Isaac Broomley and Herman Cady of Plattsburgh, New York, took $3,000 in 1836, mortgaging a house and store; and Philip Schuyler and Stephen Van Rensselaer mortgaged lands in Saratoga to secure a $20,000 note. In 1832, Astor gave Benjamin Knower, a member of New York State's dominant political faction, the Albany Regency, $20,000 at 6 percent interest. Indeed, Astor often placed loans through Thomas Olcott, another Albany Regency politico and president of the Merchants and Farmers Bank of Albany.[65]

Personal friendship was often an element in these loans. In 1834, for example, Astor made an atypical investment in manufacturing when he lent $60,000 to the Mattewan Manufacturing Company, a favorite project of his friend Philip Hone. He lent over $20,000 to his former associate in the Astoria venture, Wilson Price Hunt, to develop land near Saint Louis. Hunt never succeeded and both the principal and interest were in default for years until Hunt transfered title to Astor. The financier, though, never pressed for payment and was exceedingly gracious to his friends, "I regret indeed, that my wishes to serve you when I made you the loan did not produce a more favorable result. We cannot forsee and must abide the events."[66]

Gerrit Smith, the son of Astor's former partner and friend, Peter Smith, was perhaps the largest single borrower. In 1837, he received a loan of $200,000 at 7 percent interest for the rather vague purpose of satisfying his own creditors and escaping "pecuniary embarassment." Even though Smith continually missed interest payments in the late 1830s and throughout the 1840s, the Astors were patient. The note was not finally paid until the 1860s.[67]

Astor was only rarely concerned with managing stock or corporate investments, but the Mohawk and Hudson Railroad Company was the exception. George Featherstonhaugh and Stephen Van Rensselaer envisioned a railroad, the first in New York, to link the Hudson and Mohawk rivers between Schenectady and Albany. Astor was attracted to the project in the mid-1820s because the railroad would provide faster transportation for the movement of furs and supplies. He was an early stockholder, holding at one point over 700 of 3,000 shares, and became an active director in 1829 when the railroad had difficulty raising capital for construction. For several years, he attended board of director's meetings, many held at his New York City residence; attracted new stockholders;

and helped purchase materials and an engine. He was also instrumental in the selection of his longtime business associate, Churchill C. Cambreling, as the railroad's superintendent. Astor later sold many of his shares when their value rose. By late 1832, he held only 180 shares with an approximate value of $20,000.[68] He subsequently lent $100,000 to Albany businessman, Erastus Corning, and the directors of the Utica and Schenectady Railroad shortly after it was incorporated in 1833. Of course, the investment was self-serving because the railroad was an obvious link to the Hudson and Mohawk Railroad. Astor also purchased stock in the Utica and Schenectady Railroad, although he never assumed any managerial role.[69]

In general, Astor perceived railroad and canal stock as a reasonably safe investment, and he bought heavily in such issues throughout the 1820s and 1830s. In 1826, on the advice of his friend De Witt Clinton, he purchased nearly $1 million in Ohio State canal bonds and $250,000 of a New York State canal loan. In 1829, he held $25,000 in Pennsylvania State stock for internal improvements. Astor also invested in the Delaware and Raritan Canal, the Camden and Amboy Railroad, and the Trenton Railroad Company—all improvements providing more rapid transportation from the Philadelphia and New Jersey regions to the New York City area.[70]

The financier also purchased improvement bonds and public debt issues of state and city governments such as the New York City water loan for $100,000; Detroit and New Haven city bonds; and Alabama, Missouri, Massachusetts and Indiana state bonds. The value of state and city bonds, though, were closely monitored, and either John or William Astor constantly traded such stocks in domestic and foreign markets.[71]

Financial institutions such as commercial banks, fire insurance companies, and trust companies also attracted the financier's interest. After his brief tenure as director of the New York branch of the Second Bank of the United States (BUS) prior to the depression of 1819, Astor had shied away from banks as inherently unstable. But this attitude changed in the 1830s and he expanded his holdings in bank stock. However, his investments were spread among many different institutions for security. He once stated that bank stock should be a safe and permanent investment, "No objections to large dividends, but whether that be a little more or less is not so much a matter, as to have it perfectly safe."[72]

Astor became particularly interested in two New York City banks. In 1829, he was approached by New York City capitalists who had received a charter for the National Bank but who were unable to raise sufficient capital to open. Astor and his son William agreed to purchase stock worth $85,000 on the condition that family friend, Albert Gallatin, served as the bank's president. In 1832, he joined a number of New York merchants and bankers including Philip Hone, Isaac Bronson, and John Catlin in securing a charter and serving as a trustee for an innovative financial institution, the New York Life Insurance and Trust Company. This firm accepted large deposits from wealthy merchants for extended periods and then invested these funds in secure agricultural mortgages and personal bonds throughout the state. It was one of the first institutions to assume the functions of the private bankers, who had been the only sources for long-term city and rural mortgages. The Astor family held a stock interest of $43,000 plus John Astor's deposit account, which fluctuated between $175,000 in 1836 and $51,444 in 1845. Even though Astor was listed as a trustee in the 1830s, he attended very few meetings.[73]

Throughout his life John Astor, then, was primarily a bank investor, who traded bank stock based on its market value. In the 1830s, for example, he held stock in the: Bank of Oswego, $16,000; Bank of America, $50,000; Manhattan Company, $51,300; Merchants Bank, $50,000; Mechanics Bank, $40,000; and Bank of Ithaca, $25,000. Unfortunately there is not a complete record of these investments, but their extent and diversity was apparent when the trustees of his estate prepared a partial list of his holdings in bank and insurance stock in 1849: National Bank, $60,000; Fulton Bank, $12,000; Bank of New York, $23,500; Union Bank, $42,900; Mechanics Bank, $28,800; Merchants Bank, $60,550; New York Gas and Light Company, $5,000; North River Fire Insurance Company, $18,500; Eagle Fire Insurance Company, $10,200; Bowery Fire Insurance Company, $28,850; Howard Fire Insurance Company, $1,000; New York Marine Insurance Company, $27,500; Butchers and Drovers Bank, $30,125; Phoenix Bank, $24,000; Bank of America, $12,300; Bank of Rochester, $40,000; and Bank of Utica, $21,000[74]

In reviewing John Astor's investment policies over his entire career, there are some obvious explanations for his enormous success. He was both conservative and diversified. He operated the fur and China trades and his New York real estate business on a fixed capital and plowed back only a small portion of the profits. Excess capital was placed in bank stock, agricultural mortgages, and state and federal bonds. Occasionally he took a chance as he did with Astoria, the townsite at Astor, and the Morris purchase, yet such speculations never jeopardized his main operations. This caution and diversity was also evident in the breadth of his investments from bank stock to manufacturing companies and within his New York City real estate holdings. He built homes and offices, owned a hotel, shared an interest in a theater, leased some parcels and sold others outright. Interesting, too, was the internal logic, which may or may not have been intentional, that operated within the portfolio. He purchased railroad and canal stocks so fundamental to the transportation of retail goods and held stock in banks that provided funds for urban and rural mortgages. Finally, a distinguishing characteristic of Astor, which placed him alongside modern industrial capitalists and urban developers, was his desire to be remembered for some great work or public edifice—Astoria, the Astor House Hotel in New York, the town of Astor, and the Astor Library. With all his wealth, he wished in some way to create something larger than himself. It must have saddened the financier greatly that, as his life neared its end, only the Astor House Hotel had fulfilled this purpose.

Epilogue

DURING THE last decade of his life, John Astor remained active as a businessman and financier, but the physical infirmities of advancing age gradually narrowed his world. After returning from Europe in 1834, the elderly financier never again ventured far from New York City. He moved constantly about the city, though, and resided either at his house on Broadway or at his summer home, Hell Gate, along the East River. By 1839, he was seventy-five years old and had come to depend on a narrow circle of friends that included Joseph Green Cogswell, Fitz-Greene Halleck, his son William, and his grandson, Charles Astor Bristed.

Business remained of interest in the early 1840s, but it was no longer a constant preoccupation. He periodically checked the account books relating to his city real estate and to his various investments in bank stock and western lands. When illness prevented him from leaving home in the 1840s, his chief accountant would carry enormous ledgers to the house so Astor could make entries. By the early 1840s, Astor routinely dictated his correspondence either to his son or to Joseph Cogswell. But his closest friends revealed that business affairs quickly tired him; thus Joseph Cogswell, for example, found it impossible to move ahead on plans for the Astor Library. Astor's intellectual powers, though, remained sharp. He read voraciously and thrived on intellectual discussions with Halleck and Cogswell. His wife's nephew, Henry Brevoort, Jr., reported that Astor became increasingly more interested in religion and took an odd delight in discussions related to an afterlife.[1]

Although these final years were accompanied by constant physical ills, the financier never became an invalid and insisted on frequent forays in a carriage either around the city or into the countryside. As age changed his appearance and abilities, however, people had difficulty reconciling their image of the great titan of business and finance to the debilitated figure now before them. Walt Whitman remembered seeing Astor carried down the steps of his home, attended by a dozen servants and dressed as some aged monarch. In 1843, Philip Hone, a friend and business associate, attended a dinner party that included Astor, Cogswell, and other business and cultural leaders. Hone was stunned by Astor's appearance and revealed his inability to accept the financier's inexorable decline:

> Mr. Astor . . . yesterday, presented a painful example of the insufficiency of wealth to prolong the life of man. . . . He sat at the dinner table with his head down upon his breast, saying little, and in a voice almost unintelligible; the saliva dropping from his mouth, and a servant behind him to guide the victuals which he was eating, and to watch him as an infant is watched. His mind is good, his observation acute, and he seems to know everything that is going on. But the machinery is all broken up, and there are some people, no doubt, who think he has lived long enough.[2]

Immobility made Astor's final years quite difficult. He once commented to buinessman and reformer, Gerrit Smith, in the 1840s, "I am broken up. It is time for me to be out of the way." He died on 29 March 1848 at the age of eighty-four. His death aroused substantial public comment because New Yorkers believed that America had seen the death of its richest citizen. The *New York Herald* reported that thousands viewed the body, which was waked at William B. Astor's home at 32 Lafayette Place. The funeral was held at St. Thomas Episcopal Church at the corner of Broadway and Huston. Pallbearers included many of Astor's friends and business associates, among them were Ramsay Crooks, Philip Hone, and Washington Irving. Astor was then buried in the family vault at the back of the church.[3]

The reaction to Astor's death would likely have surprised the financier. Although he received the usual eulogies in the public press, his reputation for great wealth and his prominence because of Astoria, the American Fur Company, and the Astor House Hotel also attracted social commentary about the enormous fortunes possible in this new industrial society. In a way, this concern was somewhat ironic because many financiers and industrialists were already building fortunes on an even larger scale. John Astor's will, nevertheless, became the subject of great public interest, and its terms would seriously damage the financier's historical reputation. Astor's burden was that he had grown up with the young Republic and somehow carried the responsibility for living its rhetoric. Thus, when Astor's will became public knowledge, carried on the front page of the *New York Herald* on 5 April 1848, the debate over the financier's social consciousness began.[4]

The *New York Herald* estimated that Astor's estate amounted to $20 million, but the figure was grossly exaggerated. The first report of the estate's administrators reported approximately $5 million available for distribution, although this figure omitted many New York city properties jointly held with his son William. A few years earlier, these lands were estimated to be worth $5 million. The total value of Astor's estate, then, could not have been more than $10 million; more than likely, it was closer to $8 million. Historians and social commentators used the $20-million estimate, and thus made the financier appear more parsimonious than he was.[5]

Astor's will was not an unusual document for the time. When it was first drafted in 1836, and then later supplemented with numerous codicils, Astor demonstrated first his concern with maintaining the family unit and second with maintaining his business interests. As Astor once remarked to Peter Smith, "I do divide with my children. Like you I work for them & I wish them to have all the Good of it. The more they enjoy it, the more happy I am." Family tradition was part of his European inheritance and already a dominant characteristic of wealthy Americans.[6]

Astor thus gave the majority of his estate to his children and grandchildren through his executors, including William his son;

John Jacob, a grandson; Daniel Lord, his lawyer; and friends and business acquaintances James Gallatin, James G. King, and Washington Irving. Of special concern was his mentally incompetent son, who was given a yearly living stipend of $10,000 and a private dwelling. His daughter, Dorothea, who had married Walter Langdon, was given all his household furniture and a life income of $100,000 from stocks and bonds. Astor also mentioned his many grandchildren in the will, among them his favorite grandson, Charles Bristed, who inherited the estate at Hell Gate, eighty-four city lots, and the interest and income on $115,000. William B. Astor's daughters were each assured $200,000 at the discretion of their father, and William's sons were each given lots and buildings within the city. Astor's family bequests also extended to more distant relatives in England and Germany. His brother George, who had lived in England and preceded him in death, nonetheless, was remembered with a bequest to each of his four daughters of $20,000 and a yearly annuity to George's wife of $350. To his niece, Sophia of Neuwied, Germany, he gave $5,000. He also provided $50,000 for the establishment of an institution for the poor and the sick in Walldorf, leaving the final plans and organization to his son-in-law, Vincent Rumpff, who then lived in Europe.

William B. Astor, though, gained the most from his father's will. In essence, the financier left William B. Astor a family business that largely consisted of city real estate, buildings, bonds, and stocks. To assure that the business continued beyond a single generation, John Astor split the estate, giving William, one-half of the estate after distribution and establishing a trust with the other half. One-half of the estate, after all bequests were disbursed, amounted to $1,234,972 plus an undetermined amount in stocks, bonds, and lands in New York City. William was also to receive the income from the half of the estate that remained intact and under the control of the trustees. At William's death, whatever remained of John Jacob Astor's estate was to be divided among the children of William B. Astor. John Astor, then, had extended his influence beyond a generation, and these provisions prompted his critics to claim that he had created a dynasty. Yet the fortune was now at William's discretion; and although an American dynasty had begun, John Astor was neither the first nor the last American capitalist to create a family legacy.[7]

Astor's critics were most disturbed by his meager attempts at philanthropy. The value of his estate was approximately $8 million,

the half-million earmarked for charitable causes or public concerns was only 6 percent of the estate. Although Astor was not
quite the miserly Scrooge so permanently fixed in American literature, his charitable bequests were, nevertheless, inexplicably
mingy. Like many of his ilk, Astor came to believe that his wealth
was both deserved and a reward for hard work. Even in his bequests to public purposes, he tried to move society in directions
that he predetermined. Thus he left $20,000 to the German Soci-
ety of New York for the assistance of immigrants. Smaller bequests were given to organizations such as the Association for the
Relief of Respectable Aged Indigent Females, the Institution for
the Blind, the Society for the Relief of Half-Orphans and Destitute
Children, and the New York Lying-In Aslyum. Probably in Astor's
own mind, the $400,000 that he designated for the Astor Library
was a magnificent gesture. He probably never realized that such
grand gestures were at least partly to insure his public image.[8]
Astor's will was a stark example of how little early American capitalists had thought of wealth's responsibilities in the new industrial society.

John Astor's business career, thus, had spanned almost a half-
century. Although myths surrounding his life have continued to
our own time, his business accomplishments and the larger significance of his reputation in American history are, nevertheless,
visible beneath the conflicting data. He was clearly not a business revolutionary who radically altered an existing system. He
was, however, an entrepreneur who exerted a profound change on
an industry, as did John D. Rockefeller and Andrew Carnegie,
even though the scale of his operations was considerably less.
When compared to men such as Carnegie and Rockefeller, historians might legitimately wonder why Astor has become so
much the subject of legend. But Astor fascinated his contemporaries precisely because he so mirrored his age and its changing
business and economic patterns. He grasped the greater size
and complexity of an emerging commercial economy in post-
Revolutionary America and adopted strategies and structures
that transformed the fur and China trades. His investment in
city real estate, stocks, bonds, and even a western city made him
part of America's evolution into an urban-industrial society. For
his era, 1783 to the early 1840s, John Astor's career was remark-

able for its modernity, vision, and reflection of American economic and political values.

Astor's managerial skills were evident throughout his career. He was the first American businessman to experiment with corporate structures such as the American Fur Company and the Pacific Fur Company and to employ hundreds of people across an entire continent. His bewildering array of companies and partnerships often crossed national boundaries. The complexity of his business endeavors was a unique characteristic. The establishment of Astoria, for example, involved negotiations with three governments, scores of employees, questions of national policy, and a delicate balancing of international markets and supplies. Similarly, the American Fur Company from 1816 to 1834 was a constantly shifting horizontal integration that utilized partnerships, pools, and mergers in order to limit competition and control the continental fur trade.

Astor also understood that structures and organizations were part of a business strategy that reduced operating expenses and increased profitability. Unlike merchants of an earlier period, he had the ability to control the cost of acquiring furs and teas and to select the most advantageous markets. Thus, he followed a carefully designed strategy that increased his control over supplies, transportation, personnel, and markets. When he perceived cost advantages, he built his own ships, maintained storehouses for furs and teas in North America, Europe, and China; and expanded the number of products traded. When market prices declined, Astor's managerial expertise was evident as he tightened the company's expenses and demanded strict accounting from his middle managers on issues ranging from the number of employees to the size of inventories. When business conditions changed drastically, he quickly sold his ships, withdrew from the China trade, closed entire territories in the fur trade, and ultimately sold the American Fur Company. Astor's ability to forecast and act on perceived changes in the business system was a principal reason for his phenomenal success. Tradition had no hold on his business philosophy or practice.

No business activity fit the New Yorker into a modern cast more than his role as an urban promoter. Astor's massive involvement in New York City real estate was not solely a means of protecting his capital, rather, he treated urban development as a business that operated according to market forces as did furs and teas. He bought and sold property to make money, held other property until the markets changed or capital improvements raised its value, rented some parcels to provide a steady income and a source of reusable capital, and launched major expenditures such as the Park Theatre, Astor Library, and the Astor House Hotel. All these properties were closely monitored, and Astor knew at any given moment the relative profitability of every tract of land in his possession.

Astor also realized the close interrelationship between business and government. From his earliest days in the fur trade, he demonstrated an uncanny ability to work between British and American designs on the American West. He picked up the Canadian visions of a continental fur trade linked to British imperial ambitions; by 1808, he had pushed, before the American government, the intimate ties between an American-controlled fur trade and national expansion. Through the first three decades of the nineteenth century, Astor was a constant presence as he tried to align his business objectives and national policy. Astoria was the major example, but equally important was his role as loan contractor for the government during the War of 1812, promoter and executive of the Second Bank of the United States (BUS), and persistent advocate of the American Fur Company's needs in the American West.

Astor, though, was not only driven by a cost accountant's mentality and by the desire to increase his own net worth. His political and economic vision, the ability to think in national and international economic and political terms, while still maintaining an eye on the balance sheet, was another of his distinguishing characteristics. No individual of his time, perhaps, better exemplified the union of capitalism and the new liberal state.[9] In Astor's mind, the ultimate success of the new Republic depended on its commercial and geographic expansion. His contemporaries accepted that premise and linked his career and reputation with the economic vision of the Jeffersonian Republicans. Astor was also a dominant presence into the next generation. As he became a financier and a builder of an urban society, his notion of the great project, whether it be a theater, a hotel, or a library, set him apart from those who dreamed on a smaller scale. Eventually, he also came to symbolize, both to his contemporaries and to later historians, some of the harsh realities of American society. His death in 1848 provoked disturbing questions about the glaring existence of a new American aristocracy, the presence of an urban proletariat, and the often unethical ties between business and government. Astor has become such a major historical figure not solely because of a unique and successful career. He also was the first businessman to epitomize the successes, the failures, indeed, the character of the new Republic.

Abbreviations

AFC, LB	American Fur Company Papers, Letterbooks, Microfilm, Clarke Historical Library, Central Michigan University, Mount Pleasant
AFC, MHS	American Fur Company Papers, Minnesota Historical Society, Saint Paul
AFC, PAC	American Fur Company Papers, Public Archives of Canada
AP, BL	John Jacob Astor Papers, Baker Library, Harvard University, Microfilm Edition. (References are to reel number)
AP, Beinecke	John Astor Letters, Beinecke Library, Yale University, New Haven
AP, HSP	John Jacob Astor Papers, Historical Society of Pennsylvania, Philadelphia
AP, Mo.HS	John Astor Papers, Missouri Historical Society, Saint Louis
AP, NYHS	Astor Family Papers, New York Historical Society, New York City
AP, NYPL	John Jacob Astor Papers, New York Public Library, New York City
Chouteau Coll, Mo.HS	Chouteau Collections, Missouri Historical Society, Saint Louis
DAB	*Dictionary of American Biography*

EIC	East India Company Records, G12 Factory Diaries, India Office Library and Records, London
Edgar Papers, NYPL	William Edgar Papers, New York Public Library, New York City
GP	Albert Gallatin Papers, Microfilm Edition (References are to reel number)
HBC, NW, PAC	Hudson's Bay Company Archives, North West Company Correspondence Public Archives of Canada, Ottawa
MPHC	*Michigan Pioneer and Historical Collections,* 40 vols. (Lansing: 1874–1929)
NA, RG 36	Records of the United States Customs Service, New York Customs House, John Jacob Astor Papers, 1802–1824, National Archives, Record Group 36
NW, PAC	North West Company, Letterbooks and Accounts, Public Archives of Canada, Ottawa
Porter	Kenneth Wiggins Porter, *John Jacob Astor: Businessman,* 2 vols. (Cambridge: Harvard Univ. Press, 1931)
PRO, FO or CO	Public Records Office, Foreign Office or Colonial Office, London (References include manuscript numbers)
WHC	*Wisconsin State Historical Society Collections,* 31 vols. (Madison: 1854–)

Notes

Chapter 1

1. Washington Irving to Pierre Irving, 15 September 1834, 6 May 1835, and 10 June 1835 in "Documents on Washington Irving and Astoria," *Washington Historical Quarterly* 18 (April 1927): 133–136; John Astor to Albert Gallatin, 22 August 1836, Albert Gallatin Papers, National Historical Publications Commission, Microfilm Roll 41; Ross Cox, *Adventures on the Columbia River Including the Narrative of a Residence of Six Years on the Western Side of the Rocky Mountains . . .* (New York: J. & L. Harper, 1832); Gabriel Franchére, *Adventures at Astoria, 1810–1814* (1820; repr., Norman: Univ. of Oklahoma Press, 1967); James Lanman, "The American Fur Trade," *Hunt's Merchant Magazine* 3 (July 1840): 197. Also see the *North American Review* 44 (1837): 200–237. A discussion of public reaction to Astoria is contained in an introduction to a 1964 edition of *Astoria* by Edgeley W. Todd: see Washington Irving, *Astoria, or Anecdotes of an Enterprise Beyond the Rocky Mountains,* ed. Edgeley W. Todd (1836; repr., Norman: Univ. of Oklahoma Press, 1964), xxiii–xxv.

2. "Mercantile Biography: John Jacob Astor," *Hunt's Merchant Magazine* 11 (July 1844): 153–159; Moses Beach, *Wealth and Biography of the Wealthy Citizens of New York City: Comprising an Alphabetical Arrangement of Persons Estimated to Be Worth $100,000 and Upwards, with the Sums Appended to Each Name . . .* (New York: 1845) in Henry Lanier, *A Century of Banking in New York, 1822–1922* (New York: Gillis, 1922). In this same category of booster writings, one should consult David Jacques, "John Jacob Astor," in Freeman Hunt, ed., *Lives of American Merchants,* 2 vols. (New York: Derby & Jackson, 1858), 2:387–439.

3. Ibid.

4. *Hunt's Merchant Magazine,* 1840, 153–154.

5. See especially the analysis of New York City's promotional writers in Edward Pessen, "The Egalitarian Myth and American Social Reality: Wealth, Mobility, and Equality in the 'Era of the Common Man,'" *American Historical Review* 76 (October 1971): 1031–1034; idem, "Moses Beach Revisited: A Critical Examination of His Wealthy Citizens Pamphlets," *Journal of American History* 58 (September 1971): 415–426; and Sigmund Diamond, *The Reputation of American Businessmen* (Cambridge: Harvard Univ. Press, 1955), 26–27.

6. *Hunt's Merchant Magazine,* 1840, 152–159; Beach, *Wealth and Wealthy Citizens,* 2; and Jacques, "Astor," 380–397.

7. John Astor to Washington Irving, 25 November 1836, AP, HSP.

8. John Jacob Astor's Will, 1836, plus eight codicils, which were added up to 1843, in Porter, 2:1260–1286. Sigmund Diamond has carefully examined the newspapers and periodical press for comments surrounding Astor's death, see Diamond, *Reputation,* 6–12, 25–50. Also see James Oliver Robertson, *America's Business* (New York: Hill & Wang, 1985), 89–90.

9. *New York Weekly Tribune,* 3 April 1848; and Edward K. Spann, *The New Metropolis: New York City 1840–1857* (New York: Columbia Univ. Press, 1981), 229–233.

10. *New York Herald,* 5 April 1848; and Diamond, *Reputation,* 32–33.

11. Horace Mann, *A Few Thoughts for a Young Man* (Syracuse: L. W. Hall, 1850), 61, 58–60. Also see Diamond, *Reputation,* 47–48.

12. Mann, *Few Thoughts,* 59–60.

13. Diamond, *Reputation,* 25–50.

14. Charles Astor Bristed, *A Letter to Horace Mann* (New York: H. Kernot, 1850), 8–18. Also see Diamond, *Reputation,* 48–49.

15. Michael Kraus, *A History of American History* (New York: Farrar & Rinehart, 1937), 558–559; Milton Flower, *James Parton* (Durham: Duke Univ. Press, 1951), passim; and Charles Sellers, "Andrew Jackson Versus the Historian," *Mississippi Valley Historical Review* 44 (March 1959): 616–618.

16. James Parton, "John Jacob Astor," *Harper's Magazine* 30 (December 1864–May 1865): 311–319; and James Parton, *Life of John Jacob Astor* (New York: American News Co., 1867), iii. The article and book on Astor are nearly identical except that Parton included a short preface to the book.

17. Parton, "Astor," 309, 309–311; and Porter, 2:1300. It should be pointed out that few authorities agree on Astor's early life. Porter believes that Astor's father was most likely a struggling butcher who simply could not provide economic opportunities for all his children. See Porter, 1:4–6. However, this notion comes directly from the highly romanticized German work by W. D. von Horn ("Philip Oertel"), *Johann Jacob Astor* (Wiesbaden: Julius Riedner, 1877), 1–10.

18. Parton, "Astor," 321.

19. Ibid.

20. This story is repeated in Norman S. Gras and Henrietta Larson, *Casebook in American Business History* (New York: Appleton-Century-Crofts, 1939), 78, and in Ben Seligman, *The Potentates: Businessmen in American History* (New York: Dial, 1971), 74.

21. Vincent Nolte, *Fifty Years in Both Hemispheres or, Reminiscences of the Life of a Former Merchant* (New York: Redfield, 1854), 143; Porter, 2:1113; and Gras and Larson, *Casebook,* 78.

22. "Walter Barrett" (Joseph Scoville), *The Old Merchants of New York City,* 5 vols. (1870; repr., New York: Greenwood, 1968), 4:37; and Porter, 2:872, 1113.

23. Parton, "Astor," 316, 317–319.

24. Burton J. Hendrick, "The Astor Fortune," *McClure's Magazine* 24 (April 1905): 563–578; Kraus, *History,* 568; and Louis Filler, *Crusaders for American Liberalism* (Yellow Springs, Ohio: Antioch Press, 1939), 198–199. Also see Joseph Wall, "Burton Jesse Hendrick," *DAB,* 22 vols., 7 suppls. (New York: Scribner's, 1928–), suppl. 4, pp. 367–368.

25. Hendrick, "Astor Fortune," 564, 565–578.

26. Ibid., 574.

27. Ibid., 565–578.

28. Gustavus Myers, *History of Great American Fortunes,* 3 vols. (Chicago: Charles H. Kerr, 1911); Gustavus Myers, *History of Great American Fortunes* (New York: Random House, Modern Library, 1936).

29. Myers, *Great American Fortunes* (1936 ed.), 7–8; Filler, *Crusaders,* 118–119; and John Chamberlain, *Farewell to Reform* (Chicago: Times Books, Quadrangle, 1965), 204–206.

30. Louis Filler, "Gustavus Myers, in *DAB,* suppl. 3, pp. 545–546; Chamberlain, *Farewell,* 204–206; Kraus, *History,* 316; R. Gordon Wasson, *The Hall Carbine Affair* (New York: Pandick, 1948). Hall, in particular, demonstrated how Myers distorted evidence in writing about J. P. Morgan. The most recent evaluation of Myers by Louis Filler finds that Myers was totally one-sided with little substance to his interpretations: see Louis Filler, *Appointment at Armageddon* (Westport, Conn.: Greenwood, 1976), 345–346.

31. Stanley J. Kunitz and Howard Haycraft, eds., *Twentieth Century Authors* (New York: H. W. Wilson, 1942), 1004–1005. Myers authored this article.

32. Filler, "Myers," 545–546.

33. Gustaus Myers, "History of Public Franchises in New York City (Boroughs of Manhattan and the Bronx)," *Municipal Affairs* 4 (March 1900): 71–206.

34. Gustavus Myers, *The History of Tammany Hall,* with an introduction by Alexander Callow (1917; repr., New York: Dover, 1971), viii.

35. Myers, *Great American Fortunes,* 1:iii–ix.

36. Ibid., iv.

37. Ibid., 66.

38. Ibid., 111, 120–122. There were a few American Fur Company account books available in 1909–1910, and there were government reports from the early nineteenth century that documented the costs of fur trading (ibid., 1:125, n. 7).

39. Ibid., 1:125.

40. Ibid., 125, n. 7.

41. Porter, 2:723–725; Gras and Larson, *Casebook,* 79–80; and David Lavender, *The Fist in the Wilderness* (Garden City, N.Y.: Doubleday, 1964), 458, n. 4. Also see Seligman, *The Potentates, 73.*

42. Myers, *Great American Fortunes,* 1:104–105, 126–154.

43. Ibid., 184–185.

44. A perfect example of Myers's misinterpretation of facts was revealed in his description of Astor's living habits. He explained that Astor lived over his own store because he was such a miser that he refused to move into larger quarters. Of course, in early nineteenth-century New York many merchants lived above their businesses. See Myers, *Great American Fortunes,* 1:110.

45. James Gallatin, *A Great Peace Maker: The Diary of James Gallatin, Secretary to Albert Gallatin* (New York: Scribner's, 1914), 174; Porter, 2:596–597.

46. Gallatin, *Peace Maker,* 80, 167–169, 174. Also see Porter, 2:596–597, 1100–1101.

47. See Porter, 2:1050–1051, 623, n. 22; Gallatin, *Peace Maker,* 81, 167–169; Raymond Walters, Jr., "The James Gallatin Diary: A Fraud?" *American Historical Review* 44 (July 1957): 878–885; and Wayne Andrews, "Gallatin Revisited. Part Three: The Not So Dreadful Mr. Astor," *New York Historical Society Quarterly* 36 (1952): 175–180.

48. Harold Smith, "William James Ghent," *DAB,* suppl. 3, pp. 297–298; and William James Ghent, "John Jacob Astor," *DAB,* 1:397–399; and Filler, *Armageddon,* 256.

49. W. J. Ghent, *Our Benevolent Feudalism* (New York: Macmillan, 1902), passim.

50. H. Smith, "Ghent," 292–298; Filler, *Crusaders,* 125; Chamberlain, *Farewell,* 85; and W. J. Ghent, *The Reds Bring Reaction* (1929; repr., New York: Arno, 1977); and idem., *The Road to Oregon* (New York: Longmans, Green, 1929).

51. Ghent, "Astor," 399.

52. Arthur D. Howden-Smith, *John Jacob Astor* (Philadelphia: Lippincott, 1929), 47, 117–118, 203. Alongside Smith's unflattering portrait of Astor, the New York newspapers simultaneously carried stories of a lawsuit filed by the descendants of John Nicholas Emerick. Emerick supposedly taught Astor the fur business and then later entrusted his estate to Astor. According to the suit, Astor kept the estate for himself and thus denied Emerick's heirs a vast fortune. The suit attracted some publicity but it was dismissed by the courts on the grounds that no documents existed to substantiate the claims. However, the plaintiffs' lawyer, Calvin Hoy, later wrote a denunciation of the original Astor. The episode can be followed in the *New York Times,* 26 May 1928, 1:2; 8 March 1929, 11:4; 8 January 1930, 47:2; and 28 March 1930, 27:5. Also see Calvin Hoy, *John Jacob Astor* (Boston: Meador, 1936).

53. Elizabeth L. Gebhard, *The Life and Ventures of the Original John Jacob Astor* (Hudson, N.Y.: Bryan, 1915), xii–xiv, 22–25, 301–308.

54. Matthew H. Smith, *Bulls and Bears of New York, with the Crisis of 1873 and the Cause* (Hartford, Conn.: J. B. Burr, 1875), 95, 97, passim. There were many other works that attempted to use Astor's career to demonstrate social mobility in America. See, for example, William O. Stoddard, *Men of Business* (1893; repr., Freeport, N.Y.: Books for Libraries, 1972), 3–28; Henry Hall, ed., *America's Successful Men of Affairs: An Encyclopedia of Contemporaneous Biography,* 2 vols. (New York: New York Tribune, 1895–1896), 1:33–34; J. S. Chamberlain, *Success: Or the Triumphs and Achievements of Self-Made Men* (Chicago: Merchants' Specialty Co., 1891), 43–79; and L. C. Tuthill, *Success in Life: The Merchant* (New York: Putnam's, 1850), 105–106.

55. Elbert Hubbard, *Little Journeys to the Homes of the Great Businessman* (East Aurora, N.Y.: Roycrafters, 1916), 202, 202–225.

56. Porter, passim. On the sources available to Porter, see Porter, 2: 1299. Also see Henrietta Larson to K. Porter, 14 April 1930, AP, BL, 12.

57. See Porter, 1:7; 11; 27; 35–38; 42, n. 9; 43, n. 23; and 44, n. 41.

58. An excellent study by a psychiatrist with valuable insights on how biographers should deal with conflicting sources is William M. Runyan, *Life Histories and Psychobiography* (New York: Oxford Univ. Press, 1962), 1–63, passim.

59. Porter, 2:1071–1072, 1122–1123. Background on Porter can be found in Barbara Harte and Carol Riley, eds., *Contemporary Authors* (Detroit: Gale Research, 1963), 5:907. On Porter's early years at Harvard, see Arthur Cole, "Economic History in the United States: Formative Years of a Discipline," *Journal of Economic History* 28 (December 1968): 576–578.

60. Porter, 2:1123–1124.

61. John Terrell, *Furs by Astor* (New York: Morrow, 1963); Lucy Kavaler, *The Astors: A Family Chronicle of Pomp and Power* (New York: Dodd, Mead, 1966); Harvey O'Connor, *The Astors* (New York: Knopf, 1941); and Virginia Cowles, *The Astors* (New York: Knopf, 1979).

62. Harte and Riley, *Contemporary Authors,* 5:841; O'Connor, *Astors,* 58–59, 28–30, and passim; and *New York Times,* 19 November 1955, 10:2–3.

63. Terrell, *Furs by Astor,* 51, 102–103, 239–240. Also see Thomas Jefferson to John Astor, 24 May 1812, in Dorothy Wildes Bridgewater, ed., "John Jacob Astor Relative to His Settlement on the Columbia River," *Yale University Library Gazette* 24 (October 1949): 47–69.

64. Seligman, *The Potentates,* 75, 73–74; and Gras and Larson, *Casebook,* 78–79.

65. For example, James Henretta et al., *American History to 1877* (Chicago: Dorsey, 1987), mentions Astor only very briefly on pp. 261 and 331. In textbooks of American economic and social history, Astor receives little or no acknowledgment. See Jonathan R. T. Hughes, *American Economic History* (Glenview, Ill.: Scott, Foresman, 1983); James Henretta and Gregory Nobles, *Evolution and Revolution: American Society, 1600–1820* (Lexington, Mass.: Heath, 1987); and Stuart Bruchey, *Enterprise: The Dynamic Economy of a Free People* (Cambridge, Mass.: Harvard Univ. Press, 1990). Also see Gary Nash et al., *The American People,* 2 vols. (New York: Harper, 1986), 1:264, 312. A recent exception is a textbook in American business history that provides a capsule summary of Astor's career without the Parton-Myers interpretation. See Keith L. Bryant and Henry C. Dethloff, *A History of American Business* (Englewood Cliffs, N.J.: Prentice-Hall, 1983), 108–110, and Robertson, *America's Business,* 66–69, 89–90.

66. William L. Barney, *The Passage of the Republic* (Lexington, Mass.: Heath, 1987); and Robert H. Wiebe, *The Opening of American Society* (New York: Knopf, 1984).

67. Richard Bartlett, *The New Country* (New York: Oxford Univ. Press, 1974), 87.

68. William J. Rorabaugh, *The Alcoholic Republic* (New York: Oxford Univ. Press, 1979), 160. Other examples of modern authors who depend on nineteenth-century sources for characterizations of Astor are Robertson, *America's Business,* 89–90; and Kenneth T. Jackson, *Crabgrass Frontier* (New York: Oxford Univ. Press, 1985), 134.

69. John N. Ingham, ed., *Biographical Dictionary of American Business Leaders,* 4 vols. (Westport, Conn.: Greenwood, 1983), 1:26–28. Also see John Dobson, *A History of American Enterprise* (Englewood Cliffs, N.J.: Prentice-Hall, 1988), 82–83, and the more neutral description in C. Joseph Pusateri, *A History of American Business* (Arlington Heights, Ill.: Harlan Davidson, 1984), 94–96. Also see the excellent account of Astor's career in Chandler and Tedlow's recent book that, nevertheless, makes use of many apocryphal stories: see Alfred Chandler and Richard Tedlow, *The Coming of Managerial Capitalism* (Homewood, Ill.: Irwin, 1985), 56–

57. A popular example is Peter Baida, "Poor Jacob," *Forbes* 400 (October 26, 1987): 345–349.

70. William Waldorf Astor, "John Jacob Astor," *Pall Mall Magazine* 18 (1899): 171 and passim. On the other Astors, see William J. Ghent, "William B. Astor," "William Waldorf Astor," and "John Jacob Astor" in *DAB*, 1:397–402. Also see Cowles, *Astors*, 68–78; and O'Connor, *Astors*, passim.

71. For a fuller analysis of this argument, see John Haeger, "Business Strategy and Practice in the Early Republic: John Jacob Astor and the American Fur Trade," *Western Historical Quarterly* 19 (May 1988): 183–202. For a review of earlier literature on the fur trade, see Dale L. Morgan, "The Fur Trade and Its Historians," in Russell Fridley, ed., *Aspects of the Fur Trade: Selected Papers of the 1965 North American Fur Trade Conference* (Saint Paul: Minnesota Historical Society, 1967), 1–8; Gordon Dodds, "The Fur Trade and Exploration," in Michael Malone, ed., *Historians and the American West* (Lincoln: Univ. of Nebraska Press, 1983), 57–75; and Jaqueline Peterson and John Anfinson, "The Indian and the Fur Trade: A Review of Recent Literature," in W. R. Swagerty, *Scholars and the Indian Experience* (Bloomington: Indiana Univ. Press, 1984), 223–257. The standard treatment of the trade is Paul Phillips, *The Fur Trade*, 2 vols. (Norman: Univ. of Oklahoma Press, 1961). For newer views, see David J. Wishart, *The Fur Trade of the American West, 1807–1840* (Lincoln: Univ. of Nebraska Press, 1979), and Donald B. Freeman and Arthur J. Ray, *"Give Us Good Measure": An Economic Analysis of Relations Between the Indians and the Hudson's Bay Company Before 1763* (Toronto: Univ. of Toronto Press, 1978).

72. The literature on land speculators and land speculation is voluminous. A good starting point is Robert Swierenga, *Pioneers and Profits: Land Speculation on the Iowa Frontier* (Ames: Iowa State Univ. Press, 1968), xix–xxviii; and idem, "Land Speculation and Its Impact on American Economic Growth and Welfare: A Historiographical Review," *Western Historical Quarterly* 8 (July 1977): 283–302, and Marc A. Weiss, "Real Estate History: An Overview and Research Agenda," *Business History Review* 63 (Summer 1989): 241–282.

73. The difficulties of writing critical biographies is discussed in Runyan, *Life Histories*, 22–35; and William M. Runyan, ed., *Psychology and Historical Interpretation* (New York: Oxford Univ. Press, 1988).

74. The development of entrepreneurial and modernization theory in relation to the American West is described in John Haeger "Economic Development of the American West," in Roger Nichols, ed., *American Frontier and Western Issues* (Westport, Conn.: Greenwood, 1986), 27–31. A good summary of entrepreneurial theory is in Pusateri, *History of American Business*, 3–12. On modernization theory, the classic works include Alek Inkeles and David Smith, *Becoming Modern* (Cambridge: Harvard Univ. Press, 1974); and David McClelland, *The Achieving Society* (Princeton, N.J.: Princeton Univ. Press, 1961). Also see the application of the theory to American history in Richard Brown, *Modernization* (New York: Hill & Wang, 1976), 3–22.

75. Gras and Larson, *Casebook*, 3–15; Alfred Chandler, *The Visible Hand* (Cambridge: Harvard Univ. Press, 1977); Thomas C. Cochran, "The Business Revolution," *American Historical Review* 79 (December 1974): 1449–1466; idem, *Frontiers of Change: Early Industrialism in America* (New York: Oxford Univ. Press, 1981), 17–48, 116–127.

76. Chandler, *Visible Hand*, 15–40.

77. Cochran, "Business Revolution," 1449–1466; and *Frontiers of Change,* 17–48, 116–127. Other examples of historians who have found sophisticated business strategies in earlier periods are: Thomas Doerflinger, *A Vigorous Spirit of Enterprise* (Chapel Hill: Univ. of North Carolina Press, 1986); and Ann Carlos and Elizabeth Hoffman, "The North American Fur Trade: Bargaining to a Joint Profit Maximum Under Incomplete Information, 1804–1821," *Journal of Economic History* 46 (December 1986): 967–986; and Edwin J. Perkins, "The Entrepreneurial Spirit in Colonial America: The Foundations of Modern Business History," *Business History Review* 63 (Spring 1989): 160–186.

Chapter 2

1. James Parton, "John Jacob Astor," *Harper's Magazine* 30 (December 1864–May 1865): 309–311. Also see Porter, 2:1123–1124.

2. Joseph G. Cogswell, "The Astor Library and Its Founder," *United States Magazine of Science, Art, Manufactures, Agriculture, Commerce and Trade,* 2 (1855): 137–138; Washington Irving, *Astoria, or Anecdotes of an Enterprise Beyond the Rocky Mountains,* ed. Richard Dilworth Rust (1976; repr. Lincoln: Univ. of Nebraska Press, 1982), 15–16. The most reliable sources for Astor's early years are Washington Irving and Joseph G. Cogswell. Both men were close friends and had little reason to elaborate the story of the financier's early years. Porter admits that there is tremendous confusion about Astor's early years, particularly the character of his family life. Moses Beach, *Wealth and Biography of the Wealthy Citizens of New York City: Comprising an Alphabetical Arrangement of Persons Estimated to Be Worth $100,000 and Upwards, with the Sums Appended to Each Name . . .* (New York: 1845) in Henry Lanier, *A Century of Banking in New York* (Gillis, 1922), 2, says that Astor's father was a bailiff. James Parton, on the other hand, claimed that Astor's father was a drunk and drove him away from home. Parton, and most other authors, took this information from an undependable work, first published in the early 1860s by a popular German author, W. D. von Horn ("Philip Oertel"). My account, depends on the Irving and Cogswell accounts, even though that information is not as complete as historians might hope. See Porter, 1:3–6, 42–43; Parton, "Astor," 308–310; W. D. von Horn ("Philip Oertel"), *Johann Jacob Astor* (Wiesbaden: Julius Riedner, 1877), 1–12. Other sources of inaccurate accounts of Astor's early years are Thomas F. DeVoe, *The Market Book Containing a Historical Account of the Public Markets in the Cities of New York, Boston, Philadelphia and Brooklyn,* 2 vols. (New York: Privately printed, 1862), 1:185; and "Walter Barrett" (Joseph Scoville), *The Old Merchants of New York City,* 5 vols. (1870; repr., New York: Greenwood, 1968), 1:285, 5–11.

3. For background on towns and economic life in Baden-Württemberg, see Eda Sagara, *A Social History of Germany, 1648–1914* (London: Methuen, 1977), 63–75; W. H. Bruford, *Germany in the Eighteenth Century* (Cambridge: Cambridge Univ. Press, 1965), 136–145; Peter Stearns, *European Society in Upheaval* (New York: Macmillan, 1967), 53–54, 38–46; Mack Walker, *German Home Towns* (Ithaca: Cornell Univ. Press, 1971), 3; and James Allen Van, *The Making of a State: Württemberg, 1593–1793* (Ithaca: Cornell Univ. Press, 1984).

4. The backgrounds and patterns of German emigration to America can be followed in Albert Faust, *The German Element in the United States,* 2 vols. (New York: Arno, 1969), 2:61–67; and Maldwyn A. Jones, *American Emigration* (Chicago: Univ. of Chicago Press, 1960), 28–29.

5. Cogswell, "Astor Library," 137–138; Porter, 1:8; "Oertel," *Astor,* 12–19; and John Broadwood & Sons to Editor of the *Times* (London), reprinted in the *New York Times,* 16 March 1890, in William Kelby, "Scrapbook on the Astor Family," New York Historical Society, New York City.

6. Cogswell, "Astor Library," 137–138; and Irving, *Astoria* (1982), 15–16. Astor's departure from Walldorf was a major event for early biographers that occasioned many apocryphal stories. For example, Astor supposedly stopped outside town and promised to be honest and never gamble, then worked his way along the Rhine River and across the English Channel. See Porter, 1:7; Parton, "Astor," 340–341; and "Oertel," *Astor,* 12–15.

7. John Broadwood & Sons to Editor of the *Times,* (London), in Kelby, "Scrapbook"; Cogswell, Astor Library," 137–138; and Porter, 1:8. Those popular historians who wish to stress Astor's good character relate that he arose early each morning in London to read his Bible. However, nothing in Astor's later life suggests any reason for accepting such obviously moralistic stories. See Porter, 1:8–9; and David Jacques, "John Jacob Astor" in Freeman Hunt (ed.), *Lives of American Merchants,* 2 vols. (New York: Derby & Jackson, 1858), 2:390.

8. John Astor to Washington Irving, 25 November 1836, AP, HSP; Irving, *Astoria* (1982), 14–15; and Cogswell, "Astor Library," 137–138.

9. Ibid.

10. Ibid.; and Porter, 1:22–23.

11. For a vivid description of an English immigrant who came to America seeking a business career, see Herbert Heaton, "Yorkshire Cloth Traders in the United States, 1770–1840," *Thoresby Society Miscellanea* 37 (1944): 230–242.

12. For background on New York City, see Carl Abbott, "The Neighborhoods of New York, 1760–1775," *New York History* 45 (January 1974): 35–43; and Betsy Blackmar, "Rewalking the 'Walking City': Housing and Property Relations in New York City, 1780–1840," *Radical History Review* 21 (Fall 1979): 131–133. Also see Elizabeth Blackmar, *Manhattan for Rent, 1785–1850* (Ithaca: Cornell Univ. Press, 1989), 45–50.

13. Abbott, "Neighborhoods," 40–41; I. N. Phelps Stokes, *The Iconography of Manhattan Island, 1498–1909,* 6 vols. (New York: Robert H. Dodd, 1915), 1:68–69; Sidney I. Pomerantz, *New York: An American City, 1783–1803* (Port Washington, N.Y.: Ira Friedman, 1965), 19–22; John Reps, *The Making of Urban America* (Princeton, N.J.: Princeton Univ. Press, 1965), 296; and Hendrix Hartog, *Public Property and Private Power* (Chapel Hill: Univ. of North Carolina Press, 1983), 82–83.

14. Blackmar, *Manhattan for Rent,* 38–39; and Pomerantz, *An American City,* 21–22.

15. Ibid.; and Blackmar, "Rewalking," 136.

16. Astor to Irving, 25 November 1836, Astor Letters, HSP; and Irving, *Astoria* (1982), 15; Cogswell, "Astor Library," 137–138; and Parton, "Astor," 311–312.

17. George S. Hellman, ed., *Letter of Henry Brevoort to Washington Irving, Together with Other Unpublished Papers,* 2 vols. (New York: Putnam's, 1918), xxxi; and Porter, 1:24–25.

18. *New York Packet,* 22 May 1786; Porter, 1:26–27.

19. DeVoe, *The Market Book,* 1:185; and Porter, 1:42, n. 42.

20. Paul Phillips, *The Fur Trade,* 2 vols. (Norman: Univ. of Oklahoma Press, 1961), 1:292–306 and 2:4–10; W. J. Eccles, "The Fur Trade and Eighteenth Century Imperialism," *William and Mary Quarterly* 40 (July 1983): 352–353; Harold Innis,

The Fur Trade in Canada (Toronto: Univ. of Toronto Press, 1956), 84–180. The Hudson's Bay Company controlled a third center of the North American fur trade in northern Canada.

21. Wayne Edson Stevens, *The Northwest Fur Trade, 1763–1800,* Univ. of Illinois Studies in the Social Sciences, 14 (Urbana: Univ. of Illinois, 1928), 97; Virginia Harrington, *The New York Merchant on the Eve of the Revolution* (New York: Columbia Univ. Press, 1935), 232–234; Innis, *Fur Trade,* 173–179; Eccles, "Fur Trade," 352–353; and Harrington, *New York Merchant,* 235–236.

22. Innis, *Fur Trade,* 180–181; Stevens, *Northwest Fur Trade,* 98–100; and Phillips, *Fur Trade,* 1:627–654 and 2:14–18.

23. Stevens, *Northwest Fur Trade,* 95–101. Also see Reginald Stuart, *United States Expansionism and British North America, 1775–1871* (Chapel Hill: Univ. of North Carolina Press, 1988); and Colin G. Calloway, *Crown and Calumet: British-Indian Relations, 1783–1815* (Norman: Univ. of Oklahoma Press, 1987).

24. Stevens, *Northwest Fur Trade,* 101–102; Phillips, *Fur Trade,* 2:13–22; E. E. Rich, *The History of the Hudson's Bay Company, 1670–1870,* 2 vols. (London: Hudson's Bay Record Society, 1958–1959), 2:198; Reginald Horsman, "American Indian Policy in the Old Northwest, 1783–1815," *William and Mary Quarterly* 18 (January 1961): 35–42. Also see Samuel Flagg Bemis, *Jay's Treaty* (1923; repr., New Haven: Yale Univ. Press, 1962), 1–16.

25. Vincent Nolte, *Fifty Years in Both Hemispheres or, Reminiscences of the Life of a Former Merchant* (New York: Redfield, 1854), 140; Arthur D. Howden-Smith, *John Jacob Astor* (Philadelphia: Lippincott, 1929), 39; and Porter, 1:48, 119.

26. Irving, *Astoria* (1982), 15–16; and Cogswell, "Astor Library," 137–138.

27. *New York Packet,* 29 April, 1788; and Porter, 1:39.

28. John Astor to Peter Smith, 12 November 1794, Peter Smith Papers, George Arents Research Center, Syracuse Univ., New York, Microfilm Reel 1; William Duncan, *The New York Directory and Register for the Year 1792* (New York: Duncan, 1792), 6; and Porter, 1:39, 54.

29. Duncan, *New York Directory, 1792,* p. 6; William Laight to Peter Smith, 30 November 1794, Smith Papers, Reel 1; *New York Gazette and General Advertiser,* 24 September 1795; and *New York Weekly Tribune,* 3 April 1848.

30. Parton, "Astor," 311–312; Beach, *Wealth and Wealthy Citizens,* 2; *New York Weekly Tribune,* 3 April 1848; and Porter, 1:23.

31. *New York Directory and Register for 1789* (New York: Hodge, Allen & Campbell, 1789), 8, 14, 114, 121; Pomerantz, *An American City,* 149, 185–186; and Porter, 1:54.

32. Cornelius Heeney to Peter Smith, August 1792, in Porter, 1:365–366; *New York Gazette and General Advertiser,* 24 September 1795; *New York Weekly Tribune,* 3 April 1848; T. Longworth, *Longworth's American Almanack: New York Register and City Directory* (New York: T. & J. Swords, 1798 [Astor is listed at 149 Broadway and Heeney at 80 Water Street]). Also see Thomas F. Meehan, "A Self-Effaced Philanthropist: Cornelius Heeney, 1754–1848," *Catholic Historical Review* 4 (April 1918): 3–17. Meehan's article, however, is very confused and must be used with considerable care.

33. Cornelius Heeney to Peter Smith, August, 1792, in Porter, 1:365–366; Astor to Peter Smith, 19 February 1795 and 26 August 1795, AP, BL, 10; Porter, 1:36–37, 49–50; and Ronald Shaw, *Erie Water West* (Lexington: Univ. of Kentucky Press, 1966), 9.

34. John Inglis to George Grenville, 31 May 1790, in Gordon Davidson, *The North West Company* (Berkeley: Univ. of California Press, 1918), 272–274; "Memoir of Isaac Todd and Simon McTavish, 1794," in Davidson, *North West Company*, 277–278; Stevens, *Northwest Fur Trade*, 106–108; and Phillips, *Fur Trade*, 2:5–7.

35. Stevens, *Northwest Fur Trade*, 110–113; William E. Foley and C. David Rice, *The First Chouteaus* (Urbana: Univ. of Illinois Press, 1983), 72–75.

36. John Inglis to George Grenville, 31 May 1790, in Davidson, North West Company, 272–274; Stevens, *Northwest Fur Trade*, 106; and Rich, *Hudson's Bay Company*, 2:198–199.

37. Benjamin and Joseph Frobisher to General Haldimand, 4 October 1784; and Benjamin Frobisher to Adam Mabane, 19 April 1784, in William Stewart Wallace, ed., *Documents Relating to the North West Company* (1934; repr., New York: Greenwood, 1968), 66–75; Rich, *Hudson's Bay Company*, 2:198–200; W. Kaye Lamb, ed., *The Journals and Letters of Sir Alexander Mackenzie* (Cambridge: Cambridge Univ. Press, 1970), 4–5; Stevens, *Northwest Fur Trade*, 116–119.

38. Alexander Mackenzie, "A General History of the Fur Trade from Canada to the North-West," in Lamb, *Journals and Letters*, 65–101. Mackenzie's "General History" was part of a book he later published entitled *Voyages from Montreal Through the Continent of North America to the Frozen and Pacific Oceans in 1789 and 1793 with an Account of the Rise and State of the Fur Trade* (London: R. Noble, 1801). There are several excellent accounts by historians and economists concerning the structure of the fur-trade business. See Stevens, *Northwest Fur Trade*, 120–161; Rich, *Hudson's Bay Company*, 2:182–197; Ann Carlos, "The Birth and Death of Predatory Competition in the North American Fur Trade," *Explorations in Economic History*, 19 (July 1982): 156–183; and Ann Carlos and Elizabeth Hoffman, "The North American Fur Trade: Bargaining to a Joint Profit Maximum Under Incomplete Information, 1804–1821," *Journal of Economic History* 46 (December 1986): 967–986.

39. Mackenzie, "General History," 71–76; Stevens, *Northwest Fur Trade*, 130–133.

40. Mackenzie, "General History," 81–85; Rich, *Hudson's Bay Company*, 2:186–189; Stevens, *Northwest Fur Trade*, 132–133 and 154–157; and Innis, *Fur Trade*, 196–246.

41. Mackenzie, "General History," 78–80; Benjamin Frobisher to Adam Mabane, 19 April 1784; Benjamin and Joseph Frobisher, 4 October 1784; Simon McTavish to Joseph Frobisher, April 1787; and North West Company Agreement, 1790, in Wallace, ed., *Documents Relating to the North West Company*, 62–89. Also see Stevens, *Northwest Fur Trade*, 139–142; Innis, *Fur Trade*, 196–202; and Marjorie Wilkens Campbell, *The North West Company* (Toronto: Macmillan, 1957), 30–42.

42. Irving, *Astoria* (1982), 15–16; *Richard Dobie v. John Astor*, 21 September 1790, in Porter, 1:364; Contract of William Hands, John Astor, and Alexander Henry, 26 August 1790, in Porter, 1:362–363; and Elliott Coues, ed., *The Manuscript Journals of Alexander Henry and of David Thompson, 1799–1814*, 3 vols. (New York: Francis Harper, 1897), 1: vii.

43. Campbell, *North West Company*, 57. Also see Porter, 1:64–65.

44. Contract of John Astor and Ephraim Santford, 28 September 1789, AP, BL, 10; Contract of Hands, Astor, and Henry, 26 August 1790, in Porter, 1:362–363; *Richard Dobie v. John Astor*, 21 September 1790, in Porter, 1:364.

45. *New York Packet*, 29 April 1788.

46. Ibid., 28 October 1788. Astor ran this advertisement for some weeks in this and other New York newspapers.

47. Agreement of Rosseter Hoyle and John Astor, 30 September 1788, in Porter, 1:353–355.

48. John Astor to Pliny Moore, 25 July 1794; James Rouse to Pliny Moore, 9 August 1794; Peter Sailly to Messrs. Moore and Corbin, 24 October 1792; Alexander Henry to Pliny Moore, 21 September 1793, in "John Jacob Astor Correspondence, Part I," *Moorsfield Antiquarian* 1 (May 1937): 7–26; and D. G. Creighton, *The Commercial Empire of the St. Lawrence* (Toronto: Ryerson, 1937), 104–105; and Charles Ritcheson, *Aftermath of Revolution* (Dallas, Tex.: Southern Methodist Univ. Press, 1969), 189–190.

49. Rich, *Hudson's Bay Company,* 2:290–292.

50. Ibid., 2:206; Barry Gough, "The North West Company's Adventure to China," *Oregon Historical Quarterly* 76 (December 1975): 311–315.

51. The fur-trade route is described in Eric Morse, *Fur Trade Canoe Routes of Canada: Then and Now* (Ottawa: Queen's Printer, 1969), 51; and Gurdon S. Hubbard, *The Autobiography of Gurdon Saltonstall Hubbard* (New York: Citadel Press, 1969), 8–9. Also see Marjorie Campbell, *Northwest to the Sea: A Biography of William McGillivray* (Toronto: Clarke, Irwin & Co., 1975), 9.

52. Alexander Henry to Joseph Banks, 13 October 1781, Alexander Henry Papers, Public Archives of Canada, Ottawa; Alexander Henry to William Edgar, 1 September 1785 and 5 March 1786, North West Company Papers and Accounts Collection, Toronto Metropolitan Reference Library; Gough, "North West Company," 318–319; and James Ronda, "Astoria and the Birth of Empire," *Montana: The Magazine of Western History* 36 (Summer 1986): 26–28.

53. Mackenzie, "General History," 82–83, 415–418; and Ronda, "Astoria," 30–31.

54. Jonathan Goldstein, *Philadelphia and the China Trade* (Philadelphia: Univ. of Pennsylvania Press, 1978), 24–27; Foster Rhea Dulles, *The Old China Trade* (New York: AMS, 1970), 51–52; and Philip C. F. Smith, *The Empress of China* (Philadelphia: Philadelphia Maritime Museum, 1984), 229, passim.

55. Timothy Pitkin, *A Statistical View of the Commerce of the United States of America . . .* (New Haven: Durrie & Peck, 1835), 264; Thomas Vaughn, ed., *Soft Gold* (Portland: Oregon Historical Society, 1982), viii; Dulles, *Old China Trade,* 53–61.

56. Emory Johnson et al., *History of Domestic and Foreign Commerce of the United States,* 2 vols. (Washington, D.C.: Carnegie Institute, 1915), 2:336, 349. All these laws were continually revised. Johnson has a convenient summary on p. 349.

57. Porter, 1:24–25, 129.

58. Astor's presence at Henry's home was evident in Legal Document of Protest by *Richard Dobie* v. *John Astor,* 21 December 1790, in Porter, 1:364.

59. Alexander Henry to William Edgar, 1 September 1785 and 5 March 1786, North West Company Papers; Power of Attorney of Sampson Fleming to William Edgar, 1782; Samson-Fleming to William Fleming, 28 September 1787, Sampson-Fleming Letterbook, William Edgar Papers, New York Public Library, New York City; and Herman Edgar to Miss Mayer, 23 April 1934, Edgar Papers, Dossier File.

60. Porter dates Astor's first voyage to China as 1800, but his involvement began much earlier. See Porter, 1:118.

61. Alexander Henry to McTavish, Frobisher & Co. to Messrs. McTavish, Fraser & Co., 21 December 1792; James Hallowell to Simon McTavish, 21 August

1794, in Grace Morris, "Some Letters from 1792–1800 on the China Trade," *Oregon Historical Quarterly* 42 (1941): 48–56; Captain William Howell to William Edgar, 15 December 1793, Edgar Papers; EIC, 1792–1793, p. 104.

62. Balance Sheet, 30 November 1794; Alexander Henry to Simon McTavish, 23 November 1794; James Hallowell to Messrs. McTavish, Fraser, & Co., 2 April 1795, HBC, NW, PAC. Also see Rich, *Hudson's Bay Company,* 2:206–207; and Campbell, *North West Company,* 90.

63. James Hallowell to Simon McTavish, 22 May 1795, and Balance Sheet, 30 November 1794, HBC, NW, PAC.

64. Agreement between P. Liebert and Astor, 25 August 1792, John Jacob Astor Papers, Library of Congress, Washington, D.C.; and Agreement between Fleury Mesplet and Astor, 29 August 1792, AP, BL, 10.

65. See, for example, Petition of John Astor and Associates, 19 September 1792, Lower Canada Land Papers, Public Archives of Canada, Ottawa, Microfilm Reel C 2506, pp. 17406–17413; and Petition of Alexander Henry, 19 June 1793, Lower Canada Land Papers, Public Archives of Canada, Microfilm Reel C 2533, pp. 51529–51557. Also see Creighton, *Commercial Empire,* 122–123.

66. John Astor to Peter Smith, 7 August 1794 and William Laight to Peter Smith, 30 November 1794, Smith Papers, Reel 1. Laight is identified as a partner of William Backhouse in Duncan, *New York City Directory, 1792,* 1.

67. Announcement of Land Title of Astor, Smith and Laight in *Greenleaf's New York Journal and Patriotic Register,* 6 December 1794, in Porter, 1:387–388; Astor to Smith, 7 August 1794 and 30 November 1794, Smith Papers, Reel 1; Astor to Smith, 7 December and 29 October 1796; 3 March and 9 March 1798, AP, BL, 10. A sample deed illustrating a typical settlement with a resident is Contract of Smith, Astor, and Laight with Josiah Fuller, 10 September 1803, Smith Papers, Reel 12. Also see the excellent discussion in David M. Ellis, *Landlords and Farmers in the Hudson-Mohawk Region, 1790–1850* (New York: Farrar, Straus & Giroux, Octagon Books, 1967), 58.

68. Deed of purchase from Henry Astor to John Astor, 18 May 1789, in Porter, 1:356–359; *New York Gazette and General Advertiser,* 3 June 1794; and *Index of Conveyances Recorded in the Office of the Register of the City and County of New York* (New York: McSpedon & Baker, 1857), Grantors, vol. A, p. 166; and Grantees vol. A, p. 158; and Porter, 1:39–40.

69. Duncan, *New York Directory, 1792,* 6; William Duncan, *The New York Directory and Register for the Year 1795* (New York: T. & J. Sword, 1795), 9; and Porter, 2:1034–1040.

70. Porter, 2:953; and Robert G. Albion, *The Rise of New York Port* (New York: Scribner's, 1939), 264–265.

71. T. Longworth, *Longworth's American Almanack: New York Register and City Directory* (New York: T. & J. Swords, 1798), 77; Porter, 2:1084–1085; and Dorothie Bobbie, *De Witt Clinton* (New York: Minton, Balch, 1933), 60.

72. Charles M. Mount, *Gilbert Stuart, Biography* (New York: Norton, 1964), 177; *Gilbert Stuart: Portraitist of the Young Republic, 1755–1828* (Washington, D.C.: National Gallery of Art, 1967), 64–76; and Porter, 2:1065–1066.

Chapter 3

1. The position of Astor as a "modern" merchant fits the general views of Thomas Cochran who has argued for the significance of business change in the early Republic: see Thomas Cochran, "The Business Revolution," *American Historical*

Review 79 (December 1974): 1449–1466; and idem, *Frontiers of Change: Early Industrialism in America* (New York: Oxford Univ. Press, 1981), 17–49. Older views are found in Norman S. Gras and Henrietta Larson, *Casebook in American Business History* (New York: Appleton-Century-Crofts, 1939), 76–97. Also see Alfred Chandler, *The Visible Hand* (Cambridge: Harvard Univ. Press, 1977), 38, 15–49. A more lengthy discussion of these issues can be found in John Haeger, "Business Strategy and Practice in the Early Republic: John Jacob Astor and the American Fur Trade," *Western Historical Quarterly,* 19 (May 1988): 183–202.

2. Robert G. Albion, *The Rise of New York Port* (New York: Scribner's, 1939), 394; John H. Coatsworth, "American Trade with European Colonies in the Caribbean and South America, 1790–1812," *William and Mary Quarterly* 24 (April 1967): 243–250; Arthur P. Whitaker, *The United States and the Independence of Latin America* (Baltimore: Johns Hopkins Univ. Press, 1941), 1–23; and Peggy Liss, *Atlantic Empires* (Baltimore: Johns Hopkins Univ. Press, 1983), 112–113.

3. Curtis P. Nettels, *The Emergence of a National Economy, 1775–1815* (New York: Harper & Row, Torchbooks, 1962), 221–242; Emory Johnson et al., *History of Domestic and Foreign Commerce of the United States,* 2 vols. (Washington, D.C.: Carnegie Institute, 1915), 2:20–21. For other views on the significance of foreign trade to American growth in this period, see Douglass North, *The Economic Growth of the United States, 1790–1860* (Englewood Cliffs, N.J.: Prentice-Hall, 1961), 17–58; Claudia Goldin and Frank Lewis, "The Role of Exports in American Economic Growth During the Napoleonic Wars, 1793–1807," *Explorations in Economic History* 17 (Fall 1980): 6–25; and Donald R. Adams, "American Neutrality and Prosperity, 1793–1808: A Reconsideration," *Journal of Economic History* 40 (December 1980): 713–737.

4. Tench Coxe, *A View of the United States of America* (1794; repr., New York: August Kelley, 1965), 458–459; Nettels, *Emergence,* 110–111; and Johnson et al., *Domestic Trade,* 2:328, 337, 349.

5. Albion, *New York Port,* 8; North, *Economic Growth,* 49; Sidney I. Pomerantz, *New York: An American City, 1783–1803* (Port Washington, N.Y.: Ira Friedman, 1965), 147–162, 200–201; Grant Morrison, "Isaac Bronson and the Search for System in American Capitalism, 1789–1838" (Ph.D. diss., City Univ. of New York, 1974), 61–66.

6. John Inglis to George Grenville, 31 May 1790, in Gordon Davidson, *The North West Company* (Berkeley: Univ. of California Press, 1918), 272–274; Robert Hamilton, "Observations on the Trade of Upper Canada," 24 September 1798, *MPHC,* 25:202–205; "Memorial of Montreal Merchants—McTavish, Frobisher & Co., Forsyth Richardson & Co., and Todd McGill & Co. to John Simcoe, 9 December 1791, *MPHC,* 24: 338–342; Wayne Edson Stevens, *The Northwest Fur Trade, 1763–1800,* Univ. of Illinois Studies in the Social Sciences, 14 (Urbana: Univ. of Illinois, 1928), 106, n. 48; E. E. Rich, *The History of the Hudson's Bay Company, 1670–1870,* 2 vols. (London: Hudson's Bay Record Society, 1958–1959), 2:189; and D. G. Creighton, *The Commercial Empire of the St. Lawrence* (Toronto: Ryerson, 1937), 132–133.

7. My analysis of the Jay Treaty and the position of the Canadian fur traders depends on the following: Creighton, *Commercial Empire,* 93–95, 132–135; Charles Ritcheson, *Aftermath of Revolution* (Dallas, Tex.: Southern Methodist Univ. Press, 1969), 8–17, 123–196; Bradford Perkins, *The First Rapprochment* (Berkeley: Univ. of Calfornia Press, 1967), 3; Nelson Russell, *The British Regime in Michigan*

and the Old Northwest, 1760–1796 (Northfield, Minn.: Carleton College Press, 1939), 236–270.

8. Rich, *Hudson's Bay Company,* 2:197–198; Creighton, *Commercial Empire,* 135–142; Porter, 1:52.

9. Alexander Henry to Simon McTavish, 23 November 1794, and James Hallowell to Simon McTavish, 22 May 1795, HBC, NW, PAC; John Astor to Peter Smith, 19 February 1795, AP, BL, 10.

10. Alexander Mackenzie to McTavish, Frobisher & Co., 29 January 1798, HBC, NW, PAC; Mackenzie to McTavish, Frobisher & Co., 30 January 1798, in W. Kaye Lamb, ed., *The Journals and Letters of Sir Alexander Mackenzie* (Cambridge: Cambridge Univ. Press, 1970), 463; Alexander Mackenzie, "A General History of the Fur Trade from Canada to the North-West," in Lamb, *Journals and Letters,* 82–83; Rich, *Hudson's Bay Company,* 2:210–211; Barry Gough, "The North West Company's Adventure to China," *Oregon Historical Quarterly* 76 (December 1975): 310–321; and Barry Gough, *Distant Dominion* (Vancouver: Univ. of British Columbia Press, 1980), 140.

11. EIC, 1798, p. 123; Gough, "North West Company," 319–320; Mackenzie to McTavish, Frobisher & Co., 29 January 1798, 30 January 1798, and 4 February 1798, in Lamb, *Journals and Letters,* 460–467; Mackenzie to McTavish, Fraser & Co., 4 March 1798, and James Hallowell to McTavish, Fraser & Co., 10 October 1798, NW, PAC.

12. John Fraser to McTavish, Fraser & Co., 12 February 1800, in Grace Morris, "Some Letters from 1792–1800 on the China Trade," *Oregon Historical Quarterly* 42 (1941): 85; Letter to McTavish, Frobisher & Co., 14 December 1799; John Murray to Simon McTavish, 9 May 1800; William McGillivray to Angus McIntosh, 26 May 1800; James Hallowell to Simon McTavish, 19 May 1800, NW, PAC.

13. Statement of Furs Exported from Quebec, 1801, North West Company Records, in Davidson, *North West Company,* 283; Rich, *Hudson's Bay Company,* 2:188; Wayne Edson Stevens, "The Michigan Fur Trade," *Michigan History* 29 (October–December 1945): 498–499; Mackenzie, "General History," in Lamb, *Journals and Letters,* 83.

14. Duncan McGillivray to Proprietors of the North West Company, 23 May 1802, NW, PAC; Lamb, *Journals and Letters,* 29–32; Rich, *Hudson's Bay Company,* 2:195–213; Creighton, *Commercial Empire,* 135–142; William Stewart Wallace, *The Pedlars from Quebec* (Toronto: Ryerson, 1954), 55; Russell A. Pendergast, "The XY Company, 1798–1804 (Ph.D. diss., Ottawa Univ., 1957), 3–190.

15. "Memoir of Isaac Todd and Simon McTavish, 1794, in Davidson, *North West Company,* 177–178; David Lavender, *The Fist in the Wilderness* (Garden City, N.Y.: Doubleday, 1964), 39–40; Paul Phillips, *The Fur Trade,* 2 vols. (Norman: Univ. of Oklahoma Press, 1961), 2:99–111; and Stevens, *Northwest Fur Trade,* 102–104.

16. Porter, 1:110–125; and Gras and Larson, *Casebook,* 82–83; William Duncan, *The New York Directory and Register for the Year 1795* (New York: T. & J. Sword, 1795), 9; T. Longworth, *Longworth's American Almanack: New York Register and City Directory* (New York: T. & J. Swords, 1798); *New York Commercial Advertiser,* 3 October 1797, 1803–1804, and 1805–1806.

17. John Astor Invoices, 1799–1801, AP, BL, 13; and Customs Receipts, NA, RG 36.

18. Ibid.; Porter, 1:110, 118–123. Porter makes a major point that Astor imported many weapons, but the evidence is contradictory. Gunpowder listed in

invoices could have been gunpowder tea. The actual weapons were small in number and were used, most likely, to arm vessels in the China trade. Supposedly, one letter made reference to a Mr. Oster who imported weapons, yet the letter came from individuals who would have known the proper spelling of Astor's name. See Porter, 1:112–115; and the following documents help challenge Porter's interpretations: *New York Gazette and General Advertiser,* 6 and 27 January 1800; Customs Receipts, 14 May 1801, NA, RG 36; Entry of Merchandise Imported on Ship *Two Friends,* 1800, AP, NYHS; John Astor to Colonel Whipple, 6 July 1801 and 18 June 1799; and Letter of John Astor, 3 February 1802, AP, NYPL, Box 1.

19. Alexander Henry to John Askin, 18 January 1800, in Milo Quaife, ed., *John Askin Papers,* 2 vols. (Detroit: Detroit Library Commission, 1929), 2:274–276; James McGill to Isaac Todd, 17 October 1805, AP, BL, 13; Copies of Minutes of Beaver Club, 1810, AP, BL, 12; Samuel Bridge's Journal, 1806, in Porter, 1:412–413; Journal of Joseph Frobisher, 8 September 1806 and 17 September 1808, AP, BL, 10; Porter, 1:66–67; and J. C. Clarke, "From Business to Politics: The Ellice Family 1760–1860" (Ph.D. diss., Oxford Univ., 1974), 20, 71.

20. Astor to William Fowler, 31 August 1803, John Astor Papers, Columbia Univ. Library, New York City; Astor to Fowler, 7 June 1802, AP, HSP; Astor to Peter Smith, 13 July 1799, AP, BL, 10; Astor to Smith, 8 February 1804, Peter Smith Papers, George Arents Research Center, Syracuse Univ., New York, Microfilm Reel 1; P. l'Herbette to Henry Brevoort, Jr., 6 March 1805, in George S. Hellman, ed., *Letters of Henry Brevoort to Washington Irving, Together with Other Unpublished Papers,* 2 vols. (New York: Putnam's, 1918), 2:118–180; Astor's contract with John Williams, 12 April 1806, in Porter, 1:410–412; Thomas Blackwood to J. & A. McGill, 4 July 1806, Thomas Blackwood Papers, McGill Univ. Library, Montreal, Canada.

21. John Astor to Auguste Chouteau, 28 January 1800, in Porter, 1:389–390; Astor to John l'Herbette, 16 December 1814, AP, BL, 17; Customs Receipts for 14 October 1802, 17 July 1802, and 12 February 1800, NA, RG 36; and William E. Foley and C. David Rice, *The First Chouteaus* (Urbana: Univ. of Illinois Press, 1983), 74–75, 82–83.

22. *New York Gazette and General Advertiser,* 1 January 1799 and 10 October 1800; Porter, 1:114.

23. Customs Receipts for 28 April 1804 and 5 November 1803, and passim, NA, RG 36.

24. 1804–1807, NA, RG 36; Rich, *Hudson's Bay Company,* 2: 190–192; Stevens, *Northwest Fur Trade,* 147–149; Henry Poland, *Fur-Bearing Animals in Nature and Commerce* (London: Gurney & Jackson, 1892), liv., 54.

25. Kenneth Scott Latourette, "The History of Early Relations Between the United States and China, 1784–1844," *Transactions of the Connecticut Academy of Arts and Sciences,* 22 (August 1917): 29–30. Early statistics for the China trade are scarce before 1804 when the East India Company provided the most authoritative records. The statistics presented here come from three sources. First, the East India Company kept track of all foreign ships entering Canton and usually listed their imports and exports. For this note, these records include EIC, 1798–1799, p. 123; 1799–1800, p. 127; 1801, p. 135; 1802–1803, p. 143. In addition, the American consul in Canton maintained a list of vessels and cargoes from 1804 to 1810: "List of Exports and Imports by American Vessels, 1804–1810," in U.S. Department of State, Despatches from U.S. Consuls in Canton, 1790–1906, National Archives Microfilm no. 101 (hereafter "List of Exports," U.S. Consul). Probably the best sum-

mary of American trade appeared in tabular form during a parliamentary investigation of the East India Company: see "Statement of American Imports and Exports at Canton, 1804–1818," Great Britain, House of Commons, *Report by the Lords Committee Appointed Select Committee to Inquire into the Means of Extending and Securing the Foreign Trade of the Country, and to Report to the House . . . ,* vol. 7, 1821, pp. 314–315 (hereafter "Statement of American Trade," GB, HC, 1821). Convenient lists, containing some of the statistics listed herein, are in Foster Rhea Dulles, *The Old China Trade* (New York: AMS, 1970), 210; and Timothy Pitkin, *A Statistical View of the Commerce of the United States of America . . .* (New Haven: Durrie & Peck, 1835), 465–467.

26. "Statement of American Trade," GB, HC, 1821, pp. 314–315; and Adam Seybert, *Statistical Annals: Embracing Views of the Population, Commerce, Navigation . . . of the United States of America* (Philadelphia: Thomas Dobson, 1818), 155.

27. "Commerce of China," *Hunt's Merchant Magazine* 3 (December 1840): 467; Astor to William Bell, 27 April 1799, and Account Book of Ship *Mary,* 1799, Constable-Pierpont Collection, William Bell Papers, New York Public Library; EIC, 1798, p. 123; Brian Evans, "Ginseng: Root of Chinese-Canadian Relations," *Canadian Historical Review* 56 (March 1985): 4–25; and James Kirker, *Adventures to China* (New York: Oxford Univ. Press, 1970), 7.

28. *New York Gazette and General Advertiser,* 5 July 1799, 6 and 27 January 1800; 27 June 1800; and 21 August 1800; and Porter, 1:115.

29. John McVickar, Lawrence Van Zandt, and Coster & Co. to John Bell, 27 April 1799; Astor to William Bell, 27 April 1799; Account Book of Ship *Mary,* 1799, Bell Papers.

30. *New York Gazette and General Advertiser,* 30 June 1800; John Astor to Colonel Whipple, 6 July 1801, and Letter of Astor, 3 February 1802, AP, NYPL; D. Sutherland to John Astor, 27 November 1802, Sir Alexander Mackenzie & Co. Papers, 1798–1825, Minnesota Historical Society, Saint Paul, Minnesota.

31. EIC, 1801, p. 135; 1802, p. 140; AP, BL, 13. (This reel contains typed copies of EIC records concerning Astor's ships to and from Canton.) Also see, Porter, 1:124. Description of products and measurements in the China trade can be found in "Commerce of China," *Hunt's Merchant Magazine,* 1840, 474–477; and Philip White, *The Beekmans of New York in Politics and Commerce, 1647–1877* (New York: New York Historical Society, 1956), 646–647.

32. EIC, 1803, p. 143; 1804, p. 149; List of Astor's Vessels, AP, BL, 13; "Register of Ship *Beaver,*" 7 May 1805, in Porter, 1:407. On characteristics of the British ships, see GB, HC, *Report on Foreign Trade . . . ,* vol. 7, 1821, p. 39.

33. EIC, 1806–1807, p. 158; 1807–1808, p. 161; List of Astor's Ships, AP, BL, 13; Porter, 1:139–140.

34. List of Astor's Ships, AP, BL, 13; EIC, 1804–1805, p. 149; 1805–1806, p. 151; 1807–1808, p. 161.

35. Manifest of the *Severn,* 25 May 1804, in Porter, 1:406–407; Astor to Gerritt Van Schaick, 6, 14, and 28 April and 9 and 12 May, 1804; and 29 January 1806, Gerrit Van Schaick Papers, New York Public Library, New York City; Porter, 1:137, 141.

36. See Astor's estimates of sales in John Astor to William Bell, April 1799, Bell Papers; Estimates also came from item by item estimates in the EIC Papers and in List of Astor's Ships, AP, BL, 13.

37. "Manifest of *Severn,* in Porter, 1:406–407; and Porter, 1:146–147.

38. "Statement of American Trade, GB, HC, 1821, pp. 187 and 314–315. Prices current in Canton are estimates based on prices entered for some products in "List of Imports and Exports," U.S. Consul; and in Pitkin, *Statistical View,* 251. Reference to the importance of the American fur trade is from Testimony of Mr. Blanshard, in GB, HC, *Report on Foreign Trade . . . ,* vol. 7, 1821, p. 236.

39. John Astor to Daniel Greene, 30 September 1813, AP, BL, 3; John McVickar, Lawrence Van Zandt, and Coster & Co. to Captain Daniel Moore, 27 April 1799, and same to Daniel Moore, Bell Papers; Albion, *New York Port,* 200; Porter, 1:136–143; Tyler Dennett, *Americans in Eastern Asia* (New York: Barnes & Noble, 1941), 71; and Stuart Bruchey, *Robert Oliver: Merchant of Baltimore, 1783–1819* (Baltimore: Johns Hopkins Univ. Press, 1956), 100–165.

40. Astor to Greene, 30 September 1813, AP, BL, 3; Astor to Bell, 27 April 1799, and Account Book Ship *Mary,* Bell Papers.

41. Astor to Bell, 27 April 1799, Bell Papers; Astor to Richard Cleveland, 15 November 1817, John Astor Papers, Library of Congress, Washington, D.C.; John Astor to Chandler Price, 15 December 1814, AP, BL, 17; Account of the *Seneca,* 1819, AP, NYHS; and Porter, 1:136, 140.

42. John McVicker, Lawrence Van Zandt, and Coster & Co. to Capt. Daniel Moore, 27 April 1799, and Account Book of Ship *Mary,* Bell Papers; Mary V. Kuebel, "Merchants and Mandarins: The Genesis of American Relations with China" (Ph.D. diss., Univ. of Virginia, 1974), 13, 20–21; EIC, 1803–1804, p. 143; 1804–1805, p. 146; 1805–1806, p. 151; Dulles, *Old China Trade,* 49; and Barry Gough, *The Royal Navy and the Northwest Coast of North America, 1810–1914* (Vancouver: Univ. of British Columbia Press, 1971), 341.

43. Kuebel, "Merchants and Mandarins," 49–79; Dulles, *Old China Trade,* 14; Latourette, "Early Relations," 7ff.; and Conrad Wright, "Merchants and Mandarins: New York and the Early China Trade," in David S. Howard, *New York and the China Trade* (New York: New York Historical Society, 1984), 37–39.

44. Latourette, "Early Relations," 20–21; Kuebel, "Merchants and Mandarins," 61–62; and Yen-P'ing Hao, *The Comprador in Nineteenth Century China* (Cambridge: Harvard Univ. Press, 1970), 2–3.

45. "The China Trade," *Hunt's Merchant Magazine* 12 (January 1845): 44–47; Kuebel, "Merchants and Mandarins," 64–66; Latourette, "Early Relations," 22–23; Kirker, *Adventures,* 164–165; Accounts of Rectified Voyages to China, AP, NYHS; and Account Book of Ship *Mary,* Bell Papers.

46. Kuebel, "Merchants and Mandarins," 67–68; Carl Crossman, *The China Trade* (Princeton, N.J.: Princeton Univ. Press, 1972), 3; and Wright, "Merchants," 35–37.

47. Account Book of Ship *Mary;* and Account book of Ship *William and John,* 1816, Bell Papers.

48. Astor to George Ehninger, 6 March 1815, AP, BL, 3; Stanley Patterson and Carl Seaburg, *Merchant Prince of Boston* (Cambridge: Harvard Univ. Press, 1971), 52–54; Kirker, *Adventures,* 9, 170–174; and Jonathan Goldstein, *Philadelphia and the China Trade* (Philadelphia: Univ. of Pennsylvania Press, 1978), 16–17.

49. "Commerce of China," *Hunt's Merchant Magazine* 3 (December 1840), 466–468; "The China Trade" (1845), 48–52; List of Astor's Ships, AP, BL, 13.

50. List of Astor's Ships, AP, BL, 13; EIC, 1804–1805, p. 149; 1805–1806, p. 151; 1806–1807, p. 158; "Statement of American Trade," GB, HC, 1821; Goldstein, *Philadelphia,* 38–40.

51. McVickar, Van Zandt, and Coster to Moore, 27 April 1799, Bell Papers; List of Astor's Ships, AP, BL, 13.

52. Latourette, "Early Relations," 78, n. 138; Kuebel, "Merchants and Mandarins," 335–336; Johnson et al., *Domestic Trade*, 2:336–337; Great Britain, House of Lords, *Report from the Select Committee of the House of Lords Appointed to Enquire into the Present State of the Affairs of the East India Company . . .*, 1830, vol. 274, pp. 644–645.

53. Pitkin, *Statistical View*, 265; "The China Trade," (1845), 50; *New York Commercial Advertiser*, 7 May 1803; Rectified Account of Astor's Voyages, AP, NYHS; Porter, 1:136; Astor to John Dorr, 16 August 1813; Astor to William Lippincott, 18 September and 20 December 1813; Astor to Henry Payson & Co., 17 September 1813 and 29 October 1813, AP, BL, 3.

54. Allan Nevins, ed., *The Diary of Philip Hone, 1828–1851*, 2 vols. (1927; repr., New York: Kraus Reprint Co., 1969), 2:847–848; Pitkin, *Statistical View*, 265; NA, RG 36, passim and Customs Receipts, 21 June 1806, 12 July 1806, 27 July 1802; Rectified Account of Astor Voyages, AP, NYHS; and Astor to William Ely, 3 May 1806, AP, NYPL, Box 1.

55. Accounts of Rectified Voyages, 1816–1820, AP, NYHS; Astor to Albert Gallatin, 9 October 1815, GP, 19.

56. *Index of Conveyances Recorded in the Office of the Register of the City and County of New York* (New York: McSpedon & Baker, 1857), vol. A, pp. 157–159. Each of Astor's lot purchases also can be traced in the microfilmed Libers of Deeds and Conveyances in the Office of the City Register, New York County, New York City. Also see Porter, 2:941, 956, 989.

57. Porter, 1:124 and 2:1066–1067.

58. Porter, 1:66–67 and 2:1034.

Chapter 4

1. Washington Irving to Pierre Monroe Irving, 15 September 1834, 6 May 1835 and 10 June 1835, in "Documents on Washington Irving and Astoria," *Washington Historical Quarterly*, 18 (April 1927), 133–136; Gabriel Franchére, *Adventures at Astoria, 1810–1814* (1820; repr., Norman: Univ. of Oklahoma Press, 1967); Alexander Ross, *Adventures of the First Settlers on the Oregon or Columbia River, 1810–1813* (1849; repr., Lincoln: Univ. of Nebraska Press, 1986); Ross Cox, *Adventures on the Columbia River Including the Narrative of a Residence of Six Years on the Western Side of the Rocky Mountains . . .* (New York: J. & L. Harper, 1832); "Wilson Price Hunt's Diary of His Overland Trip Westward to Astoria in 1811–1812," in Philip A. Rollins, ed., *The Discovery of the Oregon Trail* (New York: Edward Eberstadt, 1935), 267–328; Duncan McDougall Journal, 3 vols., Rosenbach Library, Philadelphia, Pennsylvania. Also see Washington Irving, *Astoria, or Anecdotes of an Enterprise Beyond the Rocky Mountains,* ed. by Richard Dilworth Rust (Lincoln: Univ. of Nebraska Press, 1982), 355. Also see John Astor to Albert Gallatin, 2 December 1821, GP, 34; John Astor to Albert Gallatin, 22 August 1836, GP, 41; and Porter, 1:211.

2. Irving, *Astoria,* (1982) 502–504; Hubert Howe Bancroft, *History of the Northwest Coast,* vol. 2, *1800–1846* (San Francisco: A L. Bancroft, 1884), 136–138; Hiram M. Chittenden, *The American Fur Trade of the Far West,* 3 vols. (New York: Francis P. Harper, 1902), 1:243–245. James Ronda, *Astoria and Empire* (Lincoln:

Univ. of Nebraska Press, 1990). A good recent summary is found in David J. Wishart, *The Fur Trade of the American West, 1807–1840* (Lincoln: Univ. of Nebraska Press, 1979), 116–120.

3. Ann Carlos, "The Causes and Origins of the North American Fur Trade Rivalry, 1804–1806," *Journal of Economic History* 41 (December 1981): 777–778; and David Lavender, "Some American Characteristics of the American Fur Company," in Russell W. Fridley, ed., *Aspects of the Fur Trade: Selected Papers of the 1965 North American Fur Trade Conference* (Saint Paul: Minnesota Historical Society, 1967), 32.

4. Memorial of Canadian Merchants to Thomas Dunn, President of the Province of Lower Canada, 8 November 1805, in Letter of A. Merry to James Madison, 7 January 1806, in William R. Manning, ed., *Diplomatic Correspondence of the United States: Canadian Relations, 1784–1860,* vol. 1, *1784–1820* (Washington, D.C.: Carnegie Endowment for International Peace, 1940), 573–575: Memorandum to Mr. Jackson, 30 September 1809, PRO, FO, 115/20; Thomas Blackwood to Charles Chaboiller, 30 May 1806, Thomas Blackwood Papers, McGill Univ. Library, Canada; David Lavender, *The Fist in the Wilderness* (Garden City, N.Y.: Doubleday, 1964), 42, 58; D. G. Creighton, *The Commercial Empire of the St. Lawrence* (Toronto: Ryerson, 1937), 17–171; and Gary C. Anderson, "American Agents vs. British Traders: Prelude to the War of 1812 in the Far West," in Ronald Lora, ed., *The American West* (Toledo, Ohio: Univ. of Toledo, 1980), 7–10.

5. Alexander Mackenzie, "A General History of the Fur Trade from Canada to the North-West," and the same author's *Voyages from Montreal . . .* (London: R. Noble, 1801), in W. Kaye Lamb, ed., *The Journals and Letters of Sir Alexander Mackenzie* (Cambridge: Cambridge Univ. Press, 1970): 82–83, 415–418; and Donald Jackson, *Thomas Jefferson and the Stony Mountains* (Urbana: Univ. of Illinois Press, 1981), 121, 126–127.

6. Wayne Edson Stevens, *The Northwest Fur Trade, 1763–1800,* Univ. of Illinois Studies in the Social Sciences, 14 (Urbana: Univ. of Illinois, 1928), 172–178; Donald Meinig, *The Great Columbia Plain* (Seattle: Univ. of Washington Press, 1968), 34; Thomas Jefferson to Meriwether Lewis, 20 June 1803, in Reuben G. Thwaites, ed., *Original Journals of the Lewis and Clark Expedition, 1804–1806* (New York: Antiquarian Press, 1959), 7:251; Thomas Jefferson's Message to Congress, 18 January 1803, in Thwaites, *Lewis and Clark Journals,* 207–209; and Francis Paul Prucha, *The Sword of the Republic* (New York: Macmillan, 1969), 88–89.

7. James Wilkinson, Order of 26 August 1805; Anthony Merry, British Minister, to James Madison, 7 and 8 January 1806, in Manning, *Diplomatic Correspondence,* 1:574–579; and Lavender, *Fist,* 44–45, 61–62.

8. Agreement between the North West Company and the Michilimackinac Company, 31 December 1806, North West Company Minute Book, NW, PAC; Paul Phillips, *The Fur Trade,* 2 vols. (Norman: Univ. of Oklahoma Press, 1961), 2:132; Lamb, *Journals and Letters,* 39–40; and Stevens, *Northwest Fur Trade,* 288–289.

9. Meriwether Lewis to Thomas Jefferson, 23 September 1806, in Donald Jackson, ed., *Letters of the Lewis and Clark Expedition,* 2 vols. (Urbana: Univ. of Illinois Press, 1978), 1:321–322.

10. Irving, *Astoria* (1982), 30–32; James Ronda, "Astoria and the Birth of Empire," *Montana: The Magazine of Western History* 36 (Summer 1986): 34.

11. Burton Spivak, *Jefferson's English Crisis* (Charlottesville: Univ. Press of Virginia, 1979), 71–72, 78–79; Richard Mannix, "Gallatin, Jefferson, and the Em-

bargo of 1808," *Diplomatic History* 3 (Spring 1979): 1151–1152; Albert Gallatin to Henry Dearborn, 7 September 1807, GP, suppl., Reel 2; and Reginald Horsman, "On to Canada: Manifest Destiny and United States Strategy in the War of 1812," *Michigan Historical Review* 13 (Fall 1987): 9.

12. Ibid.; Thomas Jefferson to Gallatin, 7 January 1808, Thomas Jefferson Papers, Library of Congress, Microfilm Ed., Reel 40.

13. Astor to De Witt Clinton, 25 January 1808, De Witt Clinton Papers, Columbia Univ., New York City; Dorothie Bobbie, *De Witt Clinton* (New York: Minton, Balch, 1933), 143–179; William Campbell, *The Life and Writings of De Witt Clinton* (New York: Barker & Scribner, 1849), xxxi.

14. Astor to Clinton, 25 January 1808, Clinton Papers.

15. Ibid.

16. Ibid.; Lamb, *Journals and Letters,* 418; Sir Alexander Mackenzie, "Preliminaries to the Establishment of a Permanent British Fishery and Trade in Furs . . . on the Continent and West Coast of North America," in Lamb, *Journals and Letters,* 505–507; Great Britain, Parliament, House of Commons, *Third Report from the Select Committee Appointed to Consider of the Means of Improving and Maintaining the Foreign Trade of the Country, East India and China,* 1821, vol. 6, 230–231; and Barry Gough, "The North West Company's Adventure to China," *Oregon Historical Quarterly* 76 (December 1975): 313–318.

17. Ibid. Other historians have argued that Astor was after a monopoly of the fur trade and that he intended from the beginning to make the American Fur Company entirely his own. See Irving, *Astoria* (1982), 20–23; Porter, 1:166–169. However, this interpretation assesses Astor's motives on the basis of what finally transpired, not necessarily on the basis of what Astor hoped for in 1808.

18. Jefferson Message to Congress, 18 June 1803, in Thwaites, *Lewis and Clark Journals,* 7:207–209; Jefferson to Gallatin, 7 January 1808, Jefferson Papers, 40; Astor to Clinton, 25 January 1808, Clinton Papers; Astor to Gallatin, 16 May 1809, GP, 19.

19. Astor to George Clinton, 9 March 1808, AP, Beinecke; Astor to Jefferson, 25 February 1808, Jefferson Papers, 40. Although David Lavender, *The Fist,* discounts that such a meeting ever took place, the evidence is clear that it did. See Astor to Madison, 27 July 1813, in Dorothy Wildes Bridgewater, ed., "John Jacob Astor Relative to His Settlement on the Columbia River," *Yale University Library Gazette* 24 (October 1949): 61–62; Gallatin to Astor, 5 August 1835, GP, 41; Astor to George Clinton, 9 March 1808, AP, Beinecke; Gallatin to Daniel Jackson, 23 August 1836, in Henry Adams, ed., *The Writings of Albert Gallatin,* 3 vols. (New York: Antiquarian Press, 1960), 2:506–511.

20. Jefferson to Astor, 13 April 1808, Jefferson Papers, 41; Astor to Jefferson, 27 February 1808, Jefferson Papers, 40. Also important is Jefferson to Astor, 24 May 1812, in Bridgewater, "Astor," 55, in which Jefferson states that he has specifically requested Astor's proposal. Also see Astor to Madison, 27 July 1813, in Bridgewater, "Astor," 61–62.

21. Gallatin to Astor, 5 August 1835, GP, 41; Gallatin to Jackson, 23 August 1836, in Adams, *Writings of Gallatin,* 2:506–511.

22. Jefferson to Meriwether Lewis, 17 July 1808, in Paul Leicester Ford, ed., *The Works of Thomas Jefferson,* 12 vols. (New York: Putnam's, 1905), 11:37–38.

23. Samuel Mitchell to Jefferson, 12 July 1808; Jefferson to Albert Gallatin, 25 July 1808; Philadelphia Merchants to Gallatin, 10 August 1808; Gallatin to

William Jones, 17 August 1808, in Porter, 1:420–428; Gallatin to David Gelston, 3 August 1808, GP, suppl., 2; and Astor to Editor, *New York Commercial Advertiser,* 15 August 1808. Good secondary accounts of the Embargo Act and the policy of exceptions can be found in Porter, 1:143–150; and Spivak, *Jefferson's Crisis,* 160–162.

24. Astor to George Clinton, 9 March 1808, AP, Beinecke; New York, Assembly, *List of All the Incorporations in the State of New York, Except Religious Incorporations, with a Recital of All Their Important Particulars and Peculiarities* (Albany: Jesse Burt, 1819), 47; Bobbie, *Clinton,* 131; New York State, Assembly, *Journal of the Assembly of the State of New York at Their Thirty-First Session, January 1808* (Albany: John Barber, 1808), 320, 344; Articles of Incorporation of the American Fur Company, 6 April 1808, in Porter, 1:413–420.

25. American Fur Company (hereafter AFC) Charter, Porter, 1:414–415; Ronald Seavoy, *The Origins of the American Business Corporation, 1783–1855* (Westport, Conn.: Greenwood, 1982), 47, 53–73.

26. AFC Charter, 414–416; Astor to George Clinton, 9 March 1808, AP, Beinecke. On the importance that Astor attached to stockholders, see his letter to De Witt Clinton, 25 July 1811, Clinton Papers.

27. Memorial of McTavish, Fraser & Co.; and Inglis Ellice & Co.; and Sir Alexander Mackenzie to Honorable Lords of the Privy Council, 30 June 1812, in Gordon Davidson, *The North West Company* (Berkeley: Univ. of Calfornia Press, 1918), 289–291; Alexander Henry to John Askin, 26 February 1810, in Milo Quaife, ed., *John Askin Papers* (Detroit: Detroit Library Commission, 1929), 2:653–654; Astor to Gallatin, 24 September 1808, GP, 17; Marjorie Wilkins Campbell, *The North West Company* (Toronto: Macmillan, 1957), 158, 164; Porter, 1:171.

28. Astor to Gallatin, 24 September 1808, GP, 17; Astor to Gallatin, 8 February 1809, GP, 18; Astor to James Madison, 27 July 1813, in Bridgewater, "Astor," 62.

29. Astor to Gallatin, 16 May 1809 and 28 September 1809, GP, 19.

30. David Erskine to James Madison, 21 June 1808; Robert Hamilton and Thomas Dickson to Francis Gore, 21 June 1808; and Charles Bagot to James Monroe, 9 July 1816, Manning, *Diplomatic Correspondence,* 1:601–603, 800–802. Also see Lavender, *The Fist,* 100–101.

31. Memorial of Montreal Merchants to Sir James Craig, 20 October 1808, *MPHC,* 25:255–256. Also see Creighton, *Commercial Empire,* 166–167.

32. Alexander Mackenzie to Viscount Castlereagh, 10 March 1808, in Lamb, ed., *Journals and Letters,* 517–518; "The Appeal of the North West Company to the British Government to Forestall John Jacob Astor's Columbian Enterprise," *Canadian Historical Review* 17 (September 1936): 304–311; Nathaniel Atcheson, Secretary to Marquis of Wellesley, 2 April 1810, PRO, FO, 115. Also see Creighton, *Commercial Empire,* 164–165, 170.

33. Quote in this paragraph is from "Memorandum to Mr. Jackson, 30 September 1809," PRO, FO, 115. Also see Simon McGillivray to Earl of Liverpool, 10 November 1810, in "Appeal of North West Company," 310–311; Nathaniel Atcheson to Wellesley, 2 April 1810, PRO, FO, 115; Memorial of McTavish, Fraser & Co.; and Inglis, Ellice & Co.; and Sir Alexander Mackenzie to Hon. Lords of the Privy Council, 30 June 1812, in Davidson, *North West Company,* 286–292.

34. Ibid.

35. Astor to Gallatin, 8 February 1809, GP, 18; Astor to Jefferson, 14 March 1812, Jefferson Papers, 45; Astor to Gallatin, 16 May 1809, GP, 19; and Curtis P. Nettels, *The Emergence of a National Economy, 1775–1818* (New York: Harper & Row, Torchbooks, 1962), 330.

36. Astor to Gallatin, 16 May 1809, GP, 19.

37. Ibid.

38. Ibid.; Charter of the Saint Louis Missouri Fur Company 1809, in Richard Oglesby, *Manuel Lisa and the Opening of the Missouri Fur Trade* (Norman: Univ. of Oklahoma Press, 1963), 202–208; ibid., 104; Wishart, *Fur Trade*, 41–45; and William E. Foley and C. David Rice, *The First Chouteaus* (Urbana: Univ. of Illinois Press, 1983), 170.

39. Andrei Dashkov to Alexander Baranov, 7 November 1809, and Astor to Alexander Baranov, 4 November 1809, in Nina Bashkina and David Trask, eds., *The United States and Russia: The Beginnings of Relations, 1765–1815* (Washington, D.C.: U.S. Government Printing Office, 1980), 603–611.

40. Letter of the Main Directorate of the Russian-American Company to General Meeting of Shareholders, 13 February 1812, in Bashkina and Trask, *United States and Russia,* 816–819; James R. Gibson, *Imperial Russia in Frontier America* (New York: Oxford Univ. Press, 1976), 4–11, 36, 44, 155–159; Howard Kushner, *Conflict on the Northwest Coast* (Westport, Conn.: Greenwood, 1975), 8–15; James R. Gibson, "The Russian-American Fur Trade," in Carol M. Judd and Arthur J. Ray, eds., *Old Trails and New Directions: Papers of the Third North American Fur Trade Conference* (Toronto: Univ. of Toronto Press, 1980), 221; S. B. Okun, *The Russian-American Company,* trans. Carl Ginsburg (Cambridge: Harvard Univ. Press, 1951), 77–80; Nikolai Bolkhovitinov, *The Beginning of Russian-American Relations, 1775–1815,* trans. Elena Levin (Cambridge: Harvard Univ. Press, 1975), 176–190.

41. Main Directorate of the Russian-American Company to Shareholders, 13 February 1812, and Dashkov to Baranov, 26 October 1809, in Bashkina and Trask, *United States and Russia,* 816–819, 609–613; Charles Francis Adams, ed., *Memoirs of John Quincy Adams* (Philadelphia: Lippincott, 1874), 2:178–179.

42. Dashkov to Baranov, 26 October 1809, and Astor to Baranov, 4 November 1809, in Bashkina and Trask, *United States and Russia,* 603–611.

43. Astor to Bentzon, 21 January 1811, in Porter, 1:455–456.

44. Astor to Baranov, 4 November 1809, in Bashkina and Trask, *United States and Russia,* 603–604; and Porter, 1:173–174.

45. "Inventory of the *Enterprise,* 1809," in Porter, 1:433–438. This cargo may have been considerably larger. The inventory of goods sold after reaching New Archangel was not necessarily an inventory of all goods sold at Ebbets's numerous stops along the coast.

46. Astor to Jefferson, 14 March 1812, in Porter, 1:508–509; Astor to Baranov, 4 November 1809 and Astor to Ebbets, 4 November 1809, in Bashkina and Trask, *United States and Russia,* 601–604.

47. Ibid. In addition to the letters noted earlier, there is another set of instructions that Astor gave to Ebbets that is quite different than the one found in the Russian archives and printed in Bashkina and Trask. I suspect that it represents Astor's earliest instructions to Ebbets before extensive discussions with the Russian consul, Dashkov. See Astor to Ebbets, November 1809, in Porter, 1:431–432.

Chapter 5

1. John Astor to Albert Gallatin, 28 September 1809 and 26 May 1810, GP, 19; John Richardson to Thomas Forsyth, 17 February 1810, PRO, FO, 115/20; Alexander Henry to John Askin, 26 February 1810, in Milo Quaife, ed., *John Askin*

Papers, 2 vols. (Detroit: Detroit Library Commission, 1929), 2:653–654; David Lavender, *The Fist in the Wilderness* (Garden City, N.Y.: Doubleday, 1964), 123–125. The most authoritative modern source on the Astoria venture is James Ronda, *Astoria and Empire* (Lincoln: Univ. of Nebraska Press, 1990).

2. Astor to Gallatin, 26 May 1810, GP, 21; Legal contract between John Astor and Alexander McKay, Donald Mackenzie, and Duncan McDougall, 10 March 1810, AP, BL, 10; Lavender, *The Fist*, 112–115, 124; T. C. Elliott, "Wilson Price Hunt, 1783–1842," *Oregon Historical Quarterly* 32 (1931): 130–134; Porter, 1:180–182.

3. Pacific Fur Company Charter, 23 June 1810, AP, BL, 10. There are more accessible copies of the charter: see Grace Flandrau, *Astor and the Oregon Country* (Saint Paul: Great Northern Railway, n.d.), 24–34; Pacific Fur Company Charter (typed copy), 23 June 1810, Miscellaneous Folder, AP, NYHS. The similarity to the North West Company structure is also mentioned in Washington Irving, *Astoria, or Anecdotes of an Enterprise Beyond the Rocky Mountains*, ed. Richard Dilworth Rust (1836; repr., Lincoln: Univ. of Nebraska Press, 1982), 37; and in David Lavender, "Some American Characteristics of the American Fur Company," in Russell W. Fridley, ed., *Aspects of the Fur Trade: Selected Papers of the 1965 North American Fur Trade Conference* (Saint Paul: Minnesota Historical Society, 1967), 33. Also see Porter, 1:181–182, and Alexander Ross, *Adventures of the First Settlers on the Oregon or Columbia River, 1810–1813* (1849; repr., Lincoln: Univ. of Nebraska Press, 1986), 38–39.

4. Pacific Fur Company Charter, 23 June 1810, AP, BL, 10.

5. Ross, *Adventures*, 41; and Gabriel Franchére, *Adventures at Astoria, 1810–1814* (1820; repr., Norman: Univ. of Oklahoma Press, 1967), 7.

6. Ross, *Adventures*, 40–41, 174–175; Franchére, *Adventures at Astoria*, 7–9; Astor to Jefferson, 14 March 1812, Thomas Jefferson Papers, Library of Congress, Microfilm Reel 45; Astor to Gallatin, 16 May 1809, GP, 19; Lavender, *The Fist*, 128–129.

7. Ross, *Adventures*, 175–179; Irving, *Astoria* (1982), 85–91; and Lavender, *The Fist*, 129–132.

8. Ross, *Adventures*, 179–182; Irving, *Astoria* (1982), 72–96; and Lavender, *The Fist*, 132–133, 146. Robert McClellan joined the group at its winter encampment. Irving says that Hunt recruited Crooks, McClellan, and Miller during the summer of 1810 when he met them in the West. However, these names were on the 23 June 1810 contract establishing the company, thus I think it is more logical to assume that they were part of the plan from late 1809.

9. Ross, *Adventures*, 180–183; Irving, *Astoria* (1982), 97–106; and Lavender, *The Fist*, 146–147.

10. The primary accounts of the sea voyage are excellent. See Duncan McDougall's Journal, 3 vols. Rosenbach Library, Philadelphia, Pennsylvania; Franchére, *Adventures at Astoria*, 8–12; and Ross, *Adventures*, 42–44. Also see Lavender, *The Fist*, 135–136; and Porter, 1:186–187. Also see Ronda, *Astoria and Empire*, which questions whether there was an escort.

11. Franchére, *Adventures at Astoria*, 20. The best descriptions of these events are Ross, *Adventures*, 44–54, and Franchére, *Adventures at Astoria*, 18–21. Strangely McDougall's Journal, vol. 1 is far less informative.

12. Ross, *Adventures*, 89–90, 88–95; Franchére, *Adventures at Astoria*, 36–52; and McDougall's Journal, 1.

13. Ross, *Adventures,* 164–172; and Irving, *Astoria* (1982), 72–79. Also see Astor's instructions to John Ebbets warning against Indians being allowed on board ship: Astor to John Ebbets, 4 November 1809, in Porter, 1:431–432.

14. McDougall's Journal, 1; Franchére, *Adventures at Astoria,* 58; and Ross, *Adventures,* 160–162.

15. Irving describes a great hostility between the North West and Pacific Fur Company traders, but that is not evident in either McDougall's Journal or Franchére's account. Afterall, these men were acquainted and countrymen. See McDougall's Journal, 1; Ross, *Adventures,* 101–102, 115–116, 116–158; Franchére, *Adventures at Astoria,* 54–55; Duncan McDougall, David Stuart, and Robert Stuart to John Astor, 22 July 1811; Duncan McDougall, David Stuart, and Robert Stuart to David Thompson, 16 July 1811; and David Thompson to McDougall, 15 July 1811, in Dorothy Wildes Bridgewater, ed., "John Jacob Astor Relative to His Settlement on the Columbia River," *Yale University Library Gazette,* 24 (October 1949): 52–54.

16. Franchére, *Adventures at Astoria,* 58; McDougall's Journal, 1.

17. Ross, *Adventures,* 188–189, 181–185; Irving, *Astoria* (1982), 97–252; Franchére, *Adventures at Astoria,* 64–68; "Wilson Price Hunt's Diary of his Overland Trip Westward to Astoria in 1811–1812," in Philip A. Rollins, ed., *The Discovery of the Oregon Trail* (New York: Edward Eberstadt, 1935), 281–308.

18. Ibid.; Porter, 1:204.

19. Astor to Gallatin, 28 September 1809, GP, 19; John Richardson to Thomas Forsyth, 17 February 1810, PRO, FO, 115/20; Lavender, *The Fist,* 123–125.

20. Curtis P. Nettels, *The Emergence of a National Economy, 1775–1818* (New York: Harper & Row, Torchbooks, 1962), 330; E. E. Rich, *The History of the Hudson's Bay Company, 1670–1870,* 2 vols. (London: Hudson's Bay Record Society, 1958–1959), 2:250; Astor to Jefferson, 14 March 1812, Jefferson Papers, 45; and Porter, 1:510–512.

21. Copies of Minutes of the Beaver Club, 1810, AP, BL, 12; Astor to Jefferson, 14 March 1812, Jefferson Papers, 45; Wayne Edson Stevens, "Fur Trade Companies in the Northwest, 1760–1816," in *Proceedings of the Mississippi Valley Historical Association, 1916–1917* (Cedar Rapids, Iowa: Torch Press, 1918), 289–290; Nettels, *Emergence,* 330; Agreement between Montreal Michilimackinac Company and the American Fur Company, 28 January 1811, Minute Book, p. 78, NW, PAC. The document is also reprinted in Porter, 1:461–469. The document was accepted and signed by the wintering partners in July 1811. See "Documents Related to the Agreement Between Fur Firms of Montreal and Mr. Jacob Astor of New York, July 1811," Baby Collection, PAC.

22. Agreement establishing the South West Company, 28 January 1811, in Porter, 1:462.

23. Ibid., 461–464. Astor probably paid some money for his interest. See Astor to Jefferson, 14 March 1812, in Porter, 1:510–512; and Astor to Gallatin, 22 December 1810, GP, 22.

24. Agreement establishing the South West Company, 28 January 1811, in Porter, 1:468.

25. John Ebbets to Astor, 11 January 1811, in Porter 1:448–453; Astor to Baranov, 4 November 1809; and Excerpts from the Recollections of Lt. Vasilii M. Golovin, in Nina Bashkina and David Trask, eds., *The United States and Russia: The Beginnings of Relations, 1765–1815* (Washington, D.C.: U.S. Government Printing Office, 1980), 603–614, 682–685. Also see Hubert Howe Bancroft, *History the*

Northwest Coast, vol. 2, *1800–1846* (San Francisco: A. L. Bancroft, 1884), 140, n. 3; and Porter, 1:175–177. In one of the truly bizarre stories of the Astor mythology, Golovin claimed in his 1861 memoirs that Ebbets mistakenly handed Baranov a secret letter from Astor ordering him to acquire military information about the Russian colony as well as to trade goods in Spanish-American ports that were intended for New Archangel. I think the Golovin story is nonsense, written years after the event, based on a document no one else has ever seen, and by a person who may well have intended his account to prevent American expansion in the Northwest.

26. Astor to Ebbets, 4 November 1809; Astor to Baranov, 4 November 1809; Dashkov to Baranov, 7 November 1809, in Bashkina and Trask, *United States and Russia,* 601–611; Ebbets to Astor, 11 January 1811, and Baranov to Astor, 27 July 1810, in Porter, 1:442–444; and Nikolai Bolkhovitinov, *The Beginning of Russian-American Relations, 1775–1815,* trans. Elena Levin (Cambridge: Harvard Univ. Press, 1975), 269–271.

27. Ibid.; "Inventory of the Sale of the Enterprise," in Porter, 1:433–438.

28. Astor to Adrian Bentzon, 21 January 1811, in Porter, 1:455–456; Bolkhovitinov, *Russian-American Relations,* 260; and James R. Gibson, *Imperial Russia in Frontier America* (New York: Oxford Univ. Press, 1976), 161.

29. Ibid.; Fedor Pahlen to Nikolai Rumiantsev, 9 July 1810, in Bashkina and Trask, *United States and Russia,* 677–679; and Bentzon to Astor, 9 July 1810, in Porter, 1:439–442.

30. Bentzon to Astor, 9 July 1810, in Porter, 1:439–442.

31. James Madison to Albert Gallatin, 12 September 1810, in Henry Adams, ed., *The Writings of Albert Gallatin,* 3 vols. (New York: Antiquarian Press, 1960), 1:489–490; Porter, 1:195–196; Astor to Gallatin, 17 January 1811, GP, 22; Bolkhovitinov, *Russian-American Relations,* 266–267; Howard Kushner, *Conflict on the Northwest Coast* (Westport, Conn.: Greenwood, 1975), 18–22; Charles Francis Adams, ed., *Memoirs of John Quincy Adams* (Philadelphia: Lippincott, 1874), 2:151–152, 160, 168–169.

32. Report from the Main Directorate of the Russian-American Fur Company to Nikolai Rumiantsev, 8 October 1811 and 31 October 1811; Adrian Bentzon to Nikolai Rumiantsev, 14 October 1811; Dimitrii Gurev to Rumiantsev, 16 January 1812; O. P. Kozodavlev, Russian Minister of Internal Affairs to Rumiantsev, 28 January 1812; Report of Main Directorate of Russian-American Company to the Shareholders, 13 February 1812; Rumiantsev to Bentzon, 19 February 1812, in Bashkina and Trask, *United States and Russia,* 789–820.

33. Convention between the American Fur Company and the Russian-American Company, 2 May 1812, in Bashkina and Trask, *United States and Russia,* 841–843.

34. Ibid.; Kushner, *Conflict,* 16–17; Bolkhovitinov, *Russian-American Relations,* 266–269; and R. A. Tikhmenev, *A History of the Russian-American Company,* trans. Richard Pierce and Alton Donnelly (1861–1863; repr., Seattle: Univ. of Washington Press, 1978).

35. Astor to De Witt Clinton, 25 February 1811, De Witt Clinton Papers, Columbia University, New York City.

36. Ibid.; and "An Act to Incorporate the American Fur Company, 6 April 1808," in Porter, 1:413–420.

37. John Astor to Cornelius Sowle, 16 October 1811, Cornelius Sowle Papers, Library of Congress, Washington, D.C.; Article of Agreement between Astor and the Clerks and Men to Go Out on the *Beaver,* 8 October 1811, in Porter, 1:475–478; Irving, *Astoria* (1832), 349; Ross Cox, *Adventures on the Columbia River Including the Narrative of a Residence of Six Years on the Western Side of the Rocky Mountains . . .* (New York: J. & L. Harper, 1832), 25; Astor to Dashkov, 13 April 1811, AP, 45; Porter, 1:200–202.

38. Ross, *Adventures,* 160–161, 270–272; Invoice of Merchandise on board the *Beaver,* 16 October 1811, Sowle Papers; and Porter, 1:478–507.

39. Astor to Sowle, 16 October 1811, Sowle Papers; Dashkov to Baranov, 12 October 1811; Astor to Baranov, 11 October 1811, in Bashkina and Trask, *United States and Russia,* 793–797; Ebbets to Astor, 11 January 1811, and Baranov to Astor, 27 July 1810, in Porter, 1:442–453.

40. Porter, 1:150–156; Great Britain, House of Lords, *Papers Relating to the Trade with India and China . . . ,* 1829, vol. 109, p. 43; EIC, 1815–1816, pp. 161, 165, 173, 182, 187. Astor's voyages to China were the *Beaver* (1808, 1809, 1810), *Sylph* (1809), *Beaver* (1810), *Enterprise* (1809–1810). The trade year of 1811–1812 was the peak year for fur imports from the United States to Canton from 1804 to 1819, with a total number of 367,215. See "Statement of No. of Furs Imported into China by the Americans," in *Papers Relating to the Trade with India and China . . . ,* p. 43.

Chapter 6

1. John Astor to Albert Gallatin, 21 and 22 December 1810, GP, 21; Astor to Gallatin, 14 January and 21 January 1811, GP, 22; Gallatin to Madison, 5 January 1811, in Henry Adams, ed., *The Writings of Albert Gallatin,* 3 vols. (New York: Antiquarian Press, 1960), 1:494 495; Raymond Walters, Jr., *Albert Gallatin* (New York: Macmillan, 1957), 237–242; and Bray Hammond, *Banks and Politics in America* (Princeton, N.J.: Princeton Univ. Press, 1957), 223–227.

2. Donald Kagin, "Monetary Aspects of the Treasury Notes of the War of 1812," *Journal of Economic History* 44 (March 1984): 69–88; and Paul Studenski and Herman E. Krooss, *Financial History of the United States* (New York: McGraw-Hill, 1963), 76–77.

3. Astor to Gallatin, 6 and 14 February, and 20 March 1813, GP 25; Donald Adams, *Finance and Enterprise in Early America* (Philadelphia: Univ. of Pennsylvania Press, 1978), 30–31; Porter, 1:330–331; Raymond Walters and Philip Walters, "David Parish, York State Land Promoter," *New York History* 26 (April 1965): 146–147; and idem, "The American Career of David Parish," *Journal of Economic History* 4 (November 1944): 160–161.

4. Astor to Gallatin, 5 April 1813, GP, 25; Astor to David Parish, 17 May 1813, Porter, 1:320–321, 526–527.

5. Kagin, "Monetary Aspects," 86–87; and Donald Hickey, "American Trade Restrictions During the War of 1812," *Journal of American History* 68 (December 1981): 535–536.

6. Astor to James Monroe, 30 April 1814, and Astor to Parish, 27 May 1813, in Porter, 1:527–528, 554–556; Parish to Astor, 26 April, 7 and 11, and 28 May, and

4 and 14 June, 1814, in David Parish Letterbooks, vol. 5, New York Historical Society, New York City (hereafter Parish LB); Raymond Walters, Jr., *Alexander James
Dallas* (Philadelphia: Univ. of Pennsylvania Press, 1943), 183–184.

7. There are several important accounts of financial conditions leading to
the revived interest in a bank. See, for example, Hammond, *Banks and Politics,*
228–229; Raymond Walters, Jr., "The Origins of the Second Bank of the United
States," *Journal of Political Economy* 53 (1945): 115–117; Robert William Keyes,
"The Formation of the Second Bank of the United States, 1811–1817" (Ph.D. diss.,
Univ. of Delaware, 1975), 13; Richard H. Timberlake, Jr., *The Origins of Central
Banking in the United States* (Cambridge: Harvard Univ. Press, 1978), 16–22;
Ralph Catteral, *The Second Bank of the United States* (Chicago: Univ. of Chicago
Press, 1902), 2–6.

8. Astor to Adrian Bentzon, 19 June 1813, AP, BL, 3; Astor to Dashkov, 11
March 1815, AP, BL, 3; Grant Morrison, "Isaac Bronson and the Search for System
in American Capitalism, 1789–1838" (Ph.D. diss., City Univ. of New York, 1974), 172.

9. Walters, "Origins," 115–118; Keyes, "Second Bank of the U.S.," 36–37;
Jacob Barker, *Incidents in the Life of Jacob Barker* (New Orleans, La.: n.p., 1855),
44–46, 86.

10. Parish to Girard, 5 April 1814, Stephen Girard Papers, American Philosophical Society, Philadelphia, Pennsylvania; Parish to Astor, 2, 4, 8, and 9 April
1814, Parish LB, 5; and Parish to Isaac Bronson, Parish LB, 5; Walters, "Origins,"
118–120; and Keyes, *Second Bank of the U.S.,* 23–27.

11. Astor to Girard, 15 August 1814, Girard Papers; Astor to Dennis Smith,
25 August 1814 and Astor to Henry Payson, 5 September 1814, AP, BL, 3; Walters,
"Origins," 120–122; and Keyes, "Second Bank of the U.S." 39–41.

12. Isaac Bronson to David Daggett, 10 December 1814, Dagget Papers, Yale
Univ. as cited in Morrison, "Isaac Bronson," 176. Also see Parish to Astor, 28 September 1814, Parish LB, 5; Astor to Dennis Smith, 22 September and 30 October
1814, AP, BL 3; Astor to Girard, 8 November 1814, and Parish to Girard, 11 November 1814, Girard Papers.

13. Astor to John Calhoun, 23 November 1814, AP, BL, 3; Walters, "Origins,"
125–127.

14. Agreements Relating to the South West Company, 28 January 1811, in
Porter, 1:462; Astor to Gallatin, 22 December 1810, GP, 22; Astor to Jefferson, 14
March 1812, Porter, 1:508–513; Gallatin to Astor, 5 August 1835, GP, 41; John As-
tor, "Petition on British Fur Monopoly March 30, 1812," 12th Cong., House of Rep-
resentatives Report in *New American State Papers,* vol. 3, *Commerce and
Navigation* (Wilmington, Del.: Scholarly Resources, 1973), 209–213.

15. Henry Brevoort, Jr., to Washington Irving, 28 June 1811, 26 June 1811,
and 14 July 1811, in George S. Hellman, ed., *Letters of Henry Brevoort to Washington Irving, Together with Other Unpublished Papers,* 2 vols. (New York: Putnam's,
1918), 1:20–43; and Brevoort to John Whetten, 25 June 1811, and Brevoort to Astor, 9 May 1811, Hellman, *Letters of Henry Brevoort,* 2:181–184 and 201–204.

16. Astor to Jefferson, 14 March 1812, in Porter, 1:508–512; Astor, "Petition
to Congress," 209–212; Astor to Gallatin, 16 December 1811, GP, 23.

17. Astor to Gallatin, 28 March 1812, GP, 24.

18. Jefferson to Astor, 24 May 1812. Thomas Jefferson Papers, Library of
Congress, Microfilm Reel, 46; and Astor to Jefferson, 14 March 1812, in Porter,
1:508–513.

19. Astor, "Petition to Congress," 209–212; Astor to Gallatin, 13 May 1812, 30 May 1812, GP, 24; and Barker, *Incidents,* 36–37.

20. Gallatin to Astor, 5 August 1835, and Gallatin to Daniel Jackson, 23 August 1836, GP, 41; "Memorandum of Albert Gallatin Respecting the Outbreak of the War of 1812 & Mr. Astor, c. 1815," in Adams, *Writings of Albert Gallatin,* 1:678–680; John Astor to the Editor of the *Philadelphia Aurora,* 15 December 1815, in GP, 28.

21. Ibid.

22. Gallatin to Madison, 17 December 1811, James Madison Papers, Library of Congress, Microfilm Reel, 13; Astor to Gallatin, 6 July 1836, GP, 41; Astor to Gallatin, 30 June 1812, GP, 25; Captain A. Gray to Sir George Prevost, 13 January 1812, in Ernest A. Cruikshank, *Documents Relating to the Invasion of Canada and the Surrender of Detroit, 1812* (1912; repr., New York: Arno, 1971), 9–12; D. G. Creighton, *The Commercial Empire of the St. Lawrence* (Toronto: Ryerson, 1937), 176–179; and David Lavender, *The Fist in the Wilderness* (Garden City, N.Y.: Doubleday, 1964), 184–187.

23. Astor to Gallatin, 25 June 1812, GP, 25; Peter Sailly Memoirs," *Plattsburgh Republican,* 16 March and 13 April 1872; Porter, 1:262–263; Donald R. Hickey, "American Trade Restrictions During the War of 1812," *Journal of American History* 68 (December 1981): 524–527; and Allan S. Everest, *The War of 1812 in the Champlain Valley* (Syracuse: Syracuse Univ. Press, 1981), 57–58.

24. Astor to Gallatin 25 June 1812, GP, 25; Astor to Pliny Moore, 9 July 1812; A. l'Herbette, Description of Furs, 16 August 1812; and Astor to Moore, 13 October 1812, in "John Astor Correspondence, Fur Trade with Lower Canada, 1790–1817," *Moorsfield Antiquarian* 1 (1937–1938): 111–124, 191–192, and 195–196; and Forsyth, Richardson & Co. to Astor, 16 June 1812, GP, 25.

25. Astor to William Howard, 5 October 1813, AP, BL, 3. Astor's activity at this time can be followed in his letters to agents reprinted in the *Moorsfield Antiquarian* 1 (1937–1938); 194–195, 270–273. Sailly was once accused of taking a bribe from John Astor but the charge was fabricated by a steamboat captain angry over Sailly's action toward him. See John Astor to William Crawford, 31 May 1819, AP, New York State Library, Albany; and "Sailly's Memoirs," *Plattsburgh Republican,* 3 April 1872.

26. Astor to John Day, 19 October 1813, AP, BL, 3. Also see Astor to George Astor, 26 October 1813; Astor to John Day, 26 October 1813; Astor to McTavish, McGillivray & Co., 30 September 1813, AP, BL, 3.

27. Ibid.; and Astor to Pliny Moore, 13 and 17 October 1812; Moore to Astor, 26 March 1813, in *Moorsfield Antiquarian,* 191–194, 199–200.

28. Astor to Ramsay Crook, 15 November 1813, in Porter, 1:543–545; Astor to Charles Gratiot, 21 October 1813, 20 April 1814, 12 October 1814, and 10 August 1814, AP, BL, 3.

29. Astor to Crooks, 19 July 1813; 8 and 9 October 1813; 14 February 1814, AP, BL, 3. Also see Crooks to Astor, 10 April 1814, 8 May 1814, 23 January 1815, and Astor to Crooks, 14 December 1814, AP, NYPL; and Lavender, *The Fist,* 198–203.

30. Astor to Crooks, 8 October 1813, AP, BL, 3; James Monroe to Astor, 16 May 1814, AP, BL, 10; McTavish, McGillivray & Co., and Forsyth, Richardson & Co., to Sir George Prevost, 8 June 1814, *MPHC,* 15:590–592; Astor to Crooks, 15 November, 1813 and Crooks to Astor, 1 December 1813, AP, NYPL; George Prevost's Order, 9 June 1814, *WHC,* 19:354–355.

31. Crooks to Astor, 1 December 1813, *WHC*, 19:348–354; Crooks to Astor, 29 May 1814, AP, NYPL; Crooks to Astor, 21 August 1814, *WHC*, 19:360–364; Lavender, *The Fist*, 212–214.

32. Crooks to Astor, 21 August 1814, *WHC*, 19:360–364; Astor to Crooks, 15 June 1814, AP, NYPL; Astor to George Astor, 14 September 1814, in Porter, 1:564–565; Everest, *War of 1812*, 78–79; and Thomas Rosenblum, "Pelts and Patronage: The Representations Made by John Jacob Astor to the Federal Government Regarding His Fur Trade Interests in the Old North West, 1808–1816," in Thomas C. Buckley, ed., *Rendezvous: Selected Papers of the Fourth North American Fur Trade Conference* (Saint Paul: North American Fur Trade Conference, 1982), 66–67.

33. Porter, 1:282; Astor to John Bryan, 3 January and 24 December 1813, in Porter, 1:523, 548.

34. Astor to Crooks, 15 November 1813, in Porter, 1:543–545; Astor to Crooks, 19 July, 8 and 9 October 1813, AP, BL, 3; Crooks to Astor, 1 December 1813 and 14 February 1814, AP, NYPL; Astor to John Gillespie, 24 September 1813, AP, BL, 3; Astor to Lewis Farquharson, 12 October 1813, AP, BL, 3.

35. Hickey, "Trade Restrictions," 517–518; Porter, 1:213, 301; Astor to Baring Brothers, 12 December 1813, AP, BL, 3.

36. Astor to Captain Ridgeway, 3 and 13 July 1813; and Astor to Adrian Bentzon, 13 December 1813, AP, BL, 3; *New York Gazette and General Advertiser,* 23 December 1814; 30 June 1815; and Porter, 1:293–294, 306–307.

37. Astor to Baring Brothers, 12 December 1813, AP, BL, 3; Porter, 1:293–296.

38. Nikolai Bolkhovitinov, *The Beginning of Russian-American Relations, 1775–1815,* trans. Elena Levin (Cambridge: Harvard Univ. Press, 1975), 313–314; Astor to Monroe, 28 June 1813, AP, BL, 3.

39. Astor to Baring Brothers & Co., 19 June 1813, AP, BL, 3; Adrian Bentzon to Gallatin, 27 July 1813, GP, 26; Astor to Bentzon, 19 June 1813, and Astor to Curtiss Blakeman, 19 June 1813, AP, BL, 3.

40. Astor to Cambreling, 20 June 1813, AP, BL, 3; Astor to Cornelius Sowle, 10 November 1813, Cornelius Sowle Papers, Library of Congress, Washington, D.C.; Bentzon to Gallatin, 16 August 1814, GP, 27.

41. Astor to Bentzon, 19 June 1813; 27 November 1813, and 5 January 1814, AP, BL, 3; Astor to Cambreling, 30 October 1813 and 11 November 1813, AP, BL, 3.

42. Astor to C. M. Baumhauer, 13 July 1813; Astor to Baring Brothers, 12 December 1813; Astor to Joseph Ridgeway, 22 June, 3 and 10 July 1813; Astor to Megrath and Jones, 3 July 1813; AP, BL, 3; and Porter, 1:299–301.

43. Astor to Daniel Greene, 8 September 1813; Astor to Bentzon, 13 December 1813; Astor to Peter Sailly, 17 September 1813, and Astor to Crooks, 14 February 1814, AP, BL, 3.

44. Astor to Henry Payson, 4 May 1814 and 30 September 1814, AP, BL, 3.

45. Hickey, "Trade Restrictions," 532–534; Astor to Payson, 24 October 1814, in Porter, 1:574–575; Astor to William Flexner, 1 and 9 December 1813; and Astor to John Stanton, 23 October 1814, AP, BL, 3; and Porter, 1:302–304.

46. Astor to Charles Gratiot, 19 October 1814, AP, BL, 10; Astor to Chandler Price, 15 December 1814; Astor to John l'Herbette, 16 December 1814; Astor to Henry Payson, 30 September 1814; Astor to James Clark, 1 January 1815, AP, BL, 3; and Porter, 1:308–310.

47. Mary V. Kuebel, "Merchants and Mandarins: The Genesis of American Relations with China" (Ph.D. diss., Univ. of Virginia, 1974), 31–32; "Statement of

American Imports and Exports at Canton, 1804–1818," Great Britain, House of Commons, *Report by the Lords Committee Appointed Select Committee to Inquire into the Means of Extending and Securing the Foreign Trade of the Country, and to Report to the House . . .*, 1821, vol. 7, 45–47; Astor to Sowle, 11 August 1812, 24 December 1812, 10 November 1813, 11 January 1815, 3 February 1815, Sowle Papers; and Astor to Nicholas G. Ogden, 13 January 1815, in Porter, 1:581–582; EIC, 1815–1816, pp. 192, 199.

48. EIC, 1810–1811, p. 173, 1811–1812, p. 182; *New York Gazette and General Advertiser,* 11 November 1812 and 30 March 1813; Astor to William Lippincott, 20 December 1813, 7 and 18 September 1813; Astor to Joshua Lippincott, 2 July 1813; Astor to Henry Payson, 29 October 1813, 4 May 1814, and 26 November 1814, AP, BL, 3; Porter, 1:312–321. Astor on occasion shipped furs to China during the war. In 1813, for example, he sent furs valued at $10,000 from the port of New Bedford, Mass. See Astor to Henry Payson, 24 October 1814, AP, BL, 3.

49. Astor to D. A. Smith, 27 December 1814; Astor to Baring Brothers & Co., 30 January 1815; Astor to C. Blakeman, 24 February 1815, AP, BL, 3; EIC, 1815–1816, p. 199; Porter, 1:320–322.

50. William Pigot and Richard Ebbets to John Astor, 28 September 1812; William Pigot to Astor, 26 October 1814, AP, BL, 3; John Astor to the Department of State, 4 April 1813, in Porter, 1:523–525; Kenneth Porter, "The Cruise of the *Forester,*" *Washington Historical Quarterly* 23 (1932): 261–267.

51. Astor to James Monroe, Sec. of State, February 1813, and Gallatin to William Jones, 10 January 1813, in Dorothy Wildes Bridgewater, ed., "John Jacob Astor Relative to His Settlement on the Columbia River," *Yale University Library Gazette* 24 (October 1949): 50–52; and Astor to Gallatin, 6 February 1813, GP, 25.

52. Astor to Monroe, February 1813, in Bridgewater, "Astor," 50–52.

53. Astor to Monroe, February 1813, in Bridgewater, "Astor," 50–52; and Astor to Gallatin, 6 February 1813, 14 and 18 February 1813, GP, 25.

54. Astor to Gallatin, 18 February 1813, GP, 25; Samuel Northrup to Astor, March 1814, in Porter, 1:552–553.

55. Astor to Department of State, 4 April 1813, in Porter, 1:523–526; Astor to Gallatin, 20 March 1813, GP, 25; Astor to William Jones, 6 April 1813; Astor, "Memorandum for Secretary Jones," 19 April 1813, in Bridgewater, "Astor," 56–58.

56. Donald Meinig, *The Great Columbia Plain* (Seattle: Univ. of Washington Press, 1968), 41–43; Lavender, *The Fist,* 192–193; David J. Wishart, *The Fur Trade of the American West, 1807–1840* (Lincoln, Univ. of Nebraska Press, 1979), 119. The account of Stuart's journey is reprinted in Philip A. Rollins, ed., *The Discovery of the Oregon Trail* (New York: Edward Eberstadt, 1935).

57. Astor to John Dorr, 7 July 1813; Astor to Jacob Van Rennselaer, 10 July 1813, AP, BL, 3; and Astor to Secretary Jones, 6 July 1813, in Bridgewater, "Astor," 58–59.

58. Lord Cracken to James Milligan, 16 February 1813, PRO, Admiralty Series 2, 1380/360, London; Simon McGillivray, "Statement Relative to the Columbia River on the Western Coast of the Continent of North America," in McGillivray to the British Ambassador, 15 November 1817, PRO, FO, 5/123.

59. "License to Trade Granted by the East India Company, 13 January 1813," in *Report by the Lord's Committee,* 1821, 7:94–98.

60. Astor to William Jones, 6, 7, 17, and 30 July and 8 and 23 August; Astor to James Madison, 27 July 1813, Bridgewater, "Astor," 58–70; Porter, 1:219–220; and Astor to Andrei Dashkov, 19 November 1813, AP, BL, 3.

61. Astor to Jefferson, 18 October 1813, Porter, 1:541–543; Jefferson to Astor, 9 November 1813, Jefferson Papers, Reel 46.

62. Hickey, "Trade Restrictions," 529–532; James Monroe to U.S. Ministers, 22 March 1814, in William R. Manning, ed., *Diplomatic Correspondence of the United States: Canadian Relations, 1784–1860*, 3 vols. (Washington, D.C.: Carnegie Endowment for International Peace, 1940), 1:218.

63. Duncan McDougall Journal, 3 vols. Rosenbach Library, Philadelphia, Pennsylvania, 3; Gabriel Franchére, *Adventures at Astoria, 1810–1814* (1820; repr., Norman: Univ. of Oklahoma Press, 1967), 69–73; Wishart, *Fur Trade*, 119–120; Meinig, *Columbia Plain*, 50–52; Invoice of Goods on *Beaver*, October 1811, Sowle Papers; and Porter, 1:205–207.

64. Account of Sales of Cargo of *Beaver*, September 1812, Sowle Papers; Astor to Baranov, 11 October 1811, in Nina Bashkina and David Trask, eds., *The United States and Russia: The Beginnings of Relations, 1765–1815* (Washington, D.C.: U.S. Government Printing Office, 1980), 793–797; Franchére, *Adventures at Astoria*, 77–78; McDougall Diary, 3.

65. Franchére, *Adventures at Astoria*, 74; and McDougall Diary, 3.

66. Franchére, *Adventures at Astoria*, 74–77; Alexander Ross, *Adventures at the First Settlers on the Oregon or Columbia River, 1810–1813* (1849; repr., Lincoln: Univ. of Nebraska Press, 1986), 216–219; McDougall Diary, 3; and Porter, 1:221–222.

67. McDougall Diary, 3; Franchére, *Adventures at Astoria*, 75–78; Ross, *Adventures*, 236–240; "Resolution of the Partners at Astoria, 25 and 26 June 1813 and 1 July 1813," in Grace Flandrau, *Astor and the Oregon Country* (Saint Paul: Great Northern Railway, n. d.), 37–39.

68. "Resolution of the Partners at Astoria," 25 August 1813, in Flandrau, *Astor*, 39–41. Also see McDougall Diary, 3; Franchére, *Adventures at Astoria*, 77–80; Astor to Sowle, 16 October 1811, 11 August 1812, and 24 December 1812, Sowle Papers; John Astor to John Quincy Adams, 4 January 1823, in *Message from the President of the United States Communicating the Letter of Mr. Prevost, and Other Documents Relating to an Establishment Made at the Mouth of the Columbia River, 27 January 1823*, 17th Cong., 2d sess., H. Doc. No. 45 (Washington: Gales & Seaton, 1823), 11–15.

69. McDougall Diary 3; Franchére, *Adventures at Astoria*, 85–86; Astor to Adams, 4 January 1823, in *Message from the President*, 11–15; and Astor to Monroe, 17 August 1815, in Porter, 1:583–584.

70. Franchére, *Adventures at Astoria*, 86–87; Ross, *Adventures*, 243–245; "Agreement Between the Pacific Fur Company and the North West Company, 16 October 1813" and "Inventory of Sundries Delivered to the North West Company, October 1813," in *Message from the President*, 16–65.

71. Franchére, *Adventures at Astoria*, 90–92; Ross, *Adventures*, 248–250; Simon McGillivray, "Statement Relative to the Columbia River . . . ," in McGillivray to the British Ambassador, 15 November 1817, PRO, FO, 123. The best account of the extensive changes and alterations in British plans is in Barry Gough, *The Royal Navy and the Northwest Coast of North America, 1810–1914* (Vancouver: Univ. of British Columbia Press, 1971), 12–24.

72. Franchére, *Adventures at Astoria*, 101–103, 125; "North West Company in Account with John Astor, March 1814," in *Message from the President*, 64; Kenneth W. Porter, "Cruise of Astor's Brig *Pedler*, 1813–1816," *Oregon Historical Quarterly* 31 (September 1930): 223–226; Lavender, *The Fist*, 218–219; and Porter, 1:235.

73. Astor to John Adams, 4 January 1823, in *Message from the President,* 11–15; Astor to J. B. Prevost, 11 November 1817, in John Astor Papers, Library of Congress, Washington, D.C.; Astor to James Monroe, in Porter, 1:583–584; and North West Company Minute Book, July 1814, HBC, NW, PAC.

74. Astor to Donald McKenzie, 27 September 1814, AP, BL 3; *New York Gazette and General Advertiser,* 12 November 1814.

75. Astor to Monroe, 17 August 1815, in Porter, 1:583–584; Ross, *Adventures,* 235; Astor to Adams, 4 January 1823, in *Message from the President,* 11–15; Porter, 1:236–243; Washington Irving, *Astoria, or Anecdotes of an Enterprise Beyond the Rocky Mountains,* ed. Edgeley W. Todd (1836; repr., Norman: Univ. of Oklahoma Press, 1964), 481–486; Hubert Howe Bancroft, *History of the Northwest Coast,* vol. 2, *1800–1846* (San Francisco: A. L. Bancroft, 1884), 144–145; Hiram M. Chittenden, *The American Fur Trade of the Far West,* 2 vols. (1935; repr., Lincoln: Univ. of Nebraska Press, 1986), 227–237.

76. Astor to Crooks, 14 September 1814, AP, BL, 3.

Chapter 7

1. John Astor to George Ehninger, 6 March 1815; and Astor to Thomas Wilson, 21 February 1815, AP, BL, 3.

2. Astor to Nicholas Ogden, 4 March 1815; Astor to Baring Brothers & Co., 6 March 1815; Astor to William Waln, 22 February 1815; Astor to Cornelius Sowle, 3 March 1815; Astor to Megrath & Jones, 13 February 1815; AP, BL, 3; *New York Gazette and General Advertiser,* 15 March 1815; and Porter, 2:590, 604.

3. Astor to William Waln, 22 February 1815, and Astor to D. A. Smith, 21 January 1815, AP, BL, 3; EIC, 1815–1816, p. 199; Astor to Cornelius Sowle, March 1815, and Astor to Sowle, 19 April 1815, Cornelius Sowle Papers, Library of Congress, Washington, D.C.; Astor to Albert Gallatin, 1 June 1817, GP, 29; and "Statement of American Imports and Exports at Canton, 1804–1818," Great Britain, House of Commons, *Report by the Lords Committee Appointed Select Committee to Inquire into the Means of Extending and Securing the Foreign Trade of the Country, and to Report to the House . . . ,* 1821, vol. 7, 44–45; and Porter, 1:320–321, and 2:592–597.

4. Astor to Gallatin, 9 October 1815, GP, 28; Raymond Walters, *Albert Gallatin* (New York: Macmillan, 1957), 294–295; and James Gallatin, *A Great Peace Maker: The Diary of James Gallatin, Secretary to Albert Gallatin* (New York: Scribner's, 1914), 80.

5. Astor to Gallatin, 14 March 1818, GP, 30; Astor to Mrs. Gallatin, 2 August 1815, GP, 27; Astor to Gallatin, 7 October 1816, GP, 29; Astor to Charles Parish, 13 October 1813, AP, BL, 3; Astor to Ogden, 10 March 1818, Madigan Collection, New York Public Library, New York City; and Porter, 2:597–598.

6. Astor to Ogden, 4 March 1815, AP, BL, 3; Astor to Daniel Stansbury, 3 March 1815; Astor to Baring Brothers, Canton, 6 March 1815, AP, BL, 3; Astor to N. G. Ogden, 2 October 1816, in *S. G. Ogden* v. *Astor and Others,* in New York City, Superior Court, *Report of Cases Argued and Determined, 1831–1893,* 61 vols. (New York: Banks & Beers, 1892), 1850: 315–318; Porter, 2:606.

7. John Astor's Instructions to James Copland, Commander of Brig *Boxer,* 26 February 1818, James Copland Logs, 1818–1821, New York Public Library, New York City; "Rectified Accounts of Voyages to China, 1817–1822," AP, NYHS; William

Roberts to Daniel Lord, 19 March 1847, in Porter, 2:1252–1255; Astor to Ogden, 5 March 1818, AP, NYPL, Box 1; and Porter, 2:600–609.

8. Astor to Ogden, 5 March 1818, AP, NYPL: "Statement of American Imports and Exports at Canton, 1804–1818," 44–45; EIC, 1815–1816, p. 199, and 1820–1821, p. 222; Porter, 2:599–601.

9. Astor to Ogden, 10 March 1818, AP, NYPL; Astor to Ogden, 5 March 1818, NYPL, Box 1; Affidavit for Cargo of *Macedonian,* April 1816, and Customs Receipts, NA, RG 36. The Astors continued to trade occasionally in opium as late as the 1830s. See William B. Astor to George Summer, 2 April 1833; and William B. Astor to Frederick Bunker, 14 May and 27 December, 1832, AP, BL, 3. The opium trade is discussed in a number of excellent studies: Jonathan Goldstein, *Philadelphia and the China Trade* (Philadelphia: Univ. of Pennsylvania Press, 1978), 49–62; Jacques Downs, "American Merchants and the China Opium Trade, 1800–1840," *Business Historical Review,* 42 (Winter 1968): 418–442; and Charles C. Stelle, "American Trade in Opium to China Prior to 1820," *Pacific Historical Review,* 9 (1940): 425–444.

10. Porter, 2:645–647; "Statement of Imports and Exports," 1814–1818, pp. 44–45; Harold Bradley, "Hawaii and the American Penetration of the Northeastern Pacific, 1800–1845," *Pacific Historical Review,* 12 (1943): 278–280; Mary V. Kuebel, "Merchants and Mandarins: The Genesis of American Relations with China" (Ph.D. diss., Univ. of Virginia, 1974), 39–40.

11. Frederic Howay, "A List of Trading Vessels in the Maritime Fur Trade, 1820–1825," *Royal Society of Canada, Transactions,* 28 (1935): 11–20; and Porter, 2:640–665.

12. John Astor to Richard J. Cleveland and Francisco Ribas, 15 November 1817, John Astor Papers, Library of Congress, Washington, D.C.; Francisco Ribas to Thomas Halsey, 18 November 1817; Ribas to Astor, 10 March 1818 and 29 April 1818, Jeremy Robinson Papers, Peter Force Collection, Microfilm Reel 60, Library of Congress, Washington, D.C.; David F. Long, *Sailor-Diplomat: A Biography of Commodore James Biddle, 1783–1848* (Boston: Northeastern Univ. Press, 1983), 70, 80–82, 88–90; Edward Billingsley, *In Defense of Neutral Rights: The United States Navy and the Wars of Independence in Chile and Peru* (Chapel Hill: Univ. of North Carolina Press, 1967), 12–13, 29–31, 69–70; Cargo of *Beaver,* 30 June 1817, Porter, 2:1150–1153; John Astor to J. R. Poinsette, 17 May 1827, AP, HSP.

13. Barry M. Gough, *Distant Dominion* (Vancouver: Univ. of British Columbia Press, 1980), 24–25; and Frederick Merk, *The Oregon Question* (Cambridge: Harvard Univ. Press, 1967), 8.

14. Robert Stuart to Ramsey Crooks, 21 March 1815, *WHC,* 19:369–371.

15. John Astor to Albert Gallatin, 6 and 10 October 1815, GP, 28.

16. Astor to Crooks, 14 February 1814, AP, BL, 3; Astor to Crooks, 29 May 1814, AP, NYPL; and Astor to Crooks, 10 December 1814, in Porter, 1:577–578.

17. Robert Stuart to Crooks, 21 March 1815, *WHC,* 19:369–371; Astor to Crooks, 14 February 1815, *WHC,* 19:369; and David Lavender, *The Fist in the Wilderness* (Garden City, N.Y.: Doubleday, 1964), 229–230.

18. Astor to Charles Gratiot, 16 May and 9 July 1815, AP, Mo.HS; and Astor to Charles Gratiot, 16 November 1815 and 23 September 1815, AP, BL, 10.

19. William McGillivray to John Astor, 7 October 1815, Baby Collection, Public Archives of Canada, Ottawa; Astor to Gallatin, 6 and 10 October 1815, GP, 28. Astor later outlined his strategy in a letter to James Monroe, 30 December 1816, NA, RG 59, M179, Reel 35.

20. James Monroe to Anthony St. Johns Baker, 19 July 1815, in William Manning, *Diplomatic Correspondence of the United States: Canadian Relations, 1784–1860,* 3 vols. (Washington, D.C.: Carnegie Endowment for International Peace, 1940), 1:230–231; Astor to James Monroe, 17 August 1815, in Porter, 1:583–585; Simon McGillivray, "Statement Relative to the Columbia River . . . ," in McGillivray to the British Ambassador, 15 November 1817, PRO, FO, 5/123; Merk, *Oregon,* 7–8; and Barry Gough, *The Royal Navy and the Northwest Coast of North America, 1810–1914* (Vancouver: Univ. of British Columbia Press, 1971), 24–26.

21. Astor to Gallatin, 6 and 10 October 1815, GP, 28.

22. Astor to Gallatin, 9 October 1815, GP, 28; Walters, *Albert Gallatin,* 294–295.

23. Gallatin to Astor, 5 August 1835, and Astor to Gallatin, 25 July 1835, GP, 41; Gough, *Royal Navy,* 25–26; and Merk, *Oregon,* 10–12.

24. Astor to William Shaler, 16 February 1816, A. C. Bining Collection, Historical Society of Pennsylvania, Philadelphia.

25. North West Company Minute Book, July 1814, HBC, NW, PAC; William McGillivray to G. McTavish, 19 June 1815, HBC, NW, PAC; William McGillivray to James Keith, 28 April 1816; McTavish, McGillivray & Co. to James Keith, 28 July 1816, and John Richardson to James Keith, 29 April 1816, James Keith Papers, Univ. of Aberdeen Library, Scotland.

26. "An Act . . . to Regulate the Indian Trade, 29 April 1816," Department of War, *Indian Treaties, and Laws and Regulations Relating to Indian Affairs* (Washington, D.C.: Way & Gideon, 1826). The license law is discussed in Francis Paul Prucha, *The Great Father: The United States Government and the American Indians,* 2 vols. (Lincoln: Univ. of Nebraska Press, 1984), 1:96–97; and Paul Phillips, *The Fur Trade,* 2 vols. (Norman: Univ. of Oklahoma Press, 1961), 2:161–163.

27. Charles Bagot to Viscount Castlereagh, 2 December 1817, PRO, FO, 5/123; John Prevost to the Secretary of State, 11 November 1818, in *Message from the President of the United States Communicating the Letter of Mr. Prevost, and Other Documents Relating to an Establishment Made at the Mouth of the Columbia River, 27 January 1823,* 17th Cong., 2d sess., H. Doc. No. 45 (Washington: Gales & Seaton, 1823), 7–11; Astor to Gallatin, 1 June 1817, GP, 29; Long, *Sailor-Diplomat,* 63–64; and Merk, *Oregon,* 11–18.

28. Astor to Benjamin Weeden, 19 March 1817 and 20 November 1818, Sowle Papers; Nikolai Bolkhovitinov, *The Beginning of Russian-American Relations, 1775–1815,* trans. Elena Levin (Cambridge: Harvard Univ. Press, 1975), 272–275; Main Directorate of the Russian-American Company to Andrei Dashkov, 28 October 1814, in Nina Bashkina and David Trask, eds., *The United States and Russia: The Beginnings of Relations, 1765–1815* (Washington, D.C.: U.S. Government Printing Office, 1980), 1094–1095; Kenneth W. Porter, "Cruise of Astor's Brig *Pedler,* 1813–1816," *Oregon Historical Quarterly,* 31 (1930): 224–227; R. A. Tikhmenev, *A History of the Russian-American Company,* trans. Richard Pierce and Alton Donnelly (Seattle: Univ. of Washington Press, 1978), 119.

29. Bagot to Castlereagh, 2 December 1817; Simon McGillivray to British Ambassador, 15 November 1817, PRO, FO, 5/123; John Q. Adams to George W. Campbell, 28 June 1818, in Manning, *Diplomatic Correspondence,* 1:275; Samuel Flagg Bemis, *John Quincy Adams and the Foundations of American Foreign Policy* (New York: Norton, 1949), 283–286; Lord Bathurst to Agents & Partners of North West Company, 27 January 1818, PRO, FO, 5/208; Simon McGillivray to James Keith, 20 July 1818, Keith Papers.

30. William H. Shirreff to Frederick Hickey, 26 July 1818, and Copy of Statement of John Prevost, 6 October 1818, PRO, FO, 5/208; J. B. Prevost to John Quincy Adams, 11 November 1818, in Manning, *Diplomatic Correspondence,* 1:886–892; Merk, *Oregon,* 17–26; and Long, *Sailor-Diplomat,* 77–80.

31. John Q. Adams, Secretary of State, to Albert Gallatin and Richard Rush, 28 July 1818, and Gallatin and Rush to Adams, 20 October 1818, in Manning, *Diplomatic Correspondence,* 1:279–280, 878–879; and Merk, *Oregon,* 26–29.

32. John Calhoun to Henry Southard, 8 January 1819, in *The Papers of John Calhoun* 18 vols. (Columbia: Univ. of South Carolina Press, 1959–), 3:478; John Calhoun, "Alteration of a System for Trading with the Indians," 5 December 1818, 15th Cong., 2d sess., H. Doc. No. 157, *American State Papers, Documents, Executive and Legislative* (Washington, D.C.: Gales & Seaton, 1834); Thomas Hart Benton, *Thirty Years' View; or a History of the Working of Government for Thirty Years, from 1820–1850,* 2 vols. (New York: D. Appleton, 1854–1856), 1:13; John H. Schroeder, "Representative John Floyd, 1817–1829: Harbinger of Oregon Territory," *Oregon Historical Quarterly* 70 (December 1969): 333–341; Howard Kushner, *Conflict on the Northwest Coast* (Westport, Conn.: Greenwood, 1975); John Astor to Secretary of State John Q. Adams, 4 January 1823, in *Message from the President . . . ,* 11–15.

33. James Keith to Thomas Perkins, 12 June 1817; William McGillivray to James Keith, 24 July 1817; McGillivray and Mackenzie to Keith, 24 July 1817; James Keith to McTavish, McGillivray & Co., 29 August 1821, Keith Papers; Merk, *Oregon,* 72–73; Gough, *Royal Navy,* 27–28; and Gough, *Distant Dominion,* 144–145.

34. Astor to Gallatin, 1 June 1817, GP, 29; Astor to Gallatin, 7 March 1827, GP, 37; Astor to Wilson Hunt, 2 January 1832, AP, BL, 3. Also see Astor to Adams, 4 January 1823, in *Message from the President . . . ,* 11–13.

35. Astor to Charles Gratiot, 26 May 1816, in Porter, 2:1143–1144; Astor to Gratiot, 6 January 1812, 18 May 1816, 25 June 1816, 10 December 1816, AP, BL, 10; Porter, 2:691–693; and Lavender, *The Fist,* 252.

36. Astor to McTavish, McGillivray & Co., 29 March 1817 and 1 September 1817, Baby Collection, PAC; Copy of Account of John Astor with McTavish, McGillivray & Co., 20 December 1817, AP, BL, 12; Crooks to Astor, 7 February 1818, AP, NYPL.

37. Astor to Gallatin, 26 March 1817, GP, 29.

38. Astor to Crooks, 17 March 1817, *WHC,* 19:451; Astor to William Matthews, 20 December 1817, and Astor to William Astor, 1819, in Porter, 2:1154–1159 and 1164–1166.

39. Crooks & Stuart to Astor, 23 September 1817; Crooks to Barton & Craig, 18 December 1816 and 30 May 1817; Crooks to Astor, 21 July 1817; Crooks to Samuel Abbot, 3 April 1818; Crooks to Caldwell & Solomon, 20 November 1819; Crooks to W. Matthews, 10 January 1818 and 23 March 1819, AFC, LB 1.

40. Astor to Matthews, 20 December 1817, in Porter, 2:1154–1159; Crooks to Matthews, 10 January 1818, AFC, LB 1; Lavender, *The Fist,* 255–256.

41. Crooks to Astor, April 1817, AFC, LB 1; Crooks to William Morrison, 20 June 1817; Crooks to Astor, 23 June 1817; Crooks to John Johnston, 28 May 1818; Crooks to Matthews, 10 and 11 January 1818; Crooks to Astor, 25 May 1818, AFC, LB 1.

42. Crooks to Astor, 19 and 26 April 1817 and 25 May 1818; Crooks to Matthews, 10 January 1818; Crooks to Matthews, 17 December 1818, AFC, LB 1; Grace

Lee Nute, *The Voyageur* (New York: D. Appleton, 1931), 36–37; and Gurdon S. Hubbard, *The Autobiography of Gurdon Saltonstall Hubbard* (New York: Citadel Press, 1969), 2–9.

43. Nute, *Voyageurs,* 36–40; Hubbard, *Autobiography,* 7–15; Stuart to Crooks, 3 June 1818; Crooks to Messers Hunt & Lay, 22 July 1817 and 14 August 1817, AFC, LB 1; Lavender, *The Fist,* 256–260, 292–293; Crooks to Captain James Rough, 15 April 1818; Crooks to Matthews, 17 December 1818, AFC, LB 1; President of Lake Erie Steamboat Co. to John Calhoun, 4 March 1820, *Calhoun Papers,* 4; and Crooks and Stuart to Matthews, 26 February 1818, AFC, LB 1.

44. Crooks to Stuart, 26 February 1818; Crooks to Abbott, 22 October 1818, AFC, LB 1; and Hubbard, *Autobiography,* 74–75, 114–115.

45. Robert Dickson to John Lawe, 23 April 1819, *WHC,* 20: 105–107; Crooks to Astor, 21 and 29 July 1817, AFC, LB 1; Stuart and Crooks to Astor, 24 January 1818; Puthuff to Gov. Cass, 14 May 1816, *WHC,* 20:17–32 and 408–409; Matthew Irwin to John Bowyer, 24 July 1817, *WHC,* 19:468–469.

46. Astor to Monroe, 30 December 1816, NA, RG 59, M 179, Reel 35; Kenneth W. Porter, "John Jacob Astor and Lord Selkirk," *North Dakota History* 5 (1930): 8–11; George Boyd to William Morrison, 17 July 1819, *WHC,* 20:116; Crooks to Astor, 21 July 1817, AFC, LB 1; Lavender, *The Fist,* 246–247.

47. Crooks to Astor, 21 July 1817, AFC, LB 1; Jacob Franks to John Lawe, 11 March 1818, *WHC,* 20:34–36; Lavender, *The Fist,* 267.

48. Historical accounts of Astor's influence peddling would include Porter, 2:695–697, and Thomas Rosenblum, "Pelts and Patronage: The Representations Made by John Jacob Astor to the Federal Government Regarding His Fur Trade Interests in the Old North West, 1808–1818," in Thomas C. Buckley, ed., *Rendezvous: Selected Papers of the Fourth North American Fur Trade Conference* (Saint Paul: North American Fur Trade Conference, 1982), 63–71; Astor to Gallatin, 6 and 10 October 1815, GP, 28; William Crawford to Governor Cass, 10 May 1816, *WHC,* 19:406.

49. George Graham to Commanding Officer, Mackinac, and Major Puthuff, 5 June 1816; *WHC,* 19:414; Astor to Monroe, 27 May 1816, in Porter, 2:1145–1146; Crawford to Astor, 27 May 1816, in Clarence Carter, ed., *The Territorial Papers of the United States,* 26 vols. (Washington, D.C.: U.S. Government Printing Office, 1934–1962), vol. 10: *The Territory of Michigan, 1805–1820* (Washington, D.C.: U.S. Government Printing Office, 1942), 638–639; Crawford to Gov. Cass and Indian Agents, 10 May 1816, *WHC,* 19:406.

50. Cass to Puthuff, 20 July 1816, *WHC,* 19:427.

51. Astor to Monroe, 30 December 1816, as cited in Porter, 1:691; George Graham to Governor Cass, 4 May 1817, *WHC,* 19:457–458.

52. Cass to John Bowyer, 22 January 1818, *WHC,* 20:16–17; Thomas McKenney to John Calhoun, 4 March 1818, *Calhoun Papers,* 2:173; Cass to Indian Agents, 23 April 1818, *WHC,* 20:42–46; Astor to Calhoun, 14 March 1818, *Calhoun Papers,* 2:191–192.

53. Cass to Puthuff, 19 June 1817, John Lawe Papers, Letter Folder 2, Chicago Historical Society, Chicago, Illinois; Michael Dousman to John Lawe, 10 May 1818, and Jacob Franks to John Lawe, 11 March 1818, *WHC,* 20:34–36 and 55–56.

54. On government policy see especially Francis Paul Prucha, *The Great Father,* 1:8–158; idem, *The Sword of the Republic* (New York: Macmillan, 1969), 119–209; John Haeger, "A Time of Change: Green Bay, 1815–1834," *Wisconsin Magazine*

of History 54 (Summer 1971): 285–298. On the intentions of the British, see especially Colin Calloway, "The End of an Era: British-Indian Relations in the Great Lakes Region After the War of 1812," *Michigan Historical Review* 12 (Fall 1986): 1–20; Colin Calloway, *Crown and Calumet* (Norman: Univ. of Oklahoma Press, 1987); and D. G. Creighton, *The Commercial Empire of the St. Lawrence* (Toronto: Ryerson, 1937), 146, 180–201.

55. Ninian Edwards to James Monroe, Secretary of State, 3 March 1816; Major Puthuff to Gov. Lewis Cass, 14 May 1816, *WHC,* 19:401–403 and 408–409. Also see Thomas L. McKenney to George Graham, 30 September 1817, *WHC,* 19:480–482; and Matthew Irwin to Col. John Bowyer, 24 July 1817, *WHC,* 19:468–469.

56. Puthuff to Cass, 20 June 1816, *WHC,* 19:423–424; Lewis Cass's Passport for Ramsay Crooks, 7 May 1818, *WHC,* 20:55; and John Astor to Editor, *Philadelphia Aurora,* 15 December 1815, GP, 28.

57. Puthuff to Cass, 29 October 1816, in Carter, *Territorial Papers,* 10:668–669; Puthuff to Cass, 20 June 1816, *WHC,* 19:423–424.

58. Puthuff to Cass, 27 June 1816, and Acting Secretary of War Graham to Governor Cass, 29 October 1816, in Carter *Territorial Papers,* 10:654–655 and 667–668; Pierre du Rocheblave to J. Porlier, 20 June 1816, Puthuff to Cass, 20 June 1816, George Graham to Puthuff, 30 October 1816, and Cass to Puthuff, 20 July 1816, *WHC,* 19:415–444. Also see Crooks to Astor, 23 June 1817, AFC, LB 1.

59. Stuart to John Astor, 5 July 1818, AFC, LB 1; Crooks and Stuart to John Astor, 24 January 1818, *WHC,* 20:17–32; Astor to Calhoun, 10 February 1818, *Calhoun Papers,* 2:127; Cass to Calhoun, 30 July 1818, ibid., 2:441–442; Puthuff to Cass, 15 October 1818, *WHC,* 20:88–90; Cass to Calhoun, 20 October 1818, *Calhoun Papers,* 3:222. The American Fur Company was just as hard on Puthuff's successor and regularly threatened him with the use of their influence. See George Boyd to John Calhoun, 25 January 1820, ibid., 3:597–602.

60. Cass to George Boyd, 22 June 1819, in National Archives, Records of the Michigan Superintendency of Indian Affairs, M 1, Letters Received and Sent, Microfilm Reel 3, p. 90; Astor to Calhoun, 14 April 1821, in Carter, *Territorial Papers,* 11:126–127.

61. Cass to Calhoun, 30 July 1818; Col. Chambers to John Lawe, 26 April 1818, *WHC,* 20:51–62; Ramsay Crooks to Russell Farnham, 20 August 1817, AFC, LB 1; Crooks to Lewis Cass, 16 April 1818, AFC, LB 1; Crooks and Stuart to Astor, 24 January 1818, *WHC,* 20:17–32; Lavender, *The Fist,* 271–274; Francis Paul Prucha, *American Indian Policy in the Formative Years* (Cambridge: Harvard Univ. Press, 1962), 82–83; Hiram M. Chittenden, *The American Fur Trade of the Far West,* 2 vols. (1935; repr., Lincoln: Univ. of Nebraska Press, 1986), 1:312–315.

62. Crooks to Cass, 16 April 1818, AFC, LB 1; Stuart and Crooks to Astor, *WHC,* 20:29–30; and Astor to Calhoun, 10 February 1818, *Calhoun Papers,* 2:127.

63. Calhoun to Astor, 17 January 1818, *Calhoun Papers,* 2:78; Crooks to Calhoun, 2 March 1819, and Crooks to Farnham, 28 December 1818, AFC, LB 1; Calhoun to Governor William Clark, 3 March 1819, *WHC,* 20:103.

64. Crooks to Astor, 30 May 1820, and Crooks to Astor, 28 February 1819, AFC, LB 1; Crooks to T. H. Benton, 31 December 1822, AFC, LB 2.

65. Lavender, *The Fist,* 272–274, 278–279; and Prucha, *American Indian Policy,* 82–83.

66. Porter, 2:725–726, n. 57; Astor to Henry Clay, 20 May 1820, in James F. Hopkins, ed., *Henry Clay Papers* (Lexington: Univ. Press of Kentucky, 1959), 2:187;

Albert Gallatin to James Nicholson, 4 May 1816, GP, suppl., 4; Porter, 2:1061–1062; Astor to Monroe, 7 March and 20 March 1818, AP, BL, 13.

67. Raymond Walters, Jr., "The Origins of the Second Bank of the United States," *Journal of Political Economy* 53 (1945): 128–131; and Porter, 2:967–969.

68. Bray Hammond, *Banks and Politics in America* (Princeton, N.J.: Princeton Univ. Press, 1957), 244; Robert W. Keyes, "The Formation of the Second Bank of the United States, 1811–1817" (Ph.D. diss., Univ. of Delaware, 1975), 123–126, 185; Subscriptions to Stock of the Second Bank of the United States (BUS) to Astor, Peter Schenk, and Isaac Dennison, 1 July 1816, John Astor Letters, Library Company of Philadelphia, Pennsylvania.

69. Receipt of Stephen Girard to John Astor, 27 August 1816, Stephen Girard Papers, American Philosophical Society, Philadelphia, Pennsylvania; John Astor to William Jones, 2, 26 and 29 July 1816, AP, HSP; Gallatin to Astor, 7 June 1816, GP, 28; Kenneth Brown, "Stephen Girard, Promoter of the Second Bank of the United States," *Journal of Economic History,* 2 (November 1942): 134–137; Keyes, "Second Bank of the U.S.," 129–136; Walters, "Origins," 130–131; Donald Adams, *Finance and Enterprise in Early America* (Philadelphia: Univ. of Pennsylvania Press, 1978), 51–56.

70. Astor to William Jones, 21, 24 and 26 October and 14 September 1816, AP, HSP; Astor to Gallatin, 31 October 1816, GP, 29; Keyes, "Second Bank of the U.S.," 131–149, 153–154; Brown, "Stephen Girard," 138–139; D. Adams, *Finance and Enterprise,* 57–63.

71. Astor to W. Woolsey, 2 November 1816, John Astor Papers, Library of Congress, Washington, D.C.; Astor to Jones, 7 December and 28 December 1816, AP, HSP; Astor to Jones, 3 March 1817, AP, NYPL, Box 1; Porter, 2:968–969; and William B. Smith, *Economic Aspects of the Second Bank of the United States* (Cambridge: Harvard Univ. Press, 1953), 39.

72. Astor to Jones, 6 April 1817, 30 July 1817, and 4 August 1817, AP, HSP; Astor to Gallatin, 12 November 1816, GP, 29; Astor to Gallatin, 14 March and 6 December 1818, GP, 30; Smith, *Economic Aspects,* 48.

73. Hammond, *Banks and Politics,* 252–263; Leon Scheer, "The Second Bank of the United States and the Inflation After the War of 1812," *Journal of Political Economy* 68 (April 1960): 118–133; D. Adams, *Finance and Enterprise,* 63–65.

74. Astor to Gallatin, 14 and 17 March 1818, GP, 30; Porter, 2:1034.

75. Astor to Peter Smith, 13 May 1819, in Porter, 2:1161–1162; Astor to Gallatin, 5 September 1818, GP, 31.

76. John Astor Memo to William B. Astor, 1819, in Porter, 2:1163–1166; Astor to Gallatin, 15 and 25 April and 5 September 1818, GP, 30; Astor to Peter Smith, 13 May 1819, in Porter, 2:1162–1163; Astor to Gallatin, 29 March 1819, GP, 31; Astor to Gallatin, 3 February and 15 May 1820, GP, 32; Astor to Gallatin, 18, 27, and 29 July 1821, GP, 33; Astor to Gallatin, 20 August 1821, GP, 34; Astor to Gallatin, 9 September 1822, GP, 35.

Chapter 8

1. David Lavender, *The Fist in the Wilderness* (Garden City, N.Y.: Doubleday, 1964), x, passim; Alfred Chandler, *The Visible Hand* (Cambridge: Harvard Univ. Press, 1977), 36–37, 1–49.

2. Memorandum of John Astor to William B. Astor, 1819, in Porter, 2:1164–1166; Crooks to Astor, 31 October 1819, 4 December 1819, and 14 June 1820; Crooks to Matthews, 24 October 1819, AFC, LB 1.

3. Crooks to Astor, 31 October 1819, AFC, LB 1; Crooks to Berthold and Chouteau, 10 August 1820, and Crooks to W. B. Astor, 27 July 1820, AFC, LB 2.

4. Astor to Crooks, 31 December 1819, John Astor Papers, William L. Clements Library, Ann Arbor, Michigan; Crooks to Astor, 4 December 1819, AFC, LB 1; Crooks to Astor, 30 November 1821, AFC, LB 2; Robert Baird, *Transplanted Flowers or Memoirs of Mrs. Rumpff (Daughter of John Jacob Astor) and the Duchess De Broglie (Daughter of Madame De Stäel) with an Appendix by Robert Baird* (New York: John S. Taylor, 1839), 22–23; and Porter, 2:1100–1101.

5. Crooks to Astor, 29 July 1821 and 30 November 1821, AFC, LB 2.

6. The history of the factory system and Thomas L. McKenney's role is detailed in Francis Paul Prucha, *The Great Father*, 2 vols. (Lincoln: Univ. of Nebraska Press, 1984), 1:115–134; Herman Viola, *Thomas L. McKenney* (Chicago: Swallow Press, 1974), 21–70; Thomas L. McKenney, *Memoirs, Official and Personal* (1846; repr., Lincoln: Univ. of Nebraska Press, 1973), 17–24.

7. Astor to De Witt Clinton, 25 January 1808, De Witt Clinton Papers, Butler Library, Columbia Univ.; Astor to Gallatin, 10 October 1815, GP, 28.

8. The arguments against the factory system were best presented in Rev. Jedidiah Morse, *A Report to the Secretary of War of the United States on Indian Affairs, Comprising a Narrative of a Tour Performed in the Summer of 1820 . . .* (New Haven: S. Converse, 1822), 40–49, passim; Paul Phillips, *The Fur Trade*, 2 vols. (Norman: Univ. of Oklahoma Press, 1961), 2:88–96. On the operation of factors see T. L. McKenney to John Johnson, 11 March 1819, *WHC*, 20:104–105; Major Irwin to Colonel McKenney, 1819, *WHC*, 7:278; T. L. McKenney to Henry Southard, 6 January 1818, *WHC*, 20:12–16. For a defense of the system, see Prucha, *Great Father*, 1:115–134.

9. Crooks and Stuart to Astor, 24 January 1818, *WHC*, 20:17–32.

10. Crooks to Astor, 24 February 1818, AFC, LB 1; Astor to Gallatin, 14 March 1818, GP, 30; T. L. McKenney to Henry Southard, 6 January 1818, *WHC*, 20:12–16; Viola, *McKenney*, 58–61. On John Johnson, see, for example, T. L. McKenney to John Calhoun, 14 July 1818, in *The Papers of John Calhoun*, 18 vols. (Columbia: Univ. of South Carolina Press, 1959–), 2:383; Calhoun to Thomas Smith, 2 September 1819, ibid., 4:294; Crooks to James Lockwood, AFC, LB 2; and Lavender, *The Fist*, 266–267.

11. McKenney to Calhoun, 19 August 1818, *WHC*, 20:66–79; Lewis Cass to Calhoun, 14 September 1818, *WHC*, 20:86–87; John Calhoun, "Alteration of the System for Trading with the Indians, 5 December 1818," *American State Papers: Indian Affairs* (Washington, D.C.: Gales & Seaton, 1834), 2:181–185; Viola, *McKenney*, 58–60.

12. Samuel Abbott to Crooks, 12 May 1820, AFC, MHS; Crooks to William Woodbridge, 24 August 1820, AFC, LB 2; and Crooks to Astor, 30 May 1820, AFC, LB 2.

13. Crooks to Astor, 30 May 1820, AFC, LB 1; Astor to Crooks, 24 December 1820, AP, Clements Library; Astor to James Monroe, 10 January 1821, in Porter, 2:1169–1170.

14. Crooks to Astor, 30 November 1821, and Crooks to James Lockwood, 2 December 1820, AFC, LB 2.

15. Morse, *Report*, 40–53, passim; Viola, *McKenney*, 65–70; Thomas Hart Benton, *Thirty Years' View: or a History of the Working of Government for Thirty Years, from 1820–1850*, 2 vols. (New York: D. Appleton, 1854–1856), 1:13, 20–21; Samuel Flagg Bemis, *John Quincy Adams and the Foundations of American Foreign Policy* (New York: Norton, 1949), 484–490; Howard Kushner, *Conflict on the Northwest Coast* (Westport, Conn.: Greenwood, 1975), 28–29.

16. "Act to Abolish the United State Trading Establishments . . . ," 6 May 1822, and "An Act to Amend an Act entitled 'An Act to Regulate Trade and Intercourse . . . , 6 May 1822,'" in Department of War, *Indian Treaties, and Laws and Regulations Relating to Indian Affairs* (Washington, D.C.: Way & Gideon, 1826), 399–402; Crooks to Abbott, 3 January 1822, AFC, LB 2; and Viola, *McKenney*, 65–70.

17. Astor to Crooks, 27 March 1821, AP, NYPL; Crooks to Robert Stuart, 5 December 1821, and Crooks to Astor, 11 July 1821, AFC, LB 2; Gurdon S. Hubbard, *The Autobiography of Gurdon S. Hubbard* (New York: Citadel Press, 1969), 75–80; and Phillips, *Fur Trade*, 2:348–352.

18. Astor to Auguste Chouteau, 28 January 1800, and Astor to Gratiot, 26 May 1816, in Porter, 1:389–390 and 2:1143–1144; and Astor to De Witt Clinton, 9 March 1808, AP, Beinecke.

19. Crooks to Wilson Hunt, 15 April 1818; Letter of Ramsay Crooks, 19 June 1818, AFC, LB 1; Crooks to Astor, 29 July 1821, AFC, LB 2; and Lavender, *The Fist*, 78–92.

20. Crooks to Astor, 4 December 1819, AFC, LB 1; Crooks to Astor, 30 November 1821, AFC, LB 2.

21. Crooks to Samuel Abbott, 2 and 25 October 1821, AFC, LB 2; and Crooks to Astor, 23 April 1822, AFC, LB 2. Good background material is available in Lavender, *The Fist*, 310–313.

22. Astor to Robert Stuart, 16 April 1823, George Franklin and Mary Stuart Turner Papers, Minnesota Historical Society, St. Paul; Crooks to Astor, 23 April 1822 and Stuart to Crooks, 10 November 1822, AFC, LB 2.

23. Crooks to Samuel Abbott, 28 April 1822, Chouteau Coll. Mo.HS; A good description of the fur companies in Saint Louis from 1818 to 1823 is in Richard M. Clokey, *William H. Ashley* (Norman: Univ. of Oklahoma Press, 1980), 65–67, 86–87.

24. Joshua Pilcher to Crooks, 16 June 1822, in Dale Morgan, ed., *The West of William H. Ashley* (Denver: Old West Publishing Co., 1964), 15–16; Stuart to Astor & Son, 20 June 1822 and 16 August 1822, AFC, LB 2; Clokey, *Ashley*, 85–87; Lavender, *The Fist*, 337.

25. Stuart to Crooks, 10 November 1822; Crooks to Astor, 30 November 1821; Crooks to Astor, 23 April 1822, AFC, LB 2; and Astor to Stuart, 28 November 1822, Turner Papers.

26. Astor to Stuart, 28 November 1822, Turner Papers; Astor to Crooks, 27 January 1823, in Porter, 2:1172; Astor to Samuel Abbott, 13 March 1823, Chouteau Coll., Mo.HS; Crooks to Stuart, 8 February 1823, AFC, LB 2, and Lavender, *The Fist*, 341–343.

27. Astor to Crooks, 27 January 1823, in Porter, 2:1172; Crooks to Astor & Son, 31 August 1823, AFC, LB 2; Astor to Samuel Abbott, 13 March 1823, Chouteau Coll., Mo.HS; Crooks to Stuart, 8 February 1823, AFC, LB 2; Stuart to William Astor, 19 July 1823, AFC, LB 2; Crooks to Samuel Abbott, 14 March 1823, AFC, LB 3; Astor to Oliver Bostwick, 28 March 1823, Chouteau Coll., Mo.HS.; Stuart to David Stone, 19 May 1823, AFC, LB 2; and Crooks to John Stevens, 12 March 1823, AFC, LB 2.

28. Astor to Samuel Abbott, 13 March 1823, Chouteau Coll., Mo.HS; Crooks to Stuart, 8 February 1823, AFC, LB 2; Stuart to William Astor, 19 July 1823, Astor to Stuart, 28 November 1822, Turner Papers; Astor to Clinton, October 1824, Clinton Papers; Porter, 2:607, 1102–1103.

29. Stuart to Astor, 15 October 1824, AFC, LB 3; Stuart to James Abbott, 7 October 1823, AFC, LB 3; Crooks to Stuart, 8 February 1823, AFC, LB 2; Stuart to Stone, 3 and 4 July 1823, AFC, LB 3; William Astor to Stuart, 19 January 1825, AFC, MHS.

30. Stuart to James Abbott, 7 October 1823, Stuart to Stone, 4 March 1823, and Crooks to Astor & Son, 31 August 1823, AFC, LB 3; William Astor to Crooks, 5 August 1823, AFC, MHS; William Astor to Stone, 1 June 1823, AFC, MHS; Crooks to Stone, 30 August 1823, AFC, LB 3; William Astor to Stuart, 19 January 1825, AFC, MHS.

31. Crooks to Rolette, 5 September 1823, AFC, LB 3. Also see Astor to Stuart, 19 January 1825, AFC, MHS.

32. Astor to Agents of the AFC, 22 April 1823, AP, Beinecke; Astor to Abbott, 26 April 1823, Chouteau Coll., Mo.HS; Astor to Stuart, 16 April 1823, Turner Papers; Crooks to Abbott, 14 March 1823, AFC, LB 2.

33. Astor to Stuart, 16 April 1823, Turner Papers.

34. Stuart to William Morrison, 18 July 1823, AFC, LB 3; Crooks to William Astor, 22 August 1823, AFC, LB 2; and Stuart to Astor, 20 May and 14 June 1823, AFC, LB 2; and Astor to Crooks, 19 March 1824, AP, NYPL.

35. Crooks to Rolette, 2 September 1820, AFC, LB 2; Stuart to Astor & Son, 20 July 1822, AFC, LB 2; Crooks to Rolette, 5 September 1823, AFC, LB 3.

36. Crooks to Astor, 30 November 1821, AFC, LB 2; Agreement of Green Bay Traders, 1 August 1821, *WHC,* 20:206–210; John Lawe to Jacob Franks, 5 September 1823, *WHC,* 20:308; and John Haeger, "A Time of Change: Green Bay, 1815–1834," *Wisconsin Magazine of History,* 54 (Summer 1971): 293–296.

37. John Lawe to Jacob Franks, 26 August 1822, *WHC,* 20:277–278; Stuart to Crooks, 18 August 1827, AFC, LB 3. A similar strategy was later followed in Detroit. See Crooks to John Astor, 22 June 1827, AP, NYPL.

38. Astor to Crooks, 26 July 1830, AP, NYPL; Stuart to David Stone, 3 July 1823, AFC, LB 3; Gurdon Hubbard to Mrs. A. Hubbard, 12 August 1825 and 2 January 1828, Gurdon Hubbard Papers, Chicago Historical Society, Chicago, Illinois; Stuart to John Crafts and Jean Beaubien, 14 August 1825, AFC, LB 3.

39. Stuart to William Astor, 31 May 1825, AFC, LB 3; Stuart to John Kinzie, 22 October 1825, AFC, LB 3; Porter, 2:754–755; Phillips, *Fur Trade,* 2:373–377; Stuart to J. Porlier, 27 October 1822, *WHC,* 20:290; Stuart to Stone, 4 September 1824, AFC, LB 3; Jeanne Kay, "The American Fur Company and the Decline of the Green Bay Trade," in Thomas C. Buckley, ed., *Rendezvous: Selected Papers of the Fourth North American Fur Trade Conference* (Saint Paul: North American Fur Trade Conference, 1982), 76–78; and William Astor to Secretary of War, 25 November 1831, Congress, Senate, *Message of the President Relative to the Fur Trade, and Inland Trade to Mexico,* 22d Cong., 1st sess., 1832, S. Doc. 90, pp. 77–78.

40. Clokey, *Ashley,* 78–161; and David J. Wishart, *The Fur Trade of the American West, 1807–1840* (Lincoln: Univ. of Nebraska Press, 1979), 51–52, 121–124.

41. Clokey, *Ashley,* 67, 86–87, and 158–159; Lavender, *The Fist,* 378.

42. William B. Astor to David Stone, 12 June 1824, and William Astor to Stuart, 19 January 1825, AFC, MHS.

43. Astor to Albert Gallatin, 9 May 1826 and 16 October 1826, GP, 36.

44. Astor to Crooks, 11 March 1825, AP, NYPL; Astor to Crooks, 10 January 1825, in Porter, 2:1176–1178; Crooks to William Matthews, 16 May 1826, AP, NYPL; and Porter, 2:740–743.

45. William Astor to O. N. Bostwick, 22 February 1826, Chouteau Coll. Mo.HS; Astor to Bostwick, 10 May 1826; 22 September 1826 and 22 December 1826, Chouteau Coll., Mo.HS; Crooks to Astor, 13 April and 10 August 1827, AP, NYPL; Peter Michel, "The St. Louis Fur Trade: Fur Company Ledgers and Account Books in the Archives of the Missouri Historical Society," *Gateway Heritage* 6 (Fall 1985): 15; Lavender, *The Fist*, 357–378; Clokey, *Ashley*, 178–179; and Phillips, *Fur Trade*, 2:403–408.

46. Crooks to Astor, 24 May 1827, AP, NYPL.

47. Crooks to Astor, 30 April 1827, 24 May 1827, and 26 June 1827, AP, NYPL; Crooks to Joseph Rolette, 21 September 1827, AP, NYPL; Rolette to Stuart, 10 August 1829, AFC, MHS; Wishart, *Fur Trade*, 52–54; and Phillips, *Fur Trade*, 2:408–419.

48. "A Tabular Statement Showing the Number of Licenses Issued to Persons to Trade with the Indians, 1824–1832; the Amount of Capital Employed; with the Value of the Returns . . . ," and William Astor to Senate Committee, 25 November 1831, in S. Doc. 90, 1832, pp. 77–79; Lewis Cass and William Clark to Thomas Hart Benton, 27 December 1828, Congress, Senate, *Report of the Committee on Indian Affairs,* 20th Cong., 2d sess., S. Doc. 67, 1829, 1–19; "Letter from Correspondent to *New York Observer,* December 1833," *Museum of Fur Trade Quarterly* 21 (Summer 1985): 6; George Boyd to James Gardiner, 18 August 1830, in Porter, 2:765–767 and 1206–1209.

49. See descriptions of trade in Lewis Cass to President, 8 February 1832, S. Doc. 90, 1–5; William Clark and Lewis Cass to Benton, 27 December 1828, S. Doc. 67, 1828, 5–11; Prince Maximilian of Wied, *Travels in the Interior of North America, 1832–1834* (1843: repr., R. G. Thwaites, ed., *Early Western Travels* [Cleveland: Arthur H. Clark, 1906]), 22:375–378; and Wishart, *Fur Trade,* 47–114.

50. Ray H. Mattison, "Fort Union: Its Role in the Upper Missouri Fur Trade," *North Dakota History* 28 (1962): 181–208; Astor to Pierre Chouteau, 17 October 1832, Chouteau Coll., Mo.HS; Donald Jackson, *Voyages of the Steamboat Yellow Stone* (Norman: Univ. of Oklahoma Press, 1985), 50, 1–49.

51. Stuart to Gillespies, Moffatt, & Co., 10 August 1822, AFC, LB 2; Astor to Crooks, 28 September 1827, AP, NYPL; Crooks to Astor, 13 April 1827, AP, NYPL; Crooks to Stuart, 26 March 1823, AFC, LB 2; Crooks to Astor, 8 June 1827, AP, NYPL; Astor to Bernard Pratte & Co., 3 March 1828, Chouteau Coll., Mo.HS; Astor to Gillespies, Moffatt, Finlay & Co. 31 October and 15 November 1831, AP, BL, 3.

52. Crooks to Astor, 5 August 1818, AFC, LB 1; Astor to Charles Gratiot, 14 April 1815, AP, Mo.HS; Crooks to Astor, 31 August 1823, Crooks to Gerard Gillespies & Co., 5 September 1821; AFC, LB 2; James Clayton, "The American Fur Company: The Final Years" (Ph.D. diss., Cornell University, 1964), 46–48; James Clayton, "The Growth and Economic Significance of the American Fur Trade, 1790–1890," in Russell Fridley, ed., *Aspects of the Fur Trade* (Saint Paul: Minnesota Historical Society, 1967), 62–63; Astor to Stuart, 10 August 1824, AP, BL, 3; Astor to Pierre Chouteau, 20 July and 21 November 1829, Chouteau Coll., Mo.HS; and William Astor to O. Bostwick, 22 February and 10 May 1826, Chouteau Coll., Mo.HS.

53. Astor to Crooks, 17 March 1824, AP, NYPL; Astor to Stuart, 7 October 1823, Turner Papers; Crooks to Astor, 23 April 1822, AFC, LB 2; Crooks to James Abbott, 27 April 1822, AFC, LB 2; William Astor to Crooks, 5 August 1823, AFC, MHS; Astor to Stuart, 24 February 1831, Turner Papers; "Statement of Shipments Made by the American Fur Company," 1823 and "Shipments & Consignments of the American Fur Company, 1818–1829," AP, BL, 13.

54. Astor to Bernard Pratte & Co., 24 July 1834, Chouteau Coll., Mo.HS; and Astor to Pierre Chouteau, 25 September 1829, Chouteau Coll., Mo.HS.

55. Astor to Stuart, 27 September 1828, Turner Papers; Astor to Crooks, 12 April 1827, AP, NYPL; Porter, 2:822–823, 781, n. 24, and 785, n. 23; Astor to Crooks, 28 September 1827, AP, NYPL; Astor to Stuart, 26 May 1828, AP, Clements Library.

56. Astor to Crooks, 26 July 1830, AP, NYPL; Astor to Stuart, 30 April 1830 and 21 April 1831, and William Astor to Stuart, 9 May 1825, Turner Papers.

57. William Astor to Stuart, 19 January 1825, AFC, MHS. Also see Crooks to Stuart, 26 April 1822, AFC, LB 2; Astor to Stuart, 8 January 1825, Turner Papers; Astor to Samuel Abbott, 8 April 1823, Chouteau Coll., Mo.HS.

58. Astor to Stuart, 8 January 1825, Turner Papers. Also see Astor to Stuart, 3 June 1828, AP, BL, 10.

59. "Statement of the Number of Furs Imported into China by the Americans, 1804–1827," and "An Account of the Value of Imports & Exports from Canton by Subjects of the United States, 1804–1827," Great Britain, House of Lords, *Papers Relating to the Trade with China . . . ,* vol. 262, 1829, p. 43; Congress, House, "Letter from the Secretary of Treasury . . . Respecting Commerce Between the United States & China, 1821–1839," 26th Cong., 1st sess., 1840, H. Doc. 248, p. 8; and Porter, 2:666–667.

60. Robert G. Albion, *Square Riggers on Schedule* (1938; repr., New York: Shoe String Press, Archon Books, 1965), 20–69; and Robert G. Albion, *The Rise of New York Port* (New York: Scribner's, 1939), 198; Mary V. Kuebel, "Merchants and Mandarins: The Genesis of American Relations with China" (Ph.D. diss., Univ. of Virginia, 1974), 100–103, 162–164; and Henry Ogden to Nicholas Ogden, 9 March 1823, Nicholas G. Ogden Papers, Historical Society of Pennsylvania, Philadelphia.

61. Nicholas Ogden to S. G. Ogden, 3 November 1820, and H. Ogden to Nicholas Ogden, 9 March 1823, Ogden Papers; Kenneth W. Porter, "Further Notes on Benjamin Clapp," *Washington Historical Quarterly* 26 (January 1935): 26–27; Porter, 2:612–614; Astor to D. Olyphant, 8 April 1831, and Astor to N. G. Carnes, 5 June 1832, in Porter, 2:1209–1217; Astor to C. Talbot, 8 June 1832, AP, BL, 16; and William Astor to J. P. Sturgis, 23 October 1832, AP, BL, 3.

62. Astor to Bostwick, 28 April 1826, Chouteau, Mo.HS; Astor to Pierre Chouteau, 28 March and 17 October 1832, Chouteau Coll., Mo.HS; William Astor to Stuart, 9 May 1825, Turner Papers; Crooks to Samuel Abbott, 26 March 1819, AFC, LB 1; Crooks to Levy Solomon, 28 December 1821, and Stuart to John Astor, 6 July 1823, and Crooks to Stuart, 26 April 1822, AFC, LB 2; Thomas Forsyth to the Secretary of War, 24 October 1831, and "List of Various Articles for Fur Trade at St. Louis, 1831," S. Doc. 90, 1832, pp. 65–77.

63. "Mackinac Blotter, 1817–1834," AFC, PAC; Henry Schoolcraft to the Secretary of War, 24 October 1831, S. Doc. 90, 1832, pp. 70–77; Clayton, "American Fur Company," 72–78, 182; Crooks to Astor, 23 April 1822, AFC, LB 2; Crooks to

Astor, 18 April 1821, AFC, LB 2; Thomas Forsyth to the Secretary of War, 24 October 1831, S. Doc. 90, 1832, pp. 70–77.

64. Lewis Cass and William Clark to Thomas Hart Benton, 27 December 1828, S. Doc. 67, 1829, pp. 5–11; Stuart to Astor, 10 September 1822, and Stuart to Crooks, 17 October 1822, AFC, LB 2; Thomas L. McKenney to Peter B. Porter, 3 January 1829, S. Doc. 67, 1829, pp. 4–5. This theme is also discussed in Clayton, "American Fur Company," 64–65, 80–83 and has been the subject of considerable discussion among historians and anthropologists. See a review of this literature in Jacqueline Peterson and John Anfinson, "The Indian and the Fur Trade: A Review of Recent Literature," in W. R. Swagerty, *Scholars and the Indian Experience* (Bloomington: Indiana Univ. Press, 1984), 223–257.

65. John Astor, "Account Book, 1816," John Astor Papers, New York State Library, Albany; Michel, "St. Louis," 10–17; "Mackinac Blotter, 1817–1834," AFC, PAC.

66. Stuart to Astor, 29 November 1826, AFC, LB 3; Astor to Stuart, 16 April 1823, Turner Papers; Astor to Stuart, 31 October 1826, John Astor Papers, New York State Library; and Astor to Crooks, 16 February 1824, in Porter, 2:1173–1174.

67. Astor to Crooks, 2 September 1824, AP, NYPL.

68. Astor to Stuart, 13 January 1828, Turner Papers; Astor to Bostwick, 10 May 1826, Chouteau Coll., Mo.HS; Haeger, "Time of Change," 298.

69. Astor to Stuart, 7 October 1823, Turner Papers; Astor to Pierre Chouteau, August 1832, AP, BL, 10.

70. "Mr. Benton's Report to the Committee, 1829," S. Doc. 67, 1829, p. 2 and passim; Lewis Cass to the President, 8 February 1832, S. Doc. 90, 1832, pp. 1–5 and passim. Also see Congress, Senate, *Message from the President of the United States . . . Relative to the British Establishments on the Columbia and the State of the Fur Trade,* 21st. Cong., 2d sess., S. Doc. 39, 1831, pp. 1–40.

71. Astor to Robert Stuart, 26 May 1828, John Astor Papers, Clements Library; John Astor to Thomas Hart Benton, 29 January 1829, S. Doc. 90, 1832, pp. 61–62; Lewis Cass and William Clark to Benton, 27 December 1828, S. Doc. 67, 1829, pp. 5–11; and "Statement of Value of Furs Imported into the United States from Foreign Countries . . . ," S. Doc. 67, 1829, p. 19.

72. The most reliable sources of information on the changing animal population and declining fur trade were in the letters found in the several congressional reports. See, for example, Joshua Pilcher to General Clark, 1 December 1831, S. Doc. 90, 1832, pp. 11–18; William Ashley to Thomas Hart Benton, 12 November 1827, S. Doc. 67, 1829, pp. 11–12; Thomas J. Owen to Governor Porter, 10 October 1831, S. Doc. 90, 1832, pp. 57–59; A. Chouteau to the Secretary of War, 12 November 1831, S. Doc. 90, 1832, pp. 60–61; Astor to Wilson P. Hunt, 2 January 1832, AP, BL, 3.

Historians disagree on the notion of a declining trade. James Clayton has argued that the fur trade actually increased in the 1830s when hundreds of farmers and town residents participated. His statistical analysis depends on a book by Henry Poland whose statistics are based on the export of Canadian furs through the Hudson's Bay Company. I think that Clayton is wrong and that the American trade was in absolute decline. A careful analysis of the Far West trade is in Wishart, *Fur Trade,* 29–33. See Clayton, "Economic Significance," 67–72; and Henry Poland, *Fur Bearing Animals in Nature and in Commerce* (London: Gurney & Jackson, 1892), pp. xx–xxxiii.

73. Lewis Cass to the Secretary of War, 8 February 1832, S. Doc. 90, 1832, p. 2; Wishart, *Fur Trade,* 132–160; and Clokey, *Ashley,* 181–202.

74. Clokey, *Ashley,* 181–192; Wishart, *Fur Trade,* 148–152; and Hiram M. Chittenden, *The American Fur Trade of the Far West,* 2 vols. (1935; repr., Lincoln: Univ. of Nebraska Press, 1986), 1:346–363; Joshua Pilcher's Report, 1 December 1831, and William Gordon to Lewis Cass, 3 October 1831, S. Doc. 90, 1832, pp. 11–19, 26–30.

75. Crooks to Astor, 23 June 1817, AFC, LB 1; Porter, 2:792–796; Crooks to Stuart, 21 October 1819, and Crooks to Lewis Cass, 24 March 1819, AFC, LB 1; Phillips, *Fur Trade,* 2:377–378; and Prucha, *Great Father,* 1:98–102.

76. Astor to Bostwick, 29 May 1826, Chouteau Coll., Mo.HS; Albert Gallatin to James Barbour, 30 June 1826, in Porter, 2:1183–1184; Stuart to Crooks, 24 January 1825, AFC, LB 2; Stuart to Astor, 28 August 1826, AFC, LB 3; Astor to Gallatin, 23 May 1826, GP, 36; J. Snelling to James Barbour, 23 August 1825, *WHC,* 20:384; Lavender, *The Fist,* 355–363; and Porter, 2:755–759 and 791–815.

77. Astor to Oliver Bostwick, 29 May 1826, Chouteau Coll., Mo.HS; Astor to Gallatin, 23 May 1826, GP, 36; Astor to Stuart, 30 April 1830, Turner Papers; and Lavender, *The Fist,* 363.

78. Stuart to David Stone, 19 May 1823, AFC, LB 2; Stuart to John Astor, 22 May 1826, AFC, LB 3; Lewis Cass to Henry Schoolcraft, 10 June 1823, *WHC,* 20:366–367; William B. Astor to James Keith, 15 December 1829, in Porter, 2:1198; and William Smith to William Astor, 3 March 1830, in Frederick Merk, ed., *Fur Trade and Empire* (Cambridge: Harvard Univ. Press, 1931), 320–321; and E. E. Rich, *The History of the Hudson's Bay Company 1670–1870,* 2 vols. (London: Hudson's Bay Record Society, 1958–1959), 2:478.

79. The law is quoted and discussed in Francis Paul Prucha, *American Indian Policy in the Formative Years* (Cambridge: Harvard Univ. Press, 1962), p. 127; John Astor to James Doty, 19 April 1832, James Duane Doty Papers, Box 3, State Historical Society of Wisconsin, Madison; William B. Astor to Pierre Chouteau, 17 October 1832, Chouteau Coll., Mo.HS; Clokey, *Ashley,* 192–194.

80. Astor to Pratte & Co., 19 June 1832, AP, BL, 3; Astor to Wilson P. Hunt, 2 January 1832, AP, BL, 3; Porter, 2:776–777, 1103–1104; Crooks to Pierre Chouteau, 20 March 1833, Chouteau Coll., Mo.HS; Clayton, "American Fur Company," 150–152; Lavender, *The Fist,* 411–412.

81. These incidents are well known in fur-trade history. See Chittenden, *American Fur Trade,* 1:342–377; Clokey, *Ashley,* 191–196; Porter, 2:768–770. Pierre Chouteau, Jr., also had a metal struck with his image on it. See Jackson, *Voyages,* 99.

82. Crooks to Pierre Chouteau, 20 March 1833, Chouteau, Mo.HS.

83. Ibid.; Astor to Hunt, 6 December 1833, AP, BL, 3; William Astor to Pratte, Chouteau & Co., 26 August and 1 November 1833, Chouteau Coll., Mo.HS; Clayton, "American Fur Company," 150–152; Clokey, *Ashley,* 195–196; and Lavender, *The Fist,* 412–413.

84. Astor to Hunt, 4 May 1834, AP, BL, 3; Astor to Pierre Chouteau, 18 June 1836, Chouteau Coll., Mo.HS; Crooks to Pierre Chouteau, 6 March 1834, Chouteau Coll., Mo.HS.

85. Crooks to Pratte, Chouteau & Co., 31 May 1834, AP, Mo.HS; Astor to Pierre Chouteau, 18 June 1836, Chouteau Coll., Porter, 2:778–779; Clayton, "American Fur Company," 170–179; Crooks to Pierre Chouteau, 16 August 1841, Chouteau Coll., Mo.HS.

86. Crooks to Chouteau, 31 January 1835, Chouteau Coll., Mo.HS.

Chapter 9

1. Legal agreement between John Astor and Patrick Langan and David A. Grant, 16 January 1796, AP, BL, 10. For a full description of these purchases, see chap. 2, p. 61.

2. Astor to Peter Smith, 7 August 1794, and William Laight to Peter Smith, 30 November 1794, Peter Smith Papers, George Arents Research Center, Syracuse University, Syracuse, New York, Microfilm Reel 1. Also see chap. 2, pp. 61–62.

3. Astor to Smith, 10 November 1810, and Smith to Astor, 24 November 1810; Astor to Smith, 22 March 1811; Smith to Astor 11 June 1811, Smith Papers, Reel 1; David M. Ellis, *Landlords and Farmers in the Hudson–Mohawk Region, 1790–1815* (New York: Farrar, Straus & Giroux, Octagon Books, 1967), 58.

4. Account of Charlotte River and Byrnes Patent Tract, 1 January 1827, in Porter, 2:1185–1186; Astor to Smith, 19 February 1828, Smith to Astor, 25 February 1828, and Astor to Smith, 30 December 1828, Smith Papers, 2. Also see Porter, 1:96–99.

5. Astor to Smith, 27 December 1815, Smith Papers, 1; Astor to James Toohumber & Co., 15 January 1814, AP, BL, 3; Astor to John Bryan, 29 November 1813, and Astor to Obadiah German, 11 April 1834, AP, BL, 3; and John Astor, "Evaluation of Real Estate," 1847, AP, NYHS.

6. Henry Livingston to John Astor, 1 August 1810, John Astor Papers, New York State Library, Albany; *Statement and Exposition of the Title of John Jacob Astor to the Land Purchased by him from the Surviving Children of Roger Morris and Mary his Wife* (New York: n.p., 1827), 1–18; Porter, 2:878–892.

7. Astor to the Commissioners, 16 January 1819; Martin Van Buren, Thomas Oakley, and Nathan Williams to John Astor, 2 January 1819, in *Statement and Exposition*, 18–46; and Astor to De Witt Clinton, 24 December 1825, and Clinton to Astor, 27 December 1827 and 29 September 1827, De Witt Clinton Papers, Columbia University, New York City.

8. *Nathaniel Crune* v. *Lessee of Henry Gage Morris et al. and of John Jacob Astor et al.*, 6 Peters, 514–520, 632; *James Carver* v. *James Jackson on the demise of John Astor*, 4 Peters, 1–99; and Porter, 2:882–886.

9. Astor to Vincent Rumpff, 9 April 1832, in Porter, 2:1214; Astor to William Wirt, 15 January and 17 February 1832; Astor to David Ogden, 18 January 1832, AP, BL, 3.

10. The economic growth of New York City from 1789 to 1850 is treated in a number of books: I. N. Phelps Stokes, *The Iconography of Manhattan Island, 1498–1909*, 6 vols. (New York: Robert H. Dodd, 1915), 1:366–408; 3:477–680; Sidney I. Pomerantz, *New York: An American City, 1783–1803* (Port Washington, N.Y.: Ira Friedman, 1965), 200; and Robert G. Albion, *The Rise of New York Port* (New York: Scribners, 1939); Edward K. Spann, *The New Metropolis: New York, 1840–1857* (New York: Columbia Univ. Press, 1981); and Sean Wilentz, *Chants Democratic: New York City and the Rise of the American Working Class, 1788–1850* (New York: Oxford Univ. Press, 1984). A convenient collection of statistics on the city's growth is in "Commerce of the City of New York," *Hunt's Merchant Magazine* 13 (July 1845): 42–45.

11. The importance of real estate investment and building construction is the subject of an important new book by Elizabeth Blackmar, *Manhattan for Rent, 1785–1850* (Ithaca: Cornell Univ. Press, 1989). Also see Allan Pred, *The Spatial Dynamics of U.S. Urban-Industrial Growth, 1800–1914* (Cambridge: MIT Press, 1966), 180–181. Three important articles on this theme are Michael J. Doucet,

"Urban Land Development in Nineteenth Century North America," *Journal of Urban History* 8 (May 1982): 299–342; Michael J. Doucet and John Weaver, "The North American Shelter Business, 1860–1920: A Study of Canadian Real Estate and Property Management Agency," *Business History Review* 58 (Summer 1984): 234–262; and Marc A. Weiss, "Real Estate History: An Overview and Research Agenda," *Business History Review* 63 (Summer 1989): 241–282.

12. Thomas C. Cochran, "The Business Revolution," *American Historical Review* (December 1974): 1449–1466. Also see idem, *Frontiers of Change: Early Industrialism in America* (New York: Oxford Univ. Press, 1981), 17–48, 116–127.

13. The historiography of western land development is voluminous. See especially the ideas of Paul Wallace Gates in *Landlords and Tenants on the Prairie Frontier: Studies in American Land Policy* (Ithaca: Cornell Univ. Press, 1973). Also see Harry Scheiber's review of Gates's work in "The Economic Historian as Realist and Keeper of Democratic Ideals: Paul Wallace Gates's Studies of American Land Policy," *Journal of Economic History* 40 (September 1980): 585–593. The revisionist view is best represented in Allan G. Bogue, *Money at Interest* (Ithaca: Cornell Univ. Press, 1955); Robert Swierenga, *Pioneers and Profits: Land Speculation on the Iowa Frontier* (Ames: Iowa State Univ. Press, 1968); and the same author's historiographical articles: "Land Speculation and Its Impact on American Economic Growth and Welfare: A Historiographical Review," *Western Historical Quarterly* 8 (July 1977): 283–302; and "Quantitative Methods in Rural Landholding," *Journal of Interdisciplinary History* 13 (Spring 1983): 787–808. A study concentrating on western urban development is John Haeger, *The Investment Frontier* (Albany: SUNY Press, 1981).

14. See, for example, Gary L. Browne, *Baltimore in the New Nation, 1789–1861* (Chapel Hill: Univ. of North Carolina Press, 1980), 94–95; Frederic Cople Jaher, *The Urban Establishment* (Urbana: Univ. of Illinois Press, 1982), 200–201, 175–208; Edward K. Spann, *The New Metropolis: New York City 1840–1857* (New York: Columbia Univ. Press, 1981), 207–209.

15. Porter, 2:910–952; Gustavus Myers, *History of Great American Fortunes,* 3 vols. (Chicago: Charles H. Kerr, 1911), 1:104–105, 126–154, and 183–185; and Burton Hendrick, "The Astor Fortune," *McClure's Magazine* 24 (April 1905): 563–578.

16. Deed of Purchase from Henry Astor to John Astor, 18 May 1789, in Porter, 1:356–359; *Index of Conveyances Recorded in the Office of the Register of the City and County of New York* (New York: McSpedon & Baker, 1857), vol. A, pp. 157–159. Each of Astor's purchases can be traced in the microfilmed Libers of Deed and Conveyances in the Office of the City Register, New York County, New York City. On property value increases see Betsy Blackmar, "Rewalking the 'Walking City': Housing and Property Relations in New York City, 1780–1840," *Radical History Review* 21 (Fall 1979): 131–148; and idem, *Manhattan for Rent,* 38–40.

17. John Astor to Albert Gallatin, 9 October 1815, GP, 28. Several scattered volumes in the Astor family papers allow one an overview of John Astor's New York City landholdings at various times. See especially, "Maps of Property in the City and County of New York Belonging to John Jacob Astor, April, 1836"; "Abstract of Title, 1807–1880"; and "House and Land Book," 1833–1847, AP, NYHS.

18. "Evaluation of Real Estate, March, 1847," AP, NYHS.

19. The difference between speculation and development of urban lands is discussed in Doucet, "Urban Land Development," 301. On the changing views toward urban lands in this period, see Pred, *Spatial Dynamics,* 154–155.

20. William J. Macnever to John Astor, 1 May 1828, Liber 237, p. 248; Schulyer Livington to John Astor, 4 July 1801, Liber 61, p. 505; John Bainbridge to John Astor, 23 March 1802, Liber 61, p. 506; and Alexander Robertson to John Astor, 23 March 1802, Liber 61, p. 508; Protestant Episcopal Church to John Astor, 19 December 1807, Liber 79, p. 221; in Libers of Deed and Conveyances, Office of City Register, New York County. Also see Stokes, *Iconography,* 6:171, 65–175; "Maps of Property in the City of New York"; and "Evaluation of Real Estate," AP, NYHS. There are many descriptions of Astor's purchases. See Porter, 2:919–921; Arthur Pound, *The Golden Earth* (New York: Macmillan, 1935), 281; and David Jacques, "John Jacob Astor," in *Lives of American Merchants,* Freeman Hunt, ed., 2 vols. (New York: Derby & Jackson, 1858), 2:425. On the development of New York City neighborhoods, see important articles by Carl Abbott, "The Neighborhoods of New York, 1760–1775," *New York History* 45 (January 1974): 35–54; Blackmar, "Rewalking," 131–148; and Blackmar, *Manhattan for Rent,* 23–28.

21. "Map of Property in the City of New York"; "Evaluation of Real Estate"; "House and Land Book"; and "Rent Roll, 1826–1831," AP, NYHS. George Rogers Taylor, "The Beginnings of Mass Transportation in Urban America: Part I," *Smithsonian Journal of History* 1 (1966): 39. Also see Edward Pessen, *Riches, Class and Power Before the Civil War* (Lexington, Mass.; Heath, 1973), 169–179; and Blackmar, *Manhattan for Rent,* 45–47 and 78–82 for a description of changing neighborhoods owing to economic growth.

22. New York City, *Minutes of the Common Council of the City of New York, 1784–1831,* 21 vols. (New York: New York City, 1917–1930), 4:415, 612, 652; 5:144–146; 8:314, 534, 551, 703; 16:182; Porter, 2:918–919; Myers, *History of American Fortunes,* 1:144–148; Hendrix Hartog, *Public Property and Private Power: The Corporation of the City of New York in American Law, 1730–1870* (Chapel Hill: Univ. of North Carolina Press, 1983), 48–164; Ann L. Buttenwieser, *Manhattan Water-Bound* (New York: New York Univ. Press, 1987), 25–26, 40.

23. James Hardie, *A Census of New Buildings Erected in this City in the Year 1824* (New York: Samuel Marks, 1825), 12; Pred, *Spatial Dynamics,* 154–155; Blackmar, *Manhattan for Rent,* 95–100; "House and Land Book"; "Map of Property in the City of New York"; and "Evaluation of Real Estate," AP, NYHS. Individual sales can be traced also in the Libers of Deed and Conveyances. For example, see John Astor to Edward Laight, 13 October 1809, Liber 84, p. 296; John Astor to William Wyeman, 31 January 1804, Liber 70, p. 68; John Astor to Bernadus Swartout, 4 June 1803, Liber 65, p. 252.

24. *New York Gazette and General Advertiser,* 7 January 1800; "Evaluation of Real Estate"; "Map of Property in New York City," AP, NYHS; Charles Lockwood, *Manhattan Moves Uptown* (Boston: Houghton Mifflin, 1976), 57; and Stokes, *Iconography,* 1:384–385; Thomas Bender, "Washington Square in the Growing City," in Mindy Canton, ed., *Around the Square, 1830–1890* (New York: New York Univ. Press, 1982), 31–34; Bayrd Still, *Mirror for Gotham* (New York: New York Univ. Press, 1956), 71; Sarah Landau, "Greek and Gothic: Side by Side: Architecture Around the Square," in Canton, *Around the Square,* 17; and Theodore Fay, *Views in New York and Its Environs* (New York: Peabody, 1831), 46.

25. Alan L. Olmstead, *New York Savings Banks in the Antebellum Years, 1819–1861* (Chapel Hill: Univ. of North Carolina Press, 1975), 92–93, 98–99; Jaher, *The Urban Establishment,* 184–186; and Herman E. Krooss and Martin Blyn, *A History of Financial Intermediaries* (New York: Random House, 1971), 41–90. The

investment policies of the New York Life Insurance and Trust Company are discussed in Haeger, *The Investment Frontier,* 32–38. The figures on mortgage lending in 1833 come from J. Disturnell, *New York As It Is in 1833,* 171.

26. "Map of Property in New York," AP, NYHS. In this volume, Astor usually listed the terms of sale for each piece of property. Other examples are: Mortgage of Edmund Genet & John Astor, 1 April 1816; Lease of John Astor and Cornelius De-Groat, 1 February 1827, in Porter, 2:1141–1143, 1186–1190; and *John Astor* v. *Alexander Bruen,* 12 September 1837, New York City, Court of Chancery, 1691–1847, County Court Building, New York City; and "List of Bondholders, 1826–1828," AP, NYHS. The list of bondholders is found on the last pages of a book entitled "Rent Roll, 1826–1831."

The system was not foolproof for Astor. A mortgagor could fail to pay, and this usually indicated that a personal bond would be useless to the creditor. Astor could bid at auctions himself to regain title, but this was a desperation move because all other efforts to secure the debt, including extending payments, had failed. Mortgage law changed rapidly in this period and was the subject of endless debate and struggle between debtors and creditors. For discussions of these issues, see Robert Skilton, "Development of Mortgage Law and Practice," *Temple University Law Quarterly* 17 (August 1943): 315–383; and Lawrence M. Friedman, *A History of American Law* (New York: Simon & Schuster, 1973), 215–218, 374–375.

27. "Map of Property in New York," AP, NYHS; Lease of John Astor and Cornelius De Groat, 1 February 1827, in Porter, 2:1186–1190; *John Astor* v. *Philip Brusher et al.,* 23 January 1829, Miscellaneous Files of the Court, 632A; and *John Astor* v. *Alexander Bruen,* 12 September 1835, CL 247, New York City Court of Chancery, 1641–1847, County Court Building, New York City (An index card file by complainant allows a search by names. CL designations are to printed documents and BM are to miscellaneous files of the court. Most case files include the briefs of lawyers and the court's final action); List of Bondholders, 1826–1828, AP, NYHS.

28. Myers, *History of American Fortunes,* 1:138. This charge is repeated in a recent work by Kenneth T. Jackson, *Crabgrass Frontier* (New York: Oxford Univ. Press, 1985), 134.

29. Porter, 2:931.

30. New York City legal records are a valuable source of information not just about Astor's real estate but also on the subject of creditor–debtor relations. See New York City, Court of Chancery, 1641–1847, County Court Building, New York City. Sample cases that reflect the generalizations cited include: *Astor* v. *Batchelor,* 13 February 1812, CL 228; *Astor* v. *Abraham Carpenter et al.,* 28 June 1827, CL 265; *Astor* v. *John Fraser,* 28 May 1831, CL 223; *Astor* v. *Philip Brusher et al.,* 23 January 1829, BM 632A; *Astor* v. *Alexander Bruen,* 12 September 1835, CL 247; *Astor* v. *David Harris,* 25 August 1838, CL 247; *Astor* v. *Henry Coghill,* 31 October 1839, BM 634A; *Astor* v. *Samuel Swartout,* 31 August 1843, CL 264, New York City, Court of Chancery.

31. The most thorough discussion of the lease is Blackmar, *Manhattan for Rent,* 9–10, 186–189, and Blackmar, "Rewalking," 133–139.

32. Blackmar, "Rewalking," 134–136; Porter, 2:923–925; Advertisement of Property for Lease by John Astor, *New York Gazette and General Advertiser,* 27 May 1800; Lease of Astor to Cornelius De Groat, 1 February 1827, in Porter, 2:1186–

1190, and Lease of Astor to Abraham Carpenter, 28 June 1827, New York City, Chancery Court, CL 265; "Rent Roll, 1826–1831" and "Rent Roll, 1840–1848," AP, NYHS.

33. Lease of Astor and Abraham Carpenter, 28 June 1827, CL 265; Lease of Astor to John Batchelor, 13 February 1812, CL 228; Lease of Astor to John Fraser, 28 May 1831, CL 223, New York City, Chancery Court; Lease of Astor to Cornelius De Groat, 1 February 1827, in Porter, 2:1186–1190.

34. Ibid.; and "List of Bondholders, 1826–1827." The identity and occupation of tenants is often conveniently provided in the leases. Also see "Rent Roll, 1826–1831" and "Rent Roll, 1840–1848" that contain a record of payment schedules by tenants.

35. See, for example, Lease of Astor and Cornelius De Groat, 1 February 1827, and Lease of Astor and Christopher Delano, 5 October 1825, in Porter, 2:1186–1190 and 1180–1183; Lease of Astor and John Batchelor, 13 February 1812, CL 228, and Lease of Astor and John Fraser, 28 May 1831, CL 223, New York City, Chancery Court; Lease of John Astor to David Jacques, 19 February 1827, Liber 220, p. 446; and John Astor to Robert Sedgwick, 6 February 1833, Liber 315, p. 597. Also see Porter, 2:933–938.

36. "Rent Roll, 1826–1831" and "Rent Roll, 1840–1848," AP, NYHS.

37. Ibid. Francis Trollope, *Domestic Manners of the Americans* (1832; repr., New York: Oxford Univ. Press, 1984), 309. On New York City housing for the working class see Wilentz, *Chants Democratic,* 52–53; and Howard Rock, *Artisans of the New Republic* (New York: New York Univ. Press, 1984), 254–255.

38. James Parton, "John Jacob Astor," *Harper's Magazine* 30 (December 1864–May 1865): 323; and Spann, *The New Metropolis,* 233. The issue of slum development in New York City and the complicity of landlords and sublandlords is a central theme of Blackmar, *Manhattan for Rent,* 183–249, and Blackmar, "Rewalking," 131–148.

39. "House and Land Book" and "Evaluation of Real Estate," AP, NYHS; *New York Weekly Tribune,* 3 April 1848.

40. Dorothy Barck, ed., *Diary of William Dunlap* (1930; repr., New York: Benjamin Bloom, 1969), 710; Still, *Mirror for Gotham,* 60–61, 93–94; Astor to Stephen Price, 24 July 1813, Astor to John Beekman, 4 August 1832, AP, BL, 3; David Grimstead, *Melodrama Unveiled: American Theater and Culture, 1800–1850* (Chicago: Univ. of Chicago Press, 1968), 55; John A. Kouwenhoven, *The Columbia Historical Portrait of New York* (New York: Harper & Row, 1972), 103, 132, 276; "Evaluation of Real Estate," AP, NYHS; William Astor to John Beekman, 18 October 1849, William B. Astor Letterbook 1, AP, NYHS.

41. City Hotel, Miscellaneous Folder, New York Historical Society; Meryle Evans, "Knickerbocker Hotels and Restaurants, 1800–1850," *New York Historical Society Quarterly* 36 (1952): 377–378; Fay, *Views in New York,* pl. 10, p. 18; Daniel Boorstin, *The Americans: The National Experience* (New York: Random House, 1965), 134–137; Doris King, "Early Hotel Entrepreneurs and Promoters, 1793–1860," *Explorations in Entrepreneurial History* 8 (February 1956): 148–160; Doris King, "The First Clas Hotel and the Age of the Common Man," *Journal of Southern History* 23 (May 1957); 175, 173–188; and Jefferson Williamson, *The American Hotel* (New York: Knopf, 1930).

42. Fay, *Views in New York,* pl. 10, p. 18; Boorstin, *Americans,* 134–138, 145–147; Williamson, *American Hotel,* 27–38; Still, *Mirror,* 57, 70.

43. Fay, *Views of New York*, pl. 10, p. 18; "Rent Roll, 1826, 1831," "Real Estate Valuation"; Evans, "Knickerbocker," 382–384; William Astor to Seth Geer, 30 April 1833, and William Astor to Chester Jennings, 31 May 1833, AP, BL, 3; and Allan Nevins, ed., *The Diary of Philip Hone, 1828–1851,* 2 vols. (1927; repr., New York: Kraus Reprint Co., 1969), 1:91.

44. Nevins, *Hone Diary,* 1:121, 91–92, 125–129; Astor to Pratte & Co., 19 June 1832, AP, BL, 3; Porter, 2:776–777, 1103–1104.

45. Julia Ward Howe, *Reminiscences, 1819–1899* (Boston: Houghton Mifflin, 1899), 74–76; Washington Irving quoted in Nelson Adkins, *Fitz-Greene Halleck* (New Haven: Yale Univ. Press, 1930), 255; Edgeley W. Todd, intro. *Astoria, or Anecdotes of an Enterprise Beyond the Rocky Mountains* (Norman: Univ. of Oklahoma Press, 1964), xx–xxiii.

46. Nevins, *Hone Diary,* 1:125–126; John and William Astor to Albert Gallatin 29 November 1833, GP, 41; William Astor to Captain Harrington, 29 June 1832, William Astor to Philip Schulyer, 20 July 1832, W. Astor to Isaiah Roger, 25 August 1832, 5 October 1832, 20 November 1832, 29 June 1833, and 2 September 1833, W. Astor to John Dorr, 2 November 1833, AP, BL, 3.

47. John Astor to William Woodruff et al., 8 July 1834 and 9 July 1834; William Astor to Peter Bogert, 10 September 1834, and John Astor to Woodruff & Bogert, 30 October 1835, AP, BL, 3; Nevins, *Hone Diary,* 1:133; Porter, 2:995.

48. "Astor House, Miscellaneous Folder," New York Historical Society; Williamson, *American Hotel,* 32–37; Evans, "Knickerbocker," 338–339; Boorstin, *Americans,* 137; and Still, *Mirror,* 81; "Rent Roll, 1826–1831," AP, NYHS; "City Hotel," Miscellaneous Folder, New York Historical Society.

49. The costs for the Astor House are calculated in "House and Land Book," AP, NYHS. On the lease arrangements see, S. & F. Boyden and John Astor Agreement, 8 April 1836, Miscellaneous Folder, New York Historical Society; John Astor to Messrs S. & F. Boyden, 19 March 1836; and William B. Astor to John Dorr, 13 April 1836, AP, BL, 10.

50. "House and Land Book," AP, NYHS. The "House and Land Book" combined with the volume of "Maps of Property in the City of New York" make it possible to estimate the size of Astor's real estate business in the 1830s.

51. "House and Land Book," "Maps of Property in the City of New York," "Rent Roll, 1840–1848," AP, NYHS. Alfred Chandler has argued that accounting expertise did not evolve until the railroad corporations of the 1840s and 1850s. Yet the argument here is that Astor's accounts were quite advanced and that he used these accounts to make business decisions. It is difficult, however, to completely substantiate this assertion as Astor's accounts are fragmentary. It is not possible to determine profit and loss either yearly or over the course of his career. For a review of the literature on accounting practice, see Chandler, *The Visible Hand,* 36–42; Cochran, "Business Revolution," 1456; Stuart Bruchey, *Robert Oliver and Mercantile Bookkeeping in the Early Nineteenth Century* (New York: Arno, 1976), 29–31; 118–120; and idem, *Robert Oliver: Merchant of Baltimore, 1783–1819* (Baltimore: Johns Hopkins Univ. Press, 1956), 370–371.

52. Joseph Cogswell to George Ticknor, 20 July 1838, and Cogswell to C. S. Davies, 2 January 1838, *Life of Joseph Green Cogswell as Sketched in His Letters* (Cambridge: Riverside Press, 1874), 216; Joseph Cogswell, "The Astor Library and Its Founder," *United States Magazine of Science, Art, Manufactures, Agriculture, Commerce and Trade,* 2 (1855): 137–145; Harry M. Lydenburg, *History of the New*

York Public Library (New York: Astor, Lenox and Tilden Foundations, 1923), 2–4; Henry Pochmann, *German Culture in America* (Madison; Univ. of Wisconsin Press, 1957), 64–72, 100; Lilian Handlin, "Harvard and Göttingen, 1815," *Massachusetts Historical Society Proceedings* 95 (1983): 79–87; and Carl Diehl, *Americans and German Scholarship, 1770–1870* (New Haven: Yale Univ. Press, 1978), 50–70.

53. Cogswell, "Astor Library," 140–141; Lydenburg, *History,* 5–6; John Jacob Astor's Will, Third Codicil, 22 August 1839, in Porter, 2:1282–1286; Phyllis Dain, *The New York Public Library* (New York: New York Public Library, 1972), 4–5; and Porter, 2:1094–1096.

54. Nevins, *Hone Diary,* 1:595, 716; Joseph Cogswell to Mrs. George Ticknor, May 1842, in *Life of Cogswell,* 233; Cogswell, "Astor Library," 140–141.

55. Cogswell, "Astor Library," 141–142; Dain, *New York Public Library,* 4–6; and Lydenburg, *History,* 10–13.

56. John Astor to James Doty, 15 July 1835, AP, BL, 3; Porter, 2:859. Astor's involvement at Green Bay, Wisconsin, is discussed in Alice Smith, *James Duane Doty, Frontier Promoter* (Madison: State Historical Society of Wisconsin, 1954), 158–173; and John Haeger, "Capital Mobilization and the Urban Center: The Wisconsin Lakeports," *Mid-America* 60 (April–July 1978): 77–83.

57. "Statement of Proprietor's Share," 16 April 1836, AP, BL, 1; "Articles of Agreement, 5 March 1835," AP, BL, 1; Haeger, "Capital Mobilization," 75–83; and Smith, *Doty,* 158–177.

58. Astor, Ramsay Crooks, and Robert Stuart to James Doty, 5 March 1835, AP, BL, 1; Astor to Doty, 16 July 1835, in Porter, 2:1230–1231; Haeger, "Capital Mobilization," 78–79.

59. "Deeds of Sale of Charles Butler, Chester Jennings, Washington Irving, Samuel Stocking & Norris Woodruff, February–March, 1836," AP, BL, 1; Haeger, "Capital Mobilization," 79–80.

60. See, for example, Doty to Astor, 8 November 1835, 25 July 1836, 18 October 1836, and 24 April 1837, AP, BL, 1; Astor to Doty, 26 August 1835, 4 March 1836, and 9 May 1836, AP, BL, 3; Astor to Robert Stuart, 15 October 1835 and 23 November 1836, AP, BL, 3. On the bank issue, see John Haeger, *The Investment Frontier,* 94–96, 229.

61. Doty to Astor, 12 December 1837, 3 February 1838, 13 August 1839, and 13 August 1839, AP, BL, 1; Deed for Lot Sale to Jason Wilkins, 5 February 1838, AP, BL, 1; Charles Rogers to John Astor, 29 July 1839, AP, BL, 6; Porter, 2:865–867; and Alice Smith, *From Exploration to Statehood,* vol. 1, *History of Wisconsin* (Madison: State Historical Society of Wisconsin, 1973), 287–289.

62. Doty to Astor, 16 May 1840, Stuart to Astor, 9 June 1840, AP, BL, 1; Porter, 2:866; Contract of Doty and Astor, 28 December 1844, AP, BL, 1.

63. Nathan Goodell to Astor, 26 November 1842 and 14 June 1843, AP, BL, 1; William Astor to Goodell, 5 February 1846, John Astor to Robert Stuart, 9 September 1845, and Joseph Cogswell to Robert Stuart, 20 May 1847, in Porter, 2:1246–1257.

64. William Astor to Ramsay Crooks, 3 January 1850 and William Astor to Norris Woodruff, 2 January 1850, William Astor Letterbook, 1, New York Historical Society; Deeds to Green Bay Lands, 1850–1868, AP, BL, 1.

65. Astor to Thomas Olcott, 23 March 1832 and 22 May 1832; Astor to Abraham Van Vechten, 25 May 1832; Astor to Benjamin Knower, 15 June 1832, AP, BL, 3; Astor to Herman Cady and Isaac Broomley, BM 633A, New York Chancery

Court; *Astor* v. *Philip Schuyler,* 21 December 1836, 665A, New York Chancery Court; Astor to Albert Gallatin, 30 November 1830, and Bond of Thomas Worthington, 20 September 1826, GP, 40.

66. Astor to Wilson Hunt, 2 January 1832, AP, BL, 3; Nevins, *Hone Diary,* 1:130; and Porter, 2:853–855.

67. Astor to Gerrit Smith, 28 July 1837, Gerrit Smith Papers, George Arents Research Center, Syracuse University, New York, 1; Astor to Smith, 5 August 1837, and 31 May 1843, in Porter, 2:1235, 1242–1243, 898–900.

68. Astor to Gerrit Smith, 21 December 1829, 1 and 29 March 1830, 15 June 1830, 5 March 1831, G. Smith Papers, 1; William Astor to George Erving, 29 August 1832, and John Astor to Francis Granger, 27 January 1832, AP, BL, 3; and Frank W. Stevens, *The Beginnings of the New York Central Railroad* (New York: Putnam's, 1926), 2–3, 15–52; Porter, 2:996–1003.

69. John Astor and William Astor to Erastus Corning, 23 August 1836, Erastus Corning Papers, Albany Institute of History and Art, New York; Porter, 2:1003.

70. Astor to De Witt Clinton, 14 August 1826, Clinton Papers; William B. Astor to John Nagle, 23 May 1836, AP, BL, 10; Ronald Shaw, *Erie Water West* (Lexington: University Press of Kentucky, 1966), 98, 304; Spann, *The New Metropolis,* 209.

71. *Jean de Nottbeck and Cecilia De Nottbeck* v. *William B. Astor et al.* (New York: Sibell & Mott, 1851), 48; Astor to Silas Wright, 17 July 1830, Box 1, AP, NYPL; Astor to Ellice, Kinnear & Co., 7 April 1832, AP, BL, 3; Astor to Gallatin, 4 December 1829, GP, 39; "List of Stock and Bond Investments, Report on Distribution and Appropriation of the Estate," 1 June 1849, in AP, NYPL.

72. Astor to Olcott, 6 January 1832; Astor to Ellice, Kinnear & Co., 7 April 1832, AP, BL, 3; Porter, 2:971–979; List of Astor's Bank Stock, 1836, in *Nottbeck* v. *Astor,* 53.

73. Raymond Walters, Jr., *Albert Gallatin* (New York: Macmillan, 1957), 347; Porter, 2:971; Haeger, *Investment Frontier,* 18–58; Porter, 2:955; List of Astor's funds in *Nottbeck* v. *Astor,* 59, 65.

74. Astor to Gallatin Brothers, 25 January 1834, AP, BL, 3; Astor to Delafield & Bryce, 21 May 1834, AP, BL, 3; William Astor to Ambrose Lanfear, 12 June 1848, William Astor Letterbook, 1, New York Historical Society; "List of Stocks Held, 1836," in *Nottbeck* v. *Astor,* 65, "Report on Estate Disbursement," 1849.

Epilogue

1. Henry Brevoort, Jr., to Washington Irving, 28 December 1842 and 18 October 1843, in George S. Hellman, ed., *Letters of Henry Brevoort to Washington Irving, Together with Other Unpublished Papers,* 2 vols. (New York: Putnam's, 1918), 2:124–127, 130–140; "Testimony of William Bruce, Accountant," in New York, Supreme Court, *Jean De Nottbeck, and Cecilia, His Wife v. William B. Astor, Washington Irving, Daniel Lord, James Gallatin, and John Jacob Astor, Jr., Executor of the Last Will and Testament of John Jacob Astor Deceased . . .* (New York: Sibell & Mott, 1851), 68–69; Joseph Cogswell to Gerrit Smith, 17 June 1843, Gerrit Smith Papers, George Arents Research Center, Syracuse University, New York, Microfilm Reel 1; Joseph Cogswell to Mrs. Ticknor, May 1842, in Anne E. Ticknor, ed., *Life of Joseph Green Cogswell as Sketched in His Letters* (Cambridge: Riverside Press, 1874), 233; and Porter, 2:1115–1120, 1282–1286.

2. Allan Nevins, ed., 2 vols. *The Diary of Philip Hone, 1828–1851* (1927; repr., New York: Kraus Reprint Co., 1969), 716; Sigmund Diamond, *The Reputation of American Businessmen* (Cambridge: Harvard Univ. Press, 1955), 24; and Porter, 2:1115–1120.

3. Gerrit Smith to William B. Astor, 4 January 1848, in Porter, 2:1258; William B. Astor to Edward Ellice, 3 April 1848, Edward Ellice Papers, Public Archives of Canada, Ottawa; and *New York Herald*, 30 and 31 March and 2 April 1848.

4. *New York Weekly Tribune*, 3 April 1848; Diamond, *Reputation*, 25–50; *New York Herald*, 2, 5, and 9 April 1848; and Edward K. Spann, *The New Metropolis: New York City, 1840–1875* (New York: Columbia Univ. Press, 1981), 233–234.

5. John Jacob Astor's Will, 1836, plus eight codicils to 1843, AP, NYPL. Porter prints a copy of the will, 2:1260–1296. On the actual size of the Astor fortune, see "Inventory of Goods and Chattels, 9 November and 21 April 1848," and "Report on the Distribution and Appropriation of the Estate as of June 1, 1849," AP, NYPL; and "Evaluation of Real Estate, 1847," AP, NYHS.

6. John Astor to Peter Smith, 13 April 1819, in Porter, 2:1161–1162; Kathleen Conzen, "Peasant Pioneers: Generational Succession Among German Farmers in Frontier Minnesota," in *Essays in the Social History of Rural America,* Steven Hahn and Jonathan Prude, eds., (Chapel Hill: Univ. of North Carolina Press, 1985), 263–267; and Carole Shammas, Marylynn Salmon, and Michel Dahlin, *Inheritance in America* (New Brunswick, N.J.: Rutgers Univ. Press, 1987), 103–122; and Lawrence M. Friedman, "The Dynastic Trust," *Yale Law Journal* 73 (March 1964): 547–555.

7. John Astor's Will in Porter, 2:1260–1296, 1092–1096; "Report on the Distribution and Appropriation of the Estate, 1849," AP, NYPL; "Minutes of the Executors, 20 April 1848," AP, NYHS; Diamond, *Reputation*, 33–43; *New York Herald,* 5 April 1848.

8. John Astor's Will in Porter, 2:1260–1296; Joseph Cogswell, "The Astor Library and Its Founder," *United States Magazine of Science, Art, Manufacturers, Agriculture, Commerce and Trade,* 2 (1855): 139; Charles Astor Bristed, *A Letter to Horace Mann* (New York: H. Kernot, 1850), 16–18; Diamond, *Reputation*, 32–49; and *New York Herald,* 9 April 1848; and Porter, 2:1087–1097.

9. Historians have written a good deal on the significance of economic thought and practice in the new Republic. Good starting points are Thomas C. Cochran, *Frontiers of Change: Early Industrialism in America* (New York: Oxford Univ. Press, 1981); Joyce Appleby, *Capitalism and the New Social Order: The Republicans of the 1790s* (New York: New York Univ. Press, 1984); and Joyce Appleby, "Commercial Farming and the 'Agrarian Myth' in the Early Republic," *Journal of American History* 68 (March 1982): 833–849; and John R. Nelson, *Liberty and Property* (Baltimore: Johns Hopkins Univ. Press, 1987).

Selected Bibliography

Note: The endnotes provide a detailed list of primary and secondary sources, thus this bibliography includes only the items on which I relied most heavily.

1. Manuscripts

American Fur Company. Letterbooks. Burton Historical Collection, Detroit, Michigan.
———. Papers and Microfilm. Chicago Historical Society, Chicago.
———. Papers and Microfilm. Clarke Historical Library, Central Michigan Univ., Mount Pleasant.
———. Papers and Microfilm. Minnesota Historical Society, Saint Paul.
———. Papers and Microfilm. New York Public Library, New York City.
———. Papers and Microfilm. Public Archives of Canada, Ottawa.
———. Papers and Microfilm. State Historical Society of Wisconsin, Madison.
Astor Family Papers. New York Historical Society, New York City.
Astor, John Jacob. Letters. Historical Society of Pennsylvania, Philadelphia.
———. Letters. Library Company of Philadelphia, Pennsylvania.
———. Papers. Beinecke Rare Book and Manuscript Library, Yale Univ., New Haven.
———. Papers. New York Public Library, New York City.
———. Papers, RG 36: Records of the United States Customs Service, New York Customs House, National Archives, Washington, D.C.
———. Papers and Microfilm. Baker Library, Harvard Univ., Boston.
Colonial Office. Records and Papers. Public Records Office, London.
Constable-Pierrepont Collection. William Bell Papers. New York Public Library, New York City.

Chouteau Collections. Missouri Historical Society, Saint Louis.

Clinton, De Witt. Papers. Butler Library, Columbia Univ., New York City.

Court of Chancery, 1691–1847. Records. New York County Court Building, New York City.

East India Company. Factory Records. India Office Library and Records, London.

Edgar, William. Papers. New York Public Library, New York City.

———. Papers. Public Archives of Canada, Ottawa.

Gallatin, Albert. Papers and Microfilm. New York Historical Society, New York City.

Girard, Stephen. Papers. American Philosophical Society, Philadelphia, Pennsylvania.

Henry, Alexander. Papers. Public Archives of Canada, Ottawa.

Hudson's Bay Company. Papers and Microfilm. Public Archives of Canada, Ottawa.

Hunt, Wilson Price. Papers. Missouri Historical Society, Saint Louis.

Keith, James. Papers. Univ. of Aberdeen Library, Scotland.

Jefferson, Thomas. Papers and Microfilm. Library of Congress, Washington, D.C.

McDougall, Duncan. Journal. Rosenbach Library, Philadelphia, Pennsylvania.

North West Company. Papers. Metropolitan Toronto Library, Canada.

———. Papers. Public Archives of Canada, Ottawa.

Ogden, Nicholas. Papers. Historical Society of Pennsylvania, Philadelphia.

Parish, David. Letterbooks. New York Historical Society, New York City.

Smith, Peter. Papers. George Arents Research Center, Syracuse Univ., New York.

Sowle, Cornelius. Papers. Library of Congress, Washington, D.C.

2. Government Documents

American State Papers: Indian Affairs. Washington: Gales & Seaton, 1834.

Great Britain. Parliament, House of Commons. *Report by the Lords Committee Appointed Select Committee to Inquire into the Means of Extending and Securing the Foreign Trade of the Country, and to Report to the House . . .* vol. 7, London, 1821.

———. Parliament, House of Lords. *Papers Relating to the Trade with China . . .* vol. 262, London, 1829.

———. Parliament, House of Lords. *Report from the Select Committee of the House of Lords Appointed to Enquire into the Present State of the Affairs of the East India Company . . .* vol. 274, London, 1830.

Morse, Jedidiah. *A Report to the Secretary of War of the United States on Indian Affairs, Comprising a Narrative of a Tour Performed in the Summer of 1820.* New Haven: S. Converse, 1822.

U.S. Congress. House. *Message from the President Communicating the Letter of Mr. Prevost and Other Documents Relating to an Establishment Made at the Mouth of the Columbia River.* 17th Congress, 2nd sess., 1823. H. Doc. 45.

———. Senate. *Message from the President of the United States . . . Relative to the British Establishment on the Columbia, and the State of the Fur Trade.* 21st Congress, 2nd sess., 1831, S. Doc. 39.

———. Senate. *Message of the President Relative to the Fur Trade, and Inland Trade to Mexico.* 22nd Congress, 1st sess., 1832. S. Doc. 90.

———. *Report of the Committee on Indian Affairs.* 20th Congress, 2nd sess., 1829. S. Doc. 67.

3. Newspapers

New York Commercial Advertiser.
New York Gazette and General Advertiser.
New York Packet.

4. Printed Primary Sources

Ames, John S. *Abstract of All Conveyances, Leases, Releases, Recorded in the Office of the Register of the City and County of New York, Made by the Mayor, Alderman and Commonality of the City of New York, to the First Day of January 1872.* New York: Kennard & Hay Stationery and Printing Company, 1872.

Baird, Robert. *Transplanted Flowers and Memoirs of Mrs. Rumpff (Daughter of John Jacob Astor) and the Duchess De Broglie (Daughter of Madame De Staël) with an Appendix by Robert Baird.* New York: John S. Taylor, 1830.

Bashkina, Nina, and Trask, David, eds. *The United States and Russia. The Beginning of Relations 1765–1815.* Washington, D.C.: U.S. Government Printing Office, 1980.

Bridgewater, Dorothy Wildes, ed. "John Jacob Astor Relative to His Settlement on the Columbia River." *Yale University Library Gazette* 24 (October 1949): 47–69.

Bristed, Charles Astor. *A Letter to Horace Mann.* New York: H. Kernot, 1850.

Cleveland, Richard J. *Voyages and Commercial Enterprises.* New York. Leavitt & Allen, 1858.

Cogswell, J. G. "The Astor Library and Its Founder." *United States Magazine of Science, Art, Manufacturers, Agriculture, Commerce and Trade* 2 (1855): 137–145.

Cox, Ross. *Adventures on the Columbia River Including the Narrative of a Residence of Six Years on the Western Side of the Rocky Mountains . . .* New York: J. & L. Harper, 1832.

Disturnell, J. *New York As It Is in 1833.* New York: J. Disturnell, 1833.

Duncan, William. *The New York Directory and Register in the Year 1791.* New York: T. and J. Sword, 1792.

De Voe, Thomas F. *The Market Book Containing a Historical Account of the Public Markets in the Cities of New York, Boston, Philadelphia and Brooklyn.* 2 vols. New York. Privately printed, 1862.

Fay, Theodore. *Views in New York and Its Environs.* New York: Peabody & Co., 1831.

Franchére, Gabriel. *Adventures at Astoria, 1810–1814.* Trans. Hoyt Franchére. 1854. Repr., Norman: Univ. of Oklahoma Press, 1967.

Gallatin, James. *A Great Peace Maker: The Diary of James Gallatin, Secretary to Albert Gallatin.* New York: Scribner's, 1914.

Greenhow, Robert. *The History of Oregon and California and the Other Territories of the North West Coast of North America . . .* Boston: Charles C. Little & James Brown, 1844.

Hardin, James. *A Census of New Buildings Erected in This City in the Year 1828.* New York: Samuel Marks, 1825.

Hellman, George S., ed. *Letters of Henry Brevoort to Washington Irving, Together with Other Unpublished Papers.* 2 vols. New York: Putnam's, 1918.

Hopkins, Vivian C. "John Jacob Astor and De Witt Clinton: Correspondence from 25 January 1808 to 23 December 1827." *New York Public Library Bulletin* 68 (November 1964): 654–773.

Howe, Julia Ward. *Reminiscences, 1819–1899.* Boston: Houghton Mifflin, 1899.

Hunt, Freeman, ed. *Lives of American Merchants.* 2 vols. New York: Derby & Jackson, 1858.

Jackson, Donald, ed. *Letters of the Lewis and Clark Expedition with Related Documents, 1783–1854.* 2 vols. Urbana: Univ. of Illinois Press, 1978.

Irving, Washington. *Astoria, or Anecdotes of an Enterprise Beyond the Rocky Mountains.* 1836. Repr. ed. Edgeley W. Todd. Norman: Univ. of Oklahoma Press, 1964.

Lamb, W. Kaye, ed. *The Journals and Letters of Sir Alexander Mackenzie.* Cambridge: Cambridge Univ. Press, 1970.

Manning, Wiliam R., ed. *Diplomatic Correspondence of the United States: Canadian Relations, 1784–1860,* vol. 1, 1784–1820. Washington D.C.: Carnegie Endowment for International Peace, 1940. Reprint. Millwood, N.Y.: Kraus Reprint Co., 1975.

McKenney, Thomas L. *Memoirs, Official and Personal; With Sketches of Travels Among the Northern and Southern Indians: Embracing a War Excursion and Description of Scenes Along the Western Borders.* 2 vols. New York: Paine & Burgess, 1846.

Morgan, Dale, ed. *The West of William H. Ashley.* Denver, Colo.: The Old West Publishing Co., 1964.

Morris, Grace Parker, ed. "Some Letters from 1792–1800 on the China Trade." *Oregon Historical Quarterly* 42 (1941): 48–87.

Morse, Rev. Jedidiah. *A Report to the Secretary of War of the United States on Indian Affairs, Comprising a Narrative of a Tour Performed in the Summer of 1820 . . .* New Haven: S. Converse, 1822.

Nevins, Allan, ed. *The Diary of Philip Hone, 1820–1851,* 2 vols. New York: Dodd Mead, 1927. Reprint. New York: Kraus Reprint Co., 1969.

Nolte, Vincent. *Fifty Years in Both Hemispheres or, Reminiscences of the Life of a Former Merchant.* New York: Redfield, 1854.

"Oertel, Philip." *Johann Jacob Astor.* Wiesbaden: Julius Riedner, 1877.

Okun, S. B. *The Russian-American Company.* Translated by Carl Ginsburg. Cambridge: Harvard Univ. Press, 1951.

Parton, James. *Life of John Jacob Astor.* New York: American News Co., 1865.

Pitkin, Timothy. *A Statistical View of the Commerce of the United States of America.* New York: James Eastburn & Co., 1817.

Rollins, Philip Ashton, ed. *The Discovery of the Oregon Trail.* New York: Edward Eberstadt & Sons, 1935.

Ross, Alexander. *Adventures of the First Settlers on the Oregon and Columbia River, 1810–1813.* 1849. Reprint. Lincoln: Univ. of Nebraska Press, 1986.

Seybert, Adam. *Statistical Annals: Embracing Views of the Population, Commerce, Navigation, Fisheries, Public Lands, Post-Office Establishments, Expenditures, Public Debt and Sinking Fund of the United States of America.* Philadelphia: Thomas Dotson, 1818.

Spaulding, Kenneth A. *On the Oregon Trail: Robert Stuart's Journey of Discovery.* Norman: Univ. of Oklahoma Press, 1953.

Ticknor, Anne, ed. *Life of Joseph Green Cogswell.* Cambridge, Mass.: Riverside Press, 1874.

Tikhmenev, R. A. *A History of the Russian-American Company 1861–1863.* Reprint. Trans. Richard A. Pierce and Alton S. Donnelly. Seattle: Univ. of Washington Press, 1978.

Wallace, William Stewart, ed. *Documents Relating to the North West Company.* Toronto: Champlain Society, 1934. Reprint. New York: Greenwood, 1968.

Wetmore, William C., comp. *Index of Conveyances Recorded in the Office of the Registrar of the City and County of New York.* New York: McSpedan & Baker, 1857.

5. Secondary Sources: Books

Adams, Donald R., Jr. *Finance and Enterprise in Early America,* Philadelphia: Univ. of Pennsylvania Press, 1978.

Adkins, Nelson. *Fitz-Greene Halleck.* New Haven: Yale Univ. Press, 1930.

Albion, Ralph G. *The Rise of New York Port.* 1939. Reprint. Hamden, Conn.: Shoe String Press, Archon Books, 1961.

Appleby, Joyce. *Capitalism and a New Social Order: The Republican Vision of the 1790s.* New York: New York Univ. Press, 1984.

Bemis, Samuel Flagg. *John Quincy Adams and the Foundations of American Foreign Policy.* New York: Norton, 1949.

Blackmar, Elizabeth. *Manhattan for Rent, 1785–1850.* Ithaca: Cornell Univ. Press, 1989.

Bolus, Malvina, ed. *People and Pelts.* Winnipeg, Manitoba: Peguis, 1972.

Brown, Roger. *The Republic in Peril: 1812.* New York: Columbia Univ. Press, 1964.

Browne, Gary L. *Baltimore in the New Nation, 1789–1861.* Chapel Hill: Univ. of North Carolina Press, 1980.

Bruchey, Stuart. *Robert Oliver: Merchant of Baltimore, 1783–1819.* Baltimore: Johns Hopkins Univ. Press, 1956.

Buckley, Thomas C., ed. *Rendezvous: Selected Papers of the Fourth North American Fur Trade Conference.* Saint Paul: North American Fur Trade Conference, 1982.

Burton, Pierre. *Flames Across the Boarder: The Canadian-American Tragedy, 1813–1814.* Boston: Little, Brown, 1981.

Calloway, Colin G. *Crown and Calumet: British-Indian Relations, 1783–1815.* Norman: Univ. of Oklahoma Press, 1987.

Campbell, Marjorie. *The North West Company.* Toronto: Macmillan, 1957.

Chandler, Alfred D. *The Visible Hand.* Cambridge: Harvard Univ. Press, 1977.

Chittenden, Hiram M. *The American Fur Trade of the Far West.* 2 vols., 1901. Reprint. Lincoln: Univ. of Nebraska Press, 1986.

Clokey, Richard M. *William H. Ashley.* Norman: Univ. of Oklahoma Press, 1980.

Cochran, Thomas C. *Frontiers of Change: Early Industrialism in America.* New York: Oxford Univ. Press, 1981.

Creighton, D. G. *The Commercial Empire of the St. Lawrence.* Toronto: Ryerson Press, 1937.

Curtin, Philip D. *Cross-Cultural Trade in World History.* London: Cambridge Univ. Press, 1984.

Dain, Phyllis. *The New York Public Library.* New York: New York Public Library, 1972.

Diamond, Sigmund. *The Reputation of American Businessmen.* Cambridge: Harvard Univ. Press, 1955.

Doerflinger, Thomas. *A Vigorous Spirit of Enterprise.* Chapel Hill: Univ. of Pennsylvania Press, 1986.

Dulles, Foster Rhea. *The Old China Trade.* 1930. Reprint. New York: AMS, 1970.

Everest, Allan S. *The War of 1812 in the Champlain Valley.* Syracuse: Syracuse Univ. Press, 1981.

Freeman, Donald B., and Ray, Arthur J. *"Give Us Good Measure": An Economic Analysis of Relations Between the Indians and the Hudson's Bay Company Before 1763.* Toronto: Univ. of Toronto Press, 1978.

Fridley, Russell, ed. *Aspects of the Fur Trade: Selected Papers of the 1965 North American Fur Trade Conference.* Saint Paul: Minnesota Historical Society, 1967.

Gibson, James R. *Imperial Russia in Frontier America.* New York: Oxford Univ. Press, 1976.

Goldstein, Jonathan. *Philadelphia and the China Trade.* Philadelphia: 1978.

Gough, Barry M. *Distant Dominion.* Vancouver: Univ. of British Columbia Press, 1980.

————. *The Royal Navy and the Northwest Coast of North America, 1810–1914: A Study of British Maritime Ascendancy.* Vancouver: Univ. of British Columbia Press, 1971.

Gras, Norman S., and Larson, Henrietta M. *Casebook in American Business History.* New York: Appleton-Century-Crofts, 1939.

Greenberg, Michael. *British Trade and the Opening of China 1800–42.* Cambridge: Cambridge Univ. Press, 1951.

Haeger, John D. *The Investment Frontier: New York Businessmen and the Economic Development of the Old Northwest.* Albany: SUNY Press, 1981.

Hammond, Bray. *Banks and Politics in America from the Revolution to the Civil War.* Princeton, N.J.: Princeton Univ. Press, 1957.

Hartog, Hendrix. *Public Property and Private Power: The Corporation of the City of New York in American Law, 1730–1870.* Chapel Hill: Univ. of North Carolina Press, 1983.

Horsman, Reginald. *The Diplomacy of the New Republic, 1776–1815.* Arlington Heights, Ill.: Harlan Davidson, 1985.

Innis, Harold A. *The Fur Trade in Canada.* Toronto: Univ. of Toronto Press, 1956.

Jackson, Donald. *Thomas Jefferson and the Stony Mountains.* Urbana: Univ. of Illinois Press, 1981.

Jaher, Frederic Cople. *The Urban Establishment.* Urbana: Univ. of Illinois Press, 1982.

Judd, Carol M., and Ray, Arthur, eds. *Old Trails and New Directions: Papers of the Third North American Fur Trade Conference.* Toronto: Univ. of Toronto Press, 1980.

Kushner, Howard. *Conflict on the Northwest Coast; America-Russia Rivalry in the Pacific North West, 1790–1867.* Westport, Conn.: Greenwood, 1975.

Lavender, David. *The Fist in the Wilderness.* Garden City, N.Y.: Doubleday, 1964.

Long, David F. *Sailor-Diplomat: A Biography of Commodore James Biddle, 1783–1848.* Boston: Northeastern Univ. Press, 1983.

Malone, Michael, ed. *Historians and the American West.* Lincoln: Univ. of Nebraska Press, 1983.

Meinig, Donald W. *The Great Columbia Plain.* Seattle: Univ. of Washington Press, 1968.

Merk, Frederick. *Fur Trade and Empire.* Cambridge: Harvard University Press, 1968.

Miller, Douglas T. *Jacksonian Aristocracy.* New York: Oxford Univ. Press, 1967.

Moehring, Eugene. *Public Works and the Patterns of Urban Real Estate Growth in Manhattan, 1835–1914*. New York: Arno, 1981.

Morgan, Dale. *Jedidiah Smith*. Lincoln: Univ. of Nebraska Press, 1953.

Morse, Eric. *Fur Trade Canoe Routes of Canada: Then and Now*. Ottawa: Queen's Printer, 1969.

Morse, Hosea B. *The Chronicles of the East India Company Trading to China, 1635–1534*. 5 vols. New York: Paragon Books Gallery, 1966.

Myers, Gustavus. *History of Great American Fortunes*. 3 vols. Chicago: Charles H. Kerr, 1911.

Nelson, John R. *Liberty and Property*. Baltimore: Johns Hopkins Univ. Press, 1987.

North, Douglass, C. *The Economic Growth of the United States, 1790–1860*. Englewood Cliffs, N.J.: Prentice-Hall, 1961.

Oglesby, Richard E. *Manual Lisa and the Opening of the Missouri Fur Trade*. Norman: Univ. of Oklahoma Press, 1963.

Perkins, Bradford. *Prologue to War: England and the United States, 1805–1812*. Berkeley: Univ. of California Press, 1961.

Pessen, Edward. *Riches, Class, and Power Before the Civil War*. Lexington, Mass.: D.C. Heath, 1973.

Phillips, Paul C. *The Fur Trade*. 2 vols. Norman: Univ. of Oklahoma Press, 1961.

Poland, Henry. *Fur-Bearing Animals in Nature and Commerce*. London: Gurney & Jackson, 1892.

Pomerantz, Sydney I. *New York: An American City, 1783–1803*. New York: Columbia Univ. Press, 1938. Reprint. Port Washington, N.Y., 1965.

Porter, Glen, and Livesay, Harold. *Merchants and Manufacturers*. Baltimore: Johns Hopkins Univ. Press, 1971.

Porter, Kenneth Wiggins. *John Jacob Astor: Businessman*. 2 vols. Cambridge: Harvard Univ. Press, 1931.

Pred, Allan R. *Urban Growth and the Circulation of Information: The United States System of Cities*. Cambridge: Harvard Univ. Press, 1973.

Prucha, Francis Paul. *American Indian Policy in the Formative Years*. Cambridge: Harvard Univ. Press, 1962.

———. *The Great Father: The United States Government and the American Indians*. 2 vols. Lincoln: Univ. of Nebraska Press, 1984.

Rich, E. E. *The History of the Hudson's Bay Company, 1670–1870*. 2 vols. London: Hudson's Bay Record Society, 1958–1959.

Ritcheson, Charles. *Aftermath of Revolution: British Policy Toward the United States, 1783–1795*. Dallas, Tex.: Southern Methodist Univ. Press, 1967.

Ronda, James, *Astoria and Empire*. Lincoln: Univ. of Nebraska Press, 1990.

Runyan, William McKinley. *Life Histories and Psychobiography*. New York: Oxford Univ. Press, 1982.

———, ed. *Psychology of Historical Interpretation*. New York: Oxford Univ. Press, 1988.

Spann, Edward K. *The New Metropolis: New York City, 1840–1857*. New York: Columbia Univ. Press, 1981.

Stagg, J. C. A. *Mr. Madison's War: Politics, Diplomacy, and Warfare in the Early Republic, 1783–1830*. Princeton, N.J.: Princeton Univ. Press, 1983.

Stevens, Wayne Edson. *The Northwest Fur Trade, 1763–1800*. Urbana: Univ. of Illinois, 1928.

Stokes, I. N. Phelps. *The Iconography of Manhattan Island, 1498–1909*. 6 vols. New York: Robert H. Dodd, 1915.

Sunder, John E. *The Fur Trade on the Upper Missouri, 1840–1865*. Norman: Univ. of Oklahoma Press, 1965.

Taylor, George Rogers. *The Transportation Revolution 1815–1860*. New York: Harper Torchbooks, 1951.

Trennert, Robert A. *Indian Trade on the Middle Border*. Lincoln: Univ. of Nebraska Press, 1981.

Walters, Raymond, Jr. *Albert Gallatin*. New York: Macmillan, 1957.

Watts, Steven. *The Republic Reborn: War and the Making of Liberal America, 1790–1820*. Baltimore: Johns Hopkins Univ. Press, 1987.

Wiebe, Robert H. *The Opening of American Society*. New York: Knopf, 1984.

Wilentz, Sean. *Chants Democratic: New York City and the Rise of the American Working Class, 1788–1850*. New York: Oxford Univ. Press, 1984.

Wishart, David J. *The Fur Trade of the American West, 1807–1840*. Lincoln: Univ. of Nebraska Press, 1979.

Woolworth, Alan R., Birk, Douglass, and White, Bruce. *Where Two Worlds Meet: The Great Lakes Fur Trade*. Saint Paul: Minnesota Historical Society, 1982.

Viola, Herman J. *Thomas L. McKenney: Architect of America's Early Indian Policy 1816–1830*. Chicago: Swallow Press, 1974.

6. Secondary Sources: Articles and Dissertations

Adams, Donald R. "American Neutrality and Prosperity, 1793–1808: A Reconsideration." *Journal of Economic History* 40 (December 1980): 713–737.

Appleby, Joyce. "Commercial Farming and the 'Agarian Myth' in the Early Republic." *Journal of American History* 68 (March 1982): 833–849.

———. "Modernization Theory and the Formation of Modern Social Theories in England and America." *Comparative Studies in Society and History* 20 (April 1978): 259–285.

———. "Republicanism in Old and New Contexts." *William and Mary Quarterly* 43 (January 1986): 20–34.

Ashworth, John. "The Jeffersonians: Classical Republicans or Liberal Capitalists." *Journal of American Studies* 18 (December 1984): 425–435.

Banning, Lance. "Jeffersonian Ideology Revisited: Liberal and Classical Ideas in the New American Republic." *William and Mary Quarterly* 43 (January 1986): 3–19.

Blackmar, Betsy. "Rewalking the 'Walking City': Housing and Property Relations in New York City, 1780–1840." *Radical History Review* 21 (Fall 1979): 131–148.

Brown, Kenneth. "Stephen Girard, Promoter of the Second Bank of the United States." *Journal of Economic History* 2 (November 1942): 125–148.

Brown, Richard D. "Modernization and the Modern Personality in Early America, 1600–1865: A Sketch of a Synthesis." *Journal of Interdisciplinary History* 2 (1972): 201–228.

Bruchey, Stuart. "Success and Failure Factors: American Merchants in Foreign Trade in the Eighteenth and Early Nineteenth Centuries." *Business History Review* 32 (1958): 272–292.

Carlos, Ann. "The Birth and Death of Predatory Competition in the North American Fur Trade, 1810–1821." *Explorations in Economic History* 19 (April 1982): 156–183.

——— . "The Causes and Origins of the North American Fur Trade Rivalry, 1804–1810." *Journal of Economic History* 41 (December 1981): 777–794.

——— , and Hoffman, Elizabeth. "The North American Fur Trade: Bargaining to a Joint Profit Maximum Under Incomplete Information, 1804–1821." *Journal of Economic History* 46 (December 1986): 967–986.

Clayton, James. "The American Fur Company, the Final Years." Ph.D. diss., Cornell Univ., 1961.

——— . "The Growth and Economic Significance of the American Fur Trade, 1790–1890." In *Aspects of the Fur Trade Selected Papers of the 1963 North American Fur Trade Conference,* ed. Russel Fridley, (Saint Paul: Minnesota, 1967): 62–72.

Cochran, Thomas C. "The Business Revolution." *American Historical Review* 5 (December 1974): 1449–1466.

Cohen, Ira. "The Auction System in the Port of New York, 1817–1837." *Business History Review* 45 (Winter 1971): 488–510.

Doucet, Michael J. "The North American Shelter Business, 1860–1920: A Study of a Canadian Real Estate and Property Management Agency." *Business Historical Review* 58 (Summer 1984): 234–262.

Downs, Jacques. "American Merchants and the China Opium Trade, 1800–1840." *Business Historical Review* 42 (Winter 1968): 418–442.

Frankel, Jeffrey A. "The 1807–1809 Embargo Against Great Britain." *Journal of Economic History* 42 (June 1982): 291–301.

Gilman, Rhoda. "The Fur Trade in the Upper Mississippi Valley, 1630–1850." *Wisconsin Magazine of History* 50 (Autumn 1970): 3–18.

——— . "Last Days of the Upper Mississippi Fur Trade." *Minnesota History* 42 (Winter 1970): 125–140.

Goldin, Claudia, and Lewis, Frank. "The Role of Exports in American Economic Growth During the Napoleonic Wars, 1793 to 1807." *Explorations in Economic History* 17 (Fall 1980): 6–25.

Gough, Barry. "The North West Company's Adventure to China." *Oregon Historical Quarterly* 76 (December 1975): 309–331.

Greenberg, Dolores. "Reassessing the Power Patterns of the Industrial Revolution: An Anglo-American Comparison." *American Historical Review* 87 (December 1982): 1237–1261.

Haeger, John D. "Business Strategy and Practice in the Early Republic: John Jacob Astor and the Fur Trade." *Western Historical Quarterly* 19 (May 1988): 183–202.

——— . "A Time of Change, 1815–1840." *Wisconsin Magazine of History* 54 (Summer 1971): 285–298.

Hickey, Donald. "American Trade Restrictions During the War of 1812." *Journal of American History* 68 (December 1981): 517–538.

Horsman, Reginald. "On to Canada: Manifest Destiny and the United States Strategy in the War of 1812." *Michigan Historical Review* 13 (Fall 1987): 1–24.

Jensen, Richard "On Modernizing Frederick Jackson Turner." *Western Historical Quarterly* 11 (July 1980): 307–322.

Kagin, Donald. "Monetary Aspects of the Treasury Notes of the War of 1812." *Journal of Economic History* 44 (March 1984): 69–88.

Keyes, Robert William. "The Formation of the Second Bank of the United States, 1811–1817." Ph.D. diss., Univ. of Delaware, 1975.

King, Doris E. "Early Hotel Entrepreneurs and Promoters, 1793–1860." *Explorations in Entrepreneural History* 8 (February 1956): 148–160.

Kuebel, Mary Veronica. "Merchants and Mandarins: The Genesis of American Relations with China." Ph.D. diss., Univ. of Virginia, 1974.

Latourette, Kenneth Scott. "The History of Early Relations Between the United States and China, 1784–1844." *Transactions of the Connecticut Academy of Arts and Sciences* 22 (August 1917): 1–209.

Peterson, Jacqueline, and Anfinson, John. "The Indian and the Fur Trade." *Scholars and the Indian Experience.* William R. Swagerty, ed., Bloomington: Indiana Univ. Press, 1984: 223–257.

Ronda, James P. "Astoria and the Birth of Empire." *Montana Magazine of Western History* 36 (Summer 1986): 22–35.

Stevens, Wayne Edson. "Fur Trade Companies in the Northwest, 1760–1816." *Proceedings of the Mississippi Valley Historical Association* 9 (1916–1917): 283–291.

———. "The Organization of the British Fur Trade, 1760–1800." *Mississippi Valley Historical Review* 3 (1916–1917): 172–202.

Stille, Charles. "American Trade in Opium to China, 1821–1839." *Pacific Historical Review* 10 (March 1941): 57–74.

———. "American Trade in Opium to China Prior to 1820." *Pacific Historical Review* 9 (December 1940): 425–444.

Thompson, E. P. "Time, Work-Discipline, and Industrial Capitalism." *Past and Present* 38 (December 1967): 56–97.

Walters, Raymond, Jr. "The James Gallatin Diary: A Fraud?" *American Historical Review* 44 (July 1957): 878–885.

Zuckerman, Michael. "Dreams That Men Dare to Dream: The Role of Ideas in Western Modernization." *Social Science History* 2 (Spring 1978): 332–345.

Index

Titles in the Great Lakes Books Series

Waiting for the Morning Train: An American Boyhood, by Bruce Catton, 1987 (reprint)

An Afternoon in Waterloo Park, by Gerald Dumas, 1988 (reprint)

The Ambassador Bridge: A Monument to Progress, by Philip P. Mason, 1988

Contemporary Michigan Poetry: Poems from the Third Coast, edited by Michael Delp, Conrad Hilberry, and Herbert Scott, 1988

Let the Drum Beat: A History of the Detroit Light Guard, by Stanley D. Solvick, 1988

Over the Graves of Horses, by Michael Delp, 1988

Wolf in Sheep's Clothing: The Search for a Child Killer, by Tommy McIntyre, 1988

Artists in Michigan, 1900–1976: A Biographical Dictionary, introduction by Dennis Barrie, biographies by Jeanie Huntley Bentley, Cynthia Newman Helms, and Mary Chris Rospond, 1989

Copper-Toed Boots, by Marguerite de Angeli, 1989 (reprint)

Deep Woods Frontier: A History of Logging in Northern Michigan, by Theodore J. Karamanski, 1989

Detroit: City of Race and Class Violence, revised edition, by B. J. Widick, 1989

Detroit Images: Photographs of the Renaissance City, edited by John J. Bukowczyk and Douglas Aikenhead, with Peter Slavcheff, 1989

Hangdog Reef: Poems Sailing the Great Lakes, by Stephen Tudor, 1989

Orvie, The Dictator of Dearborn, by David L. Good, 1989

America's Favorite Homes: A Guide to Popular Early Twentieth-Century Homes, by Robert Schweitzer and Michael W. R. Davis, 1990

Beyond the Model T: The Other Ventures of Henry Ford, by Ford R. Bryan, 1990

Detroit Kids Catalog: The Hometown Tourist, by Ellyce Field, 1990

Detroit Perspectives: Crossroads and Turning Points, edited by Wilma Henrickson, 1990

The Diary of Bishop Frederic Baraga: First Bishop of Marquette, Michigan, edited by Regis M. Walling and Rev. N. Daniel Rupp, 1990

Life after the Line, by Josie Kearns, 1990

The Making of Michigan, 1820–1860: A Pioneer Anthology, edited by Justin L. Kestenbaum, 1990

Michigan Lumbertowns: Lumbermen and Laborers in Saginaw, Bay City, and Muskegon, 1870–1905, by Jeremy W. Kilar, 1990

The Pottery of John Foster: Form and Meaning, by Gordon and Elizabeth Orear, 1990

Seasons of Grace: A History of the Catholic Archdiocese of Detroit, by Leslie Woodcock Tentler, 1990

Waiting for the News, by Leo Litwak, 1990 (reprint)

Walnut Pickles and Watermelon Cake: A Century of Michigan Cooking, by Larry B. Massie and Priscilla Massie, 1990